Study Guide for the Telecourse

Understanding Human Behavior

Study Guide for the Telecourse

Understanding Human Behavior

Third Edition

by
Louise Matthews Hewitt

for
Coast Community College District
Costa Mesa, California

Holt, Rinehart and Winston
New York Chicago San Francisco Philadelphia Montreal Toronto
London Sydney Tokyo Mexico City Rio de Janeiro Madrid

Coast Community College District

David A. Brownell, Chancellor
Coast Community College District

William M. Vega, President
Coastline Community College

Leslie N. Purdy, Director
Office of Alternative Learning Systems

Judith Lindow McDuff
Assistant Publications Editor

"Understanding Human Behavior: A Telecourse:" is produced by the Coast Community College District in cooperation with the City Colleges of Chicago, the Dallas County Community College District, Miami-Dade Community College, the State of Florida Department of Education, the Southern California Consortium, the University of Mid-America, Northern Illinois Learning Resources Cooperative, and CBS/Holt, Rinehart and Winston.

ISBN 0-03-007263-8

To the Student

Welcome to "Understanding Human Behavior," an introductory psychology television course. Whether you are planning a career in psychology or taking the course to gain personal insights about yourself and others, we hope that you will find this a useful and interesting course of study.

The course is designed to cover the concepts, vocabulary, and subjects usually treated in an on-campus college introductory psychology course typical of any two- or four-year college or university. As with a campus course, this television course has a text, a student study guide, tests, and assignments. But, unlike a campus course, this telecourse also includes thirty half-hour television programs that cover major topics. The text is *Understanding Human Behavior*, fifth edition, by James V. McConnell (New York: Holt, Rinehart and Winston, 1986). This book, *Study Guide for the Telecourse Understanding Human Behavior*, will guide your study through the course, providing reading and viewing assignments, study activities, and practice test questions.

The Course Goals

The designers, academic advisors, and producers of this television course have defined six major goals to be achieved by students taking "Understanding Human Behavior" as a course of study. By the end of the course, we want you to be able to:

Define the term "psychology" and demonstrate command of the basic vocabulary of the discipline.

Describe the major areas in the field and identify the parameters of this discipline.

Distinguish between the three differing perspectives (social/behavioral, intrapsychic, and biological) on human thought and behavior.

Appreciate the variety of ways in which psychological data is gathered and evaluated.

Gain insight into human behavior and your own personality and personal relationships.

Discuss the ways in which psychological theories are used to assess, predict, or change human behavior.

How to Take a Television Course

If you are new to college courses in general and television courses in particular, there are some helpful hints we can offer about how to study and how to complete the course to your satisfaction. Television courses are designed for busy people—people with full-time jobs or family obligations—who want to take a course at home, fitting their studying into their own personal schedules. We hope that watching the programs and studying at home will save you the time and gasoline usually spent in driving to campus, parking, and sitting in the classroom.

The following suggestions come from students who have successfully completed television courses:

Do buy the text and study guide for the course. *Do not* try to get through the course without these books. *Do* watch each of the television programs also, for the television programs do not merely repeat information provided in the books. You will need to read and study the text and view the programs in order to pass the examinations.

Do keep up with your work for this course every week. Even if you do not have any class sessions on campus or any assignments to turn in, it is very important to read the text and do the assignments in the study guide at the same time that you watch the programs every week. The programs will make more sense to you if you follow the study sequence outlined in each chapter of this study guide and do some reading *before* viewing the programs. But, most important, try to keep up with your work; *do not* fall behind, even a week or two. Students taking telecourses find that it is difficult to catch up after missing the course work presented over a period of two weeks or longer. Set aside viewing, reading, and study time *every* week and stick to your schedule.

Do get in touch with the faculty member for this course at your college or university. The instructor can answer any questions you have about the course content, help you catch up if you are behind, advise you about additional assignments, discuss the types of test questions that will be used, or tell you where you may be able to watch the programs should you happen to miss a broadcast. The instructor also wants to hear from you to find out what you think of the course; often television courses are experimental and instructors are concerned to hear how students like the programs, the tests, and other aspects of the course. So *do not* hesitate to call, write, or visit your instructor.

Do follow the activities listed in each study guide chapter. Each chapter has been written to help you. Reading the study guide chapter will often provide you with the information you would get in a classroom if you were taking the course on campus. You will find out what to watch for in the programs, what pages to read in the chapter (Assignments), what topics covered in the lesson are the major ones (Objectives and Preview), and what particular terms and concepts you should know. Each chapter has a section where you can review the material (Study Activities) and a self-test which you should use to see if you have mastered the information. Answers to the test items are given and pages are referenced so that you can check yourself and review the material if necessary.

Do read the summaries of information at the end of each chapter in your text. While a review of the summary will not substitute for careful study of the assignment as a whole, you should read the summary carefully after reading the chapter and at other times as you study the lesson to aid your recall of important information.

Do watch the programs without interruption or distraction. Tell your family or friends that you are working on a course assignment and should not be disturbed. Each program is only thirty minutes long and, if your viewing is interrupted or you cannot concentrate, you may lose the point or miss a critical scene. We do not recommend taking detailed notes during a program, but if you want to have a pad of paper and a pencil on hand, writing down a few key words or phrases may help you remember crucial ideas. Take five minutes at the end of the program and try to summarize what you have seen, especially the important concepts covered. Some students make audiotapes of programs to use for later review and study.

If you do miss a program or fall behind, *do not give up*. Many television stations provide repeats of the programs later in the week or on weekends. Most colleges have cassette copies of the program available in libraries or media centers where you can go and review any you have missed. But *do* call on your course faculty member or manager to help you if you have problems of any kind. The faculty person is assigned specifically to help you.

Most of all, we hope you find that this course enriches your life and gives you a new understanding and appreciation of human behavior.

Office of Alternative Learning Systems

Coastline Community College

Acknowledgments

Producing the "Understanding Human Behavior" television course has been a complex team effort by many people with many skills who worked together for more than two years. Several of those persons who cooperated to create this course are listed on the copyright page of this book.

In addition, appreciation is expressed for the contributions of a number of persons who served as faculty advisors to the course. First, James V. McConnell, Ph.D., professor of psychology at the University of Michigan, was the senior academic advisor for the course, author of the textbook, and the technical consultant for the television programs. Frederick A. Newton, Ph.D., professor of psychology at California State University, San Bernardino, served as academic advisor to the course, researcher for some of the programs, and author of the bank of test questions.

Production of the course was made possible with grants from several agencies and institutions. Each of these provided a faculty advisor who made suggestions for the course and reviewed parts of it. The reviewers and the institutions they represent are:

Ron Offenstein, Ph.D. Southern California Consortium

Larry Wrightsman, Ph.D. University of Mid-America

Douglas Andrews, M.S. Miami-Dade Community College and the State of Florida Department of Education

Rufus Baehr, Ph.D. City Colleges of Chicago

George Mount, Ph.D. Dallas County Community College District

Advice and assistance were also provided by the following faculty members: Pat Adams, St. Petersburg Junior College; Ann Baldwin, Miami-Dade Community College; Teresa Kendrick, Seminole Community College; and William Mellan, Hillsborough Community College. Research packages for the television programs were prepared by Robert Butler, Eve Kincaid, Richard Searles, Frederick Newton, and Diane Newton.

Administrative assistance was provided by J. Warren Binns, Jr., State of Florida Department of Education; Sally Beaty, Southern California Consortium; Rodger Pool, Dallas County Community College District; Wayne Hartley, University of Mid-America; J. Terence Kelly, Miami-Dade Community College; and John H. Thissen, City Colleges of Chicago. Appreciation is also expressed to Holt, Rinehart and Winston for their support of the telecourse production.

Contents

Human Psychology

Viewer's Guide for Program One

As you view the television program, watch for:

Scenes that show the unfolding personality of a human being, beginning life as little more than a conscious mind in a helpless body and becoming an adult with the precious abilities to reason, to invent and create, to direct his own destiny, and to fulfill his own potential—whatever it may be. We are reminded that this unfolding and flowering of the human personality is somewhat analogous to the slow but steadily unfolding civilization of man from his beginnings in the animal world.

Glimpses of our acquisition of knowledge over time, the building of science and the evolution of the scientific method, the emergence of psychology from other disciplines, and the maturing of research in the arena of behavior.

Brief introduction to the main tenets in the biological/physical, intrapsychic, social/behavioral, and holistic approaches toward understanding human behavior.

A meeting with your host, Paul Napier, who tells you a bit about what to expect from this course and explains how it involves you personally.

Preview

Knowledge of ourselves and why we do what we do, crave what we crave, and decide what we decide is a basic human interest. We are often puzzled by, and seek to understand, the attitudes and actions of those around us. Some of us seek answers in horoscopes and stars. Others of us would say, with Cassius in Shakespeare's *Julius Caesar*, that "the fault...is not in our stars, but in ourselves."

What makes you the person you are? You are, of course, many things; but, psychologically, you are primarily the way you think and the way you behave. Because no one can actually see the way you think, your behavior is the single, most important clue to who and what you are.

The way you behave is the result of your genetic makeup, your past experience, and your present environment. Thus, to understand yourself, you must be willing to take a holistic rather than fragmented approach—which means to consider yourself from a biological, an intrapsychic, and a social/behavioral point of view. That is, you must consider your brain, neurological structure, and inborn mental potential; your internal feelings and fears; and the external forces to which you regularly respond. And because most of your behavior does not occur in isolation but in social settings, you must also consider the ways in which you interact with others.

According to James V. McConnell, the author of your text for this course, " . . . the wise and human application of the holistic approach" is, for **all** individuals, the key to achievement of personal goals in life. Thus, we must learn to view individuals as highly **complex systems** whose feelings, thoughts, and actions are always influenced by biological inheritance, personal past experiences, and the people and things presently around us. In this course, we shall examine these influences and the many ways in which they affect us. We will see how the brain normally functions and how normal brain function can be altered by illness, accident, and drugs. We will see how sensations are received, interpreted, and integrated to form our perceptions of the world around us. We will take a look at learning and memory, see how intelligence develops, and discuss whether or not it can be reliably measured. We will examine personality and then discuss what we mean by "normal" and "abnormal" and what means we have to change behavior and to alter maladaptive responses. And finally, we will look at how individuals function in the roles that society assigns them as a part of the larger human community.

The course should answer some of your questions, but it should also stimulate you to raise others, for—as you will see—we do not yet know all there is to know about the human mind. However, in our efforts to study the mind, we have learned a great deal about **what** to observe, **how** to observe objectively, and how to use the data we gather to help us understand and explain human behavior.

In this beginning lesson of our study, we will describe the differing explanations for human behavior, and we will touch upon the importance of objectivity and the use of the scientific method in exploring behavior. We will also be given a frank account of the author's personal biases, or subjective viewpoints, about people and psychology.

Learning Objectives

When you have finished viewing the program and studying your text assignments, you should be able to:

1. Describe the holistic approach used by psychologists to understand human behavior, incorporating the social/behavioral, intrapsychic, and biological viewpoints.
2. Describe the steps in the scientific method.
3. Explain why objectivity is essential to scientific study.
4. Contrast the **between-subjects** and the **within-subjects** designs in psychological research, and explain how the terms ''experimental group'' and ''control group'' apply to each design.
5. Discuss the ways in which the case of Mary Smith illustrates the social/behavioral, intrapsychic, and biological points of view, as well as a subjective versus objective approach to solving human problems.
6. Summarize McConnell's biases about the field of psychology.
7. Define and give examples of dependent, independent, and intervening variables.

Assignments

Before you become deeply involved in this course, you might find it helpful to visit your campus library or a local public library and browse through the psychology section. Familiarize yourself with the psychology resources your library has and skim through such leading publications as *American Psychologist, Psychological Bulletin, Journal of Contemporary Psychology,* and *Psychological Abstracts*. (The latter publication contains brief summaries of articles printed in the major psychological journals.) As McConnell comments in text notes, several leading popular magazines also feature worthwhile articles on the behavioral sciences. These include *Psychology Today, Discover, OMNI,* and *Science 85* (which changes to *Science 86, Science 87*, and so on, with succeeding years.) You will want to use these and other resources to answer questions you may have and help you to complete assignments, or merely to satisfy a desire for more information.

Before Viewing the Program

Read the preview at the beginning of this lesson and look over the learning objectives that precede the assignments.

Look over the subtitles for text Chapter 1, ''Introduction,'' then read the chapter, which begins on page 3.

View Program 1, ''Human Psychology''

After Viewing the Program

Review the text assignment.

Complete the study activities included here as an additional study aid for you.

Now evaluate your understanding of the lesson material by reviewing the learning objectives and taking the self-test in this study guide. Check your answers against the answer key.

According to your instructor's assignment or your own interests, choose and complete activities from among the suggestions for extra credit.

Study Activities

True-False

1. T F The case of ''Clever Hans,'' described by McConnell in Chapter 1 of your text, was important to psychology and significant to the case of Mary Smith because it demonstrated that the scientific method cannot be used to study so-called ''mind reading'' and other forms of paranormal behavior.

2. T F Scientific psychology is a major tool used by modern psychologists to observe, collect, and measure data about human behavior.
3. T F The scientific method is like solving a mystery story in that it is based on the belief that mysteries have natural and measurable causes.
4. T F The scientific method is based on observation and objective testing.
5. T F The first step in the scientific method is to make a hypothesis.
6. T F Being subjective in scientific research means allowing personal or emotional feelings to color your judgments.
7. T F For McConnell, being objective in studying Mary Smith's behavior meant recognizing the possibility that experimentation might show that Mary actually **could** ''read minds.''
8. T F Most modern scientists tend to agree that the study and treatment of human behavior should be approached from a single theoretical orientation.
9. T F If a psychologist looked at only your physical problems, or only your behavior, or only your mental processes, he or she probably would not be able to do much to help you solve your problems.
10. T F McConnell decided that the social/behavioral approach would result in the best understanding of Mary Smith and her problems.
11. T F The holistic approach to human behavior rejects the intrapsychic, biological, and social/behavioral viewpoints in favor of a new experimental approach.
12. T F As part of the scientific method, the experimenter must predict future events.
13. T F The subject's reaction in an experiment is called the intervening variable.
14. T F Independent variables are behaviors or reactions that cannot be controlled by the experimenter.
15. T F In scientific experiments of the ''between-subjects'' design, the experimental subjects are not part of the control group.

Completion

1. We humans are incredibly _____ beings. In actuality, each of us is a collection of _____ parts that behave as a _____ . In addition, each of us gives off and responds to an infinite number and variety of external _____ in the form of body _____ . These signals exert strong influence on our _____ and _____ , though most of us are largely unaware of either their occurrence or their _____ on what we feel, do, think, or say.

For these reasons, trying to understand or help ourselves and others often seems like trying to solve a detective mystery. Most of us would agree with scientists, however, that mysteries have _____ that are _____. To solve the mysteries of human behavior, psychologists employ three major _____ viewpoints. These are the biological, intrapsychic, and _____ approaches. Today many psychologists believe the best way to understand an individual or his problems is to _____ information from all three _____ in what is called the _____ approach.

perspectives
social
measurable
effect
emotions
cues
interacting
complex
holistic
combine
theoretical
causes
actions
language
system

2. If we are to understand what we are really like, we must see ourselves and others as living systems composed of _____, intrapsychic, and social _____, about which we must learn as much as we can. For example, persons who suffer brain damage, as did Mary Smith, bear physical problems which should be investigated from the _____ perspective. But advocates of this view would blame **all** of her problems on her damaged brain functions. Looking at Mary from an _____ viewpoint, an approach which stresses control of the _____ by the _____, a psychologist with this particular orientation would attempt to study Mary's _____ processes for evidence to support the claim that she could communicate by mental _____. One who subscribes to the _____ view would regard Mary as primarily a _____ being and would observe Mary's _____—her interaction with her schoolmates, teachers, and family. Before he could solve the puzzle of Mary's seeming ability to read minds, McConnell needed

to adopt the _____ technique. Thus, it became clear that the child's brain functions were indeed limited by damage; she had related _____ and mental problems; and, even though she could not speak, she had the capacity to _____ and was communicating by responding to subtle _____ given by her mother—not by reading minds.

cues
behavior
environment
behavioral
mental
body
biological
parts
learn
holistic
social
telepathy
mind
intrapsychic
biological

3. The best avenue for discovering reasons for behavior and solving problems is through an objective approach called the _____ method. In this approach, one's _____ or personal feelings are not allowed to influence the _____ of the researcher. The scientific method begins with _____ of the problem and continues through five additional sequential steps that conclude with _____ of your predictions.

perception
subjective
evaluation
judgments
scientific

4. In psychological research, any condition or behavior that can change or vary is referred to as a _____ . Three types of variables are involved in scientific research. The researcher controls one variable, the _____ variable, in order to observe and _____ its effects on a second variable, the _____ variable which may or may not change when the _____ variable is manipulated by the researcher. The subject's reactions to the independent variable are the dependent variable and these reactions can be observed and measured. A variable that comes between the independent and dependent variables and affects subjects' responses is called the _____ variable.

intervening
dependent
independent
variable
independent
measure

5. Experimental research often involves two or more groups of subjects whose responses to some variable differ and can be observed, measured, and _____ . One group, which is exposed to some variable (or variables), is called the _____ group; the second group, a comparison group which is not exposed to the variable, is called the _____ group. (Often the research design includes a third group which is deliberately led to believe it is being exposed to the variable [as with the "sugar pill" group in the hypothetical headache experiments] but actually is not exposed to the variable being manipulated.) When there is only one subject available—as in the case of Mary—the single subject is used as his own _____ .

control
compared
experimental

Short-Answer Questions

1. What are the most important differences among viewing the world from a superstitious viewpoint, viewing it subjectively, and viewing it scientifically?

2. What are the main differences between dependent and independent variables?

3. Explain the significance of the "Clever Hans" studies described by McConnell.

4. What hypothesis did McConnell develop to explain Mary Smith's alleged mind-reading powers, and how did he use Mary as both experimental and control subject to test his explanation?

Self-Test

(Select the one best answer.)

Objective 1: Describe the holistic approach used by psychologists to understand human behavior, incorporating the social/behavioral, intrapsychic, and biological viewpoints.

1. The statement that your biological aspects, your mental processes, and your social behaviors must be considered as a whole is representative of the _____ approach to understanding human behavior.
   a. scientific
   b. holistic
   c. realistic
   d. intrapsychic
   e. structuralist

2. If a teenager who had been a good student suddenly developed learning problems, a "holistic" counselor might
   a. check for hearing or visual problems.
   b. find out about the student's feelings for his or her parents.
   c. determine how classmates feel about the student.
   d. do all of the above.
   e. do only a and b.

3. Therapists or researchers who subscribe to the _____ viewpoint would make an analysis of your family history.
   a. biological
   b. experimental
   c. intrapsychic
   d. social/behavioral
   e. introspective

4. A psychologist who probes your memories and your feelings about your childhood is using the _____ approach to behavior.
   a. biological
   b. experimental
   c. intrapsychic
   d. social/behavioral
   e. structuralist

Objective 2: Describe the steps in the scientific method.

5. In the scientific method, using your initial observations to make a first guess about a solution is often called
   a. making a hypothesis.
   b. testing objectively.
   c. measuring causes.
   d. perceiving the problem.
   e. testing your results.

Objective 3: Explain why objectivity is essential to scientific study.

6. Which one of the following factors is necessary for scientific study?
   a. lack of personal biases
   b. considering all viewpoints equally valid
   c. not allowing personal biases to influence gathering of data
   d. finding facts that agree with one's opinion
   e. defending one's viewpoint

Objective 4: Contrast the **between-subjects** and the **within-subjects** designs in psychological research, and explain how the terms "experimental group" and "control group" apply to each design.

7. Suppose you give twenty people doses of caffeine at bedtime and all of them report difficulty sleeping. You then conclude that caffeine causes sleeplessness. What is wrong with your experiment?
   a. The experiment lacked an independent variable.
   b. The dependent variable is missing.
   c. Some other variable intervened.
   d. You had no experimental group.
   e. There was no control group.

8. Which of the following statements best describes the use of groups in the experimental method?
   a. Both the control group and the experimental group receive identical treatment.
   b. Only the control group is exposed to the independent variable, but the groups are treated identically otherwise.
   c. Only the experimental group is exposed to the independent variable, but the groups are treated identically otherwise.
   d. Only the control group is exposed to the dependent variable, but the groups are treated identically otherwise.
   e. Subjects are assigned to groups according to ability.

9. How can a psychological experiment be carried out if there is only one subject?
   a. The experiment must be completed without any control, but observing the results.
   b. The independent variable could be tested in some trials while no variable is tested in other trials, with the researcher observing the results each time.
   c. The experimenter could try to guess how a control subject would respond, if one were available.
   d. The experimenter could test many dependent variables, observing the results each time.
   e. The experiment could be conducted without testing any variables.

Objective 5: Discuss the ways in which the case of Mary Smith illustrates the social/behavioral, intrapsychic, and biological points of view, as well as a subjective versus objective approach to solving human problems.

10. Which psychological viewpoint would emphasize the study of Mary Smith's mental processes to explain her apparent ability to read minds?
    a. biological viewpoint
    b. intrapsychic viewpoint
    c. Gestalt learning theory
    d. social/behavioral viewpoint
    e. the holistic approach

11. Mary's mother was convinced that her daughter had special powers of communication because
    a. she blamed herself for Mary's inability to speak.
    b. the ''Clever Hans'' studies proved that it is possible to read minds.
    c. she interpreted Mary's behavior subjectively.
    d. she viewed Mary's problems from an objective viewpoint.
    e. she wanted to make her daughter famous.

12. McConnell concluded that ''body language'' cues given Mary Smith by her mother were determining the child's responses in the mind-reading trials. This conclusion tended to
    a. support the importance of the environment in shaping Mary's behavior.
    b. support the intrapsychic view of Mary's case.
    c. confirm that Mary would never be able to speak or learn because of her hydrocephalism.
    d. expose the behavior of Mary and her mother as a hoax.
    e. show that damage to Mary's nervous system was solely responsible for her behavior.

Objective 6: Summarize McConnell's biases about the field of psychology.

13. Which of the following is not among McConnell's admitted biases?
    a. Learning should be rewarding.
    b. Your intellect might need to be challenged.
    c. Facts deserve more faith than theories.
    d. Active fact-gathering is preferable to passive fact-collection.
    e. Clinical studies are neither necessary nor valuable.

Objective 7: Define and give examples of dependent, independent, and intervening variables.

14. The variable that you would observe in the experimental method is called the
    a. independent variable.
    b. feedback.
    c. dependent variable.
    d. control variable.
    e. objective method.

15. Which of these was an independent variable in McConnell's study of Mary's behavior?
    a. Mary's responses to questions put by her mother
    b. Mary's love for her mother
    c. Mrs. Smith's love for Mary
    d. physical contact between mother and daughter
    e. McConnell's belief that Mary's behavior could be explained in terms of environmental factors

16. Which of these could be an intervening variable that affected Mary's responses?
    a. Mary's ability to answer correctly the questions asked by her mother
    b. Mary's love for her mother
    c. Mrs. Smith's love for Mary
    d. physical contact between mother and daughter
    e. McConnell's belief that Mary's behavior could be explained in terms of environmental factors

Suggestions for Extra Credit

1. During this course, you will encounter many common misconceptions about psychology and human behavior. Before you proceed, just for your information, look over the statements listed below and indicate whether you believe the statements to be true or false in each case. Then, put the list aside for safekeeping until the end of the course, at which time you will want to check the list to see how accurate your perceptions are.

    a.   T F   Advertisers have been successful in brainwashing people so that they will buy certain merchandise, such as a popular brand of cold drink.

b.   T F   Scientists agree that most human beings have only five senses.
c.   T F   Sigmund Freud is considered the father of scientific psychology.
d.   T F   Parenting behavior is instinctive and not learned.
e.   T F   Basically, there are no differences between the minds of men and women.
f.   T F   A drug is best defined as a chemical substance that is either illegal or can be obtained by prescription only.
g.   T F   Because the human brain loses 100,000 neurons a day after age 30, old people do not have as much capacity for new learning as younger people do.
h.   T F   Sleep serves mainly as a rest period during which the body repairs itself.
i.   T F   A lie detector will always indicate when you are telling the truth, but it cannot always detect a lie.

2. Write a short paper in which you explain, from your present and personal knowledge, what psychology is, what psychologists do, and what makes people think and act the way they do. Put this paper somewhere for safekeeping so that you can refer to it at the end of this course.
3. Write a paragraph in which you state your reasons for taking this course, what you hope to learn from it, and how you plan to apply what you learn. Put this paragraph somewhere for safekeeping so that you can refer to it at the end of the course.
4. Open your textbook and read the table of contents. On a sheet of paper, write the titles of the chapters that interest you most and tell why each interests you.
5. Thumb through your textbook and note the boldfaced terms that are glossed at intervals in the chapters. Make a list of ten to twenty of these terms that are new to you and that you cannot readily define. Put this list somewhere for safekeeping so that you can refer to it at the end of this course.
6. From memory, list the names of some famous psychologists. Beside their names, write as much as you can recall about the theories, discoveries, or methods for which they are most famous. How many were you able to name?
7. Write a brief summary of McConnell's biases (text page 20) and mention any personal biases **you** may have, particularly in the specific areas McConnell discusses.
8. In this introductory chapter, McConnell tells the story of a young girl who seemed to be able to read minds, though she was brain damaged and had never been able to talk. As McConnell comments, scientific investigation has so far neither supported claims of mental telepathy nor proven that such communication is **not** possible. Yet reports of paranormal behavior persist, and psychologists continue to study these reports objectively in experimental situations. To support his hypothesis that Mary Smith was responding to environmental cues, not reading minds, McConnell cites the ''Clever Hans'' studies and several other literature sources. What is **your**

opinion about Mary's behavior? About the paranormal in general? Knowing what you do about the scientific method, how would you have designed an experiment to test Mary's alleged abilities? To help you marshal your thoughts, read one or more of the references cited by McConnell at the end of Chapter 1 and check your library for other recent readings that might interest you. You might also enjoy reading ''China's Psychic Savants,'' in *Omni*, January, 1985, page 62, an article about a group of children who claim to read minds from messages placed in their armpits.

Answer Key

True-False

1. F	9. T
2. F	10. F
3. T	11. F
4. T	12. T
5. F	13. F
6. T	14. F
7. T	15. T
8. F	

Completion

1. complex, interacting, system, cues, language, emotions, actions, effect, causes, measurable, theoretical, social, combine, perspectives, holistic;   2. biological, parts, biological, intrapsychic, body, mind, mental, telepathy, behavioral, social, environment, holistic, behavior, learn, cues;   3. scientific, subjective, judgments, perception, evaluation;   4. variable, independent, measure, dependent, independent, intervening;   5. compared, experimental, control.

Short-Answer Questions

1. From a superstitious viewpoint, the world is seen as controlled by mysterious forces which may defy natural laws. From a subjective viewpoint, the world is seen in terms of one's own likes and dislikes, and the subjective person may easily ''jump to a conclusion'' favoring his or her own preferences. From a scientific viewpoint, one searches for facts and tries to predict future events from these facts as objectively as possible, revising explanations as often as necessary.

2. In experimental research, scientists use variables, or conditions and behaviors that are subject to variation or change, to alter the subject's environment in some way. The scientist then observes and measures the change. The **independent variable** is the condition or behavior that the scientist controls deliberately in order to observe its effects. The **dependent variable** is the condition or behavior that is affected by the independent variable. In an experimental situation with human subjects, the subject's reaction is the dependent variable.

3. The ''Clever Hans'' studies taught psychologists that most people are continually sending out a multiplicity of signals, or cues, in the form of body language, which wield enormous influence on the feelings and behavior of those who perceive them. Most individuals are not generally aware of the great extent of the exchange of such cues between themselves and others. Pfungst's research with Hans also demonstrated for psychologists that knowlege and use of the scientific method is critical to the understanding of human behavior.

4. McConnell guessed that Mary Smith could not really read minds and that Mrs. Smith was cueing her daughter's responses through some form of body language. To test his hypothesis, McConnell set up a simple experiment, using Mary as her own control in the ''within-subjects'' design, which would allow him to test Mary several times under different conditions. In Condition A, the experimenters allowed Mrs. Smith to cue her child; in Condition B, the cues were withheld. After the two conditions were administered a number of times in random order, Mary's responses to each were compared. Without the cues, Mary was unable to respond; McConnell's hypothesis was therefore confirmed.

Self-Test

1. b (text pages 14-15)
2. d (text pages 14-15)
3. d (text page 14)
4. c (text pages 13-14)
5. a (text page 9)
6. c (text pages 9, 18-19)
7. e (text pages 16-18)
8. c (text pages 16-18)
9. b (text page 18)

10. b (text pages 13-14)
11. c (text pages 14-15)
12. a (text pages 14-15)
13. e (text page 20)
14. c (text pages 15-16)
15. d (text pages 15-16)
16. b (text pages 15-16)

The Brain 2

Viewer's Guide for Program Two

As you view the television program, watch for:

The brain model. It will help you to visualize the shape of the brain, especially its division into two halves, and to understand the relationship among the cerebral cortex, the cerebrum, the cerebral hemispheres, and the corpus callosum.

Patients who have had the "split-brain" operation, first performed in 1953. In this surgery, the corpus callosum is severed to separate the cerebral hemispheres in an effort to control the spread of epilepsy within the brain and to prevent increasingly severe (and perhaps fatal) seizures.

Diagrams of a neuron with dendrites and axon labeled and graphic sequences showing transmission of nerve impulses along the communications network that is formed.

The electron microscope photo of a synapse, the extremely narrow, fluid-filled space between two nerve cells. Note that the axonic end fibers of one cell **do not actually touch** the dendrites of the other cell. When impulses are transmitted from axonic fibers to dendrites through this fluid-filled gap, the neurons involved are said to "make synapse with each other."

Are you right-handed or left-handed? That question is deceivingly easy to answer. But do you know if you are right-brained or left-brained? That question takes a bit more thought. Where does your brain do that thinking, and how do you give the answer?

One way of looking at the question is in terms of body control. Research has shown that the left half, or hemisphere, of your brain controls the right side of your body. Thus, if you are right-handed—as 90 to 93 percent of all human beings have been since people first drew on cave walls—you could be termed "left-brained." If you are left-handed, your right brain controls the right side of your body and you may be more susceptible to some physical and cognitive difficulties. Some researchers think this is so because you may have been "attacked" before birth by the male hormone testosterone.

The arrangement of functions within the brain appears to be even more complicated. Although the two hemispheres look like mirror images of each other, each apparently specializes in quite different mental functions. For example, the left hemisphere usually controls the use of language and complex physical movement. The right hemisphere, however, is better at perceiving and remembering visual patterns and spatial relationships, and is responsible for emotional expression. You will learn about some instances in which each hemisphere has functioned and communicated as if it were a separate mind, sharing one body with its counterpart. And you will also learn some surprising facts about how your two separate minds normally function as one very efficient unit.

But what does all this mean? Do you really have two separate minds functioning in your brain? How have scientists discovered the different functions of the two hemispheres? And when—if ever—does this specialization of mental function really become important to a person?

In this lesson and the three that follow, you will be considering the observable and measurable chemical and physical phenomena that cause you to think and act as you do. In an effort to uncover and to understand the biological bases for behavior, you will look at the structure of the brain (Lesson 2), at sleep and consciousness (Lessons 3 and 4), and at the way the brain works (Lesson 5).

Learning Objectives

When you have finished viewing the program and studying your text assignments, you should be able to:

1. Describe the physical structure of the human brain.

2. Explain how the brain receives and processes information that influences behavior.
3. List and describe the major parts and functions of a neuron.
4. Describe the kind of measurement made in an EEG and name the types of brain waves that occur in everyday activities.
5. Explain how disturbances in brain functioning, such as those associated with epilepsy or with the split-brain operation, provide information about brain functioning.
6. Explain the difference between the functions of the dominant cerebral hemisphere and the minor hemisphere with regard to language, thought, and emotions.
7. Define the apparent relationships among testosterone, dominance, handedness, the autoimmune system, and language problems.

Assignments

Before Viewing the Program

Read the preview at the beginning of this lesson and look over the learning objectives that precede the assignments.

Check the section "Did You Know That . . ." at the beginning of Chapter 2 in the text, and look over the subtitles for the chapter.

Read Chapter 2, "The Brain." As you read, note the boldfaced terms and those defined in the upper right corners of right-hand pages. Use the definitions and explanations of these terms to refresh your memory and clarify their meanings **before** you view the program.

Read the story (vignette) that begins and ends the chapter. Similar stories appear throughout the book, not only to give you an interesting complement to text material but also to illumine concepts presented by the author.

View Program 2, "The Brain"

After Viewing the Program

Review the text assignments.

Read through the summary items at the end of Chapter 2 and consider the thought questions inserted by the author to stimulate your thinking. Then, to aid your understanding of the materials presented in this lesson, review all of the terms and concepts mentioned above. In particular, note these terms carefully: cortex, cerebrum, cerebral hemispheres, dominant hemisphere, handedness, autoimmune system, corpus callosum, motor epilepsy, neurons, dendrites, soma, axon, synapse, neural transmitters, receptor cells, processing cells, positive feedback loop, aphasia, electroencephalograph (EEG), holistic, grand mal.

Complete the study activities included here as an additional study aid for you.

Now evaluate your understanding of the lesson material by reviewing the learning objectives and taking the self-test in this study guide. Check your answers against the answer key.

According to your instructor's assignment or your own interests, choose and complete activities from among the suggestions for extra credit. You might also consider the recommended readings listed at the end of the chapter, especially the article by Dr. R. W. Sperry, "Some Effects of Disconnecting the Cerebral Hemispheres," *Science*, 217(1982): 1223-1226.

Study Activities

Matching

Match each phrase in the column on the right with the appropriate term in the column on the left, writing the letters of the phrases in the appropriate blanks.

_____ 1. cortex	a. nerve cells
_____ 2. cerebrum	b. "input" end of neuron
_____ 3. corpus callosum	c. cap atop brain stem
_____ 4. dominant hemisphere	d. fluid-filled space between neurons
	e. "output" end of neuron
_____ 5. minor hemisphere	f. outer layer of cerebral hemispheres
_____ 6. epilepsy	g. wave of electricity carried by the axon
_____ 7. neurons	
_____ 8. dendrite	h. "firestorm in the brain"
_____ 9. axon	i. "bridge" of nervous tissue connecting the hemispheres
_____ 10. synapse	
_____ 11. feedback loop	j. speech and writing
_____ 12. action potential	k. corpus callosum
	l. spatial perception, emotions

Completion

1. All living systems have three types of functions: inputs, _____ processes, and outputs.

internal

2. The cerebral hemispheres, also called the _____, make up the largest portion of the brain. Most brain functions related to conscious decision making are located in the thin outer covering of the cerebrum, the _____, which is about 0.65 centimeters (1/4 inch) thick.

cortex
cerebrum

3. Information about the outside world flows into your cortex along a number of routes called sensory _____, which transmit messages from receptors in your skin, ears, eyes, nose, and tongue. Your cortex attends to the messages, checks its memory files, then decides what to do. Once your cortex has processed an _____ and decided on a response, it sends command messages along _____ pathways to your body's muscles and glands.

motor
input
pathways

4. Coordination of such complex movements as walking and driving a car occurs in a motor output area of the brain which is located below, but is not a part of, the cerebrum. This lower brain center is called the _____.

cerebellum

5. An instrument that converts electrical energy of the brain into a visual pattern display is called an EEG, or _____. Through this technology, three different types of waves have been identified: the activity pattern, or _____ waves, regular but fast waves called _____ waves, and those associated with sleep or _____ waves.

alpha
delta
electroencephalograph
beta

6. The deep groove that runs down the center of the cerebrum from front to back is called the central fissure. It divides the brain into the cerebral _____, which are connected by, and communicate through, the _____ callosum, a _____ of tissue that crosses the central fissure.

bridge
hemispheres
corpus

7. Each half of the cerebral hemisphere completely controls the half of the body that is opposite to it. At birth or shortly thereafter, one hemisphere starts to gain the lead over the other in controlling the entire body. Thus, this hemisphere becomes the _____ hemisphere. If you are right-handed, your left hemisphere is your dominant hemisphere. Your right hemisphere, then, is called your _____ hemisphere.

minor
dominant

8. The dominant hemisphere is the center of writing and _____, while the minor hemisphere perceives visual _____ and processes _____ responses. If your dominant hemisphere is damaged in some way, you may be unable to recognize the meaning of words or to speak or write in meaningful terms, a condition called _____.

aphasia
emotional
patterns
speech

9. When researchers Myers and Sperry severed the corpus callosum of a cat in a surgical technique called the _____ operation, they paved the way for a successful new treatment of severe epilepsy. Epilepsy is caused by brain damage, and seizures occur when all the cells in one part of the brain begin firing in _____ instead of in small, independent clusters that normally fire separately. (These disturbances show up on an EEG as ''spikes'' in the pattern of brain _____.) But a more significant finding of the Sperry-Myers research was that _____ the two hemispheres resulted in the emergence of two independent _____ in the same body. Under normal circumstances, each hemisphere works at its own special tasks, with the dominant one of the two keeping control over the minor one. But the two hemispheres ''_____'' so well and smoothly that they operate as a functional _____ rather than _____ entities.

unit
minds
waves
split-brain
separate
communicate
separating
unison

Short-Answer Questions

1. Label the parts of these nerve cells and the fluid-filled spaces between them, then explain briefly how impulses travel from one to the other.

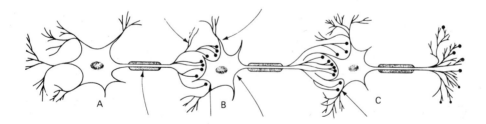

2. Describe what may happen if your input neurons are damaged or drugged and what may happen if your processing neurons are disturbed.

3. How does the size of the human cerebrum compare with that of a rabbit? What difference does the development of an organism's cerebrum make in its behavior?

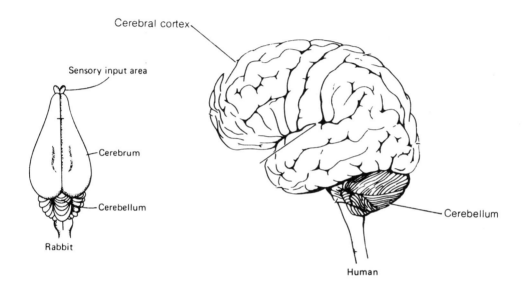

Cerebral cortex

Sensory input area

Cerebrum

Cerebellum

Rabbit

Cerebellum

Human

4. If the two cerebral hemispheres are originally identical in capability, at what point does one become dominant? How does the dominant one exercise control over the other?

5. Some researchers believe that the male hormone testosterone influences hemisphere dominance and thus handedness as well. In what ways does testosterone affect the cerebral hemispheres and handedness? What physical and perceptual or cognitive problems may be related to the effects of testosterone?

Self-Test

(Select the one best answer.)

Objective 1: Describe the physical structure of the human brain.

1. Which of the following is not a structure of the human brain?
   a. cortex
   b. cerebrum
   c. cerebellum
   d. bilateral symmetry
   e. corpus callosum

2. The cerebral cortex is responsible for
   a. maintaining "stream of consciousness."
   b. thinking moment-to-moment thought.
   c. checking memory files.
   d. making conscious decisions about what the body is going to do next.
   e. all of the functions listed above.

3. Which one of the following statements about the cerebellum is incorrect?
   a. It is divided into two hemispheres.
   b. It is one of the "lower centers" of the brain.
   c. It is not part of the cerebrum.
   d. It is involved in coordinating such complex movements as walking, playing the piano, and driving a car.
   e. It is much smaller than the cerebrum in human brains.

4. If the brain is compared to a mushroom, the cerebrum would be thought of as the
   a. rind or peel.
   b. cap.
   c. stem.
   d. roots.
   e. spores, or seeds.

5. Split-brain surgery to cut the corpus callosum, such as that performed on an epileptic in the television sequences,
   a. causes the patient to see light flashes.
   b. halts communication between the cerebral hemispheres.
   c. creates a thick "bridge" by which the hemispheres communicate.
   d. creates two separate minds in one body.
   e. produces the effects listed in both b and d.

Objective 1; and *Objective 2:* Explain how the brain receives and processes information that influences behavior.

6. What happens when the cerebrum is larger in relation to the rest of the brain?
   a. The organism is more likely to experience what we call headaches.
   b. The organism can think faster.
   c. Its behavior is likely to be more complex.
   d. Both a and b are true.
   e. None of the above statements is true.

Objective 2

7. Psychologists have made thousands of tests and filled libraries with explanations of every part of the human brain. Today
   a. we know all there is to know about the mind.
   b. the human mind remains largely unexplained.
   c. the mind is thought of as mere fabrication.
   d. the mind reigns supreme.
   e. we know precisely how the mind influences behavior.

8. All of the activities listed below are functions of the brain. The primary purpose of the brain is to
   a. receive information about the outside world.
   b. check its memory files.
   c. manufacture thoughts and behaviors.
   d. create neural, muscular, and glandular reactions.

9. Information about the outside world flows into your cortex along a number of routes called
   a. sensory pathways.
   b. filaments.
   c. motor pathways.
   d. inputs.
   e. feedbacks.

10. Command messages to your body's muscles and glands travel along
    a. filaments.
    b. sensory pathways.
    c. motor pathways.
    d. outputs.
    e. feedbacks.

11. Electrochemical impulses received by the _____ cause electrical waves to travel along the length of neurons.
    a. axons
    b. dendrites
    c. central fissure
    d. corpus callosum
    e. cerebellum

Objective 3: List and describe the major parts and functions of a neuron.

12. Neurons are made up of
    a. soma, synapses, and dendrites.
    b. receivers, transmitters, and impulses.
    c. body, clusters, and fibers.
    d. soma, axon, and dendrites.
    e. peel, stem, and cap.

13. The main part, or body, of the nerve cell is called the
    a. soma.
    b. axon.
    c. dendrite.
    d. synapse.
    e. neurotransmitter.

14. The complex chemical reactions that keep the neuron alive and functioning occur in the
    a. synapse.
    b. dendrites.
    c. axons.
    d. soma.
    e. cell wall.

15. Which of the following statements best describes the synapse?
    a. It is a transmitter chemical.
    b. It makes spike-shaped waves on an EEG.
    c. It is rapid brain-wave activity.
    d. Synapse is made when a dendrite fires.
    e. It is a microscopically small space between two neurons.

Objective 4: Describe the kind of measurement made in an EEG and name the types of brain waves that occur in everyday activities.

16. An EEG measures
    a. chemical changes in a neuron.
    b. electrical activity in an individual neuron.
    c. only energy expended by an active brain.
    d. electrical activity generated by the brain.
    e. chemical changes within the cerebrum.

17. EEG patterns called delta waves are seen when the subject is
    a. in deep sleep.
    b. resting.
    c. mentally active.
    d. physically active.
    e. depressed.

Objective 5: Explain how disturbances in brain functioning, such as those associated with epilepsy or with the split-brain operation, provide information about brain functioning.

18. Experiments with split-brain patients demonstrate that
    a. one side of the body may do "odd things."
    b. one side of the brain may not express itself verbally.
    c. the hemispheres cannot communicate when separated.
    d. each of the two minds that emerge can learn on its own.
    e. all of the above events can occur.

Objective 6: Explain the difference between the functions of the dominant cerebral hemisphere and the minor hemisphere with regard to language, thought, and emotions.

19. The dominant cerebral hemisphere is responsible for
    a. linguistic expression and coordinated movements.
    b. emotional expression.
    c. spatial perceptions.
    d. controlling the cortex.
    e. all of the above functions.

20. The minor cerebral hemisphere is responsible for
    a. language and coordinated movements.
    b. emotional expression.
    c. spatial perceptions.
    d. emotional expression and spatial perceptions.
    e. language and spatial perceptions.

Objective 6; and *Objective 7:* Define the apparent relationships among testosterone, dominance, handedness, the autoimmune system, and language problems.

21. According to recent research, which of the following statements best describes the potential effect of the male hormone testosterone on the brains and handedness of unborn babies?
    a. The individual will contract AIDS in adulthood.
    b. The development of the left brain is inhibited and the individual becomes left-handed.
    c. The development of the left brain is inhibited and the individual becomes right-handed.
    d. The development of the right brain is inhibited and the left hemisphere becomes dominant.

22. Left-handed males appear likely to suffer more language and reading disabilities than do women and right-handed men. This is so because their
    a. left hemispheres usually cannot talk or write.
    b. right and left brains cannot communicate.
    c. right hemispheres have developed dominance over the left brain and control language.
    d. left hemispheres are dominant and control language.

Suggestions for Extra Credit

1. Select a movement or series of movements you make frequently, such as throwing a ball, vacuuming the floor, or starting the car. **Without** repeating the movement, quickly jot down brief step-by-step directions for it. Can you remember **exactly** how you do it? Why? Now, perform the movement and correct or elaborate upon your directions. What steps did you leave out the first time? Why?

2. As you know, aphasia is the inability to recognize the meaning of words or to speak or write in meaningful terms. Its primary cause is damage to the major or ''language'' hemisphere of the cerebrum. Read *A Different Drum* (Englewood Cliffs, N.J.: Prentice-Hall, 1973), Constance Carpenter Cameron's account of her courageous fight to rescue her aphasic son Evan from his tragic handicap.

3. In a few paragraphs, explain why most of us frequently forget names but not the faces associated with the names. Recall what you have learned about the differing functions of the two hemispheres. You might review the story of ''Patrick'' that begins and ends Chapter 2 and review lesson material that deals with split-brain experimentation.

4. With their split-brain surgery experiments, Drs. R. W. Sperry and R. E. Myers have contributed valuable information about the functions and behavior of the mind. Dr. Sperry, a California Institute of Technology psychobiologist, has been engaged in this intriguing research for more than thirty years and has contributed extensively to the literature dealing with the study of the mind. Read the *Science* magazine article by Dr. Sperry that is listed by your author at the end of Chapter 2, then locate one or two other reports about his work written either by Sperry himself or by others. What are some implications of Dr. Sperry's findings that the brain is really **two** brains working as **one**? Can you think of any experimental studies that might be useful other than those performed by Sperry and Myers?

5. Visit a college or university library in your vicinity and try to locate references to the work of Harvard's Norman Geschwind, a neurologist, whose research suggests that there is a strong and definite relationship between testosterone, handedness, brain dominance, and certain physical and cognitive problems. If left-handed males are more subject to AIDS, it should then be true that more AIDS victims are left-handed. Is this so? Why do a few young girls and women contract AIDS? What do you think are the implications of Geschwind's research findings? Would it be possible—or ethical—to intercede and change the direction of dominance and handedness at some key point in the development process?

Answer Key

Matching

1. f
2. c
3. i
4. j
5. l
6. h

7. a
8. b
9. e
10. d
11. k
12. g

Completion

1. internal;   2. cerebrum, cortex;   3. pathways, input, motor;
4. cerebellum;   5. electroencephalograph, beta, alpha, delta;
6. hemispheres, corpus, bridge;   7. dominant, minor;   8. speech, patterns, emotional, aphasia;   9. split-brain, unison, waves, separating, minds, communicate, unit, separate.

Short-Answer Questions

1. Bursts of neural energy are the means by which neurons pass messages from one part of the body to another. A wave of electrical energy shoots along the length of the cell A and reaches the tiny fibers at the end of the axon. A chemical change occurs in the axon of A that releases a chemical transmitter into the fluid-filled space between A's axonic fibers and B's dendrites. This results in the generation of electrical activity that sweeps the length of the B cell, beginning in B's dendrites and moving wave-like to the end of B's axon.

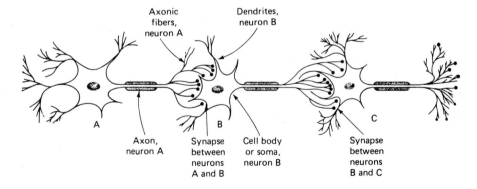

2. If your input neurons are damaged or drugged, you may see things that are not really there, hear voices when no one is speaking, or fail to detect important changes in your sensory environment. If your processing neurons are disturbed, you may suffer loss of memory, you may underreact or overreact to emotional situations, your judgment may become clouded, you may faint or fall into a coma, or your cortex may issue such confused orders that you appear to be mentally ill.
3. The human cerebrum is more than 100 times larger than the cerebrum of the rabbit. The more developed the cerebrum, the more complex the behavior of which the organism is typically capable.
4. At birth or shortly after, one hemisphere gains the lead over the other and eventually takes major control of the body. This dominant hemisphere, which specializes in language, controls the so-called minor hemisphere by inhibiting any attempt it might make to speak or control movements.
5. Testosterone is believed to "attack" the left hemispheres of unborn babies, sometimes inhibiting the development of the left brain and encouraging the normally developing right brain to assume dominance and to control language. Individuals who are right-hemisphere dominated become left-handed. About 10 percent of the world's population is left-handed. As you might expect, there are about twice as many males as females among the left-handers. Men in general tend to suffer more language difficulties than do women, but these problems are most severe in males who are left-handed. Left-handers are also three times as likely to be susceptible to migraine headaches and AIDS, the latter because testosterone also appears to attack the autoimmune system of the unborn infant. On the other hand, many more left-handers become artists, musicians, engineers, and mathematicians. (Remember that the right brain specializes in spatial perception, pattern recognition, and emotions.)

Self-Test

1. d (text pages 28-31, 37-38; television program)
2. e (text page 30)
3. a (text page 29)
4. b (text page 31; television program)
5. e (text pages 43-48; television program)
6. c (text pages 31-32)
7. b (television program)
8. d (text page 32)
9. a (text page 30)
10. c (text page 30)
11. b (television program)
12. d (text pages 32-36; television program)

13. a (text pages 32-33)
14. d (text page 33)
15. e (text page 35; television program)
16. d (text pages 36-37)
17. a (text page 37)
18. e (text pages 43-48; television program)
19. a (text pages 45-48; television program)
20. d (text pages 45-48; television program)
21. b (text pages 39-40)
22. c (text page 39)

Consciousness and Sleep

3

Viewer's Guide for Program Three

As you view the television program, watch for:

The film sequences of sleepers whose brain activity is being recorded by an electroencephalograph (EEG). With the help of the EEG, we can tell when the subjects fall asleep, and we can see that there are different stages of sleep, each with its own distinctive brain pattern.

The footage of the sleeping man experiencing rapid eye movements, or REMs, which tell us that the man is dreaming. We see that in his case, at least, dreaming can be stressful. Note, too, the brief sequences in which the sleeping cat, which has had part of its brain surgically removed, acts out its dreams. (Can you think why the man does not act out his dreams?)

The scenes in which a television reporter trying to set a new record for sleeplessness demonstrates dramatically for researchers that extreme sleep deprivation can produce serious negative effects. We watch as the reporter becomes irritable, loses the ability to concentrate, then hallucinates and develops paranoid fears.

Filmed interviews with narcolepsy victims, who describe how they fall asleep without warning and are forced to rely on daily drug doses to keep them awake.

Scenes from the research of Stanford University scientist William Dement in which Dement establishes the importance of dreams to sleep. Dement also draws many conclusions about dream deprivation and expresses opinions (not always supported by other researchers) about many popular notions concerning sleep.

Animations depicting sensory input sent from the eye to the cortex and inside the cortex, where the input is analyzed—events which are part of the process of consciousness.

Preview

That familiar and regular "interruption" in our normal stream of consciousness which we call "sleep" is the biological riddle of all times. It has been praised by poets and damned by doctors. While psychoanalysts have termed it a safety valve for our sanity, other observers have called it a curse and likened it to death. We know that sleep is a basic human need, so basic that everyone spends about one-third of his or her life satisfying it. Still, much as we need it, we understand neither the nature of sleep nor why we sleep.

Recently, scientists have been able to investigate sleep by means of observation. Using the electroencephalograph to record brain activity, they have discovered that sleep, rather than being a single psychological state, is a complex cycle of stages, a cycle we repeat several times each night. But we still do not know much about why we sleep or why we dream.

Some researchers have suggested that the main function of sleep is to allow the body to repair itself **physiologically**. Yet the body appears to be able to restore itself just about as well during "deep rest." Thus, other scientists believe that sleep serves an **adaptive** function in keeping us out of harm's way while we rest. There is also growing evidence that sleep is important **psychologically** because it allows us to dream.

Regardless of what answers science finds for the riddles of sleeping and dreaming, they are natural altered states of consciousness that appear to be necessary for sound mental health and are somehow related to the complex process of memory. It is a paradox, then, that half the world suffers from sleep disorders of some kind. (See Lesson Seventeen.)

In this lesson you will learn about consciousness, and you will be introduced to what scientists think and know about sleeping and dreaming and disorders such as night terrors, sleepwalking, and insomnia. You will also examine two distinct realities, the reality of waking and the reality of dreaming.

Learning Objectives

When you have finished viewing the program and studying your text assignments, you should be able to:

1. Describe the process of consciousness and cite at least two examples of altered states of consciousness.
2. Describe each of the basic stages of sleep and the normal cycles which occur in a night's sleep.
3. Describe the effects of interrupting sleep and dreaming.
4. Describe common sleep disorders, including night terrors, anxiety nightmares, insomnia, narcolepsy, sleepwalking, sleeptalking, and bedwetting.

Assignments

Before Viewing the Program

Read the preview at the beginning of this lesson and look over the learning objectives that precede the assignments.

Check the section "Did You Know That . . ." at the beginning of Chapter 3 in the text and look over the subtitles for the chapter.

Ask yourself what consciousness is. Have you ever fainted or lost consciousness suddenly as the result of an emotional shock or a physical injury? What do you remember about that experience?

Read pages 53-68 in Chapter 3, "Sleep, Drugs, and Altered States of Consciousness." As you read, note the boldfaced terms scattered throughout the chapter. To refresh your memory and clarify their meaning **before** you view the program, use the definitions and explanations of these terms given in the glossaries located at the top right of odd-numbered pages.

View Program 3, "Consciousness and Sleep"

After Viewing the Program

Review the text assignments.

Read through the summary items at the end of Chapter 3 and consider the thought questions in the chapter. Then, to aid your understanding of the information presented in the lesson, review all of the boldfaced terms and concepts. In particular, note these terms carefully: consciousness, physiological cycles, beta waves, delta waves, REM, night terrors, anxiety nightmares, sleep disorders, lucid dreaming.

Complete the study activities included here as an additional study aid for you.

Now evaluate your understanding of the lesson material by reviewing the learning objectives and taking the self-test in this study guide. Check your answers against the answer key.

According to your instructor's assignment or your own interests, choose and complete activities from among the suggestions for extra credit. You might also consider any recommended readings listed at the end of the chapter that might be appropriate.

Drawing by Dana Fradon; © 1973
The New Yorker Magazine, Inc.

Study Activities

True-False

1. T F According to McConnell, consciousness can best be described as the internal, or subjective process, by which we are aware of the passage of time and are kept awake and advised of what is happening in the environment and what we ourselves are doing.
2. T F One way of altering your consciousness is to fall asleep.
3. T F Scientists agree that sleep serves mainly as a rest period during which the body repairs itself physiologically.
4. T F During REM sleep, our brain paralyzes our muscles, probably to keep us from physically acting out our dreams.
5. T F We experience the deepest sleep of all about one hour after we fall asleep, during Stage 5.
6. T F Stage 0 sleep is that period between sleeping and waking when you are first trying to fall asleep.
7. T F All dreaming occurs during REM sleep.
8. T F REM sleep, or dream sleep, occurs during Stage 4 at the border of sleeping and waking.
9. T F Night terrors, or **pavor nocturnus**, occur when your physiological need for sleep is greatest.
10. T F Such sleep disturbances as insomnia and nightmares have been proven to be caused by anxiety and stress.
11. T F The sleep disturbance known as narcolepsy is believed to be inherited.
12. T F If you are deprived of REM sleep, you will compensate by dreaming during the deep sleep part of the cycle.

Completion

1. McConnell describes sleeping and dreaming as two _____ states of consciousness. Sleep is a basic human need, so basic that we spend about one-third of our lives satisfying it. Little is actually known about why and how we sleep and dream, but most researchers agree that _____ seems to serve vital _____ and _____ needs.

adaptive
altered
restorative
dreaming

2. Research with the EEG and sleeping subjects has established that sleep is not a single psychological state. It is a complex _____ that includes several distinct _____. The lower your stage of sleep, the _____ your brain waves will be on the EEG. During the first few minutes of sleep, Stage 1 of the cycle, the brain wave pattern known as the _____ rhythm predominates. The deepest sleep of the cycle is Stage _____. During this stage, your brain wave pattern will show 50 percent or more of _____ rhythm.

slower
cycle
alpha
stages
delta
4

3. About 80 minutes after your fall into slumber, your activity cycle will increase slightly. The _____ rhythm will disappear, to be replaced by an EEG _____ pattern, a pattern that actually looks more characteristic of waking than sleeping. At this time, your eyes will begin to dart around under your eyelids, and these rapid eye movements will continue for about 8 to 15 minutes. This part of the cycle is called _____ sleep.

REM
delta
activity

4. Most _____ occur during REM sleep. Most persons appear to dream about everyday events that are of interest or importance to them. Some techniques have been developed to help people control their dreams through low-level consciousness, or _____ dreaming. Dreams include two kinds of nightmares, the _____ terror and the anxiety nightmare. The more common nightmare begins late in the sleep cycle at the end of a very long REM period and is called the _____ nightmare. A much more frightening kind, the night _____, usually begins in Stage _____ and not during an REM period.

anxiety
lucid
dreams
terror
4
night

40

5. Dreaming seems to be a function of the _____ hemisphere. During REM sleep, we are prevented from acting out our dream contents by _____ inhibition, or a kind of "paralysis" of the voluntary muscles. After a period of REM sleep and dreaming, most sleepers return to Stage _____.

muscular
1
right

6. The average person gets about _____ hours of sleep a day and can tolerate up to _____ hours of sleeplessness without suffering ill effects. Each night most people experience four to _____ sleep cycles and spend a total of about _____ hours dreaming. After being severely deprived of sleep, a person's sleep cycle may temporarily increase the time spent in _____ sleep and decrease the time in _____ sleep.

five
seven and one-half to eight
two
forty-eight
REM
Stage 4 (deep)

7. Sleep disturbances such as nightmares and insomnia are common throughout the world's population. One serious sleep disturbance called _____ causes its victims to fall asleep without warning anytime. Experiments seem to show that narcolepsy is _____.

inherited
narcolepsy

Short-Answer Questions

1. Explain why McConnell calls consciousness a "primitive term" and give examples of other primitive terms.

2. List the three major points McConnell suggests should be used in trying to define consciousness.

3. Explain how some experimenters have helped some persons to be aware of and influence their dreams as they are occurring.

Self-Test

(Select the one best answer.)

Objective 1: Describe the process of consciousness and cite at least two examples of altered states of consciousness.

1. According to McConnell, "primitive terms," such as "consciousness," are
   a. out of place in scientific studies.
   b. so basic that they are hard to define.
   c. always defined in terms of themselves.
   d. a problem mainly in psychology and social science.
   e. the best way of defining concepts.

2. To understand consciousness, we must remember that it is
   a. an ongoing internal, or subjective, process.
   b. an objective event.
   c. an instantaneous event.
   d. a form of output.
   e. not definable.

3. When you begin dreaming, you have
   a. voluntarily paralyzed your muscles so that you cannot act out your dreams.
   b. altered your state of consciousness.
   c. probably entered the REM stage of sleep.
   d. altered the environment to decrease sensory input.
   e. altered your state of consciousness by entering the REM stage of sleep.

4. Which of the following is not necessarily a characteristic of the process of consciousness?
   a. You take in sensory information.
   b. You compare inputs with memories of past experiences.
   c. You interpret and make decisions about the inputs.
   d. Your neural firing increases.
   e. You respond.

Objective 2: Describe each of the basic stages of sleep and the normal cycles which occur in a night's sleep.

5. Brain wave activity tends to
   a. slow down during sleep.
   b. speed up during dreams.
   c. be slowest in deep sleep.
   d. exhibit all of the changes noted above.
   e. do none of the above.

6. If monitored by an electroencephalograph, your brain waves will show the "activity pattern" during
   a. Stage 1 sleep.
   b. Stage 2 sleep.
   c. Stage 3 sleep.
   d. Stage 4 sleep.
   e. REM sleep.

7. Voluntary muscles are temporarily paralyzed during
   a. Stage 1 sleep.
   b. Stage 2 sleep.
   c. Stage 3 sleep.
   d. Stage 4 sleep.
   e. REM sleep.

8. During REM periods, subjects are most likely to
   a. be conscious.
   b. be moving their eyes.
   c. show more delta rhythms on their EEG.
   d. show alpha rhythms on their EEG.

9. The length of the sleep cycle for an adult human is about _____ minutes.
   a. 50
   b. 60
   c. 70
   d. 80
   e. 90

10. You experience _____ sleep cycles each night.
    a. one or two
    b. two to three
    c. three to four
    d. four to five
    e. five or more

Objective 3: Describe the effects of interrupting sleep and dreaming.

11. If you are an average person, you can tolerate up to _____ hours of sleeplessness without suffering ill effects.
    a. 24
    b. 48
    c. 72
    d. 96

12. Following a period of moderate sleep deprivation,
    a. your motor reactions will be slowed, but your judgment will be unaffected.
    b. your judgment will be disturbed, but you will be more relaxed.
    c. you will show signs of stress, but mental disturbance is unlikely.
    d. you will show increased hostility and may exhibit symptoms of paranoid schizophrenia.

13. When a reporter was deprived of sleep for more than 72 hours in an experiment shown in the television program, she
    a. experienced no change in mood or use of faculties.
    b. became irritable but showed few other ill effects.
    c. had trouble making decisions but showed no other ill effects.
    d. began to hallucinate and exhibit symptoms of paranoid schizophrenia toward the end of the period.

14. Dement's dream deprivation studies showed that
    a. dream content is related to the length of time between dreams.
    b. subjects deprived of dreams will adapt so that their dream need is reduced and their dream time remains low.
    c. subjects need abnormally long periods of deep sleep to recover from dream deprivation.
    d. using sleeping pills regularly increases the incidence of nightmares.
    e. most people need to dream for psychological stability.

Objective 4: Describe common sleep disorders, including night terrors, anxiety nightmares, insomnia, narcolepsy, sleepwalking, sleeptalking, and bedwetting.

15. The sleep disturbance known as night terrors is most likely to begin during
    a. Stage 1 sleep.
    b. Stage 2 sleep.
    c. Stage 3 sleep.
    d. Stage 4 sleep.
    e. an REM period.

16. During the dream part of a night terror attack, subjects may
    a. breathe rapidly.
    b. hallucinate.
    c. sleepwalk.
    d. feel smothered by a fearful "creature."
    e. experience all of the above.

17. Which of the following descriptions does not identify a form of insomnia?
    a. falling asleep suddenly, but waking again in a few minutes
    b. inability to fall asleep at all
    c. going to sleep normally, then waking five or more times during the night and trying to go back to sleep
    d. waking up after about six hours of sleep, then remaining sleepless
    e. having too little Stage 1 REM sleep and reduced amounts of Stage 4 "deep sleep"

18. Anxiety nightmares are most likely to
    a. occur while the subject is taking sleeping pills.
    b. include vivid images of being chased, falling, or witnessing frightening events.
    c. increase in frequency during illness and high fever.
    d. occur when the subject has a physiological need for sleep.

19. Anxiety nightmares
    a. are the most terrifying night experiences known.
    b. produce very few physiological changes.
    c. last for an hour or more.
    d. make the dreamers feel they are being suffocated.

Suggestions for Extra Credit

1. Keep a dream diary for several weeks. Place a small notebook and pencil on your nightstand or in some other place near your bed. As you are falling asleep, tell yourself that you will be able to remember your dreams when you awaken. Each morning when you wake up, make an effort to remember at least one dream that you had the previous night. Before the day's events crowd out your fleeting memory of it, write a description of the dream in

your notebook. After several weeks, analyze your dreams. Do you dream in color? If so, are the colors pale or vivid? Do certain colors predominate? Do you ever observe yourself in your dreams? Is there much talking in your dreams, or do they consist mainly of actions and feelings? Can you recognize the influence of daily events on your dreams? Do you seem to have recurring dreams or themes that you can identify? Before analyzing your dreams, read Sigmund Freud's *The Interpretation of Dreams*, which you should be able to find in any college library.

2. There is growing evidence that we can control our dreams and, thereby, influence our waking state of mind. Continue keeping your dream diary for several weeks more. This time, try to influence your dreams by concentrating on certain things before you fall asleep. For example, you might relive an especially pleasant experience in your memory, rehearse the answers to test questions, or mentally list the options you face with regard to a problem you must solve or a decision you must make. Make a note in your diary of what you consciously **thought** about and then of what you **dreamed** about. Do you see a connection? What role do you think the two hemispheres of your brain might have played?

3. In December 1978, *Psychology Today* published a special edition entitled ''Dream Studies: Into Phase Three,'' which is a collection of writings by three authors who explore three different lines of inquiry into current sleep and dream research. ''Dream of Innocence,'' by David Foulkes, is a study of children's dreams. ''Happy Endings for Dreams,'' by Rosalind Dymond Cartwright, discusses the possibility of controlling our lives by controlling our dreams. And ''Where Dreams Come From: A New Theory,'' by Robert W. McCarley, presents a new hypothesis that relates some dream experiences to the physiological events of REM sleep. Read one, two, or all of the articles and write a brief report of your reactions.

4. Locate a copy of Wilse Webb's book, *Sleep: The Gentle Tyrant* (New York: Prentice-Hall, 1976), and read the sections that discuss the functions and stages of sleep. What is your opinion of the two theories offered as explanations for the mysterious phenomenon called sleep?

Answer Key

True-False

1. T	7. F
2. T	8. F
3. F	9. T
4. T	10. F
5. F	11. T
6. T	12. F

Completion

1. altered, dreaming, adaptive, restorative;   2. cycle, stages, slower, alpha, 4, delta;   3. delta, activity, REM;   4. dreams, lucid, night, anxiety, terror, 4;   5. right, muscular, 1;   6. seven and one-half to eight, forty-eight, five, two, Stage 4 (deep), REM;   7. narcolepsy, inherited.

Short-Answer Questions

1. McConnell defines primitive terms as concepts or ideas that are basic to a particular science and are so elemental that they are exceptionally difficult to define or cannot be readily defined except in terms of themselves. In psychology, consciousness is such a term. Other primitive terms include **mind, life, energy,** and **matter**. Sometimes it is easier to describe primitive terms by listing their characteristics than it is to define them in a few words.

2. The three characteristics of consciousness suggested by McConnell are: (1) Consciousness is an internal (subjective) process, and processes are difficut to define; (2) consciousness is marked by a subjective awareness of the passage of time; and (3) consciousness is distinguished by an immediate awareness or certainty that you are awake and know everything that is going on around you.

3. Some scientists report that they have been able to encourage subjects to be aware of what they are dreaming **while** they're dreaming by maintaining a low level of consciousness during the dream stage of the sleep process. One experimenter, identified by McConnell as Rosalind Cartwright, reported that she trained people not only to be aware of and remember their dreams but also to influence their outcomes. This awareness and manipulation of dreams is called "lucid" dreaming and generally occurs during the last dream cycle of the night. Such subjects are aware of the difference between a dream and reality, can evaluate a dream as it progresses, and take an active role in determining its outcome if they wish. (Dreams, including the "happy endings" manipulated by Cartwright's subjects, are apparently the work of the right, or dominant, hemisphere.)

Self-Test

1. b (text page 55)
2. a (text pages 55-56)
3. e (text pages 61-62; television program)
4. d (text pages 55-56)
5. d (text pages 59-61)
6. e (text pages 59-61; television program)

7. e (text pages 62-63; television program)
8. b (text page 61; television program)
9. e (text page 61)
10. d (text page 61)
11. b (text page 63)
12. c (text page 63)
13. d (television program)
14. e (television program)
15. d (text page 67)
16. e (text page 67)
17. a (text page 64)
18. b (text page 68)
19. b (text page 68)

Altered States of Consciousness

Viewer's Guide for Program Four

As you view the television program, watch for:

Animated sequences at the beginning of the program that will refresh your memory about the brain processes which were described in Lesson 2. You will see billions of neurons at work in body and brain, reporting experiences to the cerebral cortex, piecing together these experiences to make a complete image of our world, analyzing the "picture," and firing off commands for action. A clear understanding of how the brain functions in everyday circumstances is necessary to an understanding of how consciousness can be altered.

The electron microscope photo of a synapse and the animated sequence showing a neurotransmitter crossing the synapse. Note, too, the sequences demonstrating how certain pain-killing drugs block normal transmission of pain messages to the brain.

The model of d-lysergic acid di-ethyl-amide, better known as LSD or "acid," which belongs to the family of drugs called hallucinogens. You should also watch for the animated sequence showing how hallucinogens affect sensory input neurons in the cortex. By speeding up or slowing down their firing, they alter your mind's impression of reality and may cause you to see, hear, and feel things that are not there.

The animated sequences showing how stimulants ("uppers") and depressants ("downers") can affect the nervous system, speeding up or slowing down synaptic transmission, thereby accelerating or depressing neural activity.

The film sequence showing patients undergoing biofeedback training to regulate basic body functions like heart rate and temperature in order to gain control over asthma attacks, blood pressure, and migraine headaches.

Preview

Can you name the world's most popular drug? It is a mild stimulant that works just like amphetamines. Americans take somewhere around 160 billion doses of it each year. Its scientific name is 1-3-7 trimethylxanthine, but it is more commonly known as caffeine. And it is found in coffee, tea, and many of the dark, cola-type soft drinks.

You may have answered "aspirin" when you were asked to name the world's most popular drug. And aspirin, or salicylic acid, **is** perhaps the most common **pain-killing** drug known to humans. Some 12 million kilograms (27 million pounds) of it are consumed annually in the United States—enough to treat 17 billion headaches.

If it surprises you to think of caffeine as a drug, the reason may lie in your thinking of "drugs" as something medicinal or illegal. Within the context of this course, a drug is considered any chemical that, when taken in relatively small amounts, significantly increases or decreases activities somewhere in your body. Given that definition, you would probably have no problem identifying alcohol as being the drug that Americans abuse most. Alcohol is both a "downer" and a pain-killer, and its excessive use is exceedingly costly to us in terms of accidents, deaths, crime, lost work time, medical care, and damage to body and mind.

In this lesson, you will be looking at alcohol and numerous other drugs (including the body's own natural pain-killers) that increase or decrease nerve cell activity, that speed up or slow down neural firing. And you will learn to categorize these drugs according to whether they speed up or slow down inputs, cortical processes, outputs, or a combination of these neurological activities.

What effects—harmful and beneficial—do these changes have upon body and mind functions? Or, to phrase the question in a different way, what is consciousness and how do drugs alter it? To answer this question, you will learn the difference between direct and indirect ways of altering consciousness. And you will learn about a very old and a very new way of altering mind and body functions **without** drugs.

Learning Objectives

When you have finished viewing the program and studying your text assignment, you should be able to:

1. Distinguish between direct and indirect ways of altering consciousness and give examples of each.
2. Describe how various drugs affect neural processes and states of consciousness.
3. Describe how various forms of mental discipline, such as yoga and biofeedback, can be used to alter states of consciousness **indirectly**.
4. Discuss some suggested effects of endorphins in human response to pain.

Assignments

Before Viewing the Program

Read the preview at the beginning of this lesson and look over the learning objectives that precede the assignments.

Check the section "Did You Know That . . ." at the beginning of Chapter 3 in the text and look over the subtitles for that part of the chapter not assigned for Lesson Three.

Read the remainder of Chapter 3, beginning with the section "Altered States of Consciousness." As you read, note the boldfaced terms. To refresh your memory and clarify their meaning **before** you view the program, use the definitions and explanations of these terms which are defined in the upper right corners of right-hand pages.

View Program 4, "Altered States of Consciousness"

After Viewing the Program

Review the text assignments.

Read through all items in the summary at the end of Chapter 3 and consider the thought questions included in the chapter material. Then, to aid your understanding of the information presented in the lesson, review all of the boldfaced terms and concepts. In particular, note these terms carefully: lock and key hypothesis, receptor sites, excitation, pre- and postsynaptic inhibition, inhibitory synapse, stimulants, barbiturates, tranquilizers, analgesic, hallucinogens, enkephalin, opioid peptides, withdrawal symptoms, trance state, chemotherapy.

Complete the study activities included here as an additional study aid for you.

Now evaluate your understanding of the lesson material by reviewing the learning objectives and taking the self-test in this study guide. Check your answers against the answer key.

According to your instructor's assignment or your own interests, choose and complete activities from among the suggestions for extra credit. You might also consider the recommended readings listed at the end of the chapter.

Drawing by Chas. Addams; © 1956
The New Yorker Magazine, Inc.

Study Activities

Matching

Match the drug in the column on the left with the appropriate category in the column on the right, writing the letters of the categories in the appropriate blanks.

_____ 1. Benzedrine
_____ 2. Equanil
_____ 3. cocaine
_____ 4. aspirin
_____ 5. opium
_____ 6. barbiturates
_____ 7. caffeine
_____ 8. LSD
_____ 9. PCP
_____ 10. enkephalin
_____ 11. Novocain
_____ 12. morphine
_____ 13. marijuana
_____ 14. Dexedrine
_____ 15. alcohol

a. stimulant or "upper"
b. depressant or "downer"
c. analgesic or pain-killer
d. hallucinogen

Completion

1. Every nerve impulse must cross a _____ to pass from neuron to neuron. An electrical impulse crosses the synapse by sending a _____ messenger called a transmitter, or neurotransmitter. Transmitter molecules are released by the axonic end-fibers of one neuron and these molecules appear to fit into particularly sensitive _____ sites, or molecule pockets, on the _____ of the neuron on the opposite side of the gap. Your brain can and does block such neural _____ by "ordering" _____ neurons into action. These neurons can prevent the axon from releasing neurotransmitters into the synapse, which is called _____ inhibition, or they can keep dendrites and cell bodies from _____ to neurotransmitters, which is called postsynaptic _____.

presynaptic
transmission
receptor
synapse
responding
inhibitory
dendrites
chemical

2. Our awareness of the mental image of reality given to us by our neurons and interpreted by our cerebral cortex describes our _____. Because nerve impulses report all of the information that goes into consciousness, any chemical that could _____ their reporting process would also alter _____.

alter
consciousness
consciousness

3. Consciousness can be altered directly by drugs or _____ by means of various forms of mental discipline, such as yoga and _____. In this course, a drug is any chemical that, when taken in relatively small amounts, significantly increases or _____ activities somewhere in your body.

biofeedback
decreases
indirectly

4. One way to classify consciousness-altering drugs is by the function they perform. According to this arrangement, there are three basic categories: stimulants and depressants; analgesics (pain-killers); and hallucinogens. _____, or "uppers," increase neural firing. The best-known of this group of drugs are the _____, also referred to as "speed." "Downers," or _____, have an effect opposite to that of stimulants. They _____ neural activity and thus decrease neural firing.

inhibit
Stimulants
amphetamines
depressants

5. Sleeping pills, which are _____, are the strongest downers in general use. Tranquilizers, also depressants, are more specific in their effects, but less powerful than the barbiturates. Many tranquilizers affect the nervous system by stimulating _____ neurons.

inhibitory
barbiturates

6. Some analgesics block out neural _____ messages before they can reach the brain. Other pain-killing drugs affect the way your _____ processes painful inputs. Perhaps the most common analgesic known to humans is the mild pain-killer known to us as _____. For severe pain an opiate may be needed, but one undesirable side effect of opiates is that they are _____.

addictive
pain
brain
aspirin

7. People are said to be addicted to a drug when they become _____ or _____ dependent on that drug. The number one drug-addiction problem in America is _____. According to the Presidential Commission on Marijuana and Drug Abuse, _____ dependence was our second worst drug problem during the 1970s.

psychologically
heroin
physiologically
alcoholism

8. "Acid," or LSD, is the best-known drug in the family of _____. It is not really known exactly how hallucinogens achieve their effect, but they disturb the _____ processing area of the _____ and make the user perceive a vastly different world from the one that is really there.

central
brain
hallucinogens

9. When you slip into a state of relaxed alertness, your cortex shows an EEG pattern called alpha waves. Forms of mental discipline, such as yoga exercises, meditation, and biofeedback, lead to _____ control over _____ activity. In addition to regulating alpha activity, biofeedback patients can also learn to regulate basic body functions such as _____ rate and _____.

heart
voluntary
temperature
alpha

10. The body produces natural analgesics, called _____, or opioid peptides, which appear to have some surprising effects. Enkephalin, one of these natural substances, can cause _____. McDermott has suggested that a sudden shock may cause rapid release of these chemicals, leading to a _____ state.

trance-like
endorphins
addiction

Short-Answer Questions

1. Distingush between direct and indirect ways of altering consciousness and give examples of each.

2. While the exact biological mechanism underlying drug addiction is still not fully understood, there is a growing body of evidence to suggest that addiction to opiates is related to chemicals called endorphins, the body's natural pain-killer. Describe how addiction affects the body's supply of endorphins and how the endorphin level is related to withdrawal symptoms.

3. Review what you learned about neural firing in Lesson 2 and describe how the frequency of neural firing can affect different levels of consciousness.

Self-Test

(Select the one best answer.)

Objective 1: Distinguish between direct and indirect ways of altering
   consciousness and give examples of each.

1. Drugs are
   a. a direct means of speeding up or slowing down neural firing.
   b. an indirect means of speeding up or slowing down neural firing.
   c. any substances that significantly affect the structure or functioning of
      your body.
   d. described by the statements in both a and c.
   e. described by the statements in both b and c.

Objective 1; and *Objective 2:* Describe how various drugs affect neural processes
   and states of consciousness.

2. Which one of the following is not a class or category of drugs?
   a. stimulants and depressants
   b. analgesics, or pain-killers
   c. psilocybin
   d. hallucinogens
   e. All of the above are classes of drugs.

3. Stimulants, or "uppers," usually
   a. increase neural activity.
   b. increase heart rate.
   c. decrease appetite.
   d. decrease concentration.
   e. cause all of the above effects.

4. Which of the following drugs destroys neurons primarily in the dominant
   cerebral hemisphere?
   a. enkephalin
   b. alcohol
   c. mescaline
   d. caffeine
   e. PCP

5. Depressants, or "downers," generally do not
   a. decrease neural activity.
   b. increase the heart rate.
   c. slow the heart rate.
   d. lengthen reaction time.
   e. retard breathing rate.

6. The group of drugs called opiates does not
   a. block receptor sites.
   b. cause addiction.
   c. come from poppies.
   d. include marijuana.
   e. include morphine.

7. According to the Presidential Commission on Marijuana and Drug Abuse,
   _____ is our worst drug problem.
   a. heroin dependence
   b. alcoholism
   c. hashish
   d. cannabis
   e. PCP

Objective 2

8. Which of the following statements **best** describes the relationship between
   your mental processes and the way your neurons behave?
   a. What goes on in your mind influences the behavior of your neurons just
      as strongly as neurons influence your mental processes.
   b. The natural pain-killers known as endorphins can control your mental
      processes by inducing a trance, or state of euphoria.
   c. Your dominant hemisphere tells all of your neurons what to do.
   d. Research has shown that alcoholics who were given a placebo but
      believed they were drinking alcohol showed classic symptoms of
      intoxication.

9. The effect of any given drug on your body
   a. can be complex and is hard to predict.
   b. might differ at different times of day.
   c. is determined in part by the biochemistry of the drug.
   d. will depend on your expectations and environment.
   e. can be described by all of the foregoing statements.

10. Chemicals which are released by axonic end-fibers and cross the synaptic
    space to stimulate the dendrites of the next neuron are called
    a. transmitters, or neurotransmitters.
    b. stimulators, or activators.
    c. activators, or exciters.
    d. exciters, or stimulators.
    e. inhibitors, or exciters.

11. The small molecule "pockets" on the dendrites which seem to be sensitive to transmitter chemicals are called
    a. inhibitors.
    b. receptor sites.
    c. acceptors.
    d. sensitive sites.

Objective 3: Describe how various forms of mental discipline, such as yoga and biofeedback, can be used to alter states of consciousness **indirectly**.

12. Various forms of mental discipline, such as yoga and biofeedback, are
    a. direct means of speeding up or slowing down neural firing.
    b. indirect means of speeding up or slowing down neural firing.
    c. ways of controlling body functions such as heart rate, breathing rate, and body temperature.
    d. described by both statements a and c.
    e. described by both statements b and c.

Objective 4: Discuss some suggested effects of endorphins in human response to pain.

13. Enkephalin has been identified as
    a. a hallucinogenic drug.
    b. a harmless, short-lived tranquilizer.
    c. a natural pain-killer produced in the body.
    d. an effective treatment for morphine addiction.
    e. one of the important neurotransmitters.

14. What is the general name given to the body's naturally produced pain-killers?
    a. hallucinogens
    b. endorphins
    c. opiates
    d. mescaline
    e. stimulants

Suggestions for Extra Credit

1. Make a chart naming the different groups or types of drugs, listing examples of each, and describing how the members of each group affect neural firing. You might also want to include their primary and secondary (or side) effects.

2. In the July 5, 1985, issue of the *Journal of the American Medical Association* (JAMA), two researchers from Concordia University in Montreal, Canada, report on laboratory experiments in which rats were given free access to cocaine and heroin. Rats given cocaine died at three times the rate of those given heroin, and the researchers concluded that cocaine is both more addictive and more lethal than heroin. A second article in the same issue of JAMA describes the case of a young woman with **no previous heart problem** who suffered a heart attack following heavy cocaine abuse. Her alarmed doctors have called for further study of the effects of cocaine use on coronary health. Also in the same issue, the director of the National Institute of Drug Abuse warns editorially of cocaine's great danger and reports a 91 percent increase in cocaine-related deaths between 1980 and 1983. These articles are: "Toxicity Associated with Long-Term Intravenous Heroin and Cocaine Self-administration in the Rat," page 81; "Acute Myocardial Infarction (heart attack) Following Cocaine Abuse in a Young Woman with Normal Coronary Arteries," page 95; and "The Danger of Cocaine," page 98. If you are interested, read these three articles. What could you say about the extent and significance of cocaine abuse in this country today? What implications do the rat studies have for human drug abuse?

3. Keep a diary or chart of the drugs you take during an average day, week, or month. Note any observable speedup or slowdown in bodily function as a result of the drug. Note, also, any accompanying changes of mood or feeling. If the drug is not a prescription drug, after several days of observation, cut back on the amount you are taking and compare the results with those obtained before. Include your morning coffee or tea (how many cups?) and that glass of wine with dinner.

4. Many people have more than one disease or condition that must simultaneously be treated or controlled by drugs. For some, the dilemma lies in the fact that what controls the one disease or condition may aggravate the other so that a comfortable balance becomes difficult to achieve. This is true, for example, of diabetics with high blood pressure. Write a one-page paper describing how biofeedback might be helpful in such instances. If the subject interests you, do some research to learn how biofeedback has been used to control asthma attacks, migraine headaches, and blood pressure.

Answer Key

Matching

1. a		9. d
2. b		10. c
3. c		11. c
4. c		12. c
5. c		13. c or d
6. b		14. a
7. a		15. b
8. d		

Completion

1. synapse, chemical, receptor, dendrites, transmission, inhibitory, presynaptic, responding, inhibition;   2. consciousness, alter, consciousness;
3. indirectly, biofeedback, decreases;   4. Stimulants, amphetamines, depressants, inhibit;   5. barbiturates, inhibitory;   6. pain, brain, aspirin, addictive;   7. physiologically, psychologically, alcoholism, heroin;
8. hallucinogens, central, brain;   9. voluntary, alpha, heart, temperature;
10. endorphins, addiction, trance-like.

Short-Answer Questions

1. To alter anything directly means to change it "by the shortest or quickest route." Because the activity of the sensory and cortical nerves determines consciousness, one way to alter consciousness is to change or interfere with the firing patterns of these nerves. The quickest and, hence, the direct way of doing so is physiological. One physiological means is drugs. Drugs chemically alter the activity of these nerves or interfere with their receptivity to sensory impulses. A slower and, hence, indirect way of altering consciousness is psychological. By means of acquired mental discipline, such as that which characterizes yoga and biofeedback, the brain learns to affect and then to control the activity levels of these neurons or its interpretations of their messages.
2. Repeated use of addictive pain-killers, such as heroin and morphine, has a marked effect on how much of the endorphins the body produces. If you take a drug such as morphine long enough, it will turn off your body's normal pain-protection mechanism entirely. When you stop taking the drug, your body has no natural protection against pain and you are left vulnerable to the tortures of withdrawal symptoms until your body begins to produce its own protection once again.

3. A quantitative change in neural firing can bring about a qualitative change in your conscious experience. For example, speeding up the firing process causes the whole body to increase its tempo. As a result, your heart beats more quickly, blood rushes to the surface of the skin, you breathe more rapidly, your pupils dilate, your muscles become tense, and your reaction time is shortened. You lose your appetite. You are very alert but may find that your attention span is short and that you cannot concentrate. Slowing down the firing process slows your heart beat and breathing rate, takes blood away from the surface of your body, causes your pupils to constrict, and generally makes it more difficult for you to react quickly in an emergency.

Self-Test

  1. d (text pages 71-72)
  2. c (text pages 71-80; television program)
  3. e (text page 73; television program)
  4. b (text pages 79-80)
  5. b (text page 74)
  6. d (text pages 74-75)
  7. b (television program)
  8. a (text pages 81-82)
  9. e (text pages 71-72)
10. a (text page 68; television program)
11. b (text page 69; television program)
12. e (television program)
13. c (text pages 74-75)
14. b (text pages 74-75, 81)

Functions of the Brain

5

Viewer's Guide for Program Five

As you view the television program, watch for:

The labeled drawing that will help you understand the location and function of the four sections, or lobes, into which the cortex of each cerebral hemisphere is divided. These lobes lie just under the skull in four distinct regions: the forehead, above each ear, at top and center of the brain, and just above the back of the neck.

The sequence showing the effects of electrical stimulation of the brain. (Remember that, while the brain processes pain messages, it does not consciously experience pain. Thus, these kinds of experiments are useful for what they tell us about the exact location in the brain of control centers for various functions and are not painful for the animal or human subjects.)

The film sequence of neurologist Wilder Penfield reminiscing with a patient about her responses to and recollections of electrical stimulation of various parts of her brain.

The film sequence in which rats coexisting peacefully react with aggression to the inescapable pain of electrical shock. Frustrated at their inability to avoid or terminate the pain, they turn on each other in violent attack. Is human violence always a product of frustration?

The film sequence in which a big boy kicks small boys, who then run away and attack one smaller boy. The sequence is an example of the intrapsychic view that people fight because they are frustrated in trying to solve a problem or achieve a goal.

The telling film sequence in which children pattern their violent treatment of an inflatable doll after identical behavior by a grown-up model. Is violent behavior learned from parents, from siblings, from television, from heroes, and other authority figures and behavior models in real-life situations?

The newsreel footage of Charles Whitman, who murdered his wife and mother and then shot forty-nine people from atop a tower at the University of Texas. Could a tumor growing in the region of the limbic system and pressing on the amygdala have driven Whitman to kill?

Preview

Does your mind run your body? Does your body run your mind? Or are they both controlled by outside forces of which neither is aware? If you said without hesitation that your mind runs your body, who is in charge when you—and your mind—are asleep?

Philosophers have long speculated about the relationship between the body and the mind. They have repeatedly searched for the center of being, the seat of consciousness. Does it lie in the heart, as Aristotle believed, or in the head, as Descartes argued?

Scientists, too, have studied the problem. They have been concerned not so much with locating the mind—which they view as a reflection or product of the brain's activities—as with locating the centers of control within the brain itself. Using an electrical probe, surgery, and other methods, they have mapped the physiological and anatomical paths of the brain.

In this lesson, you will learn about the basic structure of the brain, review some new thoughts about the development of the human brain and its role, and give some thought of your own to the mind-body problem, to how mind and body interact to create and change behavior. As you do, you will realize that the relationship between them is not a simple one and is not yet completely understood, despite thousands of years of philosophical speculation and several hundred years of scientific study.

You will be reminded that there are three basic approaches to understanding mind-body interaction: the biological, the intrapsychic, and the social/behavioral. Each of these can be used to explain the aggression which Konrad Lorenz says is so characteristic of our human society. You will encounter ample evidence in the form of old and new research studies which confirm that violence cannot be adequately explained by relying exclusively on any single approach to the mind-body problem. Studies suggest that violence is a complicated behavior that may have both internal and external determinants. Rather, an understanding of violence and, one would hope, its control require knowledge of all three approaches considered in this lesson.

Learning Objectives

When you have finished viewing the program and studying your text assignments, you should be able to:

1. Discuss what is meant by the mind-body problem and explain it by comparing the three views—biological, intrapsychic, and social/behavioral.
2. Recognize the theories of Aristotle, Descartes, Gall, Flourens, Broca, and Fritsch and Hitzig as they relate to localization of brain function.
3. Name the four lobes in each cerebral hemisphere and describe their functions.
4. Describe some studies and theories that point to environmental determinants, intrapsychic determinants, and biological determinants of violent behavior.
5. Discuss why violence might be better understood as a multi-determined behavior.

Assignments

Before Viewing the Program

Read the preview at the beginning of this lesson and look over the learning objectives that precede the assignments.

Check the section "Did You Know That . . ." at the beginning of Chapter 4 in the text and look over the subtitles for the chapter.

Read Chapter 4, "Structure and Function of the Brain." As you read, note especially the boldfaced terms and those defined in the upper right corners of right-hand pages. Use the accompanying definitions or descriptions to increase your knowledge or refresh your memory concerning these terms.

View Program 5, "Functions of the Brain"

After Viewing the Program

Review the text assignments.

Read through the summary items at the end of the chapter and consider the thought questions inserted in the text. Then review all of the boldfaced terms. In particular, note these terms: mind-body problem, homunculus, phrenology, frontal lobe, temporal lobe, parietal lobe, occipital lobe, motor cortex, limbic system, amygdala, decorticate, habituate, association areas, "silent areas," body language, triune brain, limbic system, reptilian brain, thalamus, hypothalamus, instincts, repress, aggression, frustration-aggression hypothesis, psychosurgery, and biological, social/behavioral, and intrapsychic viewpoints.

Complete the study activities that are included here as an additional study aid for you.

Now evaluate your understanding of the lesson material by reviewing the learning objectives and taking the self-test in this study guide. Check your answers against the answer key.

According to your instructor's assignment or your own interests, choose and complete activities from among the suggestions for extra credit. You might also consider the recommended readings listed at the end of the chapter.

"If only he could think in abstract terms. . . ."

Study Activities

Matching

Match each phrase in the column on the right with the appropriate term in the column on the left, writing the letters of the phrases in the appropriate blanks.

____	1.	homunculus
____	2.	phrenology
____	3.	frontal lobe
____	4.	temporal lobe
____	5.	parietal lobe
____	6.	occipital lobe
____	7.	frustration-aggression hypothesis
____	8.	limbic system
____	9.	"silent areas"
____	10.	instincts
____	11.	triune brain

a. motor activity
b. vision
c. sensory inputs from skin
d. violence is instinctive
e. may have evolved from primitive animals
f. "little man"
g. speech and hearing
h. innate response patterns
i. thought to be control areas where information processing and decision making occur
j. skull bumps and depressions
k. violence and sex drive

Completion

1. The nature of the relationship between mental and physical activity and the exact place in the body where these activities interact are questions that remain unresolved, though they have puzzled philosophers and scientists for centuries. These issues are part of what philosophers refer to as the _____ problem.

mind-body

2. The famous Greek philosopher Aristotle believed that the human mind (or soul) resided in the _____, while French philosopher Rene _____ argued that mind and body were separate substances entirely. A European medical doctor, Franz Joseph _____, proposed the theory of phrenology. He was among the first to believe that psychological traits or abilities are located in _____ parts of the brain, but said these traits caused bumps on the head and that they could be "located" by "reading" the bumps on the skull. Phrenology was discredited by Pierre _____ in the 1820s on the basis of actual surgical experiments on human brains.

specific
Flourens
heart
Descartes
Gall

3. The belief that there is a specific locus in the brain for specific psychological functions or traits was upheld by French surgeon Paul _____, who identified the _____ center in the left temporal lobe of a mute "lunatic." There are four main sections, or lobes, in each cerebral hemisphere: the frontal lobe, the temporal lobe, the parietal lobe, and the _____ lobe.

occipital
speech
Broca

4. The frontal lobe contains the motor cortex; the temporal lobe is the center of speech, hearing, and emotions; the occipital lobe is the brain's visual center; and the parietal lobe receives sensory inputs from the _____ and _____. Stimulation of the nerve cells of the motor cortex in your left _____ lobe would cause the muscles on the right side of your body to twitch or jerk; you would see flashes of light if your occipital lobe were probed; temporal lobe stimulation would cause you to hear brief bursts of sound; and prickling sensations would result from stimulation of your parietal lobe.

muscles
skin
frontal

5. The three theoretical approaches to psychology and to the mind-body problem are called the biological approach, the intrapsychic approach, and the _____ approach. According to the _____ viewpoint, behavioral changes are closely related to and may be brought about by physiological changes. The intrapsychic viewpoint holds that you can become whatever you want to be because your mind controls your body. According to the _____ approach, behavior is determined by the environment in which you are reared, and to change your behavior, you must first change your _____.

environment
social/behavioral
biological
social/behavioral

6. Research indicates that some aggression and violence are generated by such environmental influences as societal attitudes, violent television programs, and behavior of parents and family. The research of Konrad Lorenz, who said that we are born with aggressive instincts that we must learn to control, is often cited by the _____ theorists. These theorists also point to research that shows both pain and frustration to be causes of _____ behavior in laboratory animals. However, most evidence seems to indicate that violence has many causes, or is _____.

aggressive
multi-determined
intrapsychic

7. Research shows that the amygdala, a structure of the limbic system, the inner border of the cerebral hemispheres, plays a definite role in violence and sexual behavior. Normally the cortex maintains control over reactions from the limbic system. _____ theorists can support the claim that removal or weakening of the cortical control, as well as pressure or stimulation of the _____, can result in violent behavior but the reverse is not necessarily true; all violent behavior is not associated with these variables. Alcohol has been shown to knock out _____ control of the _____ system. Thus, we can assume that intoxication might generate _____ behavior.

cortical
limbic
Biological
aggressive
amygdala

8. It has been suggested that humans have a complex three-part brain, which is called a _____ brain, that evolved from brains of lower animals. According to the theory, the stem of the triune brain evolved from the reptilian brain, the lower center of the cerebrum (such as the limbic system) from the old mammalian brain, and the cerebrum and cortex from the _____ mammalian brain.

new
triune

Short-Answer Questions

1. Recall the conversation between Professor Solomon P. Birdwhistle and Abner Jenkins in the television program for this lesson. On what two assumptions was phrenology based?

2. On the drawing below, label the cerebrum, the cerebellum, and the frontal, parietal, temporal, and occipital lobes.

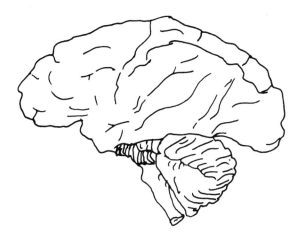

3. Explain briefly the observed effect of television violence and pornographic films on young people.

4. Psychologist Nathan Azrin and his colleagues made an accidental discovery about the association between pain and aggression. Describe their discovery.

5. Summarize Dr. McConnell's reasons for stating that violence is a multi-determined behavior.

Self-Test

(Select the one best answer.)

Objective 1: Discuss what is meant by the mind-body problem and explain it by comparing the three views—biological, intrapsychic, and social/behavioral.

1. The mind-body problem
   a. has long been the subject of discussion.
   b. is the foremost problem in psychology today.
   c. represents man's efforts to explore and explain the relationship between mental and physical activity.
   d. encompasses the complex interactions among brain, mind, and environment.
   e. is described by all of the above statements.

2. The belief that your mind controls your body and that you can become whatever you decide you should become is called the
   a. biological viewpoint.
   b. intrapsychic viewpoint.
   c. social/behavioral viewpoint.
   d. control theory.
   e. frustration-aggression theory.

3. The belief that your behavior is largely the product of the environment in which you are reared and the groups to which you belong is called the
   a. group theory.
   b. systems theory.
   c. biological viewpoint.
   d. social/behavioral viewpoint.
   e. intrapsychic viewpoint.

4. Which of the following statements does not characterize the biological stance in the mind-body controversy?
   a. Physiological psychologists take a biological approach to the mind-body problem.
   b. The biological approach holds that physical events in the nervous system are the major cause of subjective experiences in your mind.
   c. There is a definite connection between mental illness and murder.
   d. Violence can be explained in terms of brain stimulation and/or dysfunction.
   e. One-third of the murder victims in one study precipitated their own killing by taunting, goading, or threatening the murderer in some way.

Objective 2: Recognize the theories of Aristotle, Descartes, Gall, Flourens, Broca, and Fritsch and Hitzig as they relate to localization of brain function.

5. In trying to resolve the mind-body problem, Aristotle
   a. equated the mind with the "rational soul" but located it in the heart.
   b. equated the mind with the "rational soul" but located it in the head.
   c. equated the mind with the animal body and located it in the central torso or abdomen.
   d. said the mind is immortal but made no attempt to locate it.
   e. said the mind is immortal and could be discovered only through contemplation.

6. According to the textbook and the television program, Rene Decartes
   a. believed that mind and body were made of separate substances.
   b. preferred to observe the body rather than speculate on the soul.
   c. turned the mind-body problem into the mind-brain problem.
   d. did all of the above.
   e. did only a and c.

7. Franz Joseph Gall believed that a person's psychological abilities and traits could be determined by
   a. a carefully selected battery of written tests.
   b. "reading" bumps and depressions on the skull.
   c. a carefully selected series of tests administered orally.
   d. an instrument specifically designed to test both mental and motor abilities.
   e. all of the above means.

8. Gall's theory of phrenology was based on the assumptions that
   a. each trait or ability was controlled by a specific area of the brain and that, when active, these areas could be detected or "read" by an electroencephalograph (EEG).
   b. control of traits or abilities had no specific locus within the brain, but that electrical stimulation of an area while a specific behavior was being performed could "assign" its control to that area.
   c. each trait or ability was controlled by a specific area of the brain and that these brain areas would enlarge with repeated use.
   d. control of traits or abilities had no specific locus within the brain, but that specially designed mental exercises would localize these traits and abilities for "reading."

9. By scientifically observing the effects of brain surgery, Flourens
    a. proved most of Gall's theory of phrenology to be wrong.
    b. demonstrated that psychological traits or abilities have no specific locus within the brain.
    c. made many brilliant discoveries about how the brain works.
    d. discovered Gall was right about the location of a sexuality trait in the back of the head.
    e. accomplished a, b, and c.

10. Broca's work with a speechless "lunatic" showed that
    a. control of specific behaviors, like speech, is localized in specific areas of the brain.
    b. neural tissue in the left temporal lobe controls insanity.
    c. the brain controls body movement.
    d. the "lunatic" had scar tissue in his right temporal lobe.
    e. electrical stimulation of the same brain area always results in movement of the arms and legs.

11. Discovery of a motor output center (cortex) in the brain was made by _____ during experiments with soldiers dying of head wounds in the Franco-Prussian war.
    a. Penfield and Broca
    b. Hitzig and Penfield
    c. Fritsch and Hitzig
    d. Lorenz and Fritsch
    e. Flourens and Penfield

Objective 3: Name the four lobes in each cerebral hemisphere and describe their functions.

12. Each cerebral hemisphere is divided into four main lobes. Which of the following is not one of these lobes?
    a. frontal lobe
    b. temporal lobe
    c. parietal lobe
    d. callosal lobe
    e. occipital lobe

13. The frontal lobes of the brain
    a. control movement and muscle coordination.
    b. process our physical sensation of touch into mental experience.
    c. cause severe headaches and nausea.
    d. process our physical sensation of sound into a mental experience.
    e. are not a recognized part of the brain.

14. The temporal lobes in each hemisphere
    a. control movement and muscle coordination.
    b. process our physical sensation of touch into mental experience.
    c. can cause severe headaches and nausea.
    d. are not a recognized part of the brain.
    e. seem to be involved in hearing, speech production, and emotional behavior.

15. The parietal lobes
    a. control movement and muscle coordination.
    b. process our physical sensation of touch into mental experience.
    c. can cause severe headaches and nausea.
    d. are not a recognized part of the brain.
    e. seem to be involved in hearing and in speech production.

16. The occipital lobes
    a. house the motor output area and control movement and muscle coordination.
    b. are not a recognized part of the brain.
    c. house the visual input area and translate the sensation of sight into a mental experience.
    d. process our physical sensation of sound into a mental experience.
    e. process our physical sensation of touch into a mental experience.

Objective 4: Describe some studies and theories that point to environmental determinants, intrapsychic determinants, and biological determinants of violent behavior.

17. Research discussed in the text and television program suggests that environmental factors such as _____ may play a causal role in violence.
    a. pressure on the amygdala
    b. alcoholism and drug addiction
    c. removal of the amygdala
    d. family life

18. Intrapsychic theorists view violence and aggression as the natural result of
    a. pain and frustration.
    b. watching too much television.
    c. harsh punishment endured as a child.
    d. pressure on the amygdala.
    e. intoxication.

19. A society having a legal system that will arrest and try you if you kill someone subscribes to
    a. the social/behavioral explanation for violence.
    b. the intrapsychic viewpoint.
    c. the biological viewpoint.
    d. theories that all violence is caused by disturbances in the amygdala.
    e. theories that violence at home and on television are to blame for your behavior.

20. According to recent research, potential victims of crimes may be able, through "body language," to
    a. forestall a possible assault.
    b. determine the cause of violent behavior.
    c. invite a possible assault.
    d. bring about all of the above events.
    e. either prevent or invite assault.

21. According to the biological view, which of the following does not cause or intensify violent behavior?
    a. stimulating the amygdala by means of electrical shock or pressure
    b. removing the amygdala
    c. using drugs or alcohol to lessen cortical control of the limbic system
    d. removing the cortex
    e. intense pain

Objective 4; and *Objective 5:* Discuss why violence might be better understood
as a multi-determined behavior.

22. Although a tumor pressing on Charles Whitman's amygdala may have caused him to commit violence, most assaults and aggressive behaviors
    a. seem to be caused by surgery, not brain damage.
    b. are the result of frustration, not brain damage.
    c. are the direct result of television viewing.
    d. are caused by role models.
    e. seem to be caused by psychological and social factors, not by brain damage.

Objective 5

23. Which of the following statements does not support a theory of multiple causes for violent behavior?
    a. Whether a potential victim is assaulted can depend upon his or her own behavior.
    b. Television violence arouses aggression in some but not all young viewers.

c. Psychosurgery to remove the amygdala has been found to be very successful in eliminating violence, but it is a dangerous procedure.

d. Laboratory animals subjected to pain and frustration will flee rather than fight if given a choice.

Suggestions for Extra Credit

1. The three approaches to psychology explain behavior in a different way. Identify these three approaches and tell what, according to each, causes behavior. On which of the three approaches is our legal system based? For additional source material, read "Interview with Jerre Levy," p. 69, *Omni*, January 1985, or select one or more readings of your choice. Dr. Levy, who assisted Dr. Roger Sperry in the split-brain studies, forcefully defends the biological view of the "mind-body" controversy. (See Lesson 2.)

2. Discuss each of the following quotes in relation to the mind-body problem and/or to the division of responsibilities between the cerebral hemispheres:

> The soul of man is immortal and imperishable.
>
> *Plato*

> The mind of each man is the man himself.
>
> *Cicero*

> With women the heart argues, not the mind.
>
> *Matthew Arnold*

Man consists of body, mind,
and imagination. His body is
faulty, his mind untrustworthy,
but his imagination has made
him remarkable.

John Masefield

Or use *Familiar Quotations* by John Bartlett (or a similar source) to locate additional quotes on this subject.

3. Review the statistics about murder on page 99 in the text and review the section "The 'Body Language' of Victims." Then list the things you could do to decrease the likelihood that you would either commit a murder or become a murder victim.

4. For one week, keep a simple log during your normal television viewing, writing down each example of violent or aggressive behavior. (You may find it easier to keep this record if you keep your written descriptions as brief as possible, e.g. "fistfight," "gunplay," "verbal threat," "automobile pursuit.") At the end of the week, make an estimate of the number of examples of violence you might see if you watched television twenty-five hours each week. Discuss the kind of "role model" presented in these examples of violence: Are they heroes and "good guys," or deviants?

5. Devise a new rating system for television programs to indicate the amounts and types of violence so that parents can more accurately assess their suitability for children.

6. Child abuse has become an issue of great national concern in the United States today. Review the section "The 'Body Language' of Victims" in text Chapter 4, then address the thought questions the text author poses on page 103. After answering these questions, apply them to situations where the child is abused by someone **other** than parents.

Answer Key

Matching

1. f	7. d
2. j	8. k
3. a	9. i
4. g	10. h
5. c	11. e
6. b	

Completion

1. mind-body;   2. heart, Descartes, Gall, specific, Flourens;   3. Broca, speech, occipital;   4. skin, muscles, frontal;   5. social/behavioral, biological, social/behavioral, environment;   6. intrapsychic, aggressive, multi-determined;   7. Biological, amygdala, cortical, limbic, aggressive;   8. triune, new.

Short-Answer Questions

1. Franz Joseph Gall based phrenology on two assumptions: (1) that each part of the brain had a highly specific function; and (2) that, just as working the muscles makes them enlarge, so working particular centers of the brain would make them enlarge, press out on the skull, and create a bump that could be "read."

2.

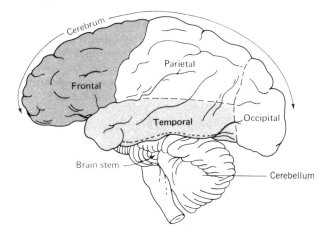

3. Studies by the U.S. Surgeon General's Office in the late 1960s and early 1970s confirmed that television viewers are bombarded with violent episodes, and in 1983 the National Institute of Mental Health concluded that " . . . while not all children (who watch such episodes) become violent, the correlation between television violence and aggressive behavior is strongly positive." William Belson, however, found that, among a group of British youths, it was the "heavy" television watcher, rather than the occasional viewer, who was much more likely to commit aggressive acts, and some 50 percent of the youths committed no violence at all. Leonard D. Eron has reported that television violence affects aggressive behavior in both boys and girls and that the children who are so affected share a number of common characteristics: they are disliked by other school children, have active aggressive fantasies, prefer masculine activities, are low school achievers, and enjoy viewing violence on television. The parents of such children were also found to share some common characteristics, such as

being aggressive themselves. A 1984 University of Wisconsin study of violence and pornography indicates that the **combination** of violence and sexuality in films desensitizes males to aggression—**not** erotic movies that are nonviolent.

4. Azrin and his colleagues discovered that administering an electrical shock to two rats that had been peacefully coexisting caused them to exhibit aggressive behavior toward each other. The stronger the shock, the longer the aggression lasted. The pain of the shock set in motion an instinctual behavior pattern that had nothing to do with sexual competition or attraction, was relatively independent of the animal's prior experience, and would allow a very small animal, such as a mouse, to attack a much larger one, such as a cat.

5. J. P. Scott believes that social and behavioral influences may be the most important causes of violence in human beings. There are also convincing studies that show intrapsychic and biological causes for violence. McConnell believes that violence, like all behaviors, is multi-determined: One's present thoughts and actions are influenced by biological heredity, past experiences, and the present environment.

Self-Test

1. e (text page 90; television program)
2. b (text page 97; television program)
3. d (text page 97)
4. e (text pages 96-97; television program)
5. a (text pages 90-91; television program)
6. d (text page 91; television program)
7. b (text pages 91-92; television program)
8. c (text pages 92-93)
9. e (text page 93)
10. a (text pages 93-94; television program)
11. c (text pages 94-95; television program)
12. d (text page 94; television program)
13. a (text pages 94-95; television program)
14. e (text page 95; television program)
15. b (text page 95; television program)
16. c (text page 95; television program)
17. d (text pages 99-103; television program)
18. a (text pages 103-106; television program)
19. b (text pages 103-106)
20. e (text pages 102-103)
21. b (text pages 108-109)
22. e (text pages 109-110; television program)
23. c (text pages 103-109)

Sensory Processes

Viewer's Guide for Program Six

As you view the television program, watch for:

The diagrams in which the three basic skin senses are identified, their importance is emphasized, and their distribution is pinpointed graphically. Note, too, the way in which the experiment with the alligator not only gives a clear understanding of how receptors react to stimuli but also allows the reaction to be measured.

The sequence in which we observe the skin sensors monitoring skin temperatures night and day as a boy proceeds through a normal, active day equipped with a special device that records reactions of the skin to temperature changes in the environment.

Animated diagrams of the trip taken by a sensory message from a receptor up the spinal cord to the somatic cortex and from there to the motor cortex, which flashes instant commands back to the appropriate muscles. Note the behavior of the frog when the message wires are "crossed."

Examples of the functioning of the so-called deep receptors in discriminating between weights, thicknesses, and shapes.

Animated sequences depicting the role of the inner ear in helping to detect and control balance and motion.

Preview

Every time you lift your hand to spoon a bit of hot soup into your mouth, do you "listen" while the nerve receptors in your mind and skin exchange information about just where and how far to go to get your spoon into your mouth on target? Do you wait while your brain and your tongue "consider" the matter before agreeing that the soup is just right—neither too hot nor too cold?

No, of course not. Your body's sensory system does these things for you continually with a careful and delicate coordination that usually does not intrude upon your conscious awareness at all. But if you were to climb a steep mountain face or build a complex robot that could go exploring for you, you would be forced to become very much aware of your sensory system and what the system does to assure your survival and that of the robot as well. To begin this lesson, you are asked to take a brief look at these two unlikely and esoteric tasks as a way of illustrating vividly how indispensable the sensory receptors really are to the body.

In this lesson, you will learn how sensory receptors located in your skin and in the deeper body tissues of muscles, joints, tendons, and bones continually monitor what your body is doing, where you are, and how you are, as well as what may be happening in the immediate world around you. The skin, which has been called your "window on the world," has special receptors that provide the brain with much of what it needs to know in the form of information about pressure, temperature, and pain. Deep receptors permit discrimination of size, weight, and shape, and they inform the brain about the changing positions of your arms and legs. Two special receptors in your inner ear keep your brain advised about your movements and balance. A special diagram presented in the television program will reinforce your understanding of the complex way in which messages are transmitted from the receptors via the spinal cord to the brain, then back to appropriate muscles in the form of a "command" to action. This lesson and the five that follow will help you to understand your senses and their relationship to how your thought processes function.

Learning Objectives

When you have finished viewing the program and studying your text assignments, you should be able to:

1. List the skin receptors, what they do, and where they are located in the body.
2. Give an example of how the corpuscles and basket cells detect complex pressure sensations of smoothness and roughness.

3. Describe how your temperature receptors operate, and explain how your interpretation of temperature might vary depending on what you have just been doing.
4. Describe the functions of the somatic cortex.
5. Distinguish between the functions of the deep receptors and the surface receptors.
6. Give examples of how rotary and linear motion are detected.
7. Distinguish between adaptation and central habituation with regard to sensation.

Assignments

Before Viewing the Program

Read the preview at the beginning of this lesson and look over the learning objectives that precede the assignments.

Check the section "Did You Know That . . ." at the beginning of Chapter 6 in the text, and look over the subtitles for the chapter.

Read Chapter 6, "Introduction to Sensory Psychology: 'Touch,' Taste, and Smell," from the beginning through the section "A Window of Skin." Note the thought questions in the chapter that relate to this lesson.

View Program 6, "Sensory Psychology"

After Viewing the Program

Review the text assignments.

Read through the summary items at the end of the chapter that relate to this lesson. Then, to facilitate your understanding of the materials presented in this lesson, study the terms and concepts that are printed in boldface and defined in the upper right corners of right-hand pages. In particular, note these terms carefully: sensory coherence, or coherent whole, corpuscles, basket cells, free nerve endings, somatic cortex, deep receptors, linear motion, saccule, utricle, semicircular canals, receptor adaptation, central habituation.

Complete the study activities that are included here as an additional study aid for you.

Now evaluate your understanding of the lesson material by reviewing the learning objectives and taking the self-test in this study guide. Check your answers against the answer key.

According to your instructor's assignment or your own interests, choose and complete activities from among the suggestions for extra credit.

Study Activities

Matching

Match each phrase in the column on the right with the appropriate term in the column on the left, writing the letters in the appropriate blanks.

____ 1. pressure
____ 2. habituation
____ 3. changing position of legs, arms
____ 4. linear motion
____ 5. temperature
____ 6. pain
____ 7. adaptation
____ 8. discriminating weight, shape
____ 9. rotary motion
____ 10. somatic cortex

a. deep receptors
b. free nerve endings
c. corpuscles, basket cells, and free nerve endings
d. semicircular canals
e. utricle and saccule
f. reduced firing rate
g. ignoring signals
h. sensory receiving area

Completion

1. To survive and to achieve other personal and social goals as well, you must receive a great assortment of _____ inputs; and if these inputs are to be useful to you, your brain must organize them into a _____ whole. The sense of touch belongs primarily to the _____. Every feeling in the skin is composed of three basic sensations: _____, _____, and _____. At the base of each hair on the skin are unique receptors called _____ cells that dispatch pressure messages to the brain. _____ are the type of skin receptors found in hairless areas that respond to the stimulation of pressure. The receptors known as _____ nerve _____ are located in greater abundance on your skin surfaces than either the basket cells or the corpuscles and are _____ to both pressure and _____.

temperature
sensory
skin
coherent
pressure
pain
temperature
basket
Corpuscles
receptive
free
endings

2. Each receptor has limits of stimuli to which it will or will not respond. Above a certain strength, the receptor cannot _____ its firing rate. Below a minimal strength, the receptor does not _____ to a stimulus.

respond
increase

3. Skin receptors help you to identify textures and substances through the experiences of _____ and _____ . Our sense of _____ is one of the most basic of all our senses and almost all areas of the _____ respond to warmth and cold. Temperature receptors are thought to respond mainly to _____ , that is, they respond to environmental stimuli that are _____ or _____ than the skin.

hotter
colder
temperature
changes
skin
temperature
pressure

4. The messages that skin receptors send to your brain tell you four things about the experience you are sensing: its _____, its _____, its _____, and its _____. The _____ cortex receives sensory messages from the skin and muscle receptors, while the _____ cortex sends sensory messages to the muscles and glands to tell them how to react.

location
motor
somatic
quality
duration
quantity

5. For each area on the body's surface, there is a corresponding area on each _____. These areas connect with one another through their own special nerve pathways. Receptors in the left side of your body send their inputs to the _____ _____ in the _____ side of your brain.

right
cortex
somatic cortex

6. We are constantly being made aware of the position of our limbs and the state of internal organs by the _____ _____. Moving your head backward or forward in a straight line stimulates the _____ nerve _____ at the base of each hair cell in the gelatinous tissue of the utricles and saccules. This action tells the _____ cortex that the body is in linear motion.

somatic
basket
deep receptors
cells

86

7. When the body moves in a circular motion, _____ inside the _____ canals presses against a small mound of gelatinous tissue at the base of each canal in the inner ear. _____ cells in the gelatin are twisted or pulled. They bend first against the motion, then with it, and finally right themselves, stimulating the _____ that carry impulses to the brain.

nerves
semicircular
fluid
Hair

8. When stimulation is constant, some receptor cells fire more slowly or stop firing altogether. This response is known as _____.

adaptation

9. Central habituation occurs when your _____ tends to _____ sensory inputs that seem unimportant. Body receptors adapt and the brain habituates to constant stimuli because survival requires attention to _____ in the environment.

ignore
changes
brain

Short-Answer Questions

1. What three things do sensory inputs from the skin tell the brain?

2. If the temperature deep inside your body does not change appreciably, why do you feel colder when it is 32°F outside than you do when the outside temperature is, say, 55°F?

3. Suppose you have just grasped a pot handle that is rather hot. Trace the complete course of the "hot message" that the skin of your hand and fingers transmits.

4. Explain how you are able to judge the weight of an object placed in your hand even if you cannot see the object.

5. What does Newton's law of inertia state? Relate this principle to your sense of motion.

Self-Test

(Select the one best answer.)

Objective 1: List the skin receptors, what they do, and where they are located in the body.

1. Almost all of the information about the world that we get from our skin comes from the receptors for
   a. pressure and temperature.
   b. softness and hardness.
   c. touch and motion.
   d. hairy and hairless regions.
   e. temperature and pain.

Objective 1; and *Objective 3:* Describe how your temperature receptors operate, and explain how your interpretation of temperature might vary depending on what you have just been doing.

2. Our sensory systems respond primarily to
   a. neuronal messages from processing centers.
   b. changes in input.
   c. the total amount of stimulation.
   d. constant stimulation from the environment.
   e. intermittent stimulation.

Objective 1

3. Which of the following statements is not correct?
   a. Receptor corpuscles in the skin detect pressure.
   b. Both pressure and temperature are sensed by free nerve endings.
   c. Basket cells on hair roots detect pressure.
   d. Deep receptors in the skin help to detect pressure.
   e. Basket cells and corpuscles in the skin detect textures and contours.

Objective 2: Give an example of how the corpuscles and basket cells detect complex pressure sensations of smoothness and roughness.

4. Complex pressure sensations of smoothness and roughness are detected by
   a. deep receptors.
   b. free nerve endings.
   c. corpuscles and basket cells.
   d. the semicircular canals.
   e. all of the above receptors.

5. When you immerse yourself for awhile in a tub of very hot water and keep the water hot, temperature receptors in your skin will
   a. be stimulated to raise your body temperature.
   b. fire rapid messages to your brain until you cool the water.
   c. automatically cool your skin.
   d. soon report the water as cooler.
   e. respond as described in both a and b.

Objective 4: Describe the functions of the somatic cortex.

6. The organization of the cortex for receiving input from the skin senses
   a. does not respond to the location of the incoming message.
   b. is similar to the organization of our motor (output) cortex.
   c. allows an approximately equal area for each subdivision of the body.
   d. makes it possible for one part of the brain to control many body parts.
   e. does not respond to changes in strength of stimuli.

Objective 5: Distinguish between the functions of the deep receptors and the surface receptors.

7. The deep receptors provide the brain with information about
   a. size and weight.
   b. pain only.
   c. pressure only.
   d. pressure and temperature.
   e. motion.

8. Muscle receptors that help tell us what our body is doing are called
   a. pressure receptors.
   b. motion receptors.
   c. deep receptors.
   d. contraction receptors.
   e. saccules and utricles.

Objective 6: Give examples of how rotary and linear motion are detected.

9. Newton's principle of inertia is involved in the function of
   a. pressure receptors.
   b. deep receptors.
   c. temperature receptors.
   d. contraction receptors.
   e. motion receptors.

10. We experience no motion when cruising steadily in a jet at 600 miles per hour because
    a. centrifugal motion creates a feeling of gravity.
    b. high altitude slows down the firing of motion receptors.
    c. the inner ear detects only changes in motion.
    d. the ear stops functioning as one approaches the speed of sound.
    e. stimulus strength is too low to sense.

Objective 7: Distinguish between adaptation and central habituation with regard to sensation.

11. Nearly all the receptor cells in the body
    a. adapt to stimulation.
    b. fire constantly at the same rate when stimulated.
    c. respond mainly to changes in the environment.
    d. fire constantly and respond mainly to environmental changes.
    e. can become habituated.

12. The response known as adaptation
    a. is an adjustment to a constant stimulus
    b. involves a slowed firing rate.
    c. occurs only in hearing.
    d. permits you to pay more attention to changes in the environment.
    e. is characterized by all of the above descriptions.

13. The brain's tendency to ignore sensory inputs that seem of little interest or importance is called
    a. habituation.
    b. adaptation.
    c. ignorance.
    d. relaxation.
    e. sensory diffusion.

Suggestions for Extra Credit

1. Read Helen Keller's *Story of My Life* (New York: Airmont, 1970). Try to repeat her experiences as nearly as possible for several hours, "hearing" and "seeing" with your skin senses and discriminating other stimuli with your deep receptors instead of with your usual complement of senses. Keep a journal of your experiences and write a report relating your experiences to those of Miss Keller.
2. If you are mechanically or artistically inclined, design a robot and draw a complete sensory system for the robot that would reasonably substitute for the functions of the human sensory system.

3. Review Lesson 4, "Altered States of Consciousness," or read additional materials on the subject, and write a brief paper describing how you think the functions of the sensory systems discussed in this chapter might be affected by drugs, particularly with respect to sensory input, motor input, and cortical processing.

4. During the 1980 winter Olympics, world pairs figure skating champions Randy Gardner and Tai Babilonia were forced to withdraw from competition because of a groin injury suffered by Gardner. He had taken an injection to numb the pain in the injured area and was left with too little feeling to tell the exact position of his leg or to judge when his weight was on his leg. Explain which receptors were probably affected by the drug. In what ways might a drug interfere with the transmission of pain messages? (Refer to Lesson 4, "Altered States of Consciousness.") What are the dangers inherent in performing a rigorous sport with pain artificially numbed but injury unhealed?

Answer Key

Matching

1. c		6. b	
2. g		7. f	
3. a		8. a	
4. e		9. d	
5. b		10. a	

Completion

1. sensory, coherent, skin, pressure, temperature, pain, basket, Corpuscles, free, endings, receptive, temperature;   2. increase, respond;   3. pressure, temperature, temperature, skin, changes, hotter, colder;   4. quality, quantity, location, duration, somatic, motor;   5. cortex, somatic cortex, right;   6. deep receptors, basket, cells, somatic;   7. fluid, semicircular, Hair, nerves; 8. adaptation;   9. brain, ignore, changes.

Short-Answer Questions

1. Receptors in the skin transmit to the brain sensory inputs about pressure, temperature, and pain. Three types of receptors receive and transmit these three sensations. Basket cells located in hairy areas of the skin, corpuscles located in hairless areas of the skin, and free nerve endings found in almost all parts of the skin are sensitive to pressure or light touch. Free nerve endings, which are the most common of the three skin receptors, respond to

both temperature and pressure changes. Damage or overstimulation of the free nerve endings results in the sensation of pain. Messages sent by the skin receptors are interpreted by the brain.

2. Because your deep body temperature must remain more or less the same, it is your skin that responds to temperature changes. If you go from a warm room to an outside temperature of 32°F, your "cold" detector receptors will fire much more vigorously at that temperature than they will at 55°F because more heat is flowing from the body through the skin at the colder temperature. This increase in the responses of the temperature receptors causes you to feel a greater sensation of cold.

3. When you grasp a pot handle that is too hot, the free nerve endings in the skin of your fingers and hand flash a message along the arm, up the spinal cord, through the lower brain centers, to the somatic cortex at the front edge of the appropriate parietal lobe in the brain. Messages from the left hand go to the right hemisphere of the brain; messages from the right hand are received on the left hemisphere. Messages from specific parts of the body, such as the hand, are received in a specific part of the somatic cortex. In the somatic cortex, the message from your hand is processed and interpreted as "hot." This interpretation is quickly flashed to the specific point on the nearby motor cortex which controls the muscles of the affected hand. The motor cortex immediately sends a command back to the hand muscles to take action. In this instance, the command would be to withdraw your hand from the pot, of course.

4. You do not need to see an object you are holding in your hand to judge its weight. Deep receptors in the muscles, joints, tendons, and bones enable us to judge weight, as well as size and shape. The heavier the object is, the harder your hand and arm muscles must work to hold the object steady. When these muscles contract (work), tiny nerve cells tell the somatic cortex what is happening. The harder the muscles contract, the faster the neurons fire. The brain interprets weight on the basis of the strength of the feedback.

5. Briefly, Newton's law of inertia states that a body at rest tends to remain at rest, while a body in motion tends to continue in motion. The human body has two types of receptor organs that detect change in motion: the semicircular canals and the saccules and utricles. Both function in obedience to Newton's law. The three semicircular canals are positioned at right angles to each other so that they can detect circular motion in the three dimensions of space. When the body moves in a circular motion, fluid and hair cells inside the canals slosh backward and forward, against the motion and with it. Then the hair cells move upright, just as your body would do if you were in a car that made a fast start, then a fast stop. The hair cells stimulate the nerves that tell the brain how and where you are moving. In linear, or straight-line, motion tiny stones in the utricles and saccules set to quivering a gelatinous mass that, in turn, shoves and pulls the hair cells back and forth. The basket cells at the base of the hair cells, stimulated by the quivering, tell the brain that the body is starting or stopping a straight-line movement.

Self-Test

1. a (text page 145)
2. b (text pages 146, 149; television program)
3. d (text page 147; television program)
4. c (text page 145)
5. d (text pages 145-146; television program)
6. b (television program)
7. a (text page 147; television program)
8. c (text page 147; television program)
9. e (text pages 147-149)
10. c (text page 149; television program)
11. d (text pages 150-151)
12. e (text pages 150-151)
13. a (text pages 150-151)

Taste, Smell, and Hearing

7

Viewer's Guide for Program Seven

As you view the television program, watch for:

The animated sequence showing the location of the taste buds on the tongue and the way they are stimulated chemically to detect four basic qualities: sweet, sour, bitter, and salty.

The animated sequence showing how specific scent molecules match with specific receptor contact points to enable us to detect and distinguish smells.

The demonstration of the way separation of our ears allows us to localize and identify sound sources.

Demonstrations of wave action and the vibrations of a tuning fork.

The animated sequence showing how sound is funneled into the auditory canal by the outer ear, amplified and passed along by the hammer, anvil, and stirrup of the middle ear to the inner ear, where hair cells fire off impulses to the brain.

Animated demonstrations of frequency and amplitude. Frequency is the number of times a sound source vibrates—or the number of cycles a sound wave makes—each second. Amplitude is the amount of sound present, or the "height" of a sound wave.

We take our senses for granted, but in the early ages of history they were the key to our survival. Taste helped us tell which foods were safe to eat. With our sense of smell, we detected danger while it was still at a distance. And we listened intently for sounds that would signal the approach of friend or foe, predator or prey.

According to popular opinion, there are but five senses—vision, hearing, taste, smell, and touch. But there are those who argue that the human sensory system also includes such "senses" as "common" sense.

Our senses are still very important to us, of course, but today we no longer fully depend upon the five senses for our survival because our survival needs have changed. At least some of these senses are more of a key to information and to our enjoyment of good food and drink, good music, and other aspects of the environment. Most of us think of these senses as they relate to our daily comforts and needs, yet we really know very little about them.

In this lesson, you will learn how the chemical senses of taste and smell and the mechanical sense of hearing work. Among other things, you will discover that people differ greatly in their sensitivity to tastes, how monosodium glutamate improves some flavors, why a cold makes food "lose its taste," why men "smell better," how smell affects sexual attraction, how sex hormones affect smell, and that at least one scientist has identified seven primary "smells," while there are believed to be only five primary taste qualities.

You will understand why the sense of hearing is so important to humankind, why dogs can hear sounds **you** can't hear, and—possibly to your surprise—you will learn that faulty hearing can result in paranoid behavior.

Learning Objectives

When you have finished viewing the program and studying your text assignments, you should be able to:

1. Describe the location and appearance of taste and smell receptors, and describe how each responds to appropriate stimuli.
2. Describe research that demonstrates how hormones influence the sense of smell and how smells in turn can affect human sexual behavior.
3. Discuss the similarities and differences between the senses of taste, smell, and hearing.

4. Describe the appearance and function of the outer, middle, and inner ear.
5. Describe frequency and amplitude of sound waves and relate them to the highness/lowness and loudness/softness of sound.

Assignments

Before Viewing the Program

Read the preview at the beginning of this lesson and look over the learning objectives that precede the assignments.

Check the section "Did You Know That . . ." at the beginning of both Chapters 6 and 7 of your text, and look over the subtitles in each chapter which relate to taste, smell, and hearing.

Read Chapter 6, "Introduction to Sensory Psychology: 'Touch,' Taste, and Smell," beginning with the section "Taste," page 151; and read Chapter 7, "Hearing and Seeing," from the beginning of the chapter through the section "Language Learning, Deafness, and Feedback" to page 172.

View Program 7, "Taste, Smell, and Hearing"

After Viewing the Program

Review the text assignments.

Read through the summary items in each chapter that apply to the assigned reading and consider the thought questions that appear throughout the chapters. Then, to facilitate your understanding of the materials presented in this lesson, study the terms and concepts that are printed in boldface and are defined in the upper right corners of right-hand pages. In particular, note these terms carefully: taste buds, papillae, acuity, taste qualities, taste blindness, olfactory membrane, smell qualities, copulins, monaural, stereo, auditory canal, separation, vibratory waves, auditory spectrum, hammer, anvil, stirrup, oval window, cochlea, organ of Corti, frequency, amplitude.

Complete the study activities that are included here as an additional study aid for you.

Now evaluate your understanding of the lesson material by reviewing the learning objectives and taking the self-test in this study guide. Check your answers against the answer key.

According to your instructor's assignments or your interests, choose and complete activities from among the suggestions for extra credit. You also might consider the section Recommended Readings which appears at the end of the chapter.

Study Activities

Matching

Match each phrase in the column on the right with the appropriate term in the column on the left, writing the letters in the appropriate blanks.

____ 1. acuity	a. chemicals released by females which act as sexual attractants for males
____ 2. copulins	b. vibrations or Hz
____ 3. monaural	c. decreased firing by receptors in the presence of a constant stimulus
____ 4. adaptation	d. strength or loudness of sound
____ 5. habituation	e. layer of tissue that contains receptors for smell
____ 6. amplitude	f. process by which the brain ignores repeated similar stimulus inputs
____ 7. frequency	g. sound that is produced by a single source
____ 8. exaltolide	h. ability to judge small differences among similar stimuli
____ 9. olfactory membrane	i. bumps on the tongue which contain taste buds
____ 10. papillae	j. compound, secreted in large amounts by men, which acts as an attractant for women
____ 11. oval window	k. separates middle and inner ear
____ 12. organ of Corti	l. site of the receptor cells for hearing

Completion

1. According to popular opinion, there are five senses. These are _____, _____, _____, _____, and _____. The two chemical senses are _____ and _____.

smell
taste
hearing
vision
smell
touch
taste

2. The primary receptors for taste are the _____ buds, which are located in mushroom-shaped bumps called _____ on the surface of the tongue. The four basic taste qualities are _____, _____, _____, and _____. We seem to inherit preferences for some tastes; for example, a baby will usually drink milk readily but spit out something _____ or _____. An inherited deficiency has been found to cause many people to be insenstive to certain tastes, a condition known as taste _____.

sour
sweet
bitter
blindness
taste
papillae
sour
salty
bitter

3. The smell receptors lie on the _____ membrane, a layer of tissue at the top of each nasal cavity. Most of the odors your nose detects come from _____ molecules that are heavier than air. A University of California researcher has identified at least seven primary _____ of smell.

qualities
olfactory
gaseous

4. Skin senses, including taste, rely on _____ receptors. Olfaction hearing, and vision rely on _____ receptors. Inputs of taste and smell each come to your brain from a single source, your nose or your tongue; therefore, these senses are said to be _____. Sound impulses, on the other hand, come to your brain from two separate sources, your ears, which are about 15 centimeters apart. For this reason, sound is a _____ sense.

monaural
distance
stereo
local

5. The separation of your ears enables your brain to detect _____ differences in sound sources. Your ear has three main divisions: the _____ ear, the middle ear, and the _____ ear. The _____ separates your outer ear from your middle ear. The middle ear contains three little bones called the _____, the _____, and the _____.

anvil
stirrup
eardrum
hammer
inner
outer
left-right

6. The oval _____ separates the middle ear from the inner ear. The inner ear has two main parts, the _____ and the _____ detectors discussed in Lesson Six. The cochlea contains the _____ receptors. These are part of the _____ of Corti, which lies atop the basilar _____.

motion
organ
auditory
membrane
cochlea
window

7. Sound waves have two aspects, their _____ and their _____. It is measured in _____, or Hz. The greater the frequency of a musical tone, the _____ it sounds. The amount of loudness of sound, _____, is measured in _____.

Hertz
decibels
frequency
amplitude
higher
amplitude

Short-Answer Questions

1. Label the three main divisions and the parts of the ear.

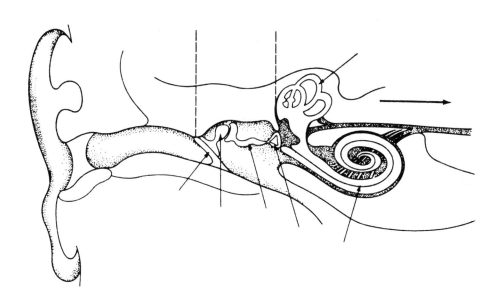

2. Discuss the similarities and differences between the senses of taste, smell, and hearing.

3. In the diagram below are three sound waves. By means of simple labels, indicate amplitude and wavelength, and then tell which sound is louder, A or B.

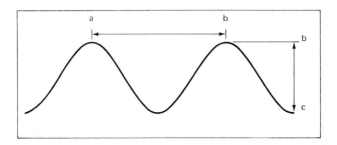

A   B

Self-Test

(Select the one best answer.)

Objective 1: Describe the location and appearance of taste and smell receptors, and describe how each responds to appropriate stimuli.

1. Which of the following qualities makes the least important contribution to how much you enjoy a good steak?
   a. smell
   b. texture
   c. taste
   d. appearance
   e. temperature

2. The taste buds are scattered in nooks and crannies all over the surface of your
   a. lips.
   b. tongue.
   c. uvula.
   d. soft palate.
   e. hard palate.

3. The sense of taste is
   a. as richly developed as smell and hearing.
   b. limited to four basic qualities.
   c. more important than the sense of hearing.
   d. more important than the sense of smell.
   e. described by all of the above.

4. Taste is
   a. a chemical sense.
   b. "monaural."
   c. a function of local receptors.
   d. described by all of the above.
   e. described by a and b only.

5. Which of the following is most important to your enjoyment of the food you eat?
   a. its texture
   b. its temperature
   c. papillae
   d. testosterone
   e. gaseous molecules

6. The chemical processes that lead to the experience of taste are not entirely known, but it appears that
   a. certain types of food molecules fill in specific receptor sites on the receptor cells that make up the taste buds.
   b. food molecules are sorted by the tongue and counted by the taste buds.
   c. the accumulation of food molecules causes particular taste buds to enlarge.
   d. all of the above statements are correct.
   e. none of the above statements is correct.

7. A rather large number of people are afflicted with taste blindness, an insensitivity to some primary qualities of taste which is thought to be caused by
   a. eating food that is too cold or hot.
   b. an inherited deficiency.
   c. too-frequent colds that dull the taste buds.
   d. the fact that taste is a monaural sense.
   e. some food molecules locking into the wrong receptor sites.

8. The olfactory rods are primarily stimulated by
   a. specific frequencies.
   b. light gaseous molecules.
   c. liquid molecules.
   d. heavy gaseous molecules.
   e. pressure and temperature.

Objective 2: Describe research that demonstrates how hormones influence the sense of smell and how smells in turn can affect human sexual behavior.

9. Olfactory acuity
   a. varies directly with the number of sex hormones present in the body.
   b. varies inversely with the number of sex hormones present in the body.
   c. varies with the degree of taste blindness.
   d. remains constant.

10. In an experiment conducted in the late 1970s by Crowley and his colleagues, sex-related odors were found to
    a. affect the feelings women students had concerning office seekers.
    b. cause some of the women to favor assertive and aggressive candidates.
    c. cause other women to favor shy and nonaggressive candidates.
    d. alter the judgments of women students.
    e. cause all of the above responses.

Objective 3: Discuss the similarities and differences between the senses of taste, smell, and hearing.

11. The sense of smell is
    a. resistant to habituation.
    b. a chemical sense.
    c. classified as a "local" receptor.
    d. a "stereo" sense.
    e. none of the above.

12. The senses of smell and taste are alike in that they both
    a. rely on chemical receptors.
    b. rely on local receptors.
    c. play an equal role in the enjoyment of food.
    d. are perceived by means of messages sent through the olfactory membrane.
    e. are perceived by means of messages sent through the basilar membrane.

13. Which of the following groupings does not belong among the seven primary smell "experiences" identified by a University of California scientist?
    a. peppermint, pungent, putrid
    b. ethereal, peppermint, floral
    c. pungent, sweet, musky
    d. musky, peppermint, putrid
    e. pungent, camphor, floral

14. In contrast to hearing, taste and smell
    a. are stronger.
    b. are weaker.
    c. rely on local rather than distance receptors.
    d. are "monaural."
    e. are connected directly to the cortex.

15. The sense of hearing is probably more important to us today than either the sense of smell or taste. One reason is that
    a. the auditory system provides a channel for communication of complex verbal symbols.
    b. research studies show that persons with impaired hearing tend to develop paranoid behavior.
    c. the ears are widely separated, while the nose and tongue are not.
    d. the senses of taste and smell are no longer important for survival.

16. We are able to determine the right-left direction of sounds because
    a. of electronic technology.
    b. the dominant hemisphere processes impulses faster.
    c. of the distance between our ears.
    d. of all of the above factors.
    e. of only those factors listed in a and b.

17. The stereophonic effect in recordings is achieved by
    a. splitting the musicians into two groups.
    b. using two widely separated microphones.
    c. turning your head to one side.
    d. placing one speaker directly over the other.
    e. cocking your head so that your ears are oriented up and down.

Objective 4: Describe the appearance and function of the outer, middle, and inner ear.

18. The middle ear
    a. contains the hammer, anvil, and stirrup.
    b. is separated from the inner ear by the basilar membrane.
    c. acts like an amplifier.
    d. contains the semicircular canals.
    e. is best described by the statements in both a and c.

19. The receptor cells in the cochlea
    a. are chemical receptors.
    b. are hair cells similar to those on the tongue.
    c. respond to amplitude but not to frequency.
    d. look like baskets.

Objective 5: Describe frequency and amplitude of sound waves and relate them to the highness/lowness and loudness/softness of sound.

20. The frequency of a musical tone
    a. cannot be heard above 2,000 Hz.
    b. is determined by the size of the cochlea.
    c. determines how loud or soft it sounds.
    d. determines how high or low it sounds.
    e. differs for sounds having different timbre.

21. The amplitude of a musical tone
    a. determines how high or low it sounds.
    b. differs for sounds having different timbre.
    c. determines how loud or soft it sounds.
    d. is determined by the size of the cochlea.
    e. is measured in Hz.

22. In general, the human organs of hearing cannot detect a sound that is
    _____ 20,000 Hz.
    a. less than
    b. greater than
    c. at a level other than
    d. at half the level of
    e. at twice the level of

Suggestions for Extra Credit

1. Conduct some taste tests to see if persons can really tell the difference between brands of similar soft drinks, tea, coffee, orange juice, beer, sparkling mineral water, or tap and bottled water without all of the usual sensory clues. Make your preparations out of sight of your subjects in order to eliminate all secondary clues, such as the shape and appearance of the container. Eliminate all other clues you think might influence your test. Serve the beverages to be compared in paper cups that are letter coded so that you know which is which and can refer to them as A, B, and C. Ask your subjects (1) to identify their favorite brand if they have previously expressed a preference or (2) to tell which one they prefer. Make a chart or graph showing how many persons can correctly identify their ''favorite'' or which brand most persons prefer.

2. Some people appear to be much more sensitive than others to the taste of certain foods. Design a simple experiment to determine whether you believe that this is true. What foods would you use? Would you include a so-called ''spicy'' food? Describe the general characteristics of the persons who participate in your ''taste test.'' Tell how you would observe and measure their responses.

3. Survey the ingredients listed on food products in your supermarket to see what additives they include. Classify these additives with regard to whether they (1) enhance flavor, (2) augment color, (3) retard spoilage, or (4) other. Make a chart or graph showing how often these additives are used and in which kinds of foods (for example, soups, sauces, prepared dinners, cheese, ice cream, yogurt). If the primary purpose of our ability to smell and taste the flavor in food is to aid us in selecting the nourishment our bodies need, is it wrong for food packers and processors to make foods artificially more enticing than they really are? What might be the long-term effects of eating foods our mouths have been tricked into accepting as desirable?

4. Tour a winery or attend a wine-tasting party sponsored by one. Note the tasting method recommended to enable you to enjoy the wine to the fullest and the use of crackers and/or cheese between tastes to resensitize your taste buds to subtle differences. What ingredients give wine its ''taste''? Make it sweet? Bitter? Which of the seven primary qualities of smell can you identify? What does the vintner mean when he speaks of ''bouquet''?

5. Review McConnell's description of the Zimbardo studies on deafness and paranoia in Chapter 7 of your text, page 172, then visit your local library to locate and read Zimbardo's own report of his studies, published in the June 26, 1981, issue of *Science* magazine. How would you then answer McConnell's question: ''If you don't 'speak up' around a person with hearing problems, how might your own behaviors increase the deaf person's feelings of paranoia?'' How does the deaf person's response affect **you**? What could you do to prevent or alter negative effects?

6. An audiometer is an instrument used to measure the acuity of hearing in the individual ear for sounds of various frequencies. If possible, have your hearing checked. What is your range of hearing in each ear? Do your ears differ? If so, what might account for this difference?

7. Hearing tests are usually given free to all students in elementary schools when they reach a specific grade level. Volunteers are often sought to help with this testing process. If your schedule permits, volunteer to help administer hearing tests in your local community or district. Learn how to interpret the test results and make some note regarding the overall characteristics of the children tested. What is their age or grade? In most children, is the range of hearing the same for both ears? Does the range of hearing differ with sex or size? Why?

Answer Key

Matching

1. h	7. b
2. a	8. j
3. g	9. e
4. c	10. i
5. f	11. k
6. d	12. l

Completion

1. vision, hearing, taste, smell, touch, taste, smell;   2. taste, papillae, sweet, sour, bitter, salty, sour, bitter, blindness;   3. olfactory, gaseous, qualities; 4. local, distance, monaural, stereo;   5. left-right, outer, inner, eardrum, hammer, anvil, stirrup;   6. window, cochlea, motion, auditory, organ, membrane;   7. frequency, amplitude, Hertz, higher, amplitude, decibels.

Short-Answer Questions

1

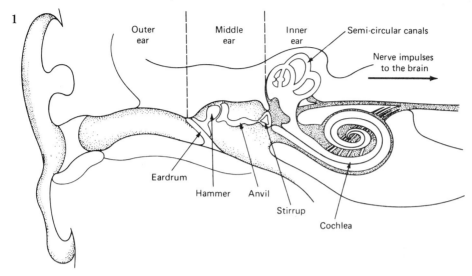

2. Because the stimuli that excite the receptors in your tongue and nose are complex chemical molecules, smell and taste are often called chemical senses. Hearing, on the other hand, is a matter of vibrations and wave action and can be termed mechanical. Because taste and smell impulses come to the brain from essentially one source, they are said to be monaural or "mono" senses. Sounds are transmitted to the brain from two separate sources, so the sense of hearing is said to be "stereo." Because foods must be in actual contact with your tongue before you can taste them, taste buds are said to rely on local receptors, while smell and hearing rely on distance receptors. Thus, these three senses differ in regard to the stimuli to which they respond (chemical or mechanical), the number of input sources (one or two), and the distance at which they function or are effective.

3.

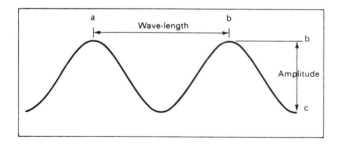

Sound B is louder.

Self-Test

1. c (text page 151)
2. b (text page 152; television program)
3. b (text page 153; television program)
4. d (text pages 158-159)
5. e (text page 155)
6. a (text pages 152-153)
7. b (text page 154)
8. d (text pages 154-155)
9. a (text pages 155-156)
10. e (text page 158)
11. b (text page 158)
12. a (text pages 158-159; television program)
13. c (text page 155)
14. d (text pages 158-159; television program)
15. a (text page 165; television program)
16. c (text pages 165-166; television program)
17. b (text page 166)
18. e (text page 167; television program)
19. b (text page 168; television program)
20. d (text page 169; television program)
21. c (text page 169; television program)
22. b (text pages 169-171)

Vision

8

Viewer's Guide for Program Eight

As you view the television program, watch for:

Animations showing shape and cross-section of the human eye and the actual film footage of a cow's eye, which is somewhat similar to your own eye. These sequences will not only give you some idea of what your own eyes are like, they will also prepare you for an understanding of the very complex process that makes vision possible.

Animations that simulate for you the way in which the lens focuses light and beams it back to the rods and cones of the retina, from where the light messages will be directed to the brain. (Be sure to observe the comparisons between the functions of the rods and cones in sensing light, color, and detail during day and night vision.)

The demonstration of light being transmitted in waves of particles called photons. Note the graph of the visible spectrum, which is what we mean when we speak of light and which appears to be white, but—as you will see—becomes all the colors of a rainbow when beamed through a prism.

Montages of colorful scenes, splashes of colors being mixed, color-coded objects and symbols. When you think of color, you basically mean "hue." These sequences illustrate strikingly that some colors are mixtures of hues, while others can be explained by saturation—that is, they are richer, more vivid, stronger and brighter shades of the same hue. (Observe how the flowers turn gray when they are "desaturated.")

Preview

Close your eyes for a moment and imagine that you have suddenly been blinded, if only temporarily. If you really were blinded, do you think that your first response might be the same feelings of panic and hysteria that overcome Alice in the fictional vignette that introduces the television program for this lesson? Your first reaction most likely would be panic. Soon, though, you too would begin to recreate in your memory the lovely colors of flowers and paintings, the graceful shapes of clouds and trees, the faces of loved ones.

But what if you had been blind from birth? What images would furnish your memory?

You may not need to be reminded of how important your eyesight is to you, for vision is the richest and most stimulating of all our senses. It is also the most complicated and most studied of all our senses. To understand what a dominant influence vision exerts on your thoughts and behaviors, you need to have knowledge of at least three things: What is the nature of light, the stimulus for vision? How does your eye convert light to a sensory input and send it on its way to your brain? And, finally, what does your brain make of such messages from the eye?

The human eye is sometimes compared to a camera, and in some ways the eye does resemble a camera. Light is the stimulus for both camera and eye. In both cases, light enters through a window (in the eye, the cornea), passes through a lens and is focused on a sensitive surface behind the lens, activating certain chemicals. But the resemblance ends about there, for the process by which your eye "photographs" the world is far more complex than the workings of the camera. For one thing, the camera records on flat film; your eye is a sphere (or ball). For another, the camera can only photograph those stimuli that pass through its lens, whereas the eye passes inputs on to the brain for interpretation, which behavioral scientists believe to be a psychological experience.

In this lesson you will learn something about how your eye processes light waves for your brain to interpret as images, what a rainbow really is, the meaning of "20-20 vision," how you are able to see so many colors, and why you do not see as well in the dark as you do in the light. You will also learn something about the causes and consequences of visual defects such as color weakness and colorblindness.

Learning Objectives

When you have finished viewing the program and studying your text assignments, you should be able to:

1. Describe the visible spectrum and discuss the characteristics of light.
2. Identify the parts of the eye and describe their functions.
3. Describe visual sensitivity, color vision, and adaptation, with reference to the rods and cones.
4. Describe near-sightedness, far-sightedness, old-sightedness (presbyopia), and the conditions that cause them.
5. Define hue, saturation, and mixtures of color.
6. Explain what is meant by the terms color weakness, partial colorblindness, and total colorblindness.

Assignments

Before Viewing the Program

Read the preview at the beginning of this lesson and look over the learning objectives that precede the assignments.

Check the section "Did You Know That . . ." at the beginning of Chapter 7 in the text, and look over the subtitles for the chapter.

Read that portion of Chapter 7, "Hearing and Seeing," (pages 172-189), which begins with the section "Vision" and continues to the end of the chapter.

View Program 8, "Vision"

After Viewing the Program

Review the text assignments.

Read through the summary items at the end of the chapter that apply to reading assignments for this lesson. Then, to facilitate your understanding of the materials presented in this lesson, study the terms and concepts that appear in boldfaced type and are defined in the upper right corners of right-hand pages. In particular, note these terms carefully: photon, visible spectrum, pupil, iris, cornea, aqueous humor, retina, vitreous humor, fovea, blind spot, rods, cones, visual acuity, astigmatism, near-sightedness, far-sightedness, old-sightedness, dark adaptation, hue, saturation, partially colorblind, additive mixtures, albinism, Holmgren wools.

Complete the study activities that are included here as an additional study aid for you.

Now evaluate your understanding of the lesson material by reviewing the learning objectives and taking the self-test in this study guide. Check your answers against the answer key.

According to your instructor's assignments or your own interests, choose and complete activities from among the suggestions for extra credit.

Study Activities

True-False

1. T F The brighter the light source, the fewer photons it produces in a given unit of time.
2. T F There is a close relationship between the wavelength of a visual stimulus and the color a person experiences.
3. T F A dim blue light has a different wavelength from that of a bright blue light.
4. T F The fovea is the point on your retina where your vision is the sharpest.
5. T F The receptors for color vision are the rods.
6. T F The cones are colorblind.
7. T F Your ability to discriminate small objects from large ones within your range of vision is called visual acuity.
8. T F You are not usually aware of your blind spot because your brain fills in this hole in your visual field by making it look like its surroundings.
9. T F Many visual problems are the result of slight abnormalities in the shape of the eyeball.
10. T F Psychologists believe that color is solely a quality of the light waves generated or reflected by the object seen.
11. T F Saturated colors are weak and diluted.
12. T F Most color-weak individuals show a deficiency in their response either to blue, yellow, or both of these hues.

Completion

1. The stimulus input for vision is light. Light is made up of _____ of very tiny energy particles called _____. If you know what the length, or _____, of a light wave is, you will know what color it will ordinarily appear to be. The height, strength, or _____ of a light wave determines the brightness of the color.

frequency
amplitude
waves
photons

2. We call the range of waves that lies between a wavelength of 400 nanometers and a wavelength of 760 nanometers the visible _____. This rainbow of colors runs from blue through green, yellow, and orange to red. Beyond the blue end of the spectrum lie the _____ rays. Beyond the red end of the spectrum lie the _____, or _____ rays.

ultraviolet
infrared
heat
spectrum

3. Light enters your eye through the cornea and _____ humor, then passes through the pupil, the lens, and the vitreous humor before striking the _____. Muscles attached to your lens pull on it to change its shape, thus allowing you to change your _____ from a near object to a more distant one.

focus
aqueous
retina

4. The inner surface of your eyeball, the retina, contains the _____ cells that translate the physical energy of a light wave into patterns of neural energy your brain interprets as "seeing." There are two structures of the retina that serve special functions—the fovea and the blind spot. The fovea, which contains only _____, is a tiny, yellow-colored pit in the center of the retina where your vision is the sharpest. The blind spot is that small part of the retina near the fovea where blood vessels and _____ fibers enter and exit from inside the eyeball, and the optic _____ is formed. There are no _____ neurons in the blind spot.

receptor
axonic
nerve
receptor
cones

5. The receptor neurons for vision are the _____ and cones. They contain chemicals that are very sensitive to _____ and allow you to "see" black and white and colors _____. The cones are your color receptors. There are three types of cones, each having its own _____ chemical. One type is sensitive to _____ light, one to _____, and one to _____. Your _____ are colorblind. Because your _____ are located primarily in the center of your retina, this part of the eye is most sensitive to color.

cones
photosensitive
rods
green
light
blue
separately
red
rods

6. _____ people typically see objects _____ to their eyes more clearly than they do objects that are _____. Far-sighted people typically see _____ objects more clearly than they do objects that are _____ to their eyes. The failure of the aging and more brittle lens to focus readily on near objects is called _____.

presbyopia
distant
close
Near-sighted

7. If a person can see a particular color only when it is very intense, the person is said to be _____. If a person cannot see a particular color no matter how intense it is, that person is said to be partially _____.

colorblind
color-weak

8. When we speak of the color of an object, we are really talking about the object's _____. Reds, greens, blues, yellows, and all shades of these "colors" are hues that are detected by your _____. Not all colors seem to be hues; some are obviously _____, as are most colors of the rainbow. But neither hue nor mixture entirely explains color experience. The vividness and richness of a color—its strength and brightness—is described as

_____.

mixtures
saturation
cones
hue

Short-Answer Questions

1. Label the parts of the eye on this diagram.

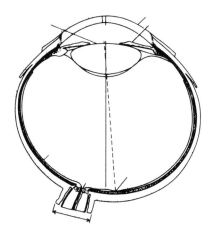

2. Explain the changes that occur in human vision at night. Describe the process of dark adaptation. Why can you see things better "out of the corner of your eye" when it is dark?

3. Fill in the table below.

Optical Defect	Structural Defect	Focal Point	Visual Defect
Near-sighted	Eyeball too long	In front of retina	

Self-Test

(Select the one best answer.)

Objective 1: Describe the visible spectrum and discuss the characteristics of light.

1. A photon is the smallest
   a. known wavelength.
   b. unit of light energy.
   c. known amplitude.
   d. unit of the visual spectrum.

2. Our perception of color is determined by
   a. amplitude.
   b. wavelength.
   c. the speed of light.
   d. nanometers.

3. Frequency is to hearing as _____ is to color vision.
   a. amplitude
   b. volume
   c. wavelength
   d. intensity

4. Amplitude determines _____ in hearing and _____ in color vision.
   a. tone, hue
   b. tone, brightness
   c. loudness, hue
   d. loudness, brightness

5. The visible spectrum, the rainbow,
   a. includes ultraviolet and infrared rays.
   b. is broader than the light from sun lamps.
   c. lies between 400 and 760 nanometers.
   d. is described by all of the above.

Objective 2: Identify the parts of the eye and describe their functions.

6. Which one of the following statements best describes the path which light takes through the eye?
   a. iris, aqueous humor, cornea, fovea
   b. lens, retina, iris, vitreous humor
   c. iris, pupil, retina, lens
   d. cornea, aqueous humor, pupil, lens, retina

7. The inner surface of the eye where images are normally focused is called the
   a. iris.
   b. cornea.
   c. retina.
   d. pupil.
   e. blind spot.

8. The retina contains
   a. the fovea.
   b. the rods.
   c. the cones.
   d. the blind spot.
   e. all of the above.

9. The blind spot is a kind of hole in the retina which is filled with
   a. rods and cones.
   b. neurons and blood vessels.
   c. receptor cells that lack color pigment.
   d. receptor cells that lack rhodopsin.

10. Your blind spot is "blind" because
   a. it contains no visual receptors.
   b. blood vessels prevent light from reaching the receptor cells.
   c. there are too many neurons in that part of the retina, and image reception becomes mixed or confused.
   d. of both a and b.
   e. of both b and c.

11. You become consciously aware that you are "seeing" something when
    a. light waves pass your blind spot.
    b. signals from your eye reach a part of your upper brain.
    c. the rods adapt to the inputs of light.
    d. the aqueous humor properly inflates your eyeballs.

Objective 2; and *Objective 3:* Describe visual sensitivity, color vision, and adaptation, with reference to the rods and cones.

12. The cones are
    a. not found in the fovea.
    b. color receptors.
    c. colorblind.
    d. insensitive to light.

13. The rods are
    a. light detectors.
    b. colorblind.
    c. found in the fovea.
    d. colorblind light detectors.
    e. light detectors found in the fovea.

14. You depend more upon your _____ vision to help you see things in fine detail.
    a. rod
    b. color
    c. cone
    d. peripheral

Objective 3

15. Dark adaptation is caused by
    a. sleepy neurons.
    b. the breaking up of photosensitive molecules in the eye.
    c. the buildup of a large store of photosensitive chemicals in the rods and cones.
    d. an abnormality in the shape of the eyeball.

Objective 4: Describe near-sightedness, far-sightedness, old-sightedness (presbyopia), and the conditions that cause them.

16. Near-sightedness
    a. results from an abnormality in the shape of the eyeball.
    b. results from old age.
    c. occurs when the eyeball is too short.
    d. results from the lens becoming brittle and unable to focus.

17. If your eyeball is too short and the lens tends to focus the visual image behind the retina, you are said to be
    a. short-sighted.
    b. near-sighted.
    c. afflicted with presbyopia.
    d. far-sighted.

18. Presbyopia is most likely to
    a. result from a ''brittle'' lens.
    b. result in a misshapen eyeball.
    c. occur in younger individuals.
    d. result in blurring of faraway objects.

Objectives 3 and *4*

19. Night-blindness is often caused by
    a. carrots.
    b. lack of Vitamin A.
    c. some disability of the rods.
    d. both a and c.
    e. both b and c.

Objective 5: Define hue, saturation, and mixtures of color.

20. The two main factors in determining our visual color experience are
    a. rods and cones.
    b. velocity and amplitude.
    c. hue and saturation.
    d. color and brightness.

21. The vividness or richness of color is what we call
    a. hue.
    b. saturation.
    c. wavelength.
    d. amplitude.
    e. color mixture.

Objective 6: Explain what is meant by the terms color weakness, partial colorblindness, and total colorblindness.

22. Color deficiency
    a. occurs more often in men than in women.
    b. is present in about 25 percent of the people in the world.
    c. is not inherited.
    d. usually involves a blue-yellow deficiency and only rarely involves a red-green deficiency.
    e. is described by all of the above.

23. The most common form of colorblindness is the result of
    a. carbon disulfide poisoning.
    b. red-green cone deficiency.
    c. lack of Vitamin A.
    d. albinism.
    e. a blind spot near the fovea.

Suggestions for Extra Credit

1. If you have not done so lately, have your eyes examined. Ask the optometrist or ophthalmologist about your visual acuity. Is it the same in each eye or does it differ from one to the other? Is your vision normal or are you near-sighted or far-sighted? Write a few paragraphs reporting your findings and, if you wear glasses, explain how they correct your vision.
2. Use a dictionary or encyclopedia to acquaint yourself with the meanings of these nine vision words.
    a. amblyopia
    b. astigmatism
    c. cataract
    d. diplopia
    e. emmetropia
    f. hyperopia
    g. myopia
    h. ophthalmologist
    i. optician
3. Call your local Braille Institute, Foundation for the Junior Blind, or other similar organization, and become acquainted with the services it provides to blind children and adults. If your schedule permits, volunteer your time to read to the blind, record ''talking'' books, write letters, care for a guide dog until it is old enough to be trained, and so on.
4. Imagine that you are about to visit someone in the hospital who has recently had successful eye surgery but has not yet had the bandages removed. What sorts of gifts might you take that would be especially useful and appealing? Obviously, the usual cards, books, and magazines are at this time not suitable. What could you take? What could you talk about?
5. Persons who are partially sighted may be classed as ''legally blind.'' Determine what the legal definition of blindness is in your state, what services are available for those so classified, and what restrictions are placed upon them.

Answer Key

True-False

1. F
2. T
3. F
4. T
5. F
6. F

7. T
8. T
9. T
10. F
11. T
12. F

Completion

1. waves, photons, frequency, amplitude;   2. spectrum, ultraviolet, heat, infrared;   3. aqueous, retina, focus;   4. receptor, cones, axonic, nerve, receptor;   5. rods, light, separately, photosensitive, red, blue, green, rods, cones;   6. Near-sighted, close, distant, presbyopia;   7. color-weak, colorblind;   8. hue, cones, mixtures, saturation.

Short-Answer Questions

1.

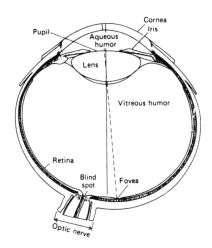

2. The round cones of your eyes, which "see" color and detail, basically function only in the daytime or in the presence of bright light. The rods in your eyes greatly outnumber the cones, but they are structured to function essentially as light detectors, not to "see" color and detail. The rods do enable you to see in the dark or when light levels are low, but you cannot of course see the color and detail that make your daytime vision so effective. When you enter a darkened area, such as a theatre, you cannot at first see very well, but in a few moments the process known as dark adaptation occurs and you can see quite well. Your eyes adapt to lower light situations because your rods and cones build up a surplus of photosensitive chemicals. You will be able to see objects better in the dark if you look at them out of the corner of your eye, not directly, because your rods (which detect light) are much more numerous around the periphery of your retina.

3.

Optical Defect	Structural Defect	Focal Point	Visual Defect
Near-sighted	Eyeball too long	In front of retina	Blurring of far objects
Far-sighted	Eyeball too short	Behind retina	Blurring of near objects
Old-sighted	Lens too brittle	In front of retina	Blurring of near objects

Self-Test

 1. b (text page 173; television program)
 2. b (text pages 173-174; television program)
 3. c (text page 173; television program)
 4. d (text page 174; television program)
 5. c (text page 175; television program)
 6. d (text pages 175-176; television program)
 7. c (text page 176; television program)
 8. e (text pages 177-178; television program)
 9. b (text page 179)
10. a (text pages 178-179)
11. b (text page 177)
12. b (text pages 177-178; television program)
13. d (text page 177; television program)
14. c (text page 180)
15. c (text pages 181-182; television program)

16. a (text page 179)
17. d (text page 179)
18. a (text page 180)
19. e (text page 182)
20. c (text pages 183-184)
21. b (text page 184)
22. a (text page 185)
23. b (text pages 185-186)

Sensory Input and Cognition

9

Viewer's Guide for Program Nine

As you view the television program, watch for:

The aerial panoramas and other film footage of Antarctica. In this dark, cold, and lonely place, scientists and explorers have met the challenge of the elements, only to be challenged anew by isolation and its sometime successor, insanity.

Film footage and photographs of Admiral Richard Byrd, the American polar explorer who managed a tiny, one-man research station throughout an entire Antarctic winter and recorded his own reactions to his isolation in his journal. From Byrd's diary we learn how he felt the solitude erode his inner calm, began to appreciate his senses as never before, and used increased sensory stimulation as a strategy for preventing apathy and preserving sanity.

Actual film of subjects taking part in the sensory deprivation experiments conducted by a group of psychologists in Donald Hebb's laboratory at McGill University. Observe that subjects of these experiments showed considerable intellectual impairment during deprivation and for some hours afterward. They also had difficulties with simple problem solving and with motor coordination.

Preview

Have you ever felt, amid the glitter and excitement of some carnival-like atmosphere, the overwhelming urge to slip out of the noisy, well-lighted scene and lose yourself in the quiet of the soft, surrounding darkness? Each of us, of course, needs occasional relief from the stimulation and stress of home, work, school, family.

A natural response to the crowded and confusing clamor of much of our urban world is the wish to get away from it all, to escape to some remote area where you can, at last, be alone with your thoughts. But where do you go and what price do you pay for going?

Of course, all sorts of travel agencies sing their siren songs of solitude and slower pace to lure you toward mountain tops, older worlds, or South Pacific seas. And, as we saw in Lesson Four, some drugs are touted as being able to induce the calm and quiet of remoteness right in the comfort of your own home.

But might there be another way? If your sensory inputs were reduced or curtailed completely, how might you react? With a sigh of relief? But what if your environment continued to be isolated for hours, then days, and possibly for months—longer than you had wanted and beyond your power to end the isolation?

Sensory deprivation (another term for isolation) is known to have both traumatic and therapeutic effects on humans. In this lesson you will learn about these effects and about some ways in which sensory deprivation has been used to bring about attitudinal and behavioral changes.

In this lesson, you will also be introduced in some depth to an absorbing area of psychological study, one that has recently emerged as one of the major concerns for psychology: the cognitive process by which we gather and use informational inputs to perceive, assess situations, make decisions, and take whatever action we deem appropriate. Your study of cognition at this point will prepare you to meet and understand considerable additional information on this highly important topic as you progress through later lessons in this course. Among other things, you will learn that cognition is a very remarkable and complex chain of interrelated processes that involves your sensory receptors and both lower and higher centers of your brain as well. As you learn, you will marvel anew over how your brain sorts through what is essentially a conglomeration of light and sound waves, plus messages from other senses, and fashions them into the thinking, reasoning, behaving being that is **you**.

Learning Objectives

When you have finished viewing the program and studying your text assignments, you should be able to:

1. Define cognition and describe the operations in the cognitive process by which the human brain makes use of informational inputs.
2. List and describe factors that influence attention, including expectancy, input, orienting reflex, arousal, novelty, significance, habituation.
3. Describe the function of the two types of sensory pathways of the central nervous system as they relate to levels of arousal.
4. Distinguish between categories and concepts and explain their role in the cognitive process.
5. List and briefly describe several important consequences of sensory isolation (input underload).
6. List the major research findings of the McGill sensory deprivation experiments.
7. Describe research findings that suggest sensory deprivation can be used as a form of therapy

Assignments

Before Viewing the Program

Read the preview at the beginning of this lesson and look over the learning objectives that precede the assignments.

Check the section "Did You Know That . . ." at the beginning of Chapter 9 in the text, and look over the subtitles for the chapter.

Read Chapter 9, "Cognition." Although a part of this chapter is related to later lessons, you will benefit from reading the entire chapter at this time, then reviewing the pertinent sections later.

View Program 9, "Sensory Deprivation"

After Viewing the Program

Review the text assignments.

Read through the summary items at the end of the chapter. Then, to facilitate your understanding of the materials presented in this lesson, study the terms and concepts that appear in boldfaced type and are defined in the upper right corners of right-hand pages. Also consider the thought questions inserted throughout the chapter. In particular, note these terms carefully: input overload, arousal, straight-line sensory system, reticular activating system (RAS), attention, brainwashing, hallucination, Restricted Environmental Stimulation Therapy (REST cure), input, screening, preconscious processing system (PPS), novelty, significance, concepts, categories, artificial intelligence, sensory isolation.

Complete the study activities that are included here as an additional study aid for you.

Now evaluate your understanding of the lesson material by reviewing the learning objectives and taking the self-test in this study guide. Check your answers against the answer key.

According to your instructor's assignments or your own interests, choose and complete activities from among the suggestions for extra credit. You might consider the recommended readings listed at the end of the chapter.

Study Activities

Matching

Match each phrase in the column on the right with the appropriate term in the column on the left, writing the letters in the appropriate blanks on the left.

_____ 1. brainwashing

_____ 2. sensory deprivation

_____ 3. habituate

_____ 4. "REST cure"

_____ 5. straight-line sensory system

_____ 6. arousal

_____ 7. preconscious processing system (PPS)

_____ 8. reticular activating system (RAS)

_____ 9. cognition

_____ 10. concepts

_____ 11. categories

_____ 12. artificial intelligence

_____ 13. parallel processing

a. a marked reduction in stimulus inputs

b. a therapy based on sensory isolation

c. the act of being awakened or stimulated to function at a peak performance level

d. screens inputs for significance

e. the "alarm" center that alerts the cortex to incoming sensory messages

f. the act or process of knowing, including awareness and judging

g. to become accustomed to, or ignore, sensory signals

h. modeling computers to process inputs the way the human brain does

i. ability of the human brain to process inputs simultaneously

j. artificial categories created by the mind as ways of perceiving situations

k. altering values, attitudes, or behavior by total isolation of an individual from his or her usual social environment

l. used by your cortex to sort out or group objects being perceived

m. a pathway leading from receptor neurons to the sensory regions of the cortex

Completion

1. Author James McConnell defines cognition as a complex chain of processes that results in the mental event we call **knowing.** Knowing includes both awareness and judgment. The cognitive process engages both the lower and the higher centers of the brain as well as the sensory organs. Cognition begins with detection and orientation toward sensory inputs, a process which is called input _____, or _____. The sensory receptors receive these inputs and process them into neural energy _____, which is called input _____. Lower centers of the nervous system select _____ features to pass along to the cortex, and they _____ out other types of information. The cortex "recognizes" _____ by matching input with stored _____. At this point, the input registers on your _____, which is the process called _____, and when this occurs, you become aware of, or _____, the input. The perception is then stored in a kind of temporary memory storage system while your cortex is occupied with the processes of reasoning, problem solving, and mental imagery—that is, deciding the question of what to do with the information. In making a decision, you can _____ the input entirely, use your long-term memory to _____ it, or you can choose to respond, which means you activate the response-_____ sequence. When your output receives a _____ from the environment, the process of _____ is reactivated.

patterns
detection
transduction
attention
screen
perception
store
patterns
cognition
memories
response
consciousness
perceive
ignore
output
critical

2. The process of paying attention to a new input involves an automatic and involuntary reaction, the orienting _____, which is at least partly innate and triggers a state of physical _____. To activate the orienting reflex, your sensory receptors must detect a sudden _____ in the environment.

How much you are aroused will depend partly on the strength and newness, or _____, and the _____, of the stimulus. Significance can be influenced by novelty, motivation (such as hunger), expectancy, and social factors. Becoming too familiar with inputs will cause you to ignore, or _____ to them, however.

change
significance
reflex
habituate
arousal
novelty

3. While studying the arousal phenomenon, Magoun and his UCLA colleagues discovered that incoming sensory inputs go to the cortex through two different pathways. One pathway leads directly to the somatic sensory cortex in the parietal lobe and is called the _____ system. The second pathway leads into the _____ _____ _____, also known as the RAS. The RAS alerts the cortex to messages incoming on the straight-line system and, from its position atop the spinal cord, the RAS monitors and filters _____ information for the cortex. The cortex, however, can either stimulate the RAS or _____ it when it doesn't "want to be bothered." The RAS is thought to be part of the preconscious processing system, which evolved from primitive lower brain centers and thus has lower input _____ than does the conscious system. The _____ processing system handles large amounts of input in a short time and can respond to some inputs _____, while the _____ system can focus on only one input at a time. The cortex is thus kept from being _____ with inputs.

critical
preconscious
overloaded
reticular activating system
inhibit
reflexively
straight-line
thresholds
conscious

4. The cortex uses critical information from the lower brain centers to sort objects into cognitive _____, or groups. These can be classified as _____ categories, those that occur in real-world situations, and _____ categories, which are inventions of the human mind. Colors are natural categories. Examples of artificial categories include departments of an organization (such as a store or college) and concepts of problems and their potential solutions. We categorize by creating _____, a kind of mental model constructed from a "first-time" experience with an object or situation. Concepts are _____ representations which function as ways of perceiving situations. In problem solving, conceptualization can sometimes lead to a perceptual difficulty known as **functional fixedness**, or mental _____, which can prevent one from viewing a problem from a new approach, as was the case with some subjects in the Maier rope studies.

mental
categories
natural
set
artificial
prototypes

5. A _____ level of sensory input is essential to human survival; however, the consequences of too much stimulation (information overload), or too little sensory input, which is variously called input _____, _____ deprivation, and sensory isolation, can be grave. Some consequences of information overload include stress and poor performance on learning tasks. The McGill research studies described in your text and in the television program that accompanies this lesson showed that subjects confined to an isolation chamber and deprived of all but basic sensory stimulation, such as food and water, showed considerable intellectual _____ and difficulties with _____ coordination, could not adapt well to _____ situations, could not concentrate, and had difficulty with organized _____. These subjects suffered blank periods when they could not _____, and 80 percent suffered visual _____. Moreover, these subjects exhibited adverse effects for several days after the experiments were concluded. Researchers reported that these subjects performed less well on simple tasks than did "normal," or control subjects; they showed _____ in handwriting and perceptual _____ of lines, spaces, and shapes. Subjects deprived of stimulation also were far more receptive to propaganda messages, or _____, than were control subjects.

changes
motor
constant
sensory
underload
thinking
hallucinations
brainwashing
think
distortions
impairment
new

6. Sensory isolation was first used for brainwashing, but research indicates that this technique can have _____ value in certain situations. REST, _____ _____ _____ Therapy, has been used successfully for meditation, relieving stress, gaining personal insight, and modification of habits such as smoking, overeating, and excessive drinking.

_____

Restricted Environmental Stimulation
therapeutic

Short-Answer Questions

1. Label this diagram to show the two pathways by which incoming sensory messages travel from the receptors to the brain.

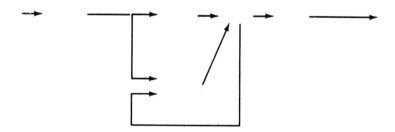

2. How does your cortex use categories and concepts in reasoning and problem solving?

3. Briefly discuss how a person's typical response to input underload, or sensory isolation, makes brainwashing possible.

4. Evaluate the evidence which suggests that sensory deprivation may serve worthwhile purposes.

Self-Test

(Select the one best answer.)

Objective 1: Define cognition and describe the operations in the cognitive process by which the human brain makes use of informational inputs.

1. The complex process known as cognition is best described as
    a. the changing of stimuli into patterns of neural energy.
    b. a chain of related events that begins with stimulus input and leads to awareness, knowledge, judgment, and potential output.
    c. a chain of related events that takes place only in the higher centers of the nervous system.
    d. the way we perceive a situation or problem after comparing it with a prototype.
    e. conceptualizing the problem.

2. Which of the following is **not** a part of the cognitive process?
   a. mental set
   b. screening out inputs
   c. input underload
   d. mental set and input underload
   e. All of these events are part of the cognitive process.

3. **Perception** is said to occur when
   a. the process of input transduction is complete.
   b. behavior modification takes place.
   c. you match input with remembered patterns and the input registers on your consciousness.
   d. sensory input triggers the orienting reflex.
   e. you decide what to do about the input.

Objective 2: List and describe factors that influence attention, including expectancy, input, orienting reflex, arousal, novelty, significance, habituation.

4. The mind experiences an input _____ when too many stimuli are received at one time.
   a. underload
   b. hunger
   c. overload
   d. hallucination
   e. control

5. Which factors are most likely to influence your attention?
   a. strong stimuli
   b. your wants and needs
   c. social standards
   d. habituation
   e. all of these factors

6. How many inputs can the brain usually attend to at one time?
   a. one
   b. three
   c. five
   d. seven
   e. nine

7. Very weak stimuli can become significant to you if
   a. you are subjected to input overload.
   b. your orienting reflex has become habituated.
   c. the stimuli reach your cortex by way of the straight-line system.
   d. you have been told what to expect.
   e. you pay close attention.

Objective 3: Describe the function of the two types of sensory pathways of the central nervous system as they relate to levels of arousal.

8. One important result of Magoun's research into arousal mechanisms was the discovery that
   a. there are two different sensory pathways.
   b. the reticular activating system blocks off input.
   c. RAS activity is triggered by the cortex.
   d. the straight-line system arouses the brain.
   e. sensory isolation can be therapeutic.

9. The two sensory pathways over which messages travel from receptors to the cortex are called the
   a. receptor-cortical routes.
   b. straight-line sensory system and the reticular activating system (RAS).
   c. alerting system and the activating system.
   d. arousal mechanism and the screening process.
   e. spinal cord and the RAS.

10. The reticular activating system is responsible for
    a. routing all sensory information along the straight-line system.
    b. making sure all sensory inputs receive the same attention.
    c. alerting the cortex to important incoming sensory information.
    d. converting receptor energy into neural patterns.
    e. preventing input overload.

11. Sensory information may be ignored by the cortex if
    a. the information is not first processed by the reticular activating system.
    b. it is not new.
    c. the straight-line system is inhibited.
    d. the cortex is focusing on too many inputs.
    e. fuzzy boundaries are present.

12. According to the television program, the RAS is crucial to existence because it
    a. satisfies "stimulus hunger."
    b. blocks off important information.
    c. can be controlled voluntarily.
    d. allows the cortex to focus on critical inputs, one at a time.
    e. works only when you are awake.

Objective 4: Distinguish between categories and concepts and explain their role in the cognitive process.

13. If a toddler insists on calling a lion "kitty," you will understand that he or she
    b. "sees" the lion as belonging to a category of household pets with similar attributes.
    c. has invented an artificial category.
    d. is perceiving the situation creatively.
    e. probably has never before seen a house cat.

14. Which of the following statements about categories and concepts is true?
    a. Categories are groupings based on similarities, concepts emphasize differences.
    b. Concepts are based on similarities, categories emphasize differences.
    c. Concepts are mental representations constructed to provide ways of perceiving given situations or problems.
    d. All of these statements are true.
    e. None of these statements is true.

15. Before some of the subjects in the Maier experiment could solve the problem of joining the ropes, they needed to
    a. take a fresh approach to conceptualization of the problem.
    b. break a mental set about pliers.
    c. see the pliers as belonging to a different cognitive category.
    d. make use of all of the devices mentioned above.
    e. be shown how to do it.

Objective 5: List and briefly describe several important consequences of sensory isolation (input underload).

16. What usually will **not** happen as a result of input underload?
    a. An individual will be motivated to seek and attend to stimuli.
    b. An individual's cortex sends inhibiting commands to the RAS.
    c. An individual becomes more changeable and flexible.
    d. An individual loses voluntary control over his thoughts.
    e. An individual may accept new inputs uncritically.

17. "Brainwashing," as described by Edward Hunter, depends largely on applying these techniques:
    a. torture or the threat of torture.
    b. education and social deprivation.
    c. encouraging the prisoner's cooperation by promising rewards.
    d. increasing the prisoner's fear while promising rewards.
    e. sensory isolation, rewards, and punishment.

Objective 6: List the major research findings of the McGill sensory deprivation experiments.

18. Most subjects in the McGill isolation experiments reported
    a. rapid alternation between periods of alertness and periods of sleep.
    b. some form of visual hallucinations.
    c. disturbances in what might be called their body images.
    d. all of the above-mentioned effects.
    e. visual hallucinations and body-image distortions.

19. According to the television program, experimenters at McGill concluded generally from their tests that
    a. sensory deprivation can produce beneficial results in some cases.
    b. incoming information reaches your cortex through two quite different pathways.
    c. a changing sensory environment is essential to normal mental activity.
    d. all of the above statements are true.
    e. only the statements in a and c are true.

Objective 7: Describe research findings that suggest sensory deprivation can be used as a form of therapy.

20. Persuasive messages used as therapy in combination with sensory deprivation will most likely
    a. often succeed because the acceptability of the message is increased.
    b. produce hallucinations.
    c. convert the subject to unquestioning obedience.
    d. cause the subject to stop paying attention.
    e. be characterized by statements a and c.

21. Which group(s) lowered drinking levels significantly as a result of the Cooper and Adams experiment?
    a. those who heard a supportive anti-alcohol message
    b. those who spent time in an isolation chamber
    c. those who heard a confrontational message about alcohol
    d. those who remained in a normal (non-isolated) environment
    e. those who heard an anti-alcohol message while in an isolation chamber

22. Restricted Environmental Stimulation Therapy can be briefly defined as a
    a. technique to control the RAS.
    b. scientific term for brainwashing.
    c. technique used to encourage changing of behavior.
    d. technique employing input overload.
    e. technique involving total immersion in water.

Suggestions for Extra Credit

1. Admiral Richard E. Byrd's autobiographical account of his struggle against isolation in Antarctica offers fascinating reading. Choose excerpts that interest you or read all of *Alone*, Byrd's diary, published in 1938 by G. P. Putnam's Sons. What could or would you have done differently if you were in Byrd's situation?
2. Read "A Long Time Between Beers," by Marvin Bird in the November 13, 1978, issue of *Sports Illustrated*. The article tells the ordeal of two fishermen lost at sea for eleven days. What impresses you most about their experience?
3. *The Prisoner*, a play written by British author Bridget Boland in the 1950s, is an unforgettable and dramatic account of the brainwashing of a brilliant and popular cardinal of the Catholic church by a Communist agent. The play is widely believed to be a fictional account of the actual experience of Cardinal Josef Mindzenty of Hungary. Check your local library for copies of the play. It may be hard to find, but the play is worth reading if it can be found. Larger libraries will have copies of *Plays of the Year*, Vol. 10, 1953-54, an anthology in which *The Prisoner* appears, published by Elek in England.
4. The concept of creativity has long been a popular subject for research in psychology, though psychologists do not agree on either the nature of creative thinking or on valid means for measuring it. It is generally agreed, however, as author James McConnell points out in this lesson, that one of the attributes of creative thinking is the blurring of boundaries between categories, or the ability to overcome mental set and perceive things as fitting into new and unusual categories. We reproduce here two short exercises which are among the best measures of creativity used in psychological research. If you are interested, administer the test to a small group of family, friends, or students.

The tests consist of a pair of word lists, which you will need to retype on separate sheets of paper and duplicate for your subjects. For Test A, ask your subjects to write down as many possible uses for each object as they can other than its normal use. (For example, if the word "brick" were listed, a subject might see the brick as a weapon and a doorstop.) Test B requires a common one-word answer for each set of three words on the list. (For example, the word for the first set on the list is "chair." The remaining responses should be (2) house, (3) foot, (4) green, (5) bar, (6) court, (7) drum, (8) call, (9) floor, and (10) jack.)

After administering the two tests, count the number of "acceptable" responses your subjects made on Test A and the "correct" number of responses to Test B. What is the most number of responses obtained on Test A? What is the average number? Were any of your subjects unable to provide all of the correct answers for B? Did some subjects do well on both tests? Do you think these tests measure creativity accurately or tell you much about its nature? How would you devise a simple way of measuring their validity?

Creativity Test A

1. toothpick
2. newspaper
3. paper clip
4. sock
5. balloon
6. sawhorse
7. beer can
8. spoon
9. shower curtain
10. candle

Creativity Test B

1. wheel, electric, high
2. paint, dog, boat
3. stool, powder, ball
4. house, village, thumb
5. bell, tender, steel
6. ship, county, basketball
7. ear, beat, oil
8. phone, girl, roll
9. plan, wood, show
10. knife, hi, ass

Answer Key

Matching

1. k	7. d
2. a	8. e
3. g	9. f
4. b	10. j
5. m	11. l
6. c	12. h
	13. i

Completion

1. detection, attention, patterns, transduction, critical, screen, patterns, memories, consciousness, perception, perceive, ignore, store, output, response, cognition;   2. reflex, arousal, change, novelty, significance, habituate;   3. straight-line, reticular activating system, critical, inhibit, thresholds, preconscious, reflexively, conscious, overloaded;   4. categories, natural, artificial, prototypes, mental, set;   5. constant, underload, sensory, impairment, motor, new, thinking, think, hallucinations, changes, distortions, brainwashing;   6. therapeutic, Restricted Environmental Stimulation.

Short-Answer Questions

1.

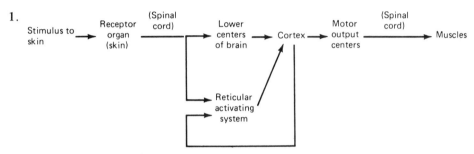

2. The cortex collects informational inputs from the lower brain centers and arranges these inputs into convenient groupings or categories, a process which allows you not only to identify likenesses but to distinguish objects from one another as well. If an object is familiar to you, your cortex will compare it to a prototype in your memory system, then will include or exclude the object as a member of the category represented by the prototype, according to whether it does or does not have certain attributes. We generally derive prototypes from what we call **basic** categories, which are neither overly broad nor narrowly specific. Some categories are **natural**, that is, they occur in real life and are immediately understandable. Natural categories include largeness or smallness, male or female, red or green, and the like. **Artificial** categories are invented classifications or concepts that are not based in nature. For example, "management" and "labor" are artificial categories, as are "freshmen" and "seniors." Problem solving requires a **conceptualization** of the problem itself as well as about elements of the problem (such as use of the pliers and the ropes in the Maier research). If conceptualization or categorization results in what is called "mental set," we may not be able immediately to conceptualize a new approach, and problem-solving behavior may be hampered.

3. Normal human functioning—even survival itself—depends upon a constant supply of appropriate sensory inputs. If you are deprived of inputs that you want and need, your motivational system will be aroused, your values may change, and you may lose control over your thoughts and actions. For example, if you are hungry but are deprived of food, food becomes more significant to you, you attend more to food-related inputs, and you will feel more rewarded when you actually get the food. The greater your need for food, the more you will change your behavior in your efforts to satisfy your hunger. Brainwashing is possible when a person is subjected to severe sensory isolation for a long period of time, then exposed to propaganda messages and rewarded for behavior that is consistent with the values and beliefs expressed in the messages.
4. The evidence seems to be that some forms of controlled sensory isolation, such as meditation and living in spartan surroundings, may encourage personal insight and dedication to purpose. In other situations, Restricted Environmental Therapy (or REST, as it is called) has been effective in treating problems of overeating, smoking, and excessive drinking. These apparent successes are based on three main factors: Subjects tend to pay more attention in situations of sensory isolation; the social value or acceptability of the inputs which are received is increased; and subjects seem to be motivated to change their behavior.

Self-Test

1. b (text pages 227-228)
2. e (text pages 228-251)
3. c (text page 228)
4. c (text page 240)
5. e (text pages 229-231)
6. a (text pages 229-230)
7. d (text page 231)
8. a (text pages 232-233; television program)
9. b (text pages 233-234)
10. c (text page 233; television program)
11. a (text page 233; television program)
12. d (television program)
13. b (text pages 240-241)
14. c (text pages 240-244)
15. d (text pages 244-245)
16. b (text pages 250-251)
17. e (text page 251)
18. e (text pages 251-252)

19. c (television program)
20. a (text pages 253-254; television program)
21. e (text pages 253-254)
22. c (text page 253)

Visual Perception 10

Viewer's Guide for Program Ten

As you view the television program, watch for:

The touching vignette that begins and ends this program with the story of a blind man who regains his sight in his middle fifties. His story has much to say to scientists about whether perception is innate or learned. What do you think after hearing Arthur Thomasino's story?

Actual film sequences of an archer shooting an arrow at a target. How does the archer's brain know the target is larger than it looks? Making a bull's eye is even more difficult than it appears because our eye cannot "see" depth or distance. When the archer hits the target, it is because he has combined what his eye "sees" with what his brain "knows" in the process we call perception.

The animated sequence of the Mueller-Lyer illusion. Why does one line look longer? Recognizing the cause of this illusion will help you to understand how the brain can organize sensations into perceptions according to our expectations about the world, though these expectations may not always be met.

The filmed demonstration of the Ames "distorted room." The brain, forced to choose between the correct size of people in the room and what it thinks is the correct shape of the room, decides to misperceive the size of the people, and an illusion results.

The landing sequence from a pilot training film. How long is the runway? One purpose of the training is to help a pilot learn to compensate or correct for perceptual distortion caused by context.

The filmed sequence of an infant's experience with the "visual cliff." The tendency of most young infants to avoid the "cliff" leads some researchers to believe that some perceptual abilities are innate.

Preview

Merely to see something is not to "perceive" it. When you perceive something, your brain automatically matches the sensory input with all the past concepts in which this particular sensory message appeared; you form some expectations about what you are going to perceive, and you therefore experience something which has some kind of meaning to you.

Of course, this is true of all sensory perception, whether it originates in your ears, your fingers, or your eyes. But your eyes ordinarily are the main sensory route by which you organize your perceptions, so the great bulk of perceptual research deals with vision.

If you were born blind or blinded very early in life, you would not, of course, be able to organize your perceptions around eyesight. You would learn to use sensory inputs other than visual ones to organize and "perceive" reality. But what if you were to miraculously regain your eyesight after a lifetime of darkness and dependence on other sensory abilities?

If you could suddenly see, would you be able to instantly experience and comprehend the great, diverse, and colorful world that your eyes now tell your brain has been out there all along? Would your brain be able to give meaning to what your eyes see? Would you know what to expect from moment to moment? The answer is no, not at first, as you will learn from the cases of "S.B.," a young French girl, and "Arthur Thomasino," which are brought to your attention in this lesson.

These and a growing number of other studies help to shed light upon—and to raise new questions about—the amazing ability of your mind to organize and apply vast numbers of sensory inputs to the functions of judging, making decisions, and remembering, which make up a most complex human cognitive process. Do you come into the world with your powers of visual perception full-blown at birth, or do you **learn** to perceive? Does your mind impose its will upon what your eyes see, as some theorists believe? Or do the sensations that stream into your sensory system through your eyes impose a direct "reality" on your brain, thus controlling what you see and perceive, as other theorists insist?

In this lesson, you will review four major theories of visual perception, including the so-called "nature-nurture" argument. You will also learn something of what scientists know about some principles of perceptual organization: how we judge distance, size, shape, and depth; why we perceive certain things but not others that our eyes "see"; why some perceptions are illusory. You may be surprised to find that your mind sometimes "censors" or "edits" your eyes if your eyes don't "agree" on what each is seeing at a given moment.

In this lesson you will also be introduced briefly to the study of speech perception, the second most important sensory tool used in the information-processing operation known as **cognition**.

Learning Objectives

When you have finished viewing the program and studying your text assignments, you should be able to:

1. Describe and compare four main theories or schools of thought that attempt to explain the nature and function of visual perception.
2. Cite evidence which suggests that some perception is genetically determined, or innate, not learned.
3. Explain how the principles of expectancy and constancy of shape and size support the belief that some perceptual abilities are learned.
4. Describe the influence of the two "organizing" principles, figure-ground relationships and visual grouping, on visual perception.
5. Discuss the clues that help us to perceive distance visually (figure-ground relationships, convergence, linear and aerial perspective, texture, shadow, motion).
6. Distinguish between illusion and hallucination and give examples.
7. Identify key differences between visual perception and speech perception.

Assignments

Before Viewing the Program

Read the preview at the beginning of this lesson and look over the learning objectives that precede the assignments.

Check the section "Did You Know That . . ." at the beginning of Chapter 8 in the text, and look over the subtitles for the chapter.

Read Chapter 8, "Visual Perception and Speech Perception."

View Program 10, "Visual Perception"

After Viewing the Program

Review the text assignments.

Read through the summary at the end of the chapter and consider the thought questions inserted in the chapter material. Then, to facilitate your understanding of the materials presented in this lesson, study the terms and concepts that appear in boldfaced type and are defined in the upper right corners of right-hand pages. In particular, note these terms carefully: perception, illusions, size constancy, depth perception, linear perspective, convergence, figure-ground relationships, shape constancy, innate, visual cliff, cognition, contour, Gestalt, empiricists, nature-nurture problem, critical features, visual grouping.

Complete the study activities that are included here as an additional study aid for you.

Now evaluate your understanding of the lesson material by reviewing the learning objectives and taking the self-test in this study guide. Check your answers against the answer key.

According to your instructor's assignments or your own interests, choose and complete activities from among the suggestions for extra credit. You might consider the recommended readings listed at the end of the chapter.

"Excuse me for shouting—I thought you were farther away."

Study Activities

True-False

1. T F Visual perception is another term for cognition.
2. T F In the nature-nurture controversy, the nurture position is that visual perception is determined by your genes.
3. T F Empiricists believe perception to be the process by which your mind "makes sense" out of sensations.
4. T F The information-processing theory focuses on innate aspects of perception.
5. T F You perceive shape visually by responding to sudden changes in lightness or darkness.
6. T F The principle of proximity explains your brain's tendency to make solid lines out of broken lines that are placed alongside one another.
7. T F If you observe that an object within your field of vision is growing brighter, you tend to conclude that the object is moving toward you.
8. T F Your mind always fuses the information into one perceptual "picture" when one of your eyes happens to see a different scene than the other is seeing.
9. T F According to the principle of size constancy, you may in some circumstances interpret an object that is very close to you as larger than it is.
10. T F Children born blind develop normally in all areas except sight.
11. T F The Mueller-Lyer illusion is thought to be based on our perception of corners.
12. T F Your early life experiences have little to do with how you later see the world.
13. T F For the most part, young babies and newborn animals do not seem to perceive the danger of a visual "cliff" introduced into the laboratory environment.
14. T F A true hallucination is dependent on stimulation from the external world.
15. T F For the most part, our eyes record the world in two dimensions.

Completion

1. The so-called nature-nurture controversy has long been one of psychology's thorniest issues. As it relates to the study of visual and speech perception, this problem causes scientists to ask whether these perceptual abilities are innate or _____. Today there are at least four well-defined positions, or approaches to the study of visual perception. Two of them, the Gestalt and Gibsonian schools, represent the "nature" side of the argument. Gestaltists believe that your brain imposes perceptual _____, such as roundness, on what your eyes tell you the world is like. Gibsonians argue that visual _____ routed to your brain through sensory receptors in your eyes determine _____ because they describe objects as they actually are. The empiricist viewpoint holds that perception is determined by present _____ and mental images (memories) of past _____. Perception itself is the process that gives _____ to sensations. According to the information-processing approach, visual inputs are _____ through a series of steps or stages on the way to the cortex, and at each stage unimportant _____ is extracted and _____ input is retained. Your higher brain then perceives a _____ which contains only the critical _____ that it needs. Information-processing theorists believe, then, that sensation, memory, and perception are part of a more complex _____ called cognition, which has many determinants.

perception
experience
information
pattern
learned
input
meaning
critical
concepts
process
stimuli
processed
sensations

2. The simplest form of visual input is a difference between light and darkness. We call a sharp or sudden change from light to dark or dark to light a _____ contour. Contour determines shape. Some studies appear to show that the first visual perception experienced by the newborn infant is the shape, or _____ of its mother's face. Thus the ability to perceive shape is thought to be _____. Shape is important to our ability to distinguish objects from their backgrounds—or "surround," as some psychologists say. In figure-ground relationships, the _____ always seems brighter and closer than the _____, and the _____ is usually continuous behind the _____. The object that stands out and appears to be a _____ "whole" is seen as the _____.

figure
innate
background
figure
contour
visual
background
figure
visual

3. Distinguishing figure-ground relationships is one of two main organizing techniques, or principles, used in visual perception; the other is the principle of grouping. By means of visual grouping, your mind tries to bring order to the chaotic jumble of infomational inputs provided by your eyes. We tend to group things together according to how close they are to one another, which is known as the principle of _____. The principle of _____ describes the tendency to group "like" objects together. When we see a collection of "parts" and try to assemble these parts into a visual "whole" by following a continuous line, we are using the _____ principle. Research has also established that when we look at a scene composed of broken lines, we tend to "close up" the lines mentally to perceive a shape or figure, a phenomenon known as _____.

continuity
proximity
closure
similarity

150

4. Your eyes report what they see as flat, or _____, but your mind creates the third dimension of _____. Because young babies can perceive a visual "cliff," the concept of depth is believed to be _____, although some other aspects of depth _____ seem to be learned. Judging distance and size visually is, for the most part, an acquired ability and is dependent upon cues from the _____ and from other environmental sources as well as upon memories of past experiences. One of the most familiar and important of these cues is our tendency to see parallel lines (such as railroad tracks) coming together at the distant horizon, a phenomenon called _____. Another is the perception that one object which blocks another in our field of vision is closer to us than the object it blocks, a perceptual influence which we call _____. Other visual _____ include aerial perspective, motion, texture, and shadow. Expectancy is a _____ behavior that wields considerable influence on visual perception. _____ causes us to see what we expect or want to see.

cues
perception
depth
learned
one-dimensional
innate
linear perspective
interposition
stimuli
Expectancy

Short-Answer Questions

1. What is the **basic** difference among the Gestalt, the Gibsonian, the empiricist, and the information-processing schools of thought on the nature of visual perception?

2. Use examples to distinguish between illusion and hallucination.

3. To what visual distance clue are you responding in perceiving the figure below?

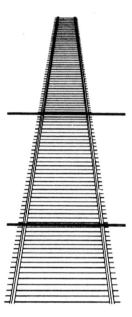

4. a. Two important principles of visual grouping are illustrated by the four sets of squares presented below. You will probably perceive the first set of squares (1) as being arranged in **rows** and the second set (2) as being arranged in **columns**. What principle is illustrated by the way you perceive these two sets of squares?

   b. You should perceive the set of squares numbered 3 as an arrangement of **columns** and set number 4 as being **rows**. What second important perceptual principle is illustrated by these squares?

1.

2.

a. _____

3.

4.

b. _____

5. Associate the figures below with perceptual relationships and principles discussed in this lesson. For example, the drawing at the left (a) contains the face and head of an old woman; illustration b shows either a wineglass or two faces nose-to-nose (but which?); and the "box" below (c) is, of course, a cube.

a. Seeing an old woman in this sketch illustrates the principle of _____.

b. Difficulty in deciding whether you see a wineglass or two heads is caused by an ambiguous

_____.

c. The cube will appear to be switching its orientation back and forth between upward and downward if you stare at it for 30 seconds or more.
This is said to be a case of _____.

Self-Test

(Select the one best answer.)

Objective 1: Describe and compare four main theories or schools of thought that attempt to explain the nature and function of visual perception.

1. The followers of Gibsonian theory
   a. explain perception by the formula "sensory inputs + memories = perception."
   b. believe sensation and perception are the same.
   c. believe that sensory inputs tell your brain to see the world exactly as it is.
   d. can be described by the statements made in both a and c.
   e. can be described by the statements made in both b and c.

2. The naturist view in the nature-nurture controversy over perception is best represented by which of the following?
   a. Gibsonian school of thought
   b. Gestalt and Gibsonian schools
   c. information-processing approach
   d. belief that mind imposes order on sensory input
   e. belief that sensory input controls the mind

3. Which of the following is **not** a part of the information-processing theory of perception?
   a. Some perceptual abilities are genetically inherited.
   b. Perceptual abilities are multi-determined.
   c. For the most part, your ability to see the world is acquired.
   d. When perception occurs, we typically see only certain critical features of the stimulus input.

Objective 2: Cite evidence which suggests that some perception is genetically determined, or innate, not learned.

4. Studies by psychologist R. L. Fantz show that young infants may have
   a. an innate ability to recognize the human face.
   b. a liking for flat objects but not round ones.
   c. an innate mechanism that keeps them from falling from high places.
   d. the ability to suppress certain images.
   e. an innate ability to see things in aerial perspective.

5. Research on the visual "cliff" provides evidence that
   a. infants cannot perceive danger.
   b. infants have innate response patterns which allow them to recognize a human face.
   c. most infants can be coaxed to hurt themselves.
   d. the ability to perceive depth may be partially innate.
   e. newborn humans and animals are perceptually unaware of danger.

6. The Haith studies appear to show that newborn infants
   a. may have an inborn ability to process faces into "wholes."
   b. cannot see in three dimensions.
   c. do not recognize the difference between flatness and a sharp drop.
   d. use auditory and skin-receptor inputs as much as visual sensations to develop visual perception.
   e. do not have an innate ability to see things in aerial perception.

Objective 3: Explain how the principles of expectancy and constancy of shape and size support the belief that some perceptual abilities are learned.

7. In a new situation, we
   a. tend to see things we have recently experienced.
   b. tend to see what we have been led to expect we will see.
   c. are likely to experience a great number of illusions.
   d. are likely to experience a great number of hallucinations.
   e. tend to keep our visual distance.

8. Scientists experimenting with the Mueller-Lyer illusion conclude that we **expect** to see one arrow as longer than the other because
   a. we tend to suppress the image of one line and concentrate on the other.
   b. the arrow with outward-pointing tips is really longer than the other arrow.
   c. we perceive the arrows in terms of what we have learned about near and far corners.
   d. our brain produces distance distortions.

9. According to the principle of expectancy, you will generally perceive an object in its "real size," no matter what the image on your retina, if
   a. the object is moving.
   b. you view the object long enough.
   c. the object is familiar to you.
   d. you use linear perspective.
   e. you close your eyes and concentrate.

10. According to the principle of size constancy, an unfamiliar object will ordinarily appear to be its "real size," regardless of its distance,
    a. if you have enough cues to judge its distance.
    b. only when the correct image appears on your retina.
    c. when you apply the principles of grouping.
    d. if you have good depth perception.
    e. when the conditions described in both a and d are present.

Objective 4: Describe the influence of the two "organizing" principles, figure-ground relationships and visual grouping, on visual perception.

11. In the Ames "distorted room" experiments, walls that join at a slant and windows shaped like trapezoids
    a. cast rectangular images on the retina.
    b. are perceived as maintaining their known rectangular shape.
    c. send signals that tell the brain to distort perceptions.
    d. product the effects noted in a and b.
    e. produce the effects noted in b and c.

12. Which of the following statements about figure-ground relationships is **not** true?
    a. The figure tends to be brighter and stand out from its background.
    b. The background tends to surround the figure.
    c. Figure and background form a "whole" that has visual properties which differ from those perceived in the separate parts.
    d. All of these statements are true.
    e. Statements b and c are not true.

13. When the relationship is ambiguous, figure and ground
    a. are not reversible.
    b. become part of the surround.
    c. become more important psychologically.
    d. are said to be salient.
    e. cannot be seen simultaneously as figure.

14. Grouping is an important process which we use to organize our perceptions about objects within our field of view. Which of the following is **not** a principle of grouping?
    a. proximity
    b. convergence
    c. continuity
    d. closure
    e. similarity

15. If you looked through some trees and saw the segments of a road behind them, you would be able to ignore the interruptions produced by the trees and would perceive the segments as parts of a single road. Your doing so illustrates the perceptual principle of
    a. continuity.
    b. shape constancy.
    c. proximity.
    d. closure.
    e. expectancy.

16. Which principles of grouping are you using when you gaze at an outdoor scene and perceive the clouds as belonging together because they look alike and the trees as belonging together because they stand close to one another?
    a. proximity and similarity
    b. similarity and continuity
    c. similarity and proximity
    d. continuity and proximity
    e. similarity and closure

Objective 5: Discuss the clues that help us to perceive distance visually (figure-ground relationships, convergence, linear and aerial perspective, texure, shadow, motion).

17. Railroad tracks and other parallel lines seem to come together as they approach the horizon. This perceptual tendency is a clue to perceiving distance which we call
    a. aerial perspective.
    b. convergence.
    c. linear perspective.
    d. figure-ground relationships.
    e. hallucination.

18. Convergence, or the turning of your eyes toward one another, is one important clue which helps you to determine the distance of a nearby object. As the distance _____, your eyes will converge _____.
    a. decreases, less and less
    b. decreases, more and more
    c. increases, more and more

19. When the air is very clear and a high mountain peak looks closer to you than it usually does (or really **is**), you are responding to the visual distance clue we call
    a. proximity.
    b. linear perspective.
    c. texture.
    d. aerial perspective.
    e. apparent motion.

Objective 6: Distinguish between illusion and hallucination and give examples.

20. The **primary** difference between illusion and hallucination is that
    a. hallucinations are extreme and dangerous forms of illusion suffered by persons who are mentally ill or on drugs.
    b. illusions are not considered abnormal; hallucinations are.
    c. many common illusions are created by one's expectations.
    d. illusions have some basis in external reality, but hallucinations occur when there is a break between mind and external reality.
    e. hallucinations are commonly created by one's expectations.

21. When the subject of the LSD experiments in the television program described watching his body "dissolve away to a skeleton," he was
    a. responding to stimuli from his sensory receptors.
    b. hallucinating.
    c. experiencing an illusion.
    d. experiencing the effects of expectancy.
    e. describing the actual deterioration of his body.

Objective 7: Identify key differences between visual perception and speech perception.

22. A basic difference between visual perception and speech perception is that
    a. the eye records input about an object all at once, while auditory perception involves input recorded in a time sequence.
    b. speech perception requires visual cues as well as auditory stimuli.
    c. the basic unit of speech is the syllable.
    d. speech perception is not subjected to as much research as is visual perception.
    e. speech perception involves communication.

Suggestions for Extra Credit

1. The theories expounded by James J. Gibson on the subject of human visual perception have attracted—and continue to provoke—spirited debate among psychologists from both sides of the so-called "nature-nurture" fence. Gibsonians have made interesting and important contributions to the understanding of perception, and the literature contains many defenses of the Gibsonian school of thought as well as critiques and rebuttals of the critiques. These writings appear in both book and journal article format. Most are quite scholarly in approach. However, the books and many of the journals (such as the *Journal for the Theory of Social Behaviour*) are readily available in university or college libraries. If you would like to study the nature-nurture problem of perception in greater depth, check the card catalogues and the journal abstracts in your favorite (or nearest) college library, select one or more articles or books that interest you, and read them. Then write a brief paper summarizing **your** views on Gibsonian theory and giving reasons for your position.

2. Optical illusions have been the subject of serious psychological study since the mid-1850s and the known object of curiosity and speculation for many centuries before that. Why do you think the study of illusions is important? What useful purpose, if any, do you think illusions serve? For example, consider the use of camouflage in nature as well as in man-created situations, such as hunting trips and military maneuvers. In his book, *Visual Illusions*, published by Dover Publications in 1965, M. Lukiesh, a lighting engineer by profession, includes a chapter on camouflage in his interesting and well-illustrated account of hundreds of familiar and unfamiliar illusions.

3. If you are interested, you might select one or two illusions pictured and described in Lukiesh's work and design a simple experiment to try on friends or family members. For example, you might use the sketch of two faces (equivocal figures) portrayed on page 73, or the trapezoid (geometrical illusion) shown on page 58. (You will recognize the trapezoid as the same one used in the pilot-training program described in the television program that accompanies this lesson.)

4. Eyewitness accounts play a decisive role in such important realms as courtroom proceedings and the reporting by the news media of crimes, major accidents, disasters, and other cataclysmic events; yet eyewitness accounts differ substantially and are often unreliable. Can you remember any experiences in which your own account of some important event differed markedly from that related by someone else who "saw" the same event? If you can find the opportunity to attend a court trial in which eyewitness testimony plays a large role (as criminal and accident trials often do), you will find the experience to be interesting and thought provoking. You might also watch your favorite newspapers and news magazines for coverage of an event which depends heavily on eyewitness descriptions (such as an automobile accident, a fistfight between two congressmen, etc.)

and compare the accounts of several persons who were interviewed. Do the accounts differ in important ways? How do you account for differences in what these persons "saw"? What do you think could be done about such discrepancies in information?

5. Some optical illusions produce tragic consequences, as authors Stanley Coren and Joan Stern Girgus point out in their 1978 book, *Seeing is Deceiving*, published by Lawrence Erlbaum Associates. A mid-air collision of two large airliners over the New York area in 1965 was blamed on a simple illusory effect called the "Poggendorff illusion," which was first identified in 1860. Psychologists commonly re-create this illusion with simple lines, and it is discussed and illustrated in the Coren and Girgus book. Coren and Girgus offer a brief history of visual illusions, explanations for the psychoanatomy of illusions, descriptions of their structure and retinal components. They also attempt to classify illusions and offer a taxonomy. If you are able to find additional evidence implicating the Poggendorff illusion in the 1965 mishap (or others of significance), write a brief report on what you find. Or, you might want to read and comment on portions of the Coren and Girgus work that interest you, particularly Chapter 14, "Illusions: Implications and Extrapolations."

Answer Key

True-False

1. F	9. T
2. F	10. F
3. T	11. T
4. F	12. F
5. T	13. F
6. F	14. F
7. T	15. T
8. F	

Completion

1. learned, concepts, stimuli, perception, sensations, experience, meaning, processed, information, critical, pattern, input, process;   2. visual, contour, innate, figure, background, background, figure, visual, figure;   3. proximity, similarity, continuity, closure;   4. one-dimensional, depth, innate, perception, stimuli, linear perspective, interposition, cues, learned, Expectancy.

Short-Answer Questions

1. The Gestaltist and Gibsonian viewpoints maintain that the properties of perception are **innate**, while the empirical and information-processing approaches emphasize the **learned** aspects of perception. To Gibsonians, the stimulus is the most important influence in perception; the other three viewpoints place emphasis on internal processing of some sort. Gestaltists, Gibsonians, and empiricists all believe that the stimulus reaches the brain with little or no prior processing, but the information-processing view is that stimuli are processed many times by lower centers in the brain and sent to the cortex in a "pattern" that contains only relevant (or "critical") information needed by the brain. Gibsonians see sensation and perception as being the same event; Gestaltists and empiricists see sensation and memory as independent processes that influence perception; and information-processing theorists believe that sensation, perception, and memory are all part of the global process known as **cognition**.

2. The basic difference between illusion and hallucination is that illusions have some basis in reality; hallucinations do not. Illusions occur frequently in visual perception and are generally caused when the brain "misperceives" stimulus input for a number of reasons that include expectancy, cultural conditioning, and the need to see shapes and sizes as constant. Hallucinations are triggered by an imagined reality, not by stimulation from the external world.

3. linear perspective

4. a. similarity
   b. proximity

5. a. expectancy (Can you also now see a **young** woman in the sketch?)
   b. figure-ground relationship
   c. reversible perspective

Self-Test

1. e (text pages 194–195)
2. b (text pages 194–195)
3. c (text pages 195–196)
4. a (text page 215)
5. d (text pages 216–217; television program)
6. d (text pages 215–216)
7. b (text page 209; television program)
8. c (text pages 210–211; television program)
9. c (text page 209)
10. a (text page 209)
11. b (text page 211; television program)

12. d (text pages 198–199)
13. e (text page 199)
14. b (text pages 201–202)
15. a (text pages 201–202)
16. c (text pages 201–202)
17. c (text pages 204–205; television program)
18. b (text page 205)
19. d (text page 207; television program)
20. d (television program)
21. b (television program)
22. a (text pages 218–219)

Subliminal Perception 11

Viewer's Guide for Program Eleven

As you view the television program, watch for:

The sword demonstration, the dancing dots, and the film sequence of an armed robbery. These will help to refresh your memory of principles studied in the preceding five lessons on sensation and perception.

The film sequence which shows United States Navy jets crossing the threshold between being earthbound and being airborne. Is this threshold—that is, the **exact** takeoff speed—always the same?

The demonstration of driving a car while the conscious mind wanders, an example of "discrimination awareness," or "overlearned responding," as your text terms this phenomenon.

The laboratory test for two-point thresholds over the skin's surface. This test is similar to the one that led to the discovery of subliminal perception, the subject of this lesson.

Famous psychic Uri Geller bending a spoon with what appears to be more mental than physical effort. Was Geller exercising ESP, or are there other explanations of the event?

The sequence in which it is noted that pigeons navigate with the help of a group of magnetized crystals behind each ear. This discovery is important because it may be evidence of a new sense.

Preview

Could you be persuaded to buy certain products or brands by means of advertising messages flashed so briefly on a movie or television screen that you would not be consciously aware of them?

In 1956, a public relations executive named James Vicary announced that he had tested this method in a movie theater and had markedly increased sales of Coca-Cola and popcorn by "subliminal suggestion." That is, he had presented the messages at a level well below the visual perception thresholds of the audiences. As you might imagine, Vicary's announcement startled both the advertising and the viewing world. Advertising executives now thought they saw a way to persuade anyone to buy anything, while some other Americans feared they would be the unwitting and unwilling dupes of a whole army of "hidden persuaders" equipped with new "mind control" techniques. Indeed, what defenses would they have against messages of which they were unaware?

Both the enthusiasm and the anguish proved to be unwarranted. While Vicary's techniques were interesting, he had used neither a control group nor other techniques of the scientific method; therefore, dozens of psychologists who have tried to repeat his study have all failed to produce the same results. It appears that any stimulus that is so weak as to be "subliminal" is probably too weak to influence your buying habits.

However, other studies suggest that subliminal perception does indeed exist, but its effects are believed to be weak and can probably be detected only under highly controlled conditions. It is suggested that subliminal perception is part of your preconscious processing system which screens informational inputs from all the sensory modalities simultaneously before sending any of them along to the conscious centers in your cortex. It is also true, as you will learn, that your lower brain centers can mount a defense against information perceived as trivial or threatening, simply by **raising** the threshold too high for the input to cross. At the same time, the same lower brain centers may be on the lookout for other kinds of messages for which they will actually **lower** the threshold. You may also be surprised to find that your brain on some occasions allows you to respond to supraliminal, or above-threshold, stimuli without being consciously aware of doing so. Can you summon readily to mind any situations where this might be so?

In this lesson, you will learn about perceptual thresholds, how they are measured, and why they are important, as well as how they are related to perceptual defense and perceptual vigilance.

Learning Objectives

1. Define threshold and explain how threshold is measured.
2. Compare supraliminal and subliminal perception.
3. Describe the effectiveness of subliminal advertising.
4. List and describe four ways of responding to supraliminal stimulus input without the mind being consciously aware of doing so (including the orienting reflex, overlearned responding, perceptual defense, and perceptual vigilance).
5. Distinguish between subliminal perception, ESP, and overlearned responding (called discrimination awareness in the television program).

Assignments

Before Viewing the Program

Read the preview at the beginning of this lesson and look over the learning objectives that precede the assignments.

Re-read those sections of Chapter 9 beginning with "Orienting Reflex" and continuing through "Habituation" and those sections beginning with "Thresholds" and continuing through "Preconscious Processing."

Review the boldfaced terms in these sections and those defined in the upper right corners of right-hand pages. In particular, note the terms threshold, subliminal advertising, supraliminal stimuli, overlearned responding, perceptual defense, perceptual vigilance, extrasensory perception, JND, and Weber's Law.

View Program 11, "Subliminal Perception"

After Viewing the Program

Review the summary items at the end of the chapter and consider the thought questions included in the assigned reading sections.

Complete the study activities that are included here as an additional study aid for you.

Now evaluate your understanding of the lesson material by reviewing the learning objectives and taking the self-test in this study guide. Check your answers against the answer key.

According to your instructor's assignment or your own interests, choose and complete activities from among the suggestions for extra credit. You might also consider any appropriate recommended readings listed at the end of the chapter.

Study Activities

Matching

Match each phrase in the column on the right with the appropriate term in the column on the left, writing the letters of the phrases in the appropriate blanks.

____ 1. threshold
____ 2. overlearned responding
____ 3. reflex orienting
____ 4. extrasensory perception
____ 5. limen
____ 6. perceptual defense
____ 7. perceptual vigilance
____ 8. subliminal
____ 9. supraliminal
____ 10. mental telepathy
____ 11. preconscious processing
____ 12. JND
____ 13. RAS

a. Latin word for "threshold"
b. lowering thresholds to certain desirable stimuli
c. below the threshold for conscious perception
d. "reading someone's thoughts"
e. halfway point, or dividing line between two places or states of being
f. screens inputs for significance
g. measure of two stimuli just noticeably different 50 percent of the time
h. repressing threatening stimuli
i. responding without being aware
j. paying attention to a new input
k. above the threshold for conscious perception
l. screening input for the cortex
m. perception without sensory inputs

Completion

1. As you know from preceding lessons, knowledge about the world around you and the world within you comes to you along your sensory pathways. A stimulus excites your sensory receptors, and the receptors send a message to your central nervous system. Before you can become conscious of the input, however, it must cross several _____, or barriers to awareness. It must be physically strong enough to cross the _____ barriers and excite your

receptor neurons. And it must be psychologically important enough to cross the _____ barrier, that is, to get past your _____ activating system, which was described earlier. In addition, for you to react to the input in any measurable way, it must cross your _____ threshold; that is, it must be strong enough or important enough to cause you to **do** something.

reticular
action
sensory
thresholds
conscious

2. Thresholds differ from person to person and from moment to moment in the same person. When you become consciously aware of a stimulus, that stimulus has crossed your _____ threshold. If a stimulus is presented to you continuously exactly at your threshold for your particular stimulus, you would be consciously aware of it only half the time. A stimulus so weak that you would not be consciously aware of it is said to be _____, meaning that it is far below your _____ threshold. While it is too weak to penetrate your conscious awareness, this kind of input is strong enough to cross your _____ threshold, however.

sensory
conscious
perceptual
subliminal

3. Stimuli that cross your difference threshold are measured in terms of JND, or Just Noticeable _____, therefore, the size of the threshold is, by definition, one _____. Weber's research resulted in the following law: The JND is always a constant fraction of the reference _____. The fraction for light was found to be 1/60; the fraction for loudness 1/10.

stimulus
difference
JND

4. Subjects in experiments in which so-called "dirty" words were presented on a subliminal level required more time to _____ disturbing, offensive, or emotionally charged words than they did to perceive normal, everyday, emotionally neutral words. McGinnies believed they were _____ defending against perceiving the disturbing words. He called this phenomenon perceptual _____. On the other hand, a few of his subjects perceived words of this type more readily. He called this tendency perceptual _____. Perceptual defense and perceptual vigilance are two ways in which we are able to respond to _____ stimuli of which we are not consciously aware. Another is called the _____ reflex, or the "Where is it?" reaction, and the fourth case is illustrated by a situation in which you might drive your car properly and safely all the way to work and not remember doing it because your mind was "on vacation," a condition called _____ responding, or responding without awareness. The stimuli in such cases are _____, however, not subliminal.

defense
orienting
overlearned
perceive
supraliminal
unconsciously
vigilance
supraliminal

5. Some _____ have sought to study _____ perception (ESP), that is, the ability to know or perceive by nonsensory means. There are many types of ESP, but two of the best known are _____ telepathy, the ability to read minds, and _____, the ability to move or bend objects mentally rather than by touching them physically. Many phenomena that are attributed to ESP are better explained in terms of _____ perception or responding without _____. At present, the "personal" _____ for ESP is stronger than the "_____" evidence.

awareness
evidence
extrasensory
experimental
mental
parapsychologists
psychokinesis
subliminal

Short-Answer Questions

1. How does the RAS "act like an automatic pilot" for your conscious mind?

2. What can be said about the effectiveness of stimuli presented at subliminal levels?

3. Recall the Great Raynaldo's experience with Mrs. Brattle in the television program for this lesson. How could she know he was a phony when he said he found **all** of his senses effective in ESP?

Self-Test

(Select the one best answer.)

Objective 1: Define threshold and explain how threshold is measured.

1. A sensory input from the outside world must be strong enough and important enough to pass over three thresholds before it results in action. In order, from least to most difficult to cross, these thresholds are
   a. sensory, action, conscious.
   b. action, sensory, conscious.
   c. action, conscious, sensory.
   d. sensory, conscious, action.
   e. conscious, sensory, action.

2. The perceptual threshold is that point at which you are conscious of a stimulus _____ percent of the time.
   a. 10
   b. 25
   c. 50
   d. 75
   e. 100

3. When you respond behaviorally to stimulus input, your _____ threshold has been crossed.
    a. action
    b. sensory
    c. perceptual or conscious
    d. subliminal
    e. supraliminal

4. Threshold is measured by
    a. the Galvanic Skin Response.
    b. the Just Noticeable Difference.
    c. how rapidly one responds to a change in the environment.
    d. stimulating perceptual vigilance.
    e. suppressing perceptual defense.

Objective 2: Compare supraliminal and subliminal perception.

5. "Subliminal" refers to stimulus input that is
    a. below the sensory and conscious thresholds.
    b. below the conscious and above the sensory threshold.
    c. below the sensory threshold.
    d. responded to without awareness.
    e. mind controlling.

6. Supraliminal perception, unlike subliminal perception,
    a. crosses both sensory and perceptual or conscious thresholds.
    b. does not cross sensory and perceptual thresholds.
    c. is useful in advertising and other forms of persuasion.
    d. is another name for overlearned responding.

Objective 3: Describe the effectiveness of subliminal advertising.

7. According to psychological experiments, subliminal advertising
    a. was a major technical breakthrough.
    b. proved to be an effective means of mind control.
    c. was neither new nor particularly effective.
    d. was a major and effective breakthrough.
    e. can be described by none of the above.

Objective 4: List and describe four ways of responding to supraliminal stimulus input without the mind being consciously aware of doing so (including the orienting reflex, overlearned responding, perceptual defense, and perceptual vigilance).

8. If you drive between two points and respond automatically to signs along the way but cannot recall any of them, you have demonstrated
    a. subliminal perception.
    b. supraliminal perception.
    c. unconscious censoring.
    d. responding without awareness, or overlearned responding.
    e. the two-point threshold.

9. Perceptual vigilance
    a. is a raising of the perceptual threshold.
    b. is a lowering of the perceptual threshold.
    c. protects you against threatening stimuli.
    d. is unconscious censoring.
    e. is an important quality in night watchmen and security guards.

10. Perceptual defense is
    a. the act of suppressing or repressing threatening stimuli.
    b. a raising of the perceptual threshold.
    c. a lowering of the perceptual threshold.
    d. described by all of the above.
    e. described by both a and b above.

11. To read ''whole'' when the word on the screen is ''whore'' is an example of
    a. perceptual vigilance.
    b. perceptual defense.
    c. letter reversal.
    d. letter substitution.
    e. reading difficulty.

12. Thinking an intruder has entered your house in the night, then listening for and hearing noises that sound like footsteps is an example of
    a. perceptual vigilance.
    b. perceptual defense.
    c. clairvoyance.
    d. overlearned responding.
    e. perceptual vigilance and overlearned responding.

Objective 5: Distinguish between subliminal perception, ESP, and overlearned responding (called discrimination awareness in the television program).

13. Psychologists have shown that people who believe they are demonstrating ESP
    a. may be responding to supraliminal perception.
    b. may be responding to subliminal perception.
    c. are really demonstrating overlearned responding.
    d. are unconsciously faking their reports.
    e. are usually ''psychic.''

14. From research regarding ESP, it is possible to conclude that
    a. many people are definitely capable of perceiving by nonsensory means.
    b. some people with special powers are capable of perceiving by nonsensory means.
    c. only mystics and psychics are able to perceive by nonsensory means.
    d. some people have extra senses.
    e. ''personal'' evidence for ESP is stronger than ''experimental'' evidence.

15. According to the television program, important factors in evaluating parapsychological research are
    a. repeatability and belief in ESP.
    b. belief in ESP and use of control groups.
    c. repeatability and use of control groups.
    d. belief in ESP and acceptance of the uncorroborated testimony of mystics and psychics.
    e. the ability to perceive subliminal stimuli and to respond without awareness.

Suggestions for Extra Credit

1. The question of subliminal perception in advertising has intrigued observers since the idea was introduced in the 1950s. Wilson Bryan Key writes authoritatively on the subject in his book, *The Clam-Plate Orgy: And Other Subliminals the Media Use to Manipulate Your Behavior*, (Prentice-Hall, 1980). The book is available at most college and university libraries. Key claims (Chapter 2) that ''ninety-nine percent'' of alcohol beverage advertising contains one or more techniques of subliminal ''excitation stimuli.'' Alcohol beverage ads abound in current magazines. Look at some of them to test Key's claim. Are they, as he states, ''the alcoholic's nightmare''?

2. Why does belief in ESP and related phenomena persist despite the ambivalence and skepticism of American psychologists about the paranormal and the occult? For a good historical account and review of anomalistic psychology and a review of psychic research and academic psychology, you will enjoy Leonard Zusne's discussion in *Perceptual and Motor Skills*, 55 (December 1982). Zusne also discusses reasons for persistent belief in ESP and the need to come to grips with the issue. For additional information and observations about ESP, UFOs, con artists, occult pretensions, and psychic phenomena, read Chapter 5, "Night Walkers and Mystery Mongers: Sense and Nonsense at the Edge of Science," pages 43 through 65 in Carl Sagan's *Broca's Brain: Reflections on the Romance of Science* (Random House, 1974).

3. Recalling what you learned about sensory deprivation and stimulus input in Lesson Nine, how do you think you might be affected by subliminal stimuli presented to you in a situation of sensory deprivation? Try to write a brief scenario describing the presentation of some particular subliminal stimulus to you in such a situation, describe your responses, and explain why you might respond as you imagine you would.

4. When a consumer makes a purchase, how is he or she influenced by the memory and attentional processes when exposed to stimuli presented below the level of consciousness? John G. Lynch and Thomas K. Srull compare memory-based judgments to stimulus-based judgments in a perceptive article in the *Journal of Consumer Research*, 9 (June 1982). For those interested in influencing or modifying decision-making, their article makes valuable reading.

Answer Key

Matching

1. e	8. c
2. i	9. k
3. j	10. d
4. m	11. l
5. a	12. g
6. h	13. f
7. b	

Completion

1. thresholds, sensory, conscious, reticular, action;   2. perceptual, subliminal, conscious, sensory;   3. Difference, JND, stimulus;   4. perceive, unconsciously, defense, vigilance, supraliminal, orienting, overlearned, supraliminal;   5. parapsychologists, extrasensory, mental, psychokinesis, subliminal, awareness, evidence, experimental.

Short-Answer Questions

1. Your reticular activating system can and does behave like an automatic pilot for you in that it handles well-learned **supraliminal** stimulus inputs by screening the inputs from your mind automatically. Thus, you can drive your car home or to work without giving your driving a conscious thought. However, if the RAS tips you off that something unusual is happening, your conscious mind takes over again.

2. Despite the claims of some advertising interests, there is no scientific proof that stimuli presented at subliminal levels can persuade people to buy certain products. Well-controlled studies in this area are nonexistent. However, laboratory studies, such as those by Miller and Kennedy, have demonstrated that perception does occur at subliminal levels and stimulus inputs at these levels can influence your behavior under certain conditions. Personal motivation seems to be the key to whether or not your mind chooses to make use of stimuli too faint for your perceptual threshold. You will tend to make use of sensory inputs that lie below your threshold of conscious awareness when you do not have enough supraliminal inputs available to you to make a decision and when you are highly motivated to make use of even your weakest sensory perceptions.

3. Mrs. Brattle asked Raynaldo which of his **senses** he found most effective in ESP. She knew he was a phony when he responded, ''All of them,'' because extrasensory perception means ''the ability to know or perceive by nonsensory means.'' Thus, he should really have replied, ''None of them.''

Self-Test

1. d (television program)
2. c (text page 236; television program)
3. a (television program)
4. b (text pages 234-235)
5. b (text page 236; television program)
6. a (text page 236; television program)
7. c (text pages 238-239; television program)
8. d (text page 236; television program)
9. b (text page 237; television program)

10. e (text page 237; television program)
11. b (text page 237)
12. a (text page 237)
13. b (television program)
14. e (television program)
15. c (television program)

Motivation and Hunger 12

Viewer's Guide for Program Twelve

As you view the television program, watch for:

The vignette, in which teenaged Lisa is described as a probable victim of anorexia nervosa, a disease that involves chronic loss of appetite. Not organic in origin, anorexia nervosa has it roots in multiple sociological and psychological influences.

The filmed experiment in which a cat responds to electrical stimulation of the feeding and satiation centers in its brain. What do you think would happen if both centers were surgically removed?

The continuous X-rays of a human chewing and swallowing and of a stomach contracting. Evidence indicates that some part of your brain actually counts the number of swallows you make as you eat. Stomach contractions begin about an hour or so before you would normally eat and will disappear an hour or so after your usual mealtime, even though you do not swallow a bite. In what way do you think these biological processes might influence your subjective experience of hunger?

Psychiatrist Robert Lynch talking about the oral stage of life. According to Freudian theory, persons who do not have sufficient opportunity to satisfy their strong oral needs while they are babies will develop an exaggerated need to "exercise their mouths" and may respond to this need by, among other things, eating and drinking too much and smoking.

Preview

Why did he do that? What **drove** him to it? What possible **motive** did he have? Why does she always act that way? We frequently ask these and similar questions when we learn of someone's act of unusual violence, courage, or annoyance.

Psychologists always ask these questions in their efforts to understand the complexitites of human actions—violent and nonviolent, courageous and cowardly, extraordinary and everyday. In the next three lessons, you will study many aspects of human motivation—which means **why** we do what we do.

Because the human body is a living thing, it has certain basic needs, things it must do and have in order to survive. These include air, food, water, and proper temperature. When these needs are not met, something within us notifies us, often uncomfortably, that we are hungry, thirsty, too hot or too cold, and we are aroused or motivated to do something to change the situation and to satisfy the need.

One need of which we are frequently aware is the need for food. But what motivates us to start and stop eating? Why do we prefer some foods to others that may be more nutritious and less fattening? Why do a large percentage of Americans become obese, while some others literally try to starve themselves to death? In this lesson, you will learn what psychologists know about the answers to these questions. You will learn, too, how such biological controls as the brain's feeding and satiation centers and "swallow counter" influence what and how much you eat.

In America we tend to stigmatize and discriminate against persons who are obese, but you may be surprised to find that obese persons may well **not** be merely "fat slobs" who can't control their own behavior; obesity is, in fact, influenced by a multitude of factors, which include the biological, the intrapsychic, and the social/behavioral. As you will see, hunger and eating in general are influenced by intrapsychic and environmental factors as well as biological ones.

While obesity is the plague of the lower classes, two other eating disorders—anorexia and bulimia—are almost exclusively problems of the upper classes of society. In this lesson, you will see the relationship of these disorders to problems of image and self-esteem and you will understand that some biological factors may actually enhance the behaviors that lead to these disorders.

This lesson also offers some specific suggestions for breaking the "hunger habit" and modifying eating habits in order to eat properly and control weight.

Learning Objectives

When you have finished viewing the program and studying your text assignments, you should be able to:

1. List the basic questions involved in any theory of motivation, and describe the concept of motivation.
2. List and explain some criticisms of the drive theory of motivation.
3. Explain how the arousal theory of motivation varies from the drive theory of motivation.
4. Describe the stages in Maslow's hierarchy of needs.
5. Briefly describe the biological basis of hunger.
6. Cite examples of intrapsychic and social/behavioral influences on obesity.
7. Summarize a behavior modification program for losing weight.
8. Describe the eating disorders anorexia and bulimia as interactions of biological, intrapsychic, and social/behavioral influences.

Assignments

Before Viewing the Program

Read the preview at the beginning of this lesson and look over the learning objectives that precede the assignments.

Check the Section "Did You Know That. . ." at the beginning of Chapter 10 and look over the subtitles for the chapter.

Read Chapter 10, "Introduction to Motivation."

View Program 12, "Motivation and Hunger"

After Viewing the Program

Review the text assignments.

Read through the summary items at the end of the chapter. Then review all of the boldfaced terms. In particular, note the terms: drive theory, primary needs, primary drive, homeostasis, secondary needs, secondary drive, arousal theory, set point, feed-forward, feedback, self-actualization, calories, insulin, sugar detector, obesity, hypothalamus, feeding center, satiation center, swallow counter, gluttony, anorexia, bulimia, endorphins, hunger habit, baseline. Also review and be able to define intrapsychic and hierarchy of needs.

Complete the study activities that are included here as an additional study aid for you.

Now evaluate your understanding of the lesson material by reviewing the learning objectives and taking the self-test in this study guide. Check your answers against the answer key.

According to your instructor's assignment or your own interests, choose and complete the activities from the suggestions for extra credit. You might also consider the recommended readings listed at the end of the chapter.

© 1972 United Feature Syndicate, Inc.

Study Activities

Matching

Match each phrase in the column on the right with the appropriate term in the column on the left, writing the letters of the phrases in the appropriate blanks.

_____ 1. drive theory
_____ 2. arousal theory
_____ 3. feed-forward
_____ 4. self-actualization
_____ 5. example of a primary need
_____ 6. a subjective experience that arouses a primary drive
_____ 7. secondary need
_____ 8. homeostasis
_____ 9. hypothalamus
_____ 10. set point
_____ 11. sugar detector
_____ 12. endorphins
_____ 13. anorexia

a. tendency of the body to reinstate its normal physiological balance
b. an optimum point which is individual, changes from time to time, and above or below which you may be motivated to action
c. explains motivation in terms of physiological needs and biological pain and pleasure
d. stimulate insulin production, which decreases blood-sugar level
e. explains motivation in terms of a departure from a norm or optimum point of neural excitation
f. hypothalamic center which monitors sugar levels of the blood
g. information which specifies future behaviors
h. self-starvation to achieve some personal goal
i. food
j. the process of developing yourself to the limits of your potential
k. neural center that influences eating and drinking
l. hunger
m. craving for steak when you are hungry

Completion

1. Because human actions are complex, trying to explain them is both fascinating and frustrating. Human actions can be analyzed in terms of the stimulating force or influence—that is, the _____ behind them. Motivation can, in turn, be seen as a series of _____: Why do we start to eat? Why do we stop eating? Why do we prefer some foods over others? Why do some persons eat to the point of obesity, while others **refuse** to eat to the point of starvation? Two well-known approaches that attempt to answer these questions are _____ theory and _____ theory.

arousal
drive
questions
motivation

2. _____ theory is based on the belief that our really important needs are physiological and that all behavior can be explained in terms of our efforts to pursue biological _____ and avoid biological _____. According to this theory, those things you must have to survive are called _____ needs, and the corresponding urges that build up within your body to satisfy these needs are called primary _____. Primary needs are _____ and are the same for all human beings. _____ needs are related to the satisfaction of primary needs but are _____ and may vary from person to person and culture to culture. A key concept of drive theory is that the human body has a "normal condition" called _____, a condition in which you are need-free, neural excitement is minimal, and bodily processes are balanced. When your _____ balance is "out of tune," you will be driven to "fix it," just as you would your car.

pleasures
primary
innate
learned
homeostatic
drive
pain
drives
Secondary
homeostasis

3. _____ theory explains motivation in terms of a departure from an optimum point of neural excitation which is called _____ _____. The optimum point may change from time to time, depending upon your biological condition, and you may be aroused or motivated by a _____ as well as an _____ in neural excitation.

increase
Arousal
set point
decrease

4. Psychologist Abraham _____ has developed a hierarchy of human _____, at the top of which is _____, the process of developing yourself to the limits of your potential. This multilevel approach to motivation pulls together _____ and _____ theory and takes perceptual and social influences into account.

drive
self-actualization
Maslow
arousal
needs

5. Eating is a _____ behavior. There are biological explanations for why you start and why you stop eating but biological influences do not explain **all** the reasons why you do or do **not** eat, how much you eat, or why you think "steak" when you're hungry and prefer oysters or clams to snails. The _____ and _____ centers in the hypothalamus exercise a strong _____ influence on eating behavior. In addition, some part of your brain actually counts the number of _____ you make as you eat and uses this information to regulate the total amount you consume. Also, if you eat regularly at certain times, your _____ anticipates these meals and sends neural signals to your stomach to begin the _____ you know as hunger pangs.

feeding
motivated
biological
satiation
brain
contractions
swallows

6. According to McConnell, approximately 10 to 25 percent of Americans are overweight; some other observers have recently estimated that as many as 40 percent of us are _____. For reasons not yet clear, obese persons do not seem to "listen" to start and stop signals given by their _____, and they may not be able to distinguish between hunger and other states of _____. In some people, eating is a response to stress, and it is known that stress produces _____, which reduces the body's _____ level. In the brain, sugar _____ help to regulate eating behavior.

insulin
arousal
bodies
detectors
obese
sugar

7. A major cause of _____, which means fatness, may be external rather than internal. Consciously or unconsciously, many parents _____ their children to overeat. Mistaking fatness for good health, they _____ their babies and encourage their children to "clean their plates." If _____ is used as a reward, the child will learn that _____ is an effective way of winning parental approval. For a variety of reasons, spouses may _____ one another for overeating and overdrinking. _____ may become synonymous with love and acceptance and may be eaten as a substitute for both. While food _____ are, to an extent, determined by religion, personal choice, and culture, the _____ of meals and the _____ of food eaten may be strongly influenced by social _____. Two other serious eating disorders that seem to be increasing in America are a form of self-starvation called _____ and bulimia, a condition in which the individual first _____ on food then _____ the body of the food. These disorders affect mostly young, upper-class women and are extremely difficult to treat.

Food
purges
obesity
choices
binges
overfeed
reward
train
food
frequency
anorexia
class
amount
eating

8. Any effective dieting plan to control obesity must include an effort to determine and bring under control the _____ and _____ factors that influence eating behavior. Many studies show that _____ _____ techniques applied over a long period of time work best in achieving weight reduction. Losing or gaining weight is really a matter of learning to eat

_____.

intrapsychic
environmental
properly
behavior modification

Short-Answer Questions

1. In Lesson Five, entitled "Functions of the Brain," we examined the biological, intrapsychic, and social/behavioral positions regarding the mind-body problem. Which of these three positions do drive theorists appear to be taking? Explain your answer.

2. Compare Maslow's explanation of human motivation with arousal and drive theories.

3. Briefly review the nine points of the cognitive behavioral modification approach to weight control described in the text.

4. Who are the major victims of anorexia and bulimia? Why are these conditions considered difficult to treat?

Self-Test

(Select the one best answer.)

Objective 1: List the basic questions involved in any theory of motivation, and describe the concept of motivation.

1. The concept of **motivation** can best be described as
   a. being characteristic of inanimate objects.
   b. drive theory.
   c. a series of questions asking why we do what we do.
   d. arousal theory.
   e. an upset in the homeostatic balance.

2. Which one of the following questions is not basic to the study of motivation?
   a. Do subliminal stimuli affect behavior?
   b. Are needs innate or learned?
   c. Does pain or pleasure cause a person to act?
   d. Does a person have choices about the way he or she behaves?
   e. What are the needs which people have?

Objective 2: List and explain some criticisms of the drive theory of motivation.

3. The drive theory of motivation states that primary needs
   a. are psychological rather than biological.
   b. can be postponed while primary drives cannot.
   c. lead to primary drives if unfulfilled.
   d. are unrelated to neural arousal.
   e. are learned or acquired.

4. In drive theory, the basic urge to keep the body in a balanced, "need-free" state is called
   a. a primary need.
   b. homeostasis.
   c. general systems theory.
   d. drive reduction.
   e. optimum.

5. Drive theory is described as a _____ approach to the problem of motivation.
   a. mechanistic and biological
   b. mechanistic and intrapsychic
   c. humanistic and intrapsychic
   d. humanistic and social/behavioral
   e. homeostatic

6. According to drive theory, an increasing level of stimulation
   a. results in homeostasis.
   b. is not related to needs.
   c. is pleasurable.
   d. is punishing.
   e. creates primary and then secondary drives.

7. Which of the following statements is a proposition of drive theory?
   a. A decrease in neural excitation can be arousing.
   b. Feelings, perceptions, and emotions affect motivation.
   c. Secondary needs can override primary needs.
   d. Drive reduction leads to homeostasis.
   e. Your homeostatic "home base" is not a state of zero excitation but rather a point of optimum stimulation.

8. Which one of the following is not an objection to drive theory?
   a. It focuses primarily on intrapsychic aspects of motivation.
   b. It fails to explain complex social behavior.
   c. It does not account for the fact that a decrease in excitation can cause an increase in arousal.
   d. It fails to take into account the perceptual and emotional aspects of motivation.
   e. Many so-called secondary needs are neither very secondary nor are they acquired through association with primary needs.

Objective 3: Explain how the arousal theory of motivation varies from the drive theory of motivation.

9. According to arousal theory, homeostasis, or "set point,"
   a. occurs when there is no stimulation.
   b. occurs when there is maximum endurable stimulation.
   c. involves an increase in stimulation.
   d. involves a decrease in stimulation.
   e. cannot be linked to any particular level of stimulation.

Objective 4: Describe the stages in Maslow's hierarchy of needs.

10. According to psychologist Abraham Maslow, which of the following represents the correct sequence of needs?
    a. physiological, love, safety, esteem, and self-actualization
    b. physiological, esteem, love, safety, and self-actualization
    c. physiological, safety, esteem, love, and self-actualization
    d. physiological, safety, love, esteem, and self-actualization
    e. physiological, love, esteem, safety, and self-actualization

11. In Maslow's hierarchy of needs, the route to self-actualization
    a. depends entirely on your need for esteem from other people.
    b. begins with belongingness or love needs and ends with physiological needs.
    c. begins with physiological needs on the bottom rung and proceeds upward.
    d. can actually be followed in random order.
    e. does not require that you progress through all five stages.

Objective 5: Briefly describe the biological basis of hunger.

12. The hypothalamic feeding center
    a. is controlled by feedback from stomach contractions.
    b. responds to the level of sugar in the blood.
    c. produces insulin to control digestion.
    d. sends messages to the swallow counter.
    e. is much enlarged in obese persons.

13. Surgical removal of the satiation center
    a. has little effect on food intake.
    b. stops stomach contractions.
    c. ends the hunger habit.
    d. cures obesity.
    e. causes dramatic overeating.

14. Surgical removal of both the feeding and satiation centers in the rat's brain will often result in
    a. an increase in the rat's food intake.
    b. a decrease in the rat's food intake.
    c. little change in the rat's usual food intake.
    d. alternate overeating and undereating.
    e. a drastic change in the obesity limit.

15. The body mechanism that is first called into play to limit food intake is the
    a. swallow counter.
    b. satiety center.
    c. feeding center.
    d. blood sugar detector.
    e. stomach contraction.

Objective 6: Cite examples of intrapsychic and social/behavioral influences on obesity.

16. According to the intrapsychic viewpoint, eating may be
    a. motivated by increased firing of the hypothalamic feeding center.
    b. the result of defective sensory input.
    c. the result of ignoring sensory input.
    d. an effort to satisfy needs for affection and acceptance.
    e. homeostatic behavior.

17. According to Freudian theory, people with oral personalities are those who may overeat because
    a. they were malnourished.
    b. the innate need to suck was not satisfied in infancy.
    c. they suffer anorexia nervosa.
    d. their swallow counter is defective.
    e. they can't discriminate between states of arousal.

18. Schacter's studies suggest that obese people
    a. will eat more than the average person even if the food tastes bad.
    b. don't discriminate between hunger and other states of arousal.
    c. eat according to external cues rather than internal drive states.
    d. eat to satisfy symbolic needs.
    e. have faulty swallow counters.

19. If you eat to relieve stress, your body may secrete more endorphins, the body's natural pain-killer, which in turn
    a. reduces insulin output and increases sugar level.
    b. increases insulin and decreases sugar level.
    c. causes you to stop eating.
    d. activates your satiation center.
    e. activates your feeding center.

20. Studies of eating behavior indicate that it is
    a. strongly influenced by social class.
    b. always influenced most by a spouse.
    c. readily changed to reflect local and religious customs.
    d. not influenced by rewards.
    e. always influenced most by intrapsychic processes.

Objective 7: Summarize a behavior modification program for losing weight.

21. Which of these steps was suggested as the first to be taken in the weight control program described in the text?
    a. Keep a record of all related activities.
    b. Exercise.
    c. Seek help and support from others.
    d. Establish a baseline of your present eating behavior.
    e. Change hunger habits.

22. Which of these approaches or attitudes will probably be most effective in a weight control program?
    a. Weight control is a matter of correcting biological drives.
    b. Overweight is an intrapsychic problem requiring professional assistance.
    c. Weight problems are due to weak character and can be overcome by will power.
    d. Weight control can be achieved by modifying secondary drives.
    e. Weight control is a matter of learning to eat properly.

Objective 8: Describe the eating disorders anorexia and bulimia as interactions of biological, intrapsychic, and social/behavioral influences.

23. A person who is anorexic usually
    a. has a pathological fear of being fat.
    b. starves voluntarily in order to satisfy some personal goal.
    c. experiences elevated endorphin levels, or "highs."
    d. belongs to a social class which values "thinness."
    e. displays all of the above behaviors.

24. One difference between anorexia and bulimia is that
    a. anorexics get "high" on food, bulimics get "high" from starving.
    b. bulimics starve themselves in order to be thin.
    c. anorexics binge on food, then purge themselves.
    d. bulimics get "high" from food, anorexics feel "high" from starving.
    e. anorexics have faulty feeding and satiation centers.

Suggestions for Extra Credit

1. In view of the medical profession's dismal failure in dealing with the problems of overeating and obesity, laypersons have founded specialized groups to provide members with the motivation and the practical dietary counseling they need for successful weight loss. Among these groups are Weight Watchers and Overeaters Anonymous. If you or someone you know has a weight problem, get in touch with one of these groups to discover

what approaches they take to weight control, what services they offer, and what information they provide. With which motivational reasons for being overweight does each of these organizations try to deal? (If you can find a copy of Marcia Millman's illuminating book, *Such a Pretty Face: Being Fat in America*, 1980, Berkley Publishing Corporation, you will find the answers to most of these questions, and you might also find the book interesting as well as informative. Millman, a social worker, offers poignant case histories and also explores the feelings and behaviors of those who are obese as well as the ways in which society treats them.)

2. Whether or not you think you need to lose weight, take your own baseline. In a notebook, record everything you eat and drink for a week. Include not only the name of the food or drink but the approximate size of the serving. And, if you prepare food for others, do not forget to write down all of those tastes, samples, handfuls, and pieces that find their way into your mouth while you cook a meal or pack a lunch. Make a note of how you felt and whom you were with when you started eating. At the end of the week, calculate your average daily calorie intake. How does it compare with that recommended for a person of your weight, age, and activity level? Are you overeating? If so, look back over your baseline record to see what changes you could make to bring your intake in line with your needs. Also, try to identify the primary motivations that influence your eating behavior.

3. According to McConnell, the way we are fed (or overfed) as children, the culture in which we grow up, and the feelings we have about ourselves have a profound influence on what, how often, and how much we eat. For a heart-warming and gently amusing account of the struggle by one man and those who love him to overcome his obsession with food, read *Fatso* by Anne Bancroft (New York: Ballantine Books, 1980).

4. In some societies of the world, being fat is a sign of wealth. Not in upper-class America, however, where many women believe you can't be too thin (or too rich). A recent National Institutes of Health panel has concluded that even five or ten pounds overweight may be hazardous to your health and obesity is a potential killer. The panel finds that 30 percent of white women in the U.S. between the ages of 45 and 55 are obese, but that among middle-aged black women obesity is a "virtual epidemic." Some 60 percent of black women in this age range are obese. Why do you think this is so? Author Gina Kolata discusses these panel findings in a brief article printed in *Science* (Vol. 227, March 1, 1985, page 1019). In a more technical article published in the same issue of *Science*, on page 1327 ("Why Do People Get Fat?"), Kolata discusses a Rockefeller University study on the role of fat cells in obesity.

5. Despite recent national attention and increased interest, anorexia nervosa is not a new affliction. At least one documented case—that of an English teenager—dates back to 1864 and, in 1873, one eminent physician described it as "mental perversity." Anorexia is, however, one of the few diseases known to be disproportionate by gender: its victims are young, affluent white women. Cherry O'Neill, the daughter of entertainer Pat Boone, has

written the story of her own struggle with anorexia (she was caught eating scraps from the family dog dish) and her recovery in her book, *Starving for Attention*. An article in *U.S. News and World Report*, Aug. 30, 1982, on page 47, offers some shocking statistics and warns of danger signals to watch for. ''The Skeleton at the Feast,'' by Anne Fadiman, *Life* (Vol. 5, February, 1982, page 62), is the moving story of a sixteen-year-old girl—one of more than 100,000 like her in the United States—and the physical and psychological damage she sustained before she began a long and difficult recovery. This article also offers some insights into the ways early physicians regarded this affliction and how they treated it.

Answer Key

Matching

1. c	8. a
2. e	9. k
3. g	10. b
4. j	11. f
5. i	12. d
6. l	13. h
7. m	

Completion

1. motivation, questions, drive, arousal;   2. drive, pleasure, pain, primary, drives, innate, Secondary, learned, homeostasis, homeostatic;   3. Arousal, set point, decrease, increase;   4. Maslow, needs, self-actualization, drive, arousal;   5. motivated, feeding, satiation, biological, swallows, brain, contractions;   6. obese, bodies, arousal, insulin, sugar, detectors;   7. obesity, train, overfeed, food, eating, reward, Food, choices, frequency, amount, class, anorexia, binges, purges;   8. environmental, intrapsychic, behavior modification, properly.

Short-Answer Questions

1. In attempting to explain motivation in terms of physiological needs and the urges to satisfy them, drive theorists have taken a strictly biological position with regard to the mind-body problem. Ignoring intrapsychic and social influences, they have attempted to explain behavioral changes solely in terms of biological ones.

2. Maslow's hierarchy of needs has, in effect, melded the principles of drive and arousal theories into a multilevel approach to motivation. Drive and arousal theorists presume that biological needs rule your life. In Maslow's hierarchy of needs, you must first satisfy physiological needs, but you must also meet equally important psychological and social/behavioral needs if you are to satisfy your highest need, the need for self-actualization. As you progress toward self-actualization, you also learn to control and change your inputs and outputs at every level.

3. 1. Establish a baseline. 2. List the rewards which could come from better control over eating. 3. Break the hunger habit. 4. Increase physical activity and exercise. 5. Consult a psychologist. 6. Obtain support from other people. 7. Record the daily routine of weight-loss related activities. 8. Don't expect too much too fast. 9. Make it a program for "learning to eat properly."

4. Anorexia involves self-induced starvation, sometimes to the point of death; bulimia is sometimes called the "binge-purge" syndrome because its victims typically gorge on as many as 15,000 calories of food in one day, but try to purge themselves of the food before the body can absorb the calories. Both disorders typically affect well-educated young women of higher socioeconomic classes, men only rarely. Both victims fear being fat, but the anorexic denies being abnormal, while the bulimic recognizes the abnormality of the behavior but is powerless to change it. Many individuals eat when frightened or stressed, but the anorexic confuses hunger with stress and interprets hunger signals as stress or fear, denying that she is hungry. Therapists find bulimics and anorexics difficult to treat because they typically have distorted body images, low esteem, and the conviction that they are not in control of their lives. Families of these victims also play an extremely important role in causing the disorders, and they are unusually insensitive to their daughters' problems and often unwilling to change their own behaviors.

Self-Test

1. c (text pages 263-287; television program)
2. a (text page 263; television program)
3. c (text pages 268, 287; television program)
4. b (text pages 268, 287)
5. a (text pages 268-270, 287)
6. d (text pages 268-269)
7. d (text pages 268-269)
8. a (text pages 269-270)
9. e (text page 271)
10. d (text pages 264-267)
11. c (text pages 264-267)
12. b (text pages 273-274; television program)

13. e (text pages 275-276)
14. c (text pages 275-276)
15. a (text pages 276-277; television program)
16. d (text pages 278-280; television program)
17. b (television program)
18. c (text pages 278-279; television program)
19. b (text page 274)
20. a (text page 279; television program)
21. d (text page 285)
22. e (text page 286)
23. e (text page 281; television program)
24. d (text page 284)

Human Sexuality 13

Viewer's Guide for Program Thirteen

As you view the television program, watch for:

The series of photographs and paintings portraying the variety of roles in which society has cast women and men over the centuries.

The animated sequences showing the fetal development of male-female differentiation and the development of additional sex characteristics during adolescence. Both processes are governed by hormones.

The series of clips from news films showing twentieth-century events—war, depression, war again—that uprooted people, brought contrasting cultures into contact and conflict, cast men and women in new roles, relaxed our attitudes, and changed our times.

The photos of Alfred Kinsey, whose surveys of sexual behavior relieved the anxieties of some and shocked others in the 1950s, and of William Masters and Virginia Johnson, whose laboratory studies of sexual responses challenged superstitions concerning sexuality in the 1960s and the 1970s.

The actual film sequence of a laboratory experiment in which the pleasure centers in a cat's brain are stimulated electrically. The cat quickly learns to press a lever to repeat the stimulation and produce the pleasant feeling. These experiments helped scientists to understand that pleasure is not limited to mere avoidance of or relief from pain.

The need for sex has long been acknowledged as one of the basic biological processes underlying motivation, but there is a crucial difference between sexual needs and other physiological needs that are discussed in Lessons Twelve and Fourteen. The difference is that air, food, water, elimination, and proper temperature are necessary for **individual** survival, while sex is essential to survival of the **species**, though not to the individual.

Notwithstanding the universal recognition of sex as an important human need, sex was—until recent years—rarely discussed and never scientifically explored.

Never, that is, until twentieth-century events turned society's Victorian attitudes inside out. War uprooted people, brought contrasting cultures into contact and conflict, and took women out of the home and into the factories to work alongside men. Gradually, people began to shed prewar restrictions on behavior and to become more relaxed and open about what they thought and did, including what they thought and did about sex.

And it was in 1948, during this early postwar period, that biologist Alfred Kinsey asked thousands of people to talk about their sex lives. His was the first survey of American sexual behavior based on a large segment of the population, and it opened the way for further scientific observation of human sexual behavior. In the 1950s gynecologist William Masters and psychologist Virginia Johnson began to study what people actually **did**, rather than what they **said** they did. Their discoveries challenged many of the old superstitions concerning human sexuality.

In this second of three lessons on motivation, you will learn about studies that illuminate the roles of genes and hormones in biasing human sexuality; the influences of sex orientation, sex identity, and pleasure in motivating sexual behavior; and the pervasive power of sex-role stereotypes, which are prescribed by society. In short, you will come to understand that while sexual **needs** are biologically based, motivation toward sexual **behavior** is imbedded in a web of intrapsychic and environmental "threads."

Learning Objectives

When you have finished viewing the program and studying your text assignments, you should be able to:

1. Describe examples of negative reactions that discouraged the early study of human sexuality.

2. Cite some contributions made by Kinsey and the team of Masters and Johnson to our knowledge of human sexual behavior.
3. State the effect of hormones on human sexuality.
4. Describe the research and conclusions of Olds and Milner on the pleasure centers of the brain.
5. Describe sex orientation, identity, roles, and pleasure as aspects of human sexual motivation.

Assignments

Before Viewing the Program

Read the preview at the beginning of this lesson and look over the learning objectives that precede the assignments.

Check the section "Did You Know That . . ." at the beginning of Chapter 11 and look over the subtitles for the chapter.

Read Chapter 11, "Sexual Motivation." As you read, note especially the boldfaced terms and those defined in the upper right corners of right-hand pages. Use the definitions or descriptions to increase your knowledge or refresh your memory concerning these terms.

View Program 13, "Sexual Motivation"

After Viewing the Program

Review the text assignments.

Read through the summary items at the end of the chapter and consider the thought questions. Then review all of the boldfaced terms. In particular, note the terms: hormones, adrenal gland, gonads, androgens, estrogens, limbic system, genitals, critical development periods, puberty, gender identity, heterosexual, orientation, sex-role stereotypes, and pleasure centers.

Complete the study activities that are included here as an additional study aid for you.

Now evaluate your understanding of the lesson material by reviewing the learning objectives and taking the self-test in this study guide. Check your answers against the answer key.

According to your instructor's assignment or your own interests, choose and complete activities from the suggestions for extra credit. You might also consider the recommended readings listed at the end of the chapter.

"I can go two weeks without <u>water</u>, but <u>sex</u> is an entirely different matter!"

Playboy, February 1969. Reproduced by special permission of PLAYBOY Magazine. Copyright © 1969 by Playboy.

Study Activities

True-False

1. T F The need for sex is not important to human survival.
2. T F During a critical period before birth, the human fetus is biased toward either male or female behavior patterns by a balance of hormones.
3. T F One significant contribution of the Kinsey studies may have been that reports of the studies relieved the anxieties of many Americans who had previously thought their sexual practices were perverted.
4. T F Masters and Johnson used a case history approach and recorded what people said about their sex lives.
5. T. F Sexual gender is determined at the moment of conception.
6. T F Once you are born, your adrenals and gonads exclusively produce either male hormones or female hormones.
7. T F Sex hormones are produced by the gonads in males and by the testes in females.
8. T F The sex organs are primary sex characteristics.
9. T F The appearance of primary but not secondary sex characteristics is controlled almost entirely by hormones.
10. T F The development of breasts and the broadening of hips at puberty in young women are secondary sex characteristics.
11. T F Sex-role stereotyping begins in puberty.

12. T F In humans, sexual behavior is predominantly under the control of hormones rather than the brain.
13. T F Sexually motivated behavior in humans seems to be aimed at reducing tension.
14. T F Olds and Milner discovered that the pleasure centers in humans are located in the genitalia.
15 T F The prevailing opinion among psychologists and psychiatrists is that homosexuality is a mental disorder.
16. T F Most societies expect their members to begin to display "appropriate" masculine or feminine behavior from birth onward.

Completion

1. As you will remember from Lesson Twelve, _____ is connected with satisfaction of needs. Sex needs are biologically based, as are needs for food and water, but motivation to satisfy sex needs differs from motivation to satisfy food and water needs in that individual _____ is not at stake. However, sex **is** essential to survival of the _____. For many years, the scientific study of human sexual behavior was regarded by the medical profession as inappropriate and was thus widely discouraged. Much of what we know today about the biology of sex is limited to animal studies. One of the first Americans to study the _____ aspects of sex was John B. Watson, a teaching psychologist at Johns Hopkins University. Watson constructed special instruments to measure female sexual _____ during intercourse. Watson's studies provided the first reliable data of its kind.

_____

survival
biological
response
motivation
species

2. In the late 1940s, biologist Alfred _____ became perhaps the first scientist to survey sexual behavior in America. Though important, Kinsey's work depended upon personal descriptions and case histories, not observation of _____. The team of William Masters and Virginia _____ began in the 1950s to study biological changes that occur during sexual excitement; their studies included both males and females. These studies ultimately gained acceptance from the medical and psychiatric communities.

responses
Johnson
Kinsey

3. Genetic gender is decided upon _____ . Each egg cell has one X chromosome, and if an egg cell receives another _____ chromosome when it is fertilized by a sperm, the result will be a genetic female. But sperm cells can have either an X chromosome or a _____ chromosome, and if the egg cell receives the Y chromosome, a genetic _____ results. The division between male and female is known as _____ dimorphism. Sexual dimorphism is affected by both male and female sex hormones secreted by the adrenal glands and the _____ . Male hormones are called **androgens**; female hormones are **estrogens**. The best-known androgen, testosterone, is known to promote sexual behavior and is believed to affect brain-hemisphere dominance and handedness in the developing fetus. In the presence of the sex hormones, the process of sexual differentiation begins soon after _____ . During differentiation, the primary sex characteristics (the sex organs) emerge. What we call _____ sex characteristics normally develop at puberty and are controlled hormonally. These include growth of face, chest, and pubic hair, development of breasts in women, and deepening of the male voice.

male
conception
Y
X
secondary
fertilization
sexual
gonads

4. When the central nervous system of the fetus begins to develop, a period which is considered to be _____ to development, the fetus will develop male genitalia and parts of the brain involved in _____ behavior will be activated if _____ are the predominant hormones. If _____ are predominant, the fetus will develop female genitalia and behaviors. Overproduction or underproduction of either androgens or estrogens at _____ will affect the timing of maturity in both men and women.

puberty
androgens
estrogens
masculine
critical

5. One important influence on human sexual behavior is the tendency to be attracted to one sex or the other (or both), which we call sexual _____. Three ways of orienting to others sexually are homosexuality, bisexuality, and _____. Other aspects of sexual motivation include sexual, or _____, identity, and socially imposed sex _____. Whether you see yourself as male or female determines sexual _____; according to sex _____ prescribed by society, you are required to show "masculine" or "feminine" behavior, according to socially accepted concepts, or _____. Sex-role begins at birth and is promoted, consciously and unconsciously, by parents.

roles
heterosexuality
identity
stereotypes
orientation
stereotyping
gender
roles

6. In lower animals, sexual behavior is cyclical and almost entirely under the control of _____ which periodically lower the thresholds for sex-related activities. In human experience, however, sexual behavior is predominantly _____ and under the control of the brain. In lower animals, sexual inhibition is instinctual. In humans, however, most sexual inhibition appears to be _____.

learned
hormones
learned

7. While mapping the _____ areas in the brains of white rats, James Olds and Peter Milner accidentally discovered the existence of "_____" centers. Until their discovery, drive theorists had assumed that the desire to avoid or reduce _____ motivated all behavior. The discovery of pleasure or reward centers suggested that there were two types of pleasure: (1) the _____ when pain ceases and (2) the sensory delight associated with _____ inputs. Later studies also showed that there are dozens of pleasure centers in the brain and that "tickling" the pleasure centers of human subjects results in "feeling good," but not in the compulsive behavior directed toward obtaining pleasurable stimulation that such tickling produces in rats.

pleasure
relief
avoidance
pleasurable
pain

Short-Answer Questions

1. What is the basic difference between the Kinsey surveys and the Masters and Johnson research? Identify the significant contribution made by these studies to the study and understanding of human sexual behavior in America.

2. What does McConnell mean when he concludes that human sexuality is "multi-determined"?

3. How do the sex hormones, androgens and estrogens, affect human development?

4. Describe sex-role stereotyping. (Refer to the Dee Shepherd-Look studies.)

Self-Test

(Select the one best answer.)

Objective 1: Describe examples of negative reactions that discouraged the early study of human sexuality.

1. Which of the following responses was (were) used to ''punish'' early attempts of researchers to study human sexual behavior?
    a. withdrawal or refusal of support money
    b. loss of job
    c. rejection by colleagues
    d. political attacks
    e. all of the responses described above

2. What was the main **reason** for rejection of the Watson study and early opposition to the work of Masters and Johnson in studying human sexual behavior?
    a. Medical journals refused to publish their work.
    b. Their colleagues disapproved.
    c. They attempted to study the biology of sex in humans.
    d. Their studies were not considered to be objective or scientific.
    e. Political pressures were applied.

3. Which of the following statements does not represent early reaction to the Masters and Johnson research?
    a. Gynecologists refused to support the research and suggested they give it up.
    b. Medical journals would not publish their findings.
    c. Political pressure prevented their obtaining governmental support of their work.
    d. Their work was unanimously condemned by the American Psychological Association.
    e. None of the above is true.

Objective 2: Cite some contributions made by Kinsey and the team of Masters and Johnson to our knowledge of human sexual behavior.

4. What was the chief **significance** of Kinsey's work in surveying sexual behavior?
    a. Kinsey used the scientific methodology, whereas Watson depended upon personal accounts of his own experience.
    b. The surveys were the first of their kind ever made.
    c. Kinsey's work opened the way for scientific study of human sexuality.

d. The Kinsey Report was the first work on human sexuality to be published.
e. All of the statements above are correct.

5. The Kinsey Report suggests that
   a. many variations in human sexual behavior are practiced by normal-appearing males.
   b. 4 percent of the men and 2 percent of the women interviewed were predominantly heterosexual.
   c. scientific studies of sexuality must depend on case history studies.
   d. his sample was biased toward women.
   e. all of the statements above are true.

6. One significant difference between the Masters and Johnson research and the Kinsey studies was that Masters and Johnson
   a. used direct measurements of bodily reactions rather than what subjects said.
   b. gave full accounts of the intrapsychic experiences of copulation.
   c. had the backing of the medical profession.
   d. used volunteer housewives as subjects.
   e. reported their work immediately in prestigious medical journals.

7. What is the significance of the Masters and Johnson research?
   a. The research was based on experimental and control groups.
   b. The research represented a detailed scientific attempt to observe and measure physiological activity during sexual behavior.
   c. The research focused on case histories, not upon actual behavior.
   d. The reasons given in both a and b are true.
   e. None of the statements above is true.

Objective 3: State the effect of hormones on human sexuality.

8. What features characterize the sex hormones known as androgens and estrogens?
   a. They are secreted by the adrenal glands and the gonads.
   b. They are present in the bodies of both males and females.
   c. They control the development of both primary and secondary sex characteristics.
   d. All of the statements above are characteristic of the sex hormones.
   e. None of the statements above is characteristic of the sex hormones.

9. Whether a fetus will develop male or female sex organs is determined by
   a. the presence of androgens, but no estrogens.
   b. the presence of estrogens, but no androgens.
   c. whether the fertilized egg received an X or Y chromosome.
   d. a balance between androgens and estrogens.
   e. what happens during brain development.

10. Secondary sex characteristics are determined by
    a. sexual gender.
    b. genetic sex.
    c. X and Y chromosomes.
    d. the relative balance between male and female hormones in the fetus.
    e. the relative balance between male and female hormones at puberty.

11. Unlike that of humans, the sexual behavior of lower animals is
    a. strongly dependent on hormonal control.
    b. not controlled by hormones.
    c. similar for both male and female species members.
    d. influenced significantly by the brain.
    e. much more complex than primate sexual behavior.

12. Hormone injections
    a. are an effective therapy for frigidity in most women.
    b. can induce birds and rats to mate out of season or cycle.
    c. can change human homosexual behavior to heterosexual behavior.
    d. are an effective therapy for impotence in most males.
    e. are the most helpful form of therapy in reducing inhibitions.

13. Women have more interest in sexual activity when they are ovulating than at other times in the month because their
    a. sexual behavior is cyclical.
    b. sexual behavior is seasonal.
    c. estrogen levels are high at this time.
    d. estrogen levels are low at this time.
    e. threshold for sexual behaviors is high at this time.

14. The Lehrman research, described by author James McConnell in the text, concludes that
    a. hormone production does not affect the mating behavior of doves.
    b. hormone production does not affect the mating behavior of humans.
    c. behavior affects hormone production as much as hormone production affects mating behavior in the dove.
    d. behavior affects hormone production as much as hormone production affects behavior in humans.
    e. male doves will not mate if injected with testosterone.

15. If androgens predominate in the body of the adolescent girl, she may reach puberty
    a. late and develop female secondary sex characteristics.
    b. late and develop male secondary sex characteristics.
    c. early and develop female secondary sex characteristics.
    d. early and develop male secondary sex characteristics.

Objective 4: Describe the research and conclusions of Olds and Milner on the pleasure centers of the brain.

16. During experiments in which electrodes were implanted in the brains of rats, Olds and Milner discovered by mistake that
    a. electrical stimulation of certain parts of the brain was pleasurable to the rats.
    b. 99 percent of the brain has pain receptors.
    c. animals will try to reduce or avoid electrical stimulation anywhere in the brain.
    d. no specific areas of the brain are related to pleasure.
    e. the reaction of cats to electrical stimulation of the brain is quite different from that of rats.

17. Dozens of "pleasure centers" have been found
    a. only in the brains of rats.
    b. only in the brains of higher animals.
    c. only in the brains of lower animals.
    d. in the brains of most mammals including humans.
    e. in the brains of most mammals except humans.

18. Until the discovery of "pleasure centers" by Olds and Milner, motivational theorists
    a. were unaware that humans experience two different kinds of pleasure.
    b. had sought to explain all behavior in terms of pain avoidance or reduction.
    c. did not know that certain sensory inputs that are "pleasurable" produce pleasurable feelings that are independent of pain reduction.
    d. thought sexual pleasure was influenced mainly by hormones.
    e. could be described by the statements in a, b, and c.

Objective 5: Describe sex orientation, identity, roles, and pleasure as aspects of human sexual motivation.

19. An individual whose sexual orientation is female
    a. always sees herself as female.
    b. always considers himself to be male.
    c. tends to be attracted primarily to women.
    d. tends to be attracted primarily to men.
    e. is generally heterosexual.

20. Which of the following statements about sexual identity is **not** true?
    a. Sexual identity is defined as attraction to the same sex or the opposite sex.
    b. Sexual identity describes a person's view of himself or herself as being "male" or "female."
    c. Sexual identity is the product of biological, intrapsychic, and social/behavioral influences.
    d. Children of homosexual parents do not have a greater-than-normal chance of becoming homosexual.

21. Heterosexuality describes the orientation of a person who
    a. is attracted to others of the same sex.
    b. is attracted to the opposite sex.
    c. is attracted to both sexes.
    d. considers himself to be male and is attracted to males.
    e. considers herself to be female and is attracted to both sexes.

22. Sex-role stereotypes
    a. define a person's identity as male or female.
    b. determine orientation toward the same or opposite sex.
    c. describe the behaviors a society expects of "males" and "females."
    d. are stamped upon the fetus by hormones present in the uterus.
    e. are formed primarily by pleasurable experiences.

23. According to Dee Shepherd-Look, research indcates that
    a. sex-role stereotypes emerge at puberty and are hormonally controlled.
    b. sex-role stereotyping begins with fertilization and is hormonally controlled.
    c. young children automatically choose their own sex roles.
    d. sex-role shaping begins at birth and is controlled by the environment.
    e. sex-role stereotyping determines orientation toward one sex or the other.

Suggestions for Extra Credit

1. Reported "miraculous appearances" of the Virgin Mary, especially to young persons, have been a recurring popular phenomenon in the Roman Catholic church for centuries. Sociologist and scholar Michael P. Carroll, of the University of Western Ontario, Canada, studies and writes extensively about these phenomena. Many of Dr. Carroll's articles appear in issues of the *Journal for the Scientific Study of Religion*. On the basis of his studies, Dr. Carroll describes many of these "visitations" as hallucinations, and he has advanced a controversial Freudian theory of sexual repression to explain the hallucinations. Dr. Carroll has documented his arguments well. For example, of eighty cases studied, he found that 80 percent of those who reported seeing visions of the Virgin Mary were either adolescents who

lacked any outlet for expressing their sexuality or they were adults who were celibate. (Dr. Carroll notes carefully that even the Catholic church approaches all reports of divine appearances with caution and has officially blessed only a very few over the centuries.) If you have access to a library which has copies of the *Journal for the Scientific Study of Religion*, try to locate one or more of Dr. Carroll's articles and write a brief paper describing what evidence the author uses to support his theories. Note your own opinions about these theories.

2. Freud wrote long ago of a link between sex and aggression, and modern psychological theory suggests an intimate and increasing relationship between the two. If the subject interests you, look through Freud's *Psychopathology of Everyday Life* and read "Bedroom Battle" on page 64 of the June 4, 1979, issue of *Time* or "Sex and Aggression: Proving the Link," by Seymour Feshbach and Neal Malamuth, on page 111 in the November 1978 isssue of *Psychology Today*.

3. If human sexual behavior is cortically controlled and so is primarily the result of developmental learning and is largely culturally determined, what problems might confront a married couple from vastly different cultural backgrounds? Might they find they do not speak the same sexual language? Tell how they might go about resolving their sexual differences and coming to understand each other.

4. The learned social behaviors and thought patterns we call sex roles are in turmoil. As H. G. Wells predicted in *The Time Machine*, a lessening of the threat to survival has made indistinct the boundaries between what were once clearly defined male and female prerogatives. Look again at Dee Shepherd-Look's description in this lesson of typical "male" and "female" stereotypes. How would you say these roles are changing? What about behavior such as expressing emotions, parenting, being artistic and creative? With the movement toward equality has come a movement toward similarity. How have changing fashions in clothing and hairstyles reflected this trend? How have changed appearances and attitudes affected sexual behavior?

Answer Key

True-False

1. F	9. F
2. T	10. T
3. T	11. T
4. F	12. F
5. T	13. F
6. F	14. F
7. F	15. F
8. T	16. T

Completion

1. motivation, survival, species, biological, response;   2. Kinsey, responses, Johnson;   3. fertilization, X, Y, male, sexual, gonads, conception, secondary;   4. critical, masculine, androgens, estrogens, puberty;
5. orientation, heterosexuality, gender, roles, identity, roles, stereotypes, stereotyping;   6. hormones, learned, learned;   7. avoidance, pleasure, pain, relief, pleasurable.

Short-Answer Questions

1. The Kinsey research was based on conversations with—and case histories of—volunteer subjects. Thus, the results might have been biased by the fact that the research did not include material from subjects unwilling to talk, and it was not based upon objective observation. Kinsey's work was, however, the first reasonably accurate sociological survey of sexual behavior ever made in the United States, and it opened the way for the Masters and Johnson research. The latter scientists worked with subjects in a laboratory setting and measured actual physiological reactions of subjects who were sexually aroused. Masters and Johnson developed many ways to help people beset with sexual problems. Partly as a result of their work, people today have a new understanding of their own sexuality and many people have more open attitudes.

2. Human sexuality is a combination of complex processes and events that is shaped first by biology, then by environment, and finally, by what the individual brain itself makes of all the influences and experiences and what it decides to do about them. Genetic sex is determined biologically at fertilization; hormones control the development of genitalia in the fetus and secondary sex characteristics in the adolescent, and they also affect areas of the brain that are related to masculine and feminine behavior. Testosterone, a male hormone, influences **levels** of adult sexual activity. But society defines ''male'' and ''female'' roles and stereotypes its members from birth onward. Nevertheless, each individual develops his or her own concept of sexual identity, chooses a sex role, and decides what kind of sexual activity is consistent with his or her personal values.

3. Sex hormones, androgens and estrogens, are secreted by the adrenal glands and the gonads and are found in both men and women. A balance, or relative amounts, of these hormones present during critical periods before birth biases the fetus toward male or female behavior patterns. If male hormones (androgens) predominate in the balance, the fetus will develop male genitalia, parts of the brain related to masculine behavior will be activated, and brain centers that mediate feminine behavior patterns will be inhibited. If estrogens (female hormones) predominate, the opposite will occur. In the adolescent male, overproduction of androgens and underproduction of

estrogens will cause early puberty; the opposite balance results in late puberty, and the youth may develop feminine physical characteristics. Overproduction of estrogens and underproduction of androgens will bring a young girl to sexual maturity early; if the reverse is true, the girl's puberty will be late, and she may develop secondary masculine charateristics. In adults, low testosterone level is related to low biological sex drive, high level to increased sex drive.

4. Text author McConnell describes "sex-role stereotype" as a cognitive "prototype" that describes how males and females are expected to dress and behave. Sex-role stereotypes are pervasive and are common to all known societies; moreover, these concepts are not only similar throughout a given society, they are also very similar from culture to culture. According to Dee Shepherd-Look, a woman is expected to be passive, affectionate, nurturant, intuitive, and supportive in her role as wife and mother. On the other hand, a man should be competitive, independent, assertive, aggressive, and dominant. Sex-role stereotypes are imposed on the consciousness of infants soon after birth by "models"—including parents—who appear to perceive male and female babies as being **inherently** different physically and behaviorally and respond to them accordingly in "cuddling" as well as in speech, in style of dress, and play activities. According to Shepherd-Look, children begin at about age two to select behaviors perceived as stereotypically "correct" for their gender. By puberty most children perceive their own sexuality in terms of a socially approved stereotype, Shepherd-Look concludes.

Self-Test

 1. e (text pages 294-296)
 2. c (text page 296)
 3. d (text page 296)
 4. c (television program)
 5. a (text pages 295-296; television program)
 6. a (text page 296; television program)
 7. b (text pages 296, 309; television program)
 8. d (text pages 297-299; television program)
 9. d (text pages 298-299)
10. e (text page 299)
11. a (text pages 299-300)
12. b (text pages 300, 303; television program)
13. c (television program)
14. c (text page 301)
15. b (text page 299)
16. a (text pages 306-308; television program)
17. d (text page 307; television program)

18. e (text page 308; television program)
19. c (text page 301)
20. a (text pages 302-303)
21. b (text pages 301-303)
22. c (text pages 303-306)
23. d (text pages 305-306)

Stress 14

Viewer's Guide for Program Fourteen

As you view the television program, watch for:

The film sequence shot inside overcrowded rat burrows. As part of an experiment to study the effects of overcrowding, the rat population in these burrows was kept at twice the number that would normally inhabit enclosures of this size. You will be able to see for yourself how the resulting stress caused normal behavior patterns to disintegrate.

The film sequence of Canadian scientist Hans Selye talking about bad stress and good stress. Good stress, which Selye calls eustress, is the amount of stress we require to function best.

The animated sequence illustrating the hypothetical personality types "A" and "B" which the Friedman-Rosenman studies have tried to link with the incidence of stress-related disease. The studies are controversial and many psychologists believe that the evidence for linking personality characteristics with disease is very weak. As you progress through the lesson, try to form your own opinions about the study.

Scenes of people using biofeedback to learn to control stress reactions. Research on meditation and biofeedback shows that subjects can consciously curb and cope with excess stress reactions.

Have you ever felt as if life were closing in on you from all sides and as if you desperately wanted to run or to hide, to escape into some tomorrowland or yesteryear, or simply to crawl into bed and pull the covers securely up over your head? If so, you are not alone, since most human beings face stressful situations at many points during their lifetimes. **Any** emotion can be stressful to your body, however, in that it can cause you to expend physical, mental, and behavioral energy. Therefore, if you are to cope with the stresses and strains of life, you must learn how to cope with your emotions.

Like most people, you probably have developed some methods of coping with stress. But do you use methods that are indirect (defensive) or techniques that are direct? Direct coping involves analyzing and meeting the challenge head on and is usually more effective than indirect methods. Persons who fall back on indirect, or defensive, resources to cope with a stressful situation usually try some form of physical escape or mental avoidance, such as Freud's famous defense mechanisms—denial, displacement, regression, and so on.

Not all stress is bad, as you will learn, and indeed all motivation is based on stress of some kind. For example, a certain level of stress enables an athlete to be ''up'' for a race or an actress to be ''on'' for a performance. According to Hans Selye, good stress, or eustress, is the amount of stress each of us requires to function at our best. Continued stress beyond this point or in addition to this amount may exact a physiological toll in the form of high blood pressure, heart disease, arthritis, and ulcers. In this lesson you will examine emotions from a holistic viewpoint. You will learn something about how physiological responses, intrapsychic factors, and social/behavioral influences all affect emotionality. You'll also learn about some interesting theories that facial expressions (which are innate) trigger subjective emotions, that learning to be ''helpless'' is one way of coping with stress, and that ''getting it off your chest'' or ''blowing off steam'' may be a devastating—not therapeutic—way to express anger.

Learning Objectives

When you have finished viewing the program and studying your text assignments, you should be able to:

1. Identify the five elements that define emotionality, and relate them to the biological, intrapsychic, and social/behavioral viewpoints in psychology.

2. Identify criticisms of the biological, intrapsychic, and social/behavioral positions on human emotionality.
3. Describe the functions of the two branches of the autonomic nervous system.
4. Discuss the effects of arousal hormones on emotional states.
5. Summarize Selye's concepts of the General Adaptation Syndrome and eustress.
6. Describe and distinguish between defensive coping and direct coping with stress.
7. Explain the concept of locus of personal control.
8. Describe the ways in which the ability to withstand stress can be increased.

Assignments

Before Viewing the Program

Read the preview at the beginning of this lesson and look over the learning objectives that precede the assignments.

Check the section "Did You Know That . . ." at the beginning of Chapter 12 and look over the subtitles for the chapter.

Read Chapter 12, "Emotion, Stress, and Coping."

View Program 14, "Stress"

After Viewing the Program

Review the text assignments.

Read through the summary at the end of the chapter and consider the thought questions throughout the chapter. Then, to facilitate your understanding of the materials presented in this lesson, study the terms and concepts that are printed in boldfaced type and are defined in the upper right corners of right-hand pages. In particular, note the terms: autonomic nervous system, sympathetic nervous system, parasympathetic nervous system (or vegetative nervous system), epinephrin, nor-epinephrin, alarm reaction, stage of resistance, stage of exhaustion, affect, hypertension, coping, defensive coping, direct coping, repression, Freud, energy theory, regression, depression, locus of control, internalizers, externalizers, eustress, parallel processing.

Complete the study activities that are included here as an additional study aid for you.

Now evaluate your understanding of the lesson material by reviewing the learning objectives and taking the self-test in this study guide. Check your answers against the answer key.

According to your instructor's assignment or your own interests, choose and complete the activities from the suggestions for extra credit. You might also consider the recommended readings listed at the end of the chapter.

"Can I kick it for you this time, Daddy?"

Reprinted courtesy of The Register and Tribune Syndicate.

Study Activities

Matching

Match each phrase in the column on the right with the appropriate term in the column on the left, writing the letters of the phrases in the appropriate blanks.

_____ 1. autonomic
nervous system

_____ 2. sympathetic
nervous system

_____ 3. parasympathetic
nervous system

_____ 4. epinephrin

_____ 5. alarm reaction

_____ 6. stage of
exhaustion

_____ 7. stage of resistance

_____ 8. energy theory

_____ 9. depression

_____ 10. internalizers

_____ 11. direct coping

_____ 12. eustress

a. "arousal hormone"

b. third stage of stress reaction

c. "turns on" emotional reactions

d. second stage of stress reaction

e. analyzing and setting goals

f. "turns off" emotional reactions

g. people who believe their actions are
under their own control

h. controls breathing, pumping of blood,
digestion, emotional reactions

i. Freudian view that all motivation
originates in the libido, or psychic energy,
produced by the body

j. the amount of good stress or motivation
each person needs to function at his or
her best

k. first stage of stress reaction

l. common form of defensive coping

Completion

1. Because you may not have time to think in an emergency, your body is set up to defend itself automatically. Many of its defensive activities are controlled by two parts of your autonomic nervous system, the _____ nervous system and the _____ nervous system. The former tends to excite or arouse you in preparation for such actions as fighting, fleeing, feeding, and sexual climax. The latter acts to _____ the bodily functions aroused by the former. The sympathetic nervous system is connected to your _____ glands. Situated atop the kidneys, these glands produce two chemicals referred to as the "arousal hormones," _____ and _____. These chemicals not only stimulate the same neural centers that the _____ nervous system has stimulated with neural impulses but also increase the firing rate of the nerve cells in the _____ system itself.

slow down
sympathetic
adrenal
parasympathetic
sympathetic
nor-epinephrin
epinephrin
sympathetic

2. Emotional arousal puts you under a variety of biological, intrapsychic, and behavioral _____ reactions. Canadian scientist Hans Selye believed that many diseases, such as high blood pressure, arthritis, and ulcers, are caused by excessive stress. Selye has identified three stages of stress _____. These are the _____ reaction, the stage of _____, and the stage of _____. Exposure to further stress during the third stage might lead to depression, insanity, or even death, because overstimulation of the _____ system may cause the heart to stop beating. We now know that death by stress is less likely to happen because the body defends itself against such exhaustion.

resistance
reaction
exhaustion
alarm
parasympathetic
stress

3. Biological theorists tend to see emotion as primarily a _____ reaction related to instinctual _____ mechanisms. Parts of your nervous system arouse your body to action, other parts suppress physical activity. Among the intrapsychic theorists, some scientists emphasize subjective feelings (affect) and moods, while _____ psychologists focus on conscious awareness and cognitive appraisal of experience. Those scientists who think of emotions primarily as behavioral responses produced by interactions with the environment represent the _____ school.

survival
social/behavioral
physical
cognitive

4. Learning to solve and adjust to the problems you face in life is called _____. There are two major kinds of coping—_____ (or indirect) and _____. The first usually involves protecting yourself from a potentially stressful situation by using some form of mental or physical _____, such as repression, projection, displacement, regression, or depression. Meeting the challenge head on is called _____ coping and is usually more effective than defensive (or indirect) coping. To cope directly you must _____ the

problem or situation objectively, decide upon clear-cut goals, and map out some ways of achieving them. Recent research studies by Seligman and Rotter seem to suggest that when a person cannot avoid or otherwise cope with an extremely stressful situation and regards his efforts as futile, he learns to be _____, and gives up.

escape
analyze
helpless
direct
defensive
coping
direct

5. Some researchers suggest that different ways of coping are directly related to each person's _____ of personal control. _____ see themselves as being in control of their own lives. Aroused by threats, they try to overcome them, and tend to use direct coping methods. Those who see their lives as being in the hands of God, fate, or Lady Luck are described as _____. They face threats passively, waiting for some outside agency to protect or care for them, or they use _____ coping methods.

externalizers
locus
defensive
Internalizers

6. Not all stress is bad. A certain level of stress simply _____ individuals and societies to provide for their needs and to perform well. According to Selye, good stress, or _____, is the amount of stress each of us requires to function best. Continued stress beyond this point or in addition to this amount may be _____ disastrous, perhaps fatal.

eustress
physiologically or psychologically
motivates

Short-Answer Questions

1. What are some specific ways mentioned in your text and in the television program for coping more satisfactorily with stress?

2. Why do people often get red in the face when they get angry?

3. Evaluate briefly the biological, intrapsychic, and social/behavioral theories of emotionality.

Self-Test

(Select the one best answer.)

Objective 1: Identify the five elements that define emotionality, and relate them to the biological, intrapsychic, and social/behavioral viewpoints in psychology.

1. Which of the following statements does **not** belong in a definition of "emotion"?
   a. physical arousal or depression
   b. feelings of pleasure or displeasure
   c. cognitive awareness and appraisal of the experience
   d. coping directly with stress
   e. environmental inputs and consequences

2. Theorists who are intrapsychically oriented believe that
   a. environmental inputs and consequences control emotions.
   b. all emotions are instinctual survival mechanisms.
   c. subjective feelings, and sometimes cognitive aspects, should be emphasized.
   d. emotion is primarily a biological event that focuses on arousal and depression.

Objective 2: Identify criticisms of the biological, intrapsychic, and social/behavioral positions on human emotionality.

3. One problem shared by both the biological and intrapsychic approaches to the study of emotionality is that they
   a. believe emotionality to be a mix of physical and psychological events.
   b. ignore the effects of environmental inputs on the emotional process.
   c. tend to believe all emotionality is the result of environmental inputs and responses.
   d. consider all emotional experiences to be stressful.

4. Tomkins' theory that facial expressions precede and give rise to autonomic arousal and all subjective feelings
   a. explains emotionality in primarily biological terms.
   b. ignores cultural differences in interpreting facial expressions.
   c. has not been supported by experimental data.
   d. is characterized by all of the statements above.
   e. is described by none of the statements above.

Objective 3: Describe the functions of the two branches of the autonomic nervous system.

5. When you encounter an emergency of some kind, your physiological reactions are
   a. handled by unconscious parts of your brain.
   b. controlled by the autonomic nervous system.
   c. consciously determined.
   d. reflexive.
   e. described by all of the above.

6. Which one of the following is not caused by action of the sympathetic nervous system?
   a. The pupils constrict.
   b. The heart pumps more blood to the brain, muscles, and surface of the skin.
   c. The lungs breathe harder and faster.
   d. The blood sugar level is elevated.
   e. The digestive process is slowed down.

7. Which one of the following is not caused by action of the parasympathetic nervous system?
   a. The heart rate slows down.
   b. The lungs breathe slower.
   c. The blood sugar level drops.
   d. The digestive process is slowed down.
   e. The perspiration rate is retarded.

8. A major difference between the sympathetic nervous system and the parasympathetic system is that the sympathetic system
   a. belongs to the autonomic nervous system.
   b. connects with many parts of the body.
   c. is connected to the adrenal glands.
   d. can create a "downer" effect.

Objective 4: Discuss the effects of arousal hormones on emotional states.

9. The "arousal" hormones secreted by the adrenal glands are
   a. androgen and estrogen.
   b. adrenalin and nor-adrenalin (now usually called epinephrin and nor-epinephrin).
   c. uppers and downers.
   d. barbiturates.
   e. progesterone and testosterone.

10. Adrenalin (epinephrin) does not
   a. increase the blood pressure.
   b. make the heart beat more rapidly.
   c. speed up breathing.
   d. lower the blood sugar level.
   e. increase perspiration.

Objective 5: Summarize Selye's concepts of the General Adaptation Syndrome and eustress.

11. The three stages of stress reaction identified by Hans Selye are, respectively,
    a. alarm reaction, stage of resistance, and stage of exhaustion.
    b. hide, fight, and flight.
    c. fighting, fleeing, and feeding.
    d. reaction formation, regression, and depression.
    e. external, internal, and generalized.

12. According to Hans Selye, the last and potentially most dangerous physiological reaction to stress comes from the
    a. adrenal glands.
    b. central nervous system.
    c. limbic system.
    d. sympathetic nervous system.
    e. parasympathetic nervous system.

13. How does Selye define eustress?
    a. an immediate reaction to an emergency
    b. a resistance to frustrating or frightening circumstances
    c. the amount of stress needed in order to function properly
    d. a state of relaxation with no stress
    e. the final counter-reaction, when all resistance resources are exhausted

Objective 6: Describe and distinguish between defensive coping and direct coping with stress.

14. Which of the following reactions would be classified as defensive coping?
    a. analyzing objectively
    b. setting realistic goals
    c. listing new approaches
    d. internalizing
    e. projecting

15. Which of the following is not an example of defensive coping?
    a. repression
    b. depression
    c. objective analysis
    d. displacement
    e. fixation

16. The refusal to consciously acknowledge a threatening situation is called
    a. reaction formation.
    b. regression.
    c. projection.
    d. repression.
    e. displacement.

Objective 7: Explain the concept of locus of personal control.

17. According to the locus of control theory, a person who feels controlled by factors in his or her environment is best described as
    a. autonomous.
    b. an externalizer.
    c. hypertensive.
    d. hyperactive.
    e. an internalizer.

18. Which of the following statements is not true of externalizers?
    a. They usually believe that God, fate, or Lady Luck controls what happens to them.
    b. When faced with stressful inputs, they block them out, ignore them, or become depressed.
    c. They feel that getting ahead in the world depends upon what befalls them.
    d. They lack skills to achieve goals in large organizations.
    e. They tend to cope directly.

19. According to McConnell, _____ is one way of learning to cope more effectively with stress.
    a. becoming an externalizer
    b. developing defense mechanisms
    c. setting realistic goals
    d. changing your locus of control
    e. reaction formation

20. Direct methods of coping can best be learned
    a. if the punishment for using indirect, or defensive, methods is sufficiently severe.
    b. if you are rewarded for progress rather than punished for failure.
    c. if indirect methods have failed.
    d. during states of depression.
    e. by fixating.

Objective 8: Describe the ways in which the ability to withstand stress can be increased.

21. Which of the following is not a healthy and effective means of coping with stress?
    a. giving up if you can't control things
    b. laughter
    c. physical exercise
    d. biofeedback training
    e. meditation

22. Recruits in the Fort Ord experiments were taught how to withstand extreme stress well by
    a. being rewarded when they did well, punished when they made mistakes.
    b. punishment for mistakes, but no rewards.
    c. using defense mechanisms, such as escape.
    d. being allowed to "sink" or "swim" on their own.
    e. being rewarded whenever they did well.

Suggestions for Extra Credit

1. Which comes first, the emotion or the facial expression? S. S. Tomkins (text page 322) believes you smile or frown innately as a reaction to stimulus input, and the expression sets off a corresponding emotion; your facial expressions then tell others exactly what you are feeling. Do facial expressions precede emotions, as Tomkins says? Can you always tell what a person is feeling from his or her facial or body expressions? Try the following experiment on your family or a group of friends. Make copies of the following nine statements taken from literary works and ask each person to identify the emotion or feeling expressed in each sentence.
    1. He gnashed his teeth until they were all but ground to dust.
    2. He drew up his leg and stood on one foot.
    3. He laughed a great ho-ho.
    4. He fanned his face with his sleeve.
    5. Every one of his hairs stood on end and pimples came out on the skin all over his body.
    6. He clapped his hands.
    7. He fain would have swallowed him at one gulp.
    8. Everyone trembled with a face the color of clay.
    9. They stuck out their tongues.
    All of these nine statements were extracted from works of Chinese literature for an experimental study conducted by Otto Klineberg in 1938. The answers are: 1. anger; 2. surprise; 3. anger; 4. anger; 5. fear; 6. worry or disappointment; 7. hatred; 8. fear; 9. surprise. How did your subjects' responses compare with the correct answers? If there were significant differences, why do you think they occurred? If you would like to learn more about Klineberg's experiments, read "Emotional Expressions in Chinese Literature," *Journal of Abnormal Psychology*, 33, (1938): 517-520.
2. How well do you deal with stress? Make lists of the positive and negative ways in which you cope with stress. Can you explain why you react the way you do? Do you see ways in which you might make changes that might result in better coping behavior? The January, 1985, issue of *Working Woman*, in a brief article entitled "The Biofeedback Card: Don't Leave Home Without It," page 80, describes a plastic card with which you can take your own "stress temperature" whenever you want and will "prescribe" specific

relaxation exercises for you if you need them. How do you think a plastic card could diagnose your situation correctly and prescribe remedies for it? You might enjoy acquiring one of the cards and designing a simple experiment to try with friends and family. Be sure to write a brief report of your experiences and conclusions.

3. As you learned in this lesson, "blowing off steam" may not be the best way of coping with stress. Read the essay "Oh, Shut Up! (The Uses of Ranting)," *Time*, August 12, 1985, page 66, then write a brief commentary on *Time's* contention that "ranting" defeats intelligent argument.

Answer Key

Matching

1. h	7. d
2. c	8. i
3. f	9. l
4. a	10. g
5. k	11. e
6. b	12. j

Completion

1. sympathetic, parasympathetic, slow down, adrenal, epinephrin, nor-epinephrin, sympathetic, sympathetic;   2. stress, reaction, alarm, resistance, exhaustion, parasympathetic;   3. physical, survival, cognitive, social/behavioral;   4. coping, defensive, direct, escape, direct, analyze, helpless;   5. locus, Internalizers, externalizers, defensive;   6. motivates, eustress, physiologically or psychologically.

Short-Answer Questions

1. Good stress management techniques include coping directly with stressful events, using positive reinforcement by rewarding successes while refraining from punishing failures, physical exercise (such as jogging), laughter, meditation, and biofeedback training. Experiments involving recruits in Fort Ord's well-known "sink or swim" officer-training program showed conclusively that a positive reinforcement program resulted in fewer suicides, fewer AWOLs, and better general performance, not only in the training program but also in action in Vietnam.

2. With minor exceptions, the physiological changes that accompany strong emotional arousal are much the same whether the emotion is fear, anger, hostility, or sexual aggressiveness. During any one of these "emergencies," the sympathetic nervous system prepares the body to flee, fight, or reach sexual climax. The pupils dilate to let in more light. Breathing becomes deeper, and the rate is speeded up so that more oxygen becomes available to the body. The blood sugar level is elevated to increase available energy. The digestion process is slowed down so that the body's efforts and energies can be concentrated elsewhere. And the heart pumps more blood to the brain, muscles, and skin. It is this pumping of blood to the skin that accounts for a reddening of the face in times of anger.

3. Biological theorists claim that emotion is a biological event involving arousal and depression by the sympathetic and parasympathetic systems respectively, and that these events are under the control of the hormones epinephrin and nor-epinephrin. This tends to reduce all emotionality to mere hormonal and neural activity. Intrapsychic theorists concede that while bodily reactions do play an important role in creating and sustaining emotions, the "feelings" and "cognitions" (or conscious awareness and appraisal function), which you develop with experience, exert control over emotions. Both theories fail to consider emotionality in the context of environmental inputs and outputs. According to McConnell, the best interpretation of all three theories considered together is that we have two separate systems that process different kinds of input. The **motivational/emotive** system—which involves the limbic system, the RAS and the autonomic system—processes energy inputs; the **perceptual/cognitive** system processes informational inputs for the cortex via the straight-line system. Both systems operate in parallel fashion (at the same time), but the motivational/emotive system energizes your thoughts and behaviors while the perceptual/cognitive system guides your emotions.

Self-Test

1. d (text page 316)
2. c (text page 316)
3. b (text pages 325-331)
4. d (text page 322)
5. e (text page 317; television program)
6. a (text page 318; television program)
7. d (text page 318; television progam)
8. c (text pages 318-319)
9. b (text page 319; television program)
10. d (text page 318; television program)

11. a (text page 320; television program)
12. e (text page 320; television program)
13. c (text page 333; television program)
14. e (text page 331)
15. c (text page 331)
16. d (text page 331)
17. b (text page 328)
18. e (text page 328)
19. c (text page 331; television program)
20. b (text page 333)
21. a (text pages 327-328; television program)
22. e (text pages 332-333; television program)

Conditioning and Desensitization 15

Viewer's Guide for Program Fifteen

As you view the television program, watch for:

The film sequences of a therapist treating a male patient who developed a phobia of snakes as he worked in his yard one day. We observe the therapist beginning to desensitize the patient's fear, using the same techniques of conditioning by which the fear was learned.

The reenactment of Pavlov's basic experiment in which a dog that salivates naturally when presented with food is conditioned to associate, or pair, the sound of a metronome with food and then to salivate in response to the sound alone. In this and other experiments, Pavlov developed classical conditioning and contributed extensively to the scientific study of the form of learning known as conditioning.

A chart to be noted briefly to help you to remember the elements and the process of classical conditioning to which you will be introduced in this lesson.

The montage of symbols, such as McDonald's golden arches, the Jolly Green Giant, the FTD florist logo, and the American flag, which are advertising techniques for conditioning you to associate certain responses to previously neutral stimuli. For example, you might become conditioned to want to eat a hamburger whenever you see the arches, and you may be moved to patriotic behavior of some kind when the flag is presented to you.

Preview

Do you have the same strong reaction to a particular situation or experience each time it occurs but find yourself unable consciously to control, change, or explain it? For example, do you always want a cigarette right after dinner? Do you become immobilized with fear when you see a snake or faint at the sight of blood? Are you overcome with panic when you find yourself in a closed space? Or do you feel you have to eat just because it's mealtime? If you said yes to any of these examples, you were acknowledging a conditioned response, that is, one you have learned by repeated association or pairing.

Conditioning is the simple and common form of learning by which we acquire many of our behaviors. The response habits we establish in this way may be positive and useful or they may be negative and impair our ability to function effectively. The blind and unreasoning fears we know as phobias are an example of conditioned responses that impair functioning. While normal amounts of fear protect us in dangerous situations and enable us to defend ourselves or to escape, a phobic reaction may cause us to become paralyzed at the mere mention of a snake or even the sight of peanut butter. Because most phobic reactions are learned, however, many therapists believe they can be unlearned by means of the step-by-step processes of counter-conditioning and desensitization. Through a process of measured exposure and gradual approach, patients have overcome their fears of everything from hypodermic syringes to airplanes.

However, you will find that some psychologists and psychiatrists criticize counter-conditioning and desensitization methods of extinguishing negative behavior on grounds that only the symptoms are being treated, and the underlying causes and problems (which could be severe) are being ignored. Many of our emotions, including fears and phobias, are conditioned early in life. Experimenters frequently use a familiar piece of equipment to measure these emotional reactions: the polygraph, or "lie detector," as it is too often called. The point is made rather strongly in this lesson that the polygraph is very valuable in many kinds of research, since it measures physical evidence of emotionality, but the polygraph does **not** detect "lies," and it has been proven unreliable at this task by a number of studies.

In this lesson, you will also learn about a very important aspect of learning—classical conditioning—and about the ways habitual behaviors are learned and can be unlearned. In the two lessons that follow, you'll take a look at another form of conditioning—called operant conditioning—and then explore the mysteries of memory.

228

Learning Objectives

When you have finished viewing the program and studying your text assignments, you should be able to:

1. Identify Ivan Pavlov and briefly describe his experiments with conditioned reflexes.
2. Name, define, and describe the key elements in establishing a conditioned response.
3. Distinguish between conditioned and unconditioned responses.
4. Define and give an example of an extinguished response.
5. Distinguish between generalization and discrimination and give an example of each.
6. Explain what implications the research by Watson, Himle, and Shorkey has for behavioral therapy, and cite specific examples.
7. Give an example of how desensitization might be used to eliminate a phobic reaction and describe the psychological principles underlying this therapy.

Assignments

Before Viewing the Program

Read the preview at the beginning of this lesson and look over the learning objectives that precede the assignments.

Check the section "Did You Know That . . ." at the beginning of Chapter 13 in the text and look over the subtitles for the chapter.

Read Chapter 13, "Conditioning and Desensitization." As you read, note the boldfaced terms and concepts that appear throughout the lesson and are defined in the upper right corners of right-hand pages. Use the definitions and explanations of these terms to refresh your memory and clarify their meanings before you view the program.

View Program 15, "Conditioning"

After Viewing the Program

Review the text assignments.

Read through the summary at the end of Chapter 13 and consider the thought questions in the chapter. Then, to aid your understanding of the materials presented in this lesson, review all of the boldfaced terms and concepts. In particular, note these terms carefully: patellar reflex, conditioned reflex, unconditioned stimulus (UCS), unconditioned response (UCR), neutral stimulus, conditioned stimulus (CS), conditioned response (CR), classical conditioning, extinguished, spontaneous recovery, discrimination training, generalization, counter-conditioning, phobia, desensitization therapy, hierarchy of fears, polygraph.

Complete the study activities included here as an additional study aid for you.

Now evaluate your understanding of the lesson material by reviewing the learning objectives and taking the self-test in this study guide. Check your answers against the answer key.

According to your instructor's assignment or your own interests, choose and complete activities from among the suggestions for extra credit. You might also consider the recommended readings listed at the end of the chapter.

Study Activities

Matching

Match each phrase in the column on the right with the appropriate term in the column on the left, writing the letters of the phrases in the appropriate blanks.

_____ 1. knee jerk
_____ 2. unconditioned response
_____ 3. conditioned stimulus
_____ 4. conditioned response
_____ 5. extinguish
_____ 6. spontaneous recovery
_____ 7. stimulus generalization
_____ 8. counter-conditioning
_____ 9. respondent (classical) conditioning
_____ 10. phobia
_____ 11. discrimination
_____ 12. conditioned emotional response
_____ 13. cognitive desensitization

a. neutral stimulus which, through frequent pairing with an unconditioned stimulus, acquires the ability to elicit an unconditioned response
b. changes in attitudes and conscious perceptions of feared objects or situations
c. known as the patellar reflex
d. a form of therapy based on extinguishing inappropriate habits or breaking stimulus-response bonds
e. innately determined response pattern or reflex
f. reaction set off by a conditioned stimulus
g. a process by which a previously neutral stimulus gains the power to evoke a conditioned response
h. increased frequency of a learned response after extinction and without additional training
i. intense, irrational fear
j. the tendency to make the same response to two or more similar stimuli
k. conscious or unconscious training to respond to emotional situations with autonomic arousal
l. to eradicate a learned response
m. distinguishing between stimuli that are similar

Completion

1. While studying the patellar reflex (knee jerk) in the early 1900s, American University student E. B. Twitmyer accidentally discovered the _____ reflex. Because American psychologists paid little attention to his discovery, Twitmyer did not pursue his findings. And so it is that Russian physiologist Ivan _____ is credited with discovering that the _____ reflex is learned when the subject associates a neutral stimulus with a stimulus that evokes an innate reflex, such as the knee jerk. Pavlov had won a Nobel prize for experiments with dogs in which he proved for the first time that the nervous system coordinates all digestive processes. He knew that salivation was an innate response elicited by the _____ input of food in the dog's mouth. Food was, thus, the _____ stimulus. His research taught him that a _____ stimulus, such as the sound of a bell, could be empowered to elicit the same salivation response through the process called _____ . Salivating in response to the bell tone is called the _____ response.

unconditioned
stimulus
conditioned
neutral
conditional or conditioned
conditioned
conditioning
Pavlov

2. During the many years Pavlov studied the conditioning process, he discovered that the more frequently the unconditioned response and conditioned stimulus are paired, the _____ conditioned response becomes and that conditioned responses can be unlearned, or _____, as easily as they are learned. Pavlov also trained a dog to _____ between a circle and an ellipse by rewarding the dog with food only when the circle appeared. When Pavlov was convinced the dog could tell the difference between the two figures and would _____ only at the sight of the _____ , he made the ellipse appear more and more like the circle. Unable to discriminate, the dog was overcome by _____ and displayed behavior patterns that, in humans, would be termed _____ .

extinguished
discriminate
stronger
salivate
stress
neurotic
circle

3. John B. _____ conditioned a child named Albert to be afraid of a gentle white rat by sounding a terrifying noise while the child was playing with the animal. Thus, the scientist used the noise to establish a _____ of fear between the sight of the animal and the arousal of Albert's nervous system. Once the bond had been established, the response _____ so that it could be elicited by any furry object. This discovery showed that many fears and _____ result from _____. Mary Cover Jones, a student of Watson, used a method now called _____ to "cure" fear. By pairing an animal stimulus with a "happy," or pleasant situation, she taught children to play with animals that had previously terrified them.

bond
Watson
generalized
autonomic
conditioning
counter-conditioning
phobias

4. Yet another example of the therapeutic use of counter-conditioning is the case of Anne M., who became so terrified of moving vehicles after her mother was killed by a car that she had to be hospitalized in a mental institution. Psychologists David _____ and Clayton _____ then attempted to "cure" Anne with a form of counter-conditioning called _____ therapy. In their talks with her, they drew up a _____ of fears; that is, they listed all of the car-related stimuli she found disturbing from the _____ to the _____ frightening. Then, using a _____ process of substituting _____ for panic as she experienced each _____ of the hierarchy, they gradually desensitized Anne to her fears until, at last, she was able to board a bus and take a trip. Because phobic reactions such as Anne's usually involve some form of sensitization to stimuli that arouse the _____ nervous system and create muscular _____, a major aspect of desensitization therapy is voluntary muscular _____.

Shorkey
Himle
hierarchy
desensitization
stimulus
least relaxation
step-by-step
most

5. None of the three viewpoints that represent the study of psychology looks upon the treatment of conditioned learning disorders from a _____ viewpoint. However, many therapists from the three schools do use one another's techniques without seeming to be aware that they do. In quarrelling over appropriate therapy, the prime goal of helping the patient to recover is sometimes forgotten, McConnell says.

holistic

Short-Answer Questions

1. Diagram the innate reflex in terms of dog, food, and salivation.

2. Diagram the pairing of conditioned stimulus with the unconditioned stimulus and response.

3. Why is relaxation a major part of desensitization therapy?

4. For the sake of the sufferer, if for no other reason, abnormal fears and phobias should be extinguished. But can you think of some conditioned responses that should **not** be extinguished?

Self-Test

(Select the one best answer.)

Objective 1: Identify Ivan Pavlov and briefly describe his experiments with conditioned reflexes.

1. Which of the following correctly states the nationality and life-span of Ivan Pavlov?
   a. German scientist, 1802-1866
   b. Russian scientist, 1849-1936
   c. Lithuanian scientist, 1872-1939
   d. American scientist, 1841-1931
   e. Norwegian scientist, 1848-1929

2. Pavlov first recognized what he called ''psychic stimulations'' when, in an experiment,
   a. dogs stopped reacting to food and reacted only to another stimulus.
   b. dogs became fearful of food because of another stimulus.
   c. dogs would consume food only when exposed to another stimulus.
   d. dogs acted as if food was already there when exposed to another stimulus.
   e. dogs lost interest in food and preferred another stimulus.

Objective 1; and *Objective 2:* Name, define, and describe the key elements in establishing a conditioned response.

3. In his experiments with dogs, Pavlov called the bell sound that elicited salivation a ''conditional'' stimulus because its effect depended on
   a. an association between sound and the stimulus of food.
   b. salivation whenever the dog saw the bell.
   c. the frequency of the bell sound.
   d. the amplitude of the bell sound.
   e. none of the above.

4. According to McConnell, conditioning can **best** be defined as
   a. a reflexive action of which you are not aware.
   b. learning to respond automatically to a previously neutral stimulus.
   c. learning to respond automatically to an unconditioned stimulus.
   d. learning to respond automatically to an unconditioned response.
   e. extinguishing a response which you have learned.

Objective 2: Name, define, and describe the key elements in establishing a
conditioned response.

5. The typical sequence of events during early classical conditioning is
    a. US, CS, UR.
    b. CS, UR, CR.
    c. neutral stimulus, US, UR.
    d. US, neutral stimulus, UR.
    e. none of the above combinations.

6. Meat powder, when placed in a dog's mouth, is a(n)
    a. reinforcement.
    b. conditioned stimulus.
    c. appetizer.
    d. unconditioned stimulus.
    e. neutral stimulus.

Objective 2; and *Objective 3:* Distinguish between conditioned and
unconditioned responses.

7. Which of the following stimulus-response connections are learned?
    a. CR and UCS
    b. CS and UCS
    c. CS and UCR
    d. UCR and UCS
    e. CS and CR

Objective 3

8. Which of the following is **not** an unconditioned response?
    a. patellar reflex
    b. salivation
    c. phobia
    d. blinking
    e. sucking

Objective 4: Define and give an example of an extinguished response.

9. Repeated presentation of the conditioned stimulus without the
unconditioned stimulus eventually causes
    a. stress.
    b. extinction.
    c. exhaustion.
    d. neurotic behavior.
    e. conditioned responses.

10. The extinction process for a classically conditioned response occurs when the
    a. CS is presented alone, without the US.
    b. UR becomes stronger than the CR.
    c. CR becomes stronger than the UR.
    d. CS no longer elicits the US.

11. The fact that a conditioned stimulus can be extinguished is the basis of a form of therapy called
    a. sensitization therapy.
    b. generalization training.
    c. discrimination training.
    d. counter-conditioning.
    e. respondent conditioning.

Objective 5: Distinguish between generalization and discrimination and give an example of each.

12. Discrimination training requires
    a. a positive unconditioned stimulus.
    b. a negative unconditioned stimulus.
    c. two conditioned stimuli.
    d. two unconditioned stimuli.
    e. circles and ellipses.

13. Stimulus generalization might best be described as
    a. transferring a conditioned response to a new stimulus.
    b. distinguishing between two similar conditioned stimuli.
    c. transferring a conditioned stimulus to a new response.
    d. distinguishing between two similar conditioned responses.
    e. making a slightly different reaction to the same stimulus.

14. Little Albert's fear of any furry object could best be explained as
    a. sensitization.
    b. extinction.
    c. discrimination.
    d. generalization.
    e. spontaneous recovery.

Objective 3; and *Objective 6:* Explain what implications the research by Watson, Himle, and Shorkey has for behavioral therapy, and cite specific examples.

15. In John B. Watson's experiments with Albert, the unconditioned stimulus was
    a. a loud noise.
    b. an electric shock.
    c. a food pellet.
    d. a furry, white rat.
    e. Albert's autonomic nervous system.

Objective 6

16. Once Albert was conditioned to fear the white rat, Watson was able to elicit a fear response with
    a. food.
    b. any furry object.
    c. a knee jerk.
    d. the polygraph test.
    e. any loud noise.

17. Showing a fear response to any furry object after being conditioned to fear a rat is called
    a. discrimination.
    b. breaking the S-R bond.
    c. counter-conditioning.
    d. generalization.
    e. desensitization.

18. Researchers Himle and Shorkey developed a counter-conditioning therapeutic technique known as
    a. discrimination training.
    b. the patellar reflex.
    c. hierarchy of fears.
    d. relaxation therapy.
    e. desensitization.

Objective 7: Give an example of how desensitization might be used to eliminate a phobic reaction and describe the psychological principles underlying this therapy.

19. Counter-conditioning is based on the fact that
    a. many incompatible responses may be given to one CS.
    b. no CS can elicit more than one response.
    c. you cannot give two incompatible responses to the same CS.
    d. small animals are lovable creatures.
    e. eating is a pleasurable experience.

20. In counter-conditioning, a fear-producing
    a. stimulus is attached to a new and pleasurable response.
    b. UCS is extinguished.
    c. S-R bond is broken.
    d. S-R bond is broken and the stimulus is associated with a pleasurable response.
    e. stimulus does none of the above.

21. Desensitization therapy
    a. is a form of counter-conditioning.
    b. consists of teaching a person to relax voluntarily.
    c. often uses a hierarchy of fears.
    d. includes a step-by-step process.
    e. includes all of the above.

22. For best results, desensitization training
    a. should not continue beyond the point at which the phobic reaction can be counteracted by voluntary muscular relaxation.
    b. overstimulates the patient.
    c. elicits a phobic reaction until the response is exhausted.
    d. results from perceptual changes.
    e. is relatively useless as a therapeutic tool.

Suggestions for Extra Credit

1. A circus that features a famous clown who loves children will soon play an engagement in your town. Your small son, once frightened in early infancy when a toy balloon popped in his crib, is terrified of clowns because they usually carry balloons and shoot toy pistols. The clown hears about your son and invites him to visit his dressing room so that he can see there is nothing to fear from the clown. Remembering what you have learned in this lesson, describe how you would use this situation to desensitize your child and "cure" his phobia.

2. The television program mentions the way we are conditioned to respond to certain symbols. List a few common symbols. Classify them according to whether they are commercial, political, patriotic, religious, and so on, and then describe in a few words your reaction to each. Do the ones you have listed elicit the intended response? Would you classify these symbols as truly "neutral" stimuli that fit the definition of conditioned stimuli?

3. The polygraph, or so-called "lie-detector," has come under increasing criticism in recent years, though it still figures prominently in criminal processes and is used regularly by government and major corporations for purposes which are sometimes questionable. But the polygraph cannot distinguish "lies" from "truth"; it can only record changes in emotions.

Still, at times, it has sent the innocent to prison, set the guilty free, and resulted in lost jobs. If you are interested, read D. T. Lykken's 1980 book, *A Tremor in the Blood* (New York: McGraw-Hill) or "The Validity of Polygraph Testing: Scientific Analysis and Public Controversy," by L. Saxe, D. Dougherty, and T. Cross (*American Psychologist*, 40, 1985, pages 355-366). Do you think the polygraph is being misused? Is it ethical for government and big corporations to use it in some situations?

4. At one time or another most of us suffer from fears or mild phobias that might be inconvenient and a bit discomforting, but some of us spend much of our daily lives coping with **large** fears that amount to real phobias. Below is a list of "phobias" borrowed from Ted Bernstein's *Reverse Dictionary*, published by Times Books, New York, 1975. (Bernstein lists a dozen or so more, and the *Psychiatric Dictionary*, New York, Oxford University Press, 1981, may list others.) If you or someone you know suffers from one (or more) of these abnormal fears, try to determine how the phobia was conditioned. What events triggered the phobia? What were your (or their) mental and physical reactions to the occurrence? What do you think might be done about the phobia? Write a brief account of your findings.

Irrational Fear of	Disorder
air, drafts, airplanes	aerophobia
animals	zoophobia
being touched	haptephobia
burial alive	taphephobia
cats	ailurophobia
crowds	demophobia
death	thanatophobia
dogs	cynophobia
eating	phagophobia
England, the English	anglophobia
fire	pyrophobia
foreigners, strangers	xenophobia
heights	acrophobia
lice	pediculophobia
marriage	gamophobia
men	androphobia
night	nyctophobia
number 13	triskaidekaphobia
ocean	thalassophobia
open spaces	agoraphobia
pain	algophobia
poison	toxicophobia
red	erythrophobia
solitude	autophobia
speaking	lalophobia
thunderstorms	astraphobia
women	gynophobia

Answer Key

Matching

1. c
2. e
3. a
4. f
5. l
6. h
7. j
8. d
9. g
10. i
11. m
12. k
13. b

Completion

1. conditioned, Pavlov, conditioned, stimulus, unconditioned, neutral, conditioning, conditional or conditioned;　2. stronger, extinguished, discriminate, salivate, circle, stress, neurotic;　3. Watson, bond, autonomic, generalized, phobias, conditioning, counter-conditioning;　4. Himle, Shorkey, desensitization, hierarchy, least, most, step-by-step, relaxation, stimulus; 5. holistic.

Short-Answer Questions

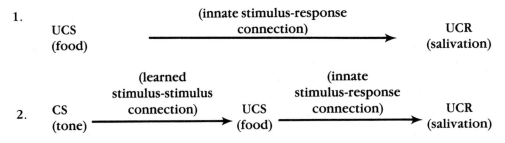

3. Phobic reactions usually involve some form of sensitization to stimuli that arouse the autonomic nervous system. As we saw in Lesson Fourteen, arousal of the sympathetic division of this system prepares you to fight, flee, or feed and causes you to experience the biological changes we associate with such emotional states as anger, fear, and hunger. Because these changes include muscular tension, they can be counteracted in part by voluntary muscular relaxation. Thus, a major part of desensitization therapy consists of teaching the patient to relax voluntarily.

4. Some conditioned responses that you might not want to extinguish could include reading and obeying traffic signals without conscious thought; applying your brakes reflexively to avoid hitting another car or person; avoiding contact with fire or objects that are very hot; looking for fire when you smell smoke; automatically looking at your speedometer and slowing down when you see a highway patrol officer; being reluctant to go into areas that are dark and deserted; expecting fire equipment or an ambulance when you hear sirens; running or walking away if you see a menacing-looking stranger approaching you on a deserted street; closing your windows when you see boiling black clouds and hear a thunderclap; answering the telephone when it rings; refusing to eat something that smells spoiled. (Are all of these behaviors conditioned? Can you think of others to add to this list?)

Self-Test

1. b (text page 345)
2. d (text page 346)
3. a (text pages 346-347; television program)
4. b (text page 348; television program)
5. c (text pages 346-347; television program)
6. d (text page 346; television program)
7. e (text page 347; television program)
8. c (text pages 353-354; television program)
9. b (text page 348)
10. a (text page 348)
11. d (text pages 349, 353-354; television program)
12. c (text pages 349-350)
13. a (text pages 349-350)
14. d (text page 351)
15. a (text page 351)
16. b (text page 351)
17. d (text page 351)
18. e (text pages 354-356)
19. c (text page 353)
20. d (text page 353; television program)
21. e (text pages 354-356; television program)
22. a (text page 355)

Operant Conditioning and Cognitive Skills 16

Viewer's Guide for Program Sixteen

As you view the television program, watch for:

Scenes from the circus. Trained animals have long fascinated young and old alike. How are lions tamed and bears taught? Can old dogs learn new tricks?

Harvard professor B. F. Skinner teaching a pigeon to turn in a circle in a laboratory demonstration of his theory of operant conditioning. Skinner, perhaps the most influential living psychologist, has devoted the past fifty years to what he calls experimental analysis of behavior.

Conductor Zubin Mehta using Skinnerian techniques—verbal rewards and physical reinforcement—to shape the performance of musicians in an orchestra. Note too the scenes of therapists using "love and ice cream" to teach a severely retarded child to walk.

A chimpanzee with a problem—and a solution. The chimpanzee figures out **on its own** how to join two sticks together so that they are long enough and strong enough to enable him to reach out and pull in a bunch of bananas. No one rewarded his successive steps toward the goal. Instead, he somehow realized in a flash of insight how his problem could be solved.

The demonstration of aversive therapy, which is used to alter destructive behaviors, such as overeating, smoking, or excessive drinking. Here, a mild shock indicates to the alcoholic that he is drinking much too fast.

Sequences that illustrate graphically some major criticisms of Skinnerian theory.

Preview

The circus casts its spell on young and old alike—the music, the costumes, the lights; the sounds, the smells, the sights. And the animals. Perhaps, more than anything else, the circus is animals—exotic animals, everyday animals, animals that do things animals ordinarily just do not do. Or do they?

Most animal trainers would be quick to point out that no animal can be taught to do anything it does not normally do. The training of animals consists of persuading them to perform on cue, in sequence, or with special props—behaviors they perform naturally but randomly. In other words, it is normal for a seal to bob its head and torso; it can be trained to use this motion to throw a ball or pick up rings.

But how does random behavior come to be shaped into a particular sequence? One answer is a learning or training process called operant conditioning, a theory proposed by Harvard psychologist B. F. Skinner to explain one way in which humans and animals learn. In Lesson Fifteen, we examined Pavlov's experiments in classical (or respondent) conditioning and the habitual response patterns that are established in dogs. In respondent conditioning, as it is more often called, repeated pairing of an unconditioned stimulus (for example, food) with a conditioned stimulus (sound) of a bell causes the unconditioned response (salivation) to become a conditioned one; that is, salivation occurs not only in response to the actual presence of food but also in anticipation of its presence, as signalled by a bell.

Respondent conditioning teaches animals to associate an established response with a new **stimulus**, while operant conditioning attaches a new **response** to stimulus inputs that are already present. Operant conditioning is the more complicated of the two techniques and involves modifying, or "shaping," behaviors toward a predetermined goal. Progress toward the goal is rewarded (positively reinforced).

As McConnell comments, both theories have exerted powerful influence on learning techniques everywhere—not just in laboratories or under the big top. Skinner's work, according to McConnell, has given psychology what is so far its best technology for helping people to change their behaviors. Skinnerian theory does have wide applications, but it also has some grave flaws. You will review some criticisms of operant conditioning in this lesson. You will also learn of the evolution of **cognitive behavior modification** from Skinnerian theory and something about the application of cognitive behavior modification and psychotherapy combined to treat behavior disorders, such as alcoholism.

Learning Objectives

When you have finished viewing the program and studying your text assignments, you should be able to:

1. Describe Thorndike's two basic laws of learning.
2. Describe findings that support the existence of two types of learning: trial and error and insight (Gestalt).
3. Describe the steps and their correct sequence in Skinner's theory of operant conditioning.
4. Distinguish between fixed-ratio and variable-ratio reinforcement schedules.
5. Compare operant and respondent (classical) conditioning.
6. Describe the use of biofeedback to alter bodily functions.
7. Identify some flaws in Skinner's theory of operant conditioning, especially in light of cognitive theories of learning.

Assignments

Before Viewing the Program

Read the preview at the beginning of this lesson and look over the learning objectives that precede the assignments.

Check the section "Did You Know That . . ." at the beginning of Chapter 14 in the text, and look over the subtitles for the chapter. Read Chapter 14, "Operant Conditioning and Cognitive Skills." As you read, note the boldfaced terms and concepts that appear throughout the lesson and are defined in the upper right corners of right-hand pages. Use the accompanying definitions or descriptions to increase your knowledge or refresh your memory concerning these terms.

View Program 16, "Operant Conditioning"

After Viewing the Program

Review the text assignments.

Read through the summary at the end of Chapter 14 and consider the thought questions that appear at intervals in the chapter. Then to aid your understanding of the materials presented in this lesson, review all of the boldfaced terms and concepts. In particular, note these terms carefully: trial and error, law of exercise, law of effect, insight, cognitive map, behaviorists, terminal response, baseline behavior, successive approximations, reinforced, shaping, chained, fixed-ratio reinforcement, variable-ratio reinforcement, operant conditioning, respondent conditioning, biofeedback, feed-forward, S-R connections, negative reinforcement, aversion training, cognitive behavior modification.

Complete the study activities included here as an additional study aid for you.

Now evaluate your understanding of the lesson material by reviewing the learning objectives and taking the self-test in this study guide. Check your answers against the answer key.

According to your instructor's assignment or your own interests, choose and complete activities from among the suggestions for extra credit. You might also consider the recommended readings listed at the end of the chapter.

"Mommy, we keep saying 'go home, kitty-cat'—but she just keeps hanging around here!"

Reprinted courtesy of The Register and Tribune Syndicate, Inc.

Study Activities

True-False

1. T F Tolman's experiments with cognitive maps led to the identification of what is now called the "learning curve."
2. T F If you receive raises whenever your supervisor feels that you deserve them, your performance is being rewarded on a variable-ratio schedule.

3. T F According to respondent conditioning techniques, the organism must be able to monitor its actions and observe the consequences of those actions.
4. T F Operant conditioning theoretically involves autonomic activities, such as heart rate, while respondent techniques are more suitable for acquiring voluntary responses like bowling.
5. T F Negative reinforcement increases the probability that a response will be repeated.
6. T F Skinner believes that punishment is a key concept in operant conditioning.
7. T F The "law of exercise" states that repetition strengthens S-R bonds.
8. T F Skinner believes that intrapsychic reinforcers are as important as environmental satisfiers.
9. T F Experiments by Gestalt psychologist Koehler appear to support the theory that animals are capable of insight learning.
10. T F The use of biofeedback to help patients learn to reduce the pain of headaches and other discomforts was developed from operant conditioning techniques.
11. T F An important contribution of Skinnerian theory is that it insists on viewing behavior objectively in terms of goals and events that can be measured.
12. T F Cognitive behavior modification techniques have so far not been successful in changing the thoughts and feelings of patients.

Completion

1. Columbia University psychologist E. L. _____ is believed to have been responsible for the first laboratory studies made of animal intelligence. His early experiments involved cats and "puzzle boxes," which the animals had to learn to unlatch in order to get out. From these experiments, Thorndike concluded that cats solved problems by trial and _____ learning. He graphed the improving performance of the cats as they learned and noted that learning seemed to follow the same general pattern, or "curve," for humans as it did for cats. Thorndike looked at learning as being a connection, or bond, between stimulus and _____. That is, if a cat unlatched the box, escaped, and received food as a reward, an S-R bond was probably made between unlocking the box and the rewarding events of escaping and being given food. Thorndike theorized that the more often the bond was exercised, the stronger it became. Thorndike called this theory the law of _____. His theory that S-R bonds made by the cats were strengthened by the results of unlocking the boxes (freedom and food) is called the law of _____.

response
exercise
Thorndike
error
effect

2. Psychologist Wolfgang Koehler argued that animals and men are capable of greater intellectual accomplishments and can discern _____ between objects and events and respond appropriately. In experiments with a chimpanzee named Sultan, Koehler appeared to demonstrate that the chimpanzee learned to secure a banana placed out of reach of his locked cage by perceiving that two sticks could be fitted together to make a single stick that was long enough to reach the fruit. This is called learning by _____. Gestalt psychologist E. C. Tolman suggested that rats rewarded with food when they found their way out of a maze were able to solve the maze because they understood _____ relationships and made mental "maps." Tolman called these _____ maps. His research tended to _____ theories of insight learning.

insight
cognitive
relationships
spatial
support

3. Harvard professor B. F. Skinner attempted to fit learning theories into a workable educational system which includes _____ response, _____, and repetition. He believed that when an organism learns to make responses that yield a reward it is "operating" upon its environment, so Skinner named his theory _____ (or instrumental) conditioning. Skinner believes that the organism responds freely and that the environment rewards some behaviors and _____ others. One reward is positive _____. Skinner holds that strengthening, or _____ of a response by rewards, tends to _____ the probability that the organism will make the same response again.

increase
feedback
reward
operant
innate
punishes
reinforcement

4. Skinner's techniques of operant conditioning involve five steps. First, the experimenter establishes a measurable goal, or _____ response. Next, the behavior of the organism prior to the experiment must be measured, then those behaviors that are to be "shaped" toward the goal are selected, a step Skinner called taking a _____. Baseline behaviors that advance the organism toward the terminal response are _____, while all others are ignored. Each small step toward the goal is reinforced, a technique called "successive approximations toward a goal," or _____.

rewarded (reinforced)
terminal
baseline
shaping

5. Skinner's system has great value in that it insists upon _____ goals and events, but it reduces the role of genes (biology) to mere "programmers" of responses to the _____, and denies the influence of such _____ aspects as feelings, perceptions, and thoughts. Operant conditioning makes no attempt to explain creativity, insight, art, conscious choice, motivation, or language learning.

environment
intrapsychic
measurable

Short-Answer Questions

1. College catalogs often state that the goal of higher education is to turn students into "creative individuals" who are "good citizens" and "productive members of modern-day society." What might B. F. Skinner say about the measurability of such objectives?

2. Skinner's theory has proved extremely worthwhile in explaining certain types of learning and is the basis for behavior modification, yet McConnell

says Skinner's approach is narrow. In what ways is it narrow? Is there evidence of types of learning that it does **not** adequately explain?

3. What do the Marlatt experiments seem to show about operant conditioning (or behavior modification) and the treatment of alcoholism? Explain briefly.

Self-Test

(Select the one best answer.)

Objective 1: Describe Thorndike's two basic laws of learning.

1. The theory that repetition strengthens S-R bonds is related to Thorndike's law of
   a. trial and error.
   b. fixed-ratio reinforcement.
   c. exercise.
   d. effect.
   e. insight.

2. The law of effect, a principle of learning that is similar to the idea of positive reinforcement, proposes that S-R bonds are strengthened by
   a. reward.
   b. repetition.
   c. insight.
   d. practice.
   e. punishment.

3. A part of Thorndike's early law of effect may have had harmful consequences for educational practices. This part of the law held that
   a. learning occurs by trial and error.
   b. satisfiers weaken S-R bonds.
   c. punishers weaken or break S-R bonds.
   d. variable-ratio schedules strengthen S-R bonds.
   e. variable-ratio schedules weaken S-R bonds.

Objective 2: Describe findings that support the existence of two types of learning: trial and error and insight (Gestalt).

4. When Thorndike's cats accidentally learned the solution to unlatching their puzzle box after making many random mistakes, they were demonstrating _____ learning.
   a. insightful
   b. trial and error
   c. law of exercise
   d. law of effect
   e. Gestalt

5. The theory that organisms can learn by insight was supported initially by
   a. studies of cats that unlatched boxes to get food.
   b. studies of a chimpanzee that fitted two sticks together to reach a banana.
   c. Darwin's theory of evolution.
   d. the "insight" experience in classroom situations.
   e. the work of Pavlov with dogs.

Objective 3: Describe the steps and their correct sequence in Skinner's theory of operant conditioning.

6. Which of the following pairs is not related?
   a. baseline behavior, shaping
   b. terminal response, baseline
   c. reinforcement, goal-directed behavior
   d. shaping, cognitive map
   e. successive approximations, terminal behavior

7. Which of the following pairs is out of sequence?
   a. baseline behavior, terminal response
   b. terminal response, baseline behavior
   c. taking a baseline, successive approximations
   d. rewarding goal-directed behaviors, terminal response
   e. ignoring nongoal-directed behaviors, shaping

8. In the Skinnerian system, shaping occurs during
   a. selection of the terminal response.
   b. negative reinforcement.
   c. determination of entering behavior.
   d. the moment of insight.
   e. successive approximations to the goal.

Objective 4: Distinguish between fixed-ratio and variable-ratio reinforcement schedules.

9. To keep players from outguessing the machines, casino owners program slot machines to pay off on a _____ schedule.
   a. monthly
   b. fixed-ratio
   c. variable-ratio
   d. variable interval
   e. periodic

10. If an animal responds slowly after reinforcement but increases its response rate at periodic intervals, it is showing a behavior pattern typical of
    a. variable-ratio reinforcement.
    b. fixed-ratio reinforcement.
    c. successive approximations.
    d. respondent conditioning.
    e. operant conditioning.

Objective 5: Compare operant and respondent (classical) conditioning.

11. If you were to train your pet dog to ring a doorbell whenever the animal wishes to go in or out of the house, you would be using a form of
    a. respondent conditioning.
    b. classical conditioning.
    c. cumulative record.
    d. biofeedback.
    e. operant conditioning.

12. A major difference between respondent and operant conditioning is that
    a. in operant conditioning, the organism learns to manipulate the environment.
    b. in operant conditioning, the organism responds involuntarily to the environment.
    c. respondent conditioning works best with negative reinforcement.
    d. operant conditioning is called classical conditioning.
    e. operant conditioning is reinforced but respondent is not.

Objective 6: Describe the use of biofeedback to alter bodily funtions.

13. Biofeedback devices have made it possible to
    a. measure the "insight" experience.
    b. demonstrate that there are no differences between respondent and operant conditioning.
    c. bring autonomic responses under respondent control.
    d. bring autonomic responses under operant control.
    e. support theories of Gestalt learning.

Objective 7: Identify some flaws in Skinner's theory of operant conditioning, especially in light of cognitive theories of learning.

14. If you put yourself on a strict diet and lose thirty pounds without help or telling anyone about your plan, your success in reaching your goal is an example of
    a. the use of biofeedback techniques.
    b. Skinner's theory of shaping.
    c. respondent conditioning techniques.
    d. Skinner's emphasis on controlling external stimuli.
    e. Skinner's failure to explain intrapsychic factors.

15. Which of the following behaviors is (are) not explained by the Skinnerian system?
    a. shaping
    b. insight
    c. trial and error learning
    d. all of the above
    e. none of the above

16. Unlike Skinner, cognitive behaviorists
    a. see individuals as passive organisms whose behavior is selected by the environment.
    b. refuse to deal with such concepts as perceptions and self-awareness.
    c. believe that changing one's thoughts and feelings leads to the modification of behavior.
    d. believe that alcoholism is a biologically based disease.
    e. consider the study of group behavior a waste of time.

Suggestions for Extra Credit

1. If you or your children have a pet (rodent, bird, dog, or cat), attempt to use operant conditioning to teach it some trick. Keep a log of your efforts. At the top of the first page, briefly describe the animal's baseline behavior. At the bottom, explain the desired terminal response. On the lines in between, write some behaviors you might recognize as successive approximations to your goal. On succeeding pages in your log, record the date, duration, and accomplishments of each training session. Make a special note of any procedural changes you decide are necessary or of any modifications you make in your original goal. Write a one-page summary of your results. If your efforts succeed, decide upon an appropriate terminal behavior for another similar experiment. If your efforts fail, analyze the reason for the failure, modify your desired terminal response or your conditioning method, and try again.

2. In his book *Walden Two*, which was published by Macmillan in 1976, Skinner describes his idea of a utopian society based on behaviorism. Read the book or special portions of it that interest you, and write a two- or three-page report, giving your opinions of Skinner's ideas.

3. When used in classrooms, Skinnerian behavior modification techniques are often criticized by parents and older or more introspective students for being "dehumanizing" and for conditioning students to work for external rewards rather than for the internal satisfaction that comes from a job well done. How would you respond to such a criticism?

Answer Key

True-False

1. F	7. T
2. T	8. F
3. F	9. T
4. F	10. T
5. T	11. T
6. F	12. F

Completion

1. Thorndike, error, response, exercise, effect;   2. relationships, insight, spatial, cognitive, support;   3. innate, reward, operant, punishes, feedback, reinforcement, increase;   4. terminal, baseline, rewarded (reinforced), shaping;   5. measurable, environment, intrapsychic.

Short-Answer Questions

1. Harvard professor B. F. Skinner is, perhaps, the most influential living psychologist. He has devoted the past fifty years to what he terms experimental analysis of behavior. According to Skinner's theory of learning, termed **operant conditioning**, you must begin any teaching, or training, project by defining precisely what it is that you want to accomplish; that is, you must describe the final step in the desired chain of behaviors. Skinner called this final step the **terminal response**. One of his greatest contributions to psychological method is his insistence that this final step be measurable. The objection he would probably raise to terminal responses or objectives, such as those expressed in the catalogue goal statement, is that creativity, good citizenship, and productivity within a society are impossible to measure unless they can be defined or described in terms of a list of recognizable behaviors. What is it that creative, productive, good citizens do?

2. While Skinner is the most influential living psychologist and his theory has widespread application, it does have limitations. McConnell cites specifically its emphasis on **biological** rewards to the exclusion of intrapsychic ones. Because of this emphasis, it cannot adequately account for the intellectual pleasure that comes from insightful learning. Also, because Skinner's theory states that all learning is under the direct control of **external** stimuli, it does not explain the self-directed behavioral changes of which humans are capable.

3. While neither medical intervention, intrapsychic techniques, nor behavior modification alone has proven to be very effective in the long-term treatment of alcoholism, the Marlatt studies at the University of Washington seem to show that a combination of strategies from the various perspectives at different stages of treatment may offer the best hope. Drinking behavior in some alcoholics could be decreased temporarily by punishment, the pairing of electrical shocks with drinking (a form of aversion training), but, over a period of time, most of the alcoholic subjects resumed drinking, and those who were punished drank **more** than subjects who were given abstinence training but not punishment (electric shocks). Patients who were most successful in maintaining decreased alcohol consumption were those who were trained and practiced in coping and self-management skills during the period when drinking behavior was suppressed. Marlatt concluded that different treatment procedures and different patient skills are required at different stages of the change process.

Self-Test

1. c (text page 368)
2. a (text pages 368-369)
3. c (text page 369)
4. b (text page 368)
5. b (text page 370; television program)
6. d (text pages 370-373; television program)
7. a (text pages 372-373; television program)
8. e (text page 373; television program)
9. c (text pages 376-377)
10. b (text pages 376-377)
11. e (text pages 377-378)
12. a (text pages 377-378)
13. d (text page 379)
14. e (text page 381; television program)
15. b (text page 382; television program)
16. c (text pages 380-382)

Memory 17

Viewer's Guide for Program Seventeen

As you view the television program, watch for:

The staged attack on the college professor and the auto accident to which you become an eyewitness. Can you describe the professor's assailant? How accurately can you recall what happened in the accident?

The sequences that introduce and illustrate the three stages of memory (sensory information storage, short-term memory, long-term memory), as well as some causes of forgetting.

The cocktail party sequence in which a memory expert explains associational techniques that can be used to program information into your mind in a way that will help you remember it more accurately and retrieve it more easily.

The film sequence of neurologist Wilder Penfield reminiscing with a patient about her responses to and recollections of electrical stimulation of various parts of her brain. Touching an electric probe to the same spot in the brain raises the same memory again and again. Does this suggest that memory has a physical location or that a physical change takes place in the brain each time you store some item in your long-term memory?

The film sequence of planarian flatworms being conditioned to associate exposure to light with electric shock and "learning" to flinch in anticipation of the shock when exposed to the light. "Training" the worm in this fashion made possible a number of subsequent experiments that seem to suggest a chemical basis for memory and support the hypothesis that memory can be transferred.

Preview

What time is it? That is a simple question and one that you probably are asked frequently. To answer, you must recognize and recall the meanings of the words that frame the question, remember that a watch or clock is the instrument we use to measure time, know where the nearest watch or clock is and how to read and interpret the numbers on its face, and then locate within your memory the right words to use in conveying your answer to the one asking the question. And you must do all of these things much more rapidly than we can list them and you can read them, or the inquirer will grow impatient and ask you again or pose the question to someone else.

How do you locate these bits of information that are stored in your brain? How do you remember? Why do you forget?

In this lesson you will study the mysteries of memory. Memory is a very complex aspect of mental functioning; and, to be truthful, we have only the vaguest notions of how it actually works. But we do know that your brain has a more elaborate memory system than any computer. In fact, you have not one memory but many different kinds of memories. As efficient as your personal "memory banks" are in remembering, however, your brain also is capable of forgetting massive amounts of input.

From what we have leaned about memory, we can deduce ways of coding and storing information to make recall easier, more accurate, and more certain. Memory devices, associations, interpretations, careful categorizing, and retrieval all play a part in the memory process.

Some research indicates that memory depends upon electrical circuits and neural firings in the brain, particularly involving the synapses and the "switches" that may control them. Scientists also believe that memory may be encoded in an "engram," a chemical molecule or "physical representation" of memory, though there is as yet no proof that engrams exist. Research also shows that certain chemicals increase or retard neural processes associated with memory storage and recall. Caffeine, strychnine, and RNA, for example, appear to facilitate long-term memory storage, while the enzyme ribonuclease may "erase" memories by decreasing RNA in the brain.

You will be interested in the planarian research studies conducted by McConnell over a period of years and discussed in this lesson, for these studies indicated that memory could be "transferred" by some worms fed parts of other worms trained in specific tests. Worms that ate "educated" worms were able to learn the same tasks faster than other worms **not** fed parts of the "educated" worms.

In this lesson, you will also take a look at what scientists now know about the memory disorders amnesia, aphasia, Alzheimer's disease, and memory loss in old people. If memory does have a mainly chemical base, what significance could this fact have for persons suffering these disorders? Might we one day acquire an "education" simply by swallowing extracts or pills or taking injections?

Learning Objectives

When you have finished viewing the program and studying your text assignments, you should be able to:

1. Describe the characteristics of the three memory systems: sensory information storage, short-term memory, and long-term memory.
2. Describe and give examples of cataloging and verbal schemes for information retrieval.
3. Give several reasons why forgetting occurs, and discuss several types of memory disorders.
4. Define "engram" and distinguish between the electrical and chemical theories of how it might be formed.
5. Describe the research that suggests memory has a biochemical basis.
6. Briefly state the reasons supporting the reliability and validity of memory transfer experimentation.

Assignments

Before Viewing the Program

Read the preview at the beginning of this lesson and look over the learning objectives that precede the assignments.

Check the section "Did You Know That . . ." at the beginning of Chapter 15 in the text and look over the subtitles for the chapter.

Read Chapter 15, "Memory."

View Program 17, "Memory"

After Viewing the Program

Review the text assignments.

Read through the summary at the end of the chapter. Then, to facilitate your understanding of the materials presented in this lesson, study the terms and concepts that are printed in boldfaced type and are defined in the upper right corners of right-hand pages. In particular, note these terms carefully: sensory information storage, short-term memory, long-term memory, aphasia, RNA, amnesia, retrograde amnesia, anterograde amnesia, mnemonics, consolidation period, engram, senility, planarian, validity, reliability, chemical "erasers," strychnine, Alzheimer's disease.

Complete the study activities that are included here as an additional study aid for you.

Now evaluate your understanding of the lesson material by reviewing the learning objectives and taking the self-test in this study guide. Check your answers against the answer key.

According to your instructor's assignments or your own interests, choose and complete activities from the suggestions for extra credit. You might consider the recommended readings listed at the end of the chapter.

"Partial amnesia, Doc. Doesn't know his name, but remembers the Alamo."

The New Yorker, May 3, 1976. Drawing by Handelsman; © 1976
The New Yorker Magazine, Inc.

Study Activities

Matching

Match each phrase in the column on the right with the appropriate term in the column on the left, writing the letters of the phrases in the appropriate blanks.

____ 1. memory
____ 2. mnemonics
____ 3. amnesia
____ 4. engram
____ 5. senility
____ 6. RNA and/or protein
____ 7. validity
____ 8. reliability
____ 9. aphasia
____ 10. clangs
____ 11. serial position effect

a. physical representation of a memory
b. process by which information is stored in the brain and retrieved to recreate past perceptions, emotions, thoughts, actions
c. words that sound alike
d. inability to recall the middle words in a series, while remembering those at the beginning and end
e. mental tricks to help you remember
f. trustability
g. process by which information is not stored, is blocked from access, or is erased from the brain
h. the molecules that may be involved in memory formation
i. loss of physical or mental ability that sometimes accompanies advanced age
j. repeatability
k. impaired ability to remember or use language

Completion

1. To think, to speak, to answer any question, you must make use of your _____. Memory is basic to consciousness, and there are at least three stages of memory. During the first stage of memory, called sensory information _____ (SIS), a more or less exact copy of each stimulus input is made by the receptors and briefly "put on hold" while the brain is making a first interpretation of the stimulus. In the second or _____ (STM) stage, auditory descriptions of six or seven items are collected and stored together for a few seconds longer while the brain decides how best to respond. If your brain desires to make a permanent record of an experience, the experience will be tucked away in your _____ (LTM) memory. Only _____ facts and events are processed by your _____ memory banks. Novelty, meaning, and emotionality of input assure a strong memory.

2. Your brain can and does forget massive amounts of input through a number
of processes that begin as memory does—in the sensory _____. Some
sensory inputs never reach the higher centers of the brain because they
_____ when receptor neurons adapt to them or they are _____ by
new inputs. Another simple form of forgetting occurs when "new" items
_____ to erase, or push out, "old" items. Some inputs are _____ by
the lower centers of your brain because they are meaningless or
unimportant, while some others are _____ by the emotional centers of
your brain before you can make a conscious effort to remember them.
Psychological amnesia, a form of _____, can cause you to forget
everything that happened during an entire day and sometimes longer.
Damage to the temporal lobe of the brain can cause the inability to remember
or use language, an impairment called _____. Victims of Alzheimer's
disease suffer anterograde amnesia, a type of forgetting in which _____
items can be easily retrieved, but some kinds of _____ can't be filed in
_____ storage.

3. The twenty or thirty minutes which it takes your brain to file an input or experience away in long-term memory is known as the _____ period. Any physical or psychological trauma that might occur to you during this period can prevent the item from being recorded and thus cause _____ amnesia, the forgetting of events that happened twenty or thirty minutes before the mishap. _____ damage can also lead to _____—the "wiping out" of memories already in permanent storage, or in the process of being stored. When you translate experiences from short-term to long-term memory, many _____ can be lost. As they are being consolidated in your long-term memory, some items get _____ and thus are not readily retrieved. Filing errors seem to occur most frequently when your memory mechanism is _____.

Brain
misplaced
consolidation
overloaded
amnesia
details
retrograde

4. Scientists believe that some physical change occurs in the brain when learning takes place. They call this physical representation of a memory an _____. Scientists have speculated that the engram might be an _____ circuit. Other research suggests that the engram must involve some _____ change at the synapse. Memory transfer experiments with planaria (flatworms), rats, and goldfish led to the conclusion by some scientists that memory formation involves the creation of new _____. As proof of the _____ of these experiments, researchers point out that **untrained** planarians who were fed the chopped up bodies of **trained** planarians learned to perform tasks already learned by the trained worms much _____ than did the worms that had not been fed the _____ worms. The slowest learners were those worms that got _____ instructions by being fed a mix of worms that had been taught opposite tasks. The fact that experiments by more than 100 scientists yielded evidence supporting the memory transfer hypothesis is cited to support the _____ of the studies.

electrical
validity
conflicting
engram
trained
chemical
faster
reliability
molecules

Short-Answer Questions

1. Fill in the columns of Table 17-1 with information about the three types of memory.

Table 17-1. Comparison of Three Stages of Memory

Characteristics	Stages of Memory			
	Sensory Information Storage	Short-term Memory	Consolidation Period	Long-term Memory
Stage				
Location				
Duration				
Capacity				
Function				
Description				

2. In Table 17-2, list nine types of forgetting and give a brief description of each.

Table 17-2. Types of Forgetting

TYPE	DESCRIPTION

3. Cite arguments for the reliability and validity of the memory transfer experiments.

4. Briefly describe the "search for the engram." What do some psychologists think the engram may be?

Self-Test

(Select the one best answer.)

Objective 1: Describe the characteristics of the three memory systems: sensory information storage, short-term memory, and long-term memory.

1. Memory begins in the
   a. sense receptors.
   b. peripheral nervous system.
   c. central nervous system.
   d. frontal lobes.
   e. cerebellum.

2. Memory in the receptor organs is called
   a. short-term memory (STM).
   b. intermediate-term memory.
   c. long-term memory (LTM).
   d. sensory information storage (SIS).
   e. none of the above.

3. During the sensory information stage
   a. sensory impressions are formed into patterns.
   b. a nearly perfect replica of the sensory impression is held or stored.
   c. meaning is extracted from sensory impressions.
   d. your brain consolidates items.
   e. both b and d take place.

4. Your short-term memory system
   a. holds all stimulus patterns for several minutes.
   b. translates, or codes, a visual stimulus pattern into an auditory representation.
   c. remembers up to several dozen items at a time.
   d. remembers only highlights and landmarks.
   e. remembers none of the above.

5. Your short-term memory cannot
   a. retain anything for more than thirty seconds.
   b. hold on to more than six or seven items at once.
   c. hold an auditory representation of a stimulus pattern.
   d. do both a and b.
   e. do both b and c.

6. When an item fades from short-term memory, it
   a. is usually gone forever.
   b. can be recalled when needed.
   c. is retained only as a sensory impression.
   d. is retained only as an emotional impression.
   e. is placed in sensory information storage.

7. As explained in the television program, long-term memories fall into two basic categories:
   a. logical and intuitive.
   b. verbal and nonverbal.
   c. semantic and episodic.
   d. analytic and artistic.
   e. mental and emotional.

8. Adults are sometimes capable of giving vivid details of childhood events because they can
   a. retrieve all sensory impressions of these events.
   b. rely on their long-term memory to retrieve them in perfect form.
   c. recall the emotional tone of these events.
   d. catalogue them in a logical way.
   e. reconstruct the experience piece by piece based on a few highlights or landmark events.

9. According to the television program, the process of reconstruction makes memory treacherous because
   a. sensory impressions fade rapidly.
   b. you might end up with a "real" memory that you can actually "see" of an event that never happened.
   c. long-term memory is imperfect and incomplete.

d. emotions color your memory of events.

e. highlight or landmark events are few and far between.

Objective 2: Describe and give examples of cataloguing and verbal schemes for information retrieval.

10. According to Harold Goodglass, items in long-term memory seem to be filed by

a. specific categories.

b. a variety of mnemonics.

c. complex stimulus patterns.

d. serial position effects.

e. time of occurrence.

11. Which of the following pairs is not included in Goodglass's memory filing system?

a. class and context

b. attributes and sensory associations

c. function and reproductive information

d. clangs and visual patterns

e. cataloguing and serial position

12. Artificial tricks and devices used for remembering are

a. called mnemonics.

b. used only for short-term memory.

c. often based on association.

d. described by both a and b.

e. described by both a and c.

Objective 3: Give several reasons why forgetting occurs, and discuss several types of memory disorders.

13. Which of these is not one of the nine types of forgetting?

a. neural decay

b. input rejection

c. experience repression

d. acoustical coding

e. stimulus interference

14. Two of the simplest types of forgetting are

a. semantic confusion and input rejection.

b. rejection and repression.

c. neural decay and interference.

d. retrograde and psychological amnesia.

e. translation and filing errors.

15. Forgetting occurs because
    a. you have too many "index cards."
    b. you have too few "index cards."
    c. you overload your memory mechanism by trying to learn too much all at once.
    d. new memories interfere with your ability to recall older ones.
    e. of all of the above.

16. The disorder known as aphasia is the result of brain damage. A person who suffers aphasia
    a. has no consolidation period for long-term memory.
    b. experiences difficulty in remembering and using words.
    c. suffers breakdown of all three stages of retrieval.
    d. has no engrams in the left brain hemisphere.
    e. usually also suffers anterograde amnesia.

17. Victims of Alzheimer's disease (a form of senility) suffer a memory disorder called anterograde amnesia, which causes the person to
    a. forget events that happened just prior to a trauma of some sort.
    b. experience permanent erasure of all long-term memory items.
    c. forget "old" items, but still be able to recall "new" ones filed in long-term storage.
    d. be able to remember "old" items but not file "new" ones in long-term memory.
    e. typically experience difficulty in remembering and using language.

Objective 4: Define "engram" and distinguish between the electrical and chemical theories of how it might be formed.

18. Most scientists believe that the brain functions much like a computer in this way:
    a. the memory units of both are electrical loops or circuits.
    b. the brain's synapses function like switches in computers.
    c. the memory storage capacity of both is limited.
    d. the memory units of both are mechanical.
    e. both use the same kind of memory "filing system."

19. The engram of memory is thought to be
    a. an artificial memory strategy.
    b. a computer bank that works like our memory.
    c. located in the dendrites of cortical neurons.
    d. a synaptic switch.
    e. a change in the physical structure of the brain.

20. The engram forms the basis for
    a. sensory information storage.
    b. short-term memory.
    c. intermediate-term memory.
    d. long-term memory.
    e. all of the above.

21. Which of the following statements is not true?
    a. The electrical loop theory holds that the engram is a combination of switches and a circuit of some kind.
    b. According to the electrical loop theory, all memory will be erased if most electrical activity in the brain ceases.
    c. According to the electrical loop theory, an engram is a chemical molecule of some sort.
    d. Electrical loop theorists believe that the engram functions as long as electricity flows through the proper pathway in the brain.

Objective 4; and *Objective 5:* Describe the research that suggests memory has a biochemical basis.

22. The results of memory transfer experiments, such as those conducted with planarian flatworms,
    a. support the memory molecule theory of learning.
    b. discredit the memory molecule theory of learning.
    c. verify the electrical current hypothesis.
    d. discredit the electrical current hypothesis.
    e. are inconclusive.

23. Research in the biochemistry of memory shows that
    a. memory is mainly a function of electrical circuits and switches.
    b. the organism's experiences cause chemical changes in neurons.
    c. genes cannot be influenced by an animal's experiences.
    d. the amount of RNA in the brain is decreased by activity and experience.
    e. all of the above are true.

Objective 6: Briefly state the reasons supporting the reliability and validity of memory transfer experimentation.

24. In the memory transfer experiments, planarian worms that were fed _____ were the _____ learners.
    a. "dark arm" instructions, slowest
    b. "opposite-color arm" instructions, fastest
    c. "opposite-color arm" instructions, slowest
    d. "conflicting" instructions, slowest
    e. "conflicting" instructions, fastest

25. According to McConnell, the transfer studies seem reliable because
    a. the same results have been obtained from every experiment.
    b. the odds of getting successful results are 100 to 1.
    c. blind testing techniques are used in experiments.
    d. "cannibal" planarians absorbed the memory molecules of the worms they devoured.
    e. positive results in similar experiments have been reported by more than 100 scientists.

Suggestions for Extra Credit

1. If you didn't do the "eyewitness reliability" exercise, item 4 in the suggestions for extra credit in Lesson Ten, "Visual Perception," you may want to try that project now that you have completed your study of this lesson. Try to think of all the explanations you can for inconsistences and discrepancies in subjects' memories and accounts. For example, what about perceptual defense and perceptual vigilance, as well as aspects of remembering and forgetting which you reviewed in this lesson? What can you conclude on the basis of what you have so far learned in this course?

2. In the past several years, scientists, health professionals, and the general public have become increasingly aware of the great incidence and impact of the brain disorder known as Alzheimer's disease, a major form of senility. More than 2,000,000 Americans are believed to be victims of Alzheimer's disease, and the disease has become a major priority for scientific research. There is as yet no cure for Alzheimer's disease. Some recent research, however, suggests that accumulations of metal in the brain, especially aluminum, may contribute to development of the disease. If you are interested, read "Progress Report on Alzheimer's Disease: Volume II," published in July, 1984, by the Public Health Service and the National Institutes of Health, under the auspices of the U.S. Department of Health and Human Services. The report summarizes current research on Alzheimer's. For a well-written description of the effects of this disease on its sufferers and their families and an account of how at least one institution approaches the care and treatment of Alzheimer's patients, read "A Calamity to the Victim and Family, Alzheimer's Yields Slowly to New Facilities and Medical Science," by Carl Arrington, *People Weekly*, May 20, 1985, page 122.

3. A three-hour college course meets for about thirty-three hours of lecture in a twelve-week quarter. Based on what you know about memory, learning, and forgetting, list and explain five reasons for spreading exposure to course content out over a ten- to twelve-week period rather than compressing it into a solid three- or four-day period.

4. List five or more ways you can change your study habits to take advantage of what you have learned about memory, retrieval, and forgetting. Actually, try several of these ways over a period of time (nine weeks, a quarter, or a semester), and make a note of the results. Which methods helped you learn faster? Remember better? Which methods are most effective for you?

5. Author William F. Rickenbacker gives an amusing, but informative, account of the somewhat bizarre influence of meaning and his emotions and preferences on his own memory in a brief article published in the May 17, 1985, issue of *National Review*. The article, entitled, ''Who Dat?,'' begins on page 38. You may want to read this short piece, then analyze the effects of your emotions and preferences and the ''meaningfulness'' of certain things on your own memory. Are there some things you regularly **forget**? Why? Hans J. and Michael Eysenck, authors of *Mindwatching* (Anchor Press/ Doubleday, 1983), remind us that forgetting can be painful and embarrassing as well as amusing—as was the case with the hapless individual who stood in the crowd waving goodbye to the British royal family as the royal plane lifted off an African runway, forgetting completely that **he** was supposed to be aboard the plane. Read ''Why Do We Forget?'' (Chapter 2, pages 230-241, in *Mindwatching*) for a discussion of some new thoughts and theories about memory. You should, of course, also read Freud's classic, *The Psychopathology of Everyday Life*, on forgetting. Describe and analyze your findings in a brief paper. Give some illustrations from your own experience.

Answer Key

Matching

1. b	7. f
2. e	8. j
3. g	9. k
4. a	10. c
5. i	11. d
6. h	

Completion

1. memory, storage, short-term, long-term, important, long-term;
2. receptors, decay, erased, interfere, rejected, repressed, repression, aphasia, old, new, long-term;   3. consolidation, retrograde, brain, amnesia, details, misplaced, overloaded;   4. engram, electrical, chemical, molecules, validity, faster, trained, conflicting, reliability.

Short-Answer Questions

1   **Table 17-1. Comparison of Three Stages of Memory**

Characteristics	Stage of Memory			
	Sensory Information Storage	Short-term Memory		Long-term Memory
Stage	First	Second		Third
Location	Sensory receptors	Brain		Brain
Duration	Brief—lasts a fraction of a second	Brief—last a few seconds		Lasts a lifetime
Capacity	Limited to one image, input, or impression at a time	Limited to six or seven items	Consolidation Period	Unlimited
Function	Hold for transfer	Hold for interpretation		Permanent storage
Description	Is in the form of visual or photographic images	Auditory code or representation		Items are filed and retrieved by categories

2. **Table 17-2. Types of Forgetting**

TYPE	DESCRIPTION
Neural decay	Receptor neurons adapt to the input— that is, in the continued presence of the stimulus, they fire less and less frequently. Thus, the neural pattern decays.
Interference	A new input can interfere with the storage and recall of new memories; and a new input may also interfere with old memories by transforming or distorting them.
Rejection	The lower centers of your mind reject items that are unimportant or meaningless to you.
Repression	The emotional centers of your brain deliberately forget, misplace, or misfile an incoming stimulus that is threatening or disturbing.
Cataloging errors	The brain seems to "make a mental index card" for every long-term memory. A cataloging error may occur if too many things must be learned at one time, such as association of the wrong name with a person's face.
Filing errors	An item of memory may be misfiled in a place reserved for a similar, already-stored item.
Retrieval errors	A particular memory "index card" may be filed with many similar memories, remaining hidden or "lost." Even a new memory may be impossible to retrieve, because there are too few cues as to its location in the memory's filing system.
Amnesia	Brain damage or emotional trauma erases or temporarily "wipes out" memories already in permanent storage or in the process of being stored.
Aphasia	Aphasics are individuals having impairments in the ability to use or remember language. The condition usually results from damage to the left hemisphere of the brain.

3. If the memory transfer tests are valid, then **specific memories** will be passed along from trained planarians to the untrained worms that devour them. McConnell cites his own experiments with planarians to show that this transfer does occur. Planarians that ate worms trained to go to either the light arm or the dark arm of a water maze learned the fastest when trained to go to the same arm as had been the "victim" worm; planarians trained to go to the opposite arm learned more slowly but still faster than planarians that had not eaten trained worms; and planarians that ate untrained worms learned at the same speed as did planarians that ate no other planarians at all. Those planarians that were fed a mixture of worms trained to go in both directions showed confusion and indecision and were the slowest to learn.

   The memory transfer studies are apparently reliable, because positive results have been reported by more than 100 scientists. However, James Dyal has found that a number of scientists have been unable to repeat the experiments successfully.

4. Scientists believe that storage of items in your permanent memory banks necessitates a physical change of some kind in the brain. They call the physical representation of a memory an "engram." But, despite considerable research, no scientist has been able to see or identify an engram. It has been speculated that the engram might be an electrical circuit, but experiments with animals showed that cessation and restoration of electrical activity in the brain had no effect on memory of learned tasks. However, when parts of the human brain are stimulated electrically, memories are aroused repeatedly. So the engram seems to have an electrical connection. Most scientists believe that synapses in the brain function like the switches in computers, routing information from one point to another. Many now believe that some kind of chemical action must occur to open or close the synaptic switch. Experiments in recent years suggest that RNA or protein may be the chemical substance essential to memory.

Self-Test

1. a (text page 393; television program)
2. d (text page 393; television program)
3. b (text page 393)
4. b (text pages 396-397; television program)
5. d (text pages 395-397)
6. a (text pages 395, 397)
7. c (television program)
8. e (text pages 398-399; television program)
9. b (television program)

10. a (text page 400)
11. e (text page 400)
12. e (text page 400; television program)
13. d (text pages 401-406; television program)
14. c (text pages 401-406; television program)
15. e (text pages 401-406; television program)
16. b (text pages 405-406)
17. d (text pages 404-405)
18. b (text page 407)
19. e (text pages 407, 411-412; television program)
20. d (text page 406; television program)
21. c (text pages 406-407)
22. a (text pages 411-413; television program)
23. b (text pages 407-408)
24. d (text pages 411-412)
25. e (text page 412)

Pain and Hypnosis 18

Viewer's Guide for Program Eighteen

As you view the television program, watch for:

Actual film footage of a man pushing a huge needle through his own arm without exhibiting outward signs of pain. The man, an experimental subject in UCLA's Pain Clinic, explains that the secret lies in a state of concentration in which his mind is dissociated from the pain reported by his body.

The animated sequence showing the way a boy's nervous system processes the message of pain when a crab nips his finger. The hurt finger is withdrawn in an automatic reflex triggered at the spine. Thus, the finger is out of danger before the brain knows danger exists.

The animated sequence showing touch and pain pathways. Notice the difference in the axonic fibers. Touch fibers are large and send impulses to the brain quite rapidly. Pain fibers are smaller and carry their messages more slowly.

The film sequences of women undergoing surgery and childbirth while hypnotized. Does hypnosis prevent them from **feeling the pain or from remembering** it afterwards?

Scenes from a "double blind" experiment in which neither the patients nor the doctors knew that the so-called pain-killer given after wisdom tooth extraction was really a placebo. Results of the study indicated that the mind's faith in a placebo actually stimulates the body to release endorphins and control its own pain.

Preview

"For as long as there have been flesh to wound, eyes to weep, and mouths to cry out, there has been pain to endure. And for equally as long, individuals and cultures have sought to halt its gnawing, nagging, throbbing, pounding, stabbing, and to free themselves from its enslaving grip. They have tried drugs and dance, incantations and trance." After this rather dramatic introduction to the study of pain, the television program for this lesson adds that no one pain-killing method works for everyone and, in fact, we don't yet really understand what pain is.

What is pain? For years pain has been thought of as a signal that warns us of damage to our body or of illness or abnormality that needs prompt remedial attention, but it has also been observed to occur when no apparent body damage exists. We really don't know where pain comes from or how we sense it. No one has ever found a nerve ending solely concerned with the sensation of pain or a part of the brain where stimulation produces the experience of pain. Pain is far from being a simple input, such as pressure or temperature. Instead, it is a highly complex psychological experience, affected by many factors, whose mechanisms are still largely a mystery.

Among the "potions" we use to secure surcease from pain are the pain-killing drugs, placebos, patent medicines, and the body's own pain-killers, called enkephalins and endorphins. We are also learning that, for at least some people, it is possible to substitute conscious control of pain for the chemical pain-killers that are now so widely used. Among the "processes" in which we take refuge from pain are meditation, hypnosis, acupuncture, biofeedback, and some other cognitive strategies which depend partly upon operant conditioning techniques. In this lesson, you will learn about how these potions and processes work (or don't work), and you will be given a step-by-step account of a plan for conscious control of pain which has been used successfully by researchers. You will find, too, that, while science still can't define or specifically "locate" pain, some of the mechanisms **are** understood. For example, it seems certain that the body uses **two** separate pain control systems. One involves the release of the pain-killing endorphins and the other controls a "gate" in the spinal cord which can be "closed" to block painful input. If there is such a gate, can we learn to control it?

Learning Objectives

When you have finished viewing the program and studying your text assignments, you should be able to:

1. Explain the placebo effect.
2. Briefly describe Mesmer's, Braid's, and Freud's views of hypnosis.
3. Discuss differing interpretations of hypnosis (e.g., those of Hull, Braid, Hilgard, Baker, and Barber).
4. Describe some of the effects and limitations of hypnosis.
5. Compare "conscious strategies" and hypnosis as methods of dealing with pain.
6. Describe the biological processes involved in experiencing pain, including the "spinal gate" theory.

Assignments

Before Viewing the Program

Read the preview at the beginning of this lesson and look over the learning objectives that precede the assignments.

Check the section "Did You Know That . . ." at the beginning of Chapter 16 and look over the subtitles for the chapter.

Read Chapter 16, "Hypnosis, Pain, and Placebos."

View Program 18, "Pain and Hypnosis"

After Viewing the Program

Review the text assignments.

Read through the summary items at the end of the chapter and consider the thought questions included in the chapter. Then review all of the boldfaced terms and those defined in the upper right corners of right-hand pages. In particular, note the terms: placebo, endorphin, mesmerism, suggestibility, hypnosis, hypnotic age regression, hypnotic role-playing, conscious strategy, fast fibers, slow fibers, spinal cord, spinal gate, reticular system, dissociation.

Complete the study activities that are included here as an additional study aid for you.

Now evaluate your understanding of the lesson material by reviewing the learning objectives and taking the self-test in this study guide. Check your answers against the answer key.

According to your instructor's assignment or your own interests, choose and complete the activities from among the suggestions for extra credit. You might also consider the recommended readings listed at the end of the chapter.

Study Activities

True-False

1. T F Patients given a placebo may recover much faster than if they had not been given one.
2. T F For placebos to be effective as pain-killers, the doctor should tell the patient that the "medicine" is a placebo.
3. T F If you are given a placebo, you may feel less pain because your body is producing more endorphins.
4. T F Anton Mesmer discovered hypnosis but made no effort to investigate its causes and effects scientifically.
5. T F Mesmer thought his "cures" were the result of suggestion and imagination rather than magnetism.
6. T F Scottish physician James Braid gave the name hypnosis to mesmerism because he considered it an intense or abnormal form of sleep.
7. T F Sigmund Freud renounced hypnosis as a therapeutic tool and developed psychoanalysis.
8. T F Clark L. Hull was unable to find any trait that was a definite index of "hypnotizability."
9. T F The research of Barber and Hilgard suggests that there is a relationship between suggestibility and an active fantasy life.
10. T F Persons under the influence of hypnosis can perform feats of strength they ordinarily could not do because hypnosis enhances their physical powers.
11. T F Psychologist Martin Orne concluded that hypnotic age regression can be explained by the fact that every experience a person has is recorded indelibly deep in the brain.
12. T F Cognitive strategies of pain reduction have proven to be no better as an analgesic than drugs or hypnosis.
13. T F Fibers that carry pain messages are smaller and slower than fibers that carry touch messages.
14. T F Scientists believe that slower fibers and faster fibers interlock to close a "gate" against pain.
15. T F When your slower pain fibers send more messages to your brain than your touch fibers, your pain gate will close and you will not experience pain.

16. T F Scientists believe that the "gate" that determines whether or not you feel an incoming pain message is located atop your spinal cord.

Completion

1. Pain is a highly complex _____ experience and one we do not fully understand. No "pain center" has ever been found in the cortex and no special pain _____ organs have been found. We do know, though, that pain messages travel through the _____ cord enroute to the brain. We also know that pain messages are transmitted to the brain along slow axonic fibers that are not insulated, while touch messages travel along _____ axonic fibers that **are** insulated. Slow-fiber activity turns pain _____, while fast-fiber activity turns pain _____.

fast
off
receptor
on
psychological
spinal

2. There is no single definition of pain, nor is there any way to investigate pain _____ because it cannot be objectively _____. Thus, we have to rely on the sufferer's own _____ of what he or she is feeling. Our society controls pain mainly by _____, such as morphine. Some harmless non-drug substances, called _____, have been found to be as effective as drugs in decreasing pain in some subjects. Their analgesic properties appear to lie in one's _____ in them. Experiments have shown that, under certain conditions, placebos cause some people to produce additional amounts of natural pain-killing chemicals called _____.

drugs
belief
scientifically
description
measured
endorphins
placebos

3. Anton _____ accidentally discovered _____ in the 1700s but made no scientific investigation of its causes and effects. Later investigators claimed

they could induce hypnotized subjects to return in their minds in time to periods long before they were born, a phenomenon known as hypnotic age _____. Martin Orne and others have suggested, however, that this phenomenon represents a kind of _____ on the part of the subject. Hilgard believes that hypnosis is merely an altered state of _____, and subjects who report no pain in experiments really feel pain at some _____ level but are consciously _____ it.

suppressing
hypnosis
role-playing
Mesmer
unconscious
regression
consciousness

4. According to the Melzack-Wall theory of pain, there is a _____ in your spinal cord that can be _____ to the pain experience according to the _____ amount of neural activity occurring along the fast and slow fibers. You will feel pain if there is _____ activity in your slow fibers than there is in your fast fibers and no pain if there is _____ activity in your slow fibers than in your fast ones.

relative
less
gate
more
closed

5. Blocking of _____ at the spinal gate is one of the body's two separate systems for pain control. Though the function of the gate is innate, it is now known that it can be brought under _____ control through _____ conditioning. The other system is an emotion-_____ process which encourages the release of endorphins and _____ neural activity in the reticular system.

suppressing
input
operant
reduces
conscious

Short-Answer Questions

1. In Lesson Fourteen, entitled ''Stress,'' we examined Julian Rotter's concept of the locus of personal control. From what you learned in that lesson and this one, which would you say would be a better hypnotic subject, an internalizer or an externalizer?

2. Under what conditions do placebos work best?

3. Explain what is meant by ''cognitive strategies of pain control.''

Self-Test

(Select the one best answer.)

Objective 1: Explain the placebo effect.

1. The results of the ''double blind'' studies described in the television program seemed to prove that
    a. faith in the placebo stimulates the body to release endorphins.
    b. placebos inhibit the work of the body's natural pain-killers.
    c. the patients did not have faith in the doctors who treated them.
    d. patients should be told they are receiving a placebo.
    e. drugs are the best form of treatment for pain associated with tooth extraction.

Objective 2: Briefly describe Mesmer's, Braid's, and Freud's views of hypnosis.

2. When he accidentally discovered hypnosis, Mesmer believed that his patients were "cured" because
   a. of the power of suggestion.
   b. of the placebo effect.
   c. they were exposed to magnetism.
   d. they were in a trance-like state.

3. Scottish physician James Braid was the first to study hypnotism scientifically, pointing out that it appeared to be
   a. a disease of epidemic proportions.
   b. closely related to hysteria.
   c. useless as a therapeutic tool.
   d. a state of narrowly focused attention.
   e. an intense form of sleep.

4. After experimenting with hypnosis, Sigmund Freud
   a. declared that Mesmer's theory of magnetism is correct.
   b. renounced hypnosis as a therapeutic tool in favor of psychoanalysis.
   c. decided that hypnotic age regression is chiefly role playing.
   d. developed an accurate index of hypnotizability.
   e. concluded that everyone can be hypnotized.

Objective 3: Discuss differing interpretations of hypnosis (e.g., those of Hull, Braid, Hilgard, Baker, and Barber).

5. Barber's research on suggestibility and fantasy implies that
   a. males are far better hypnotic subjects than females because they are more suggestible.
   b. subjects who do not fantasize are better subjects for hypnosis.
   c. there is no relationship between fantasizing and susceptibility to hypnosis.
   d. there is a high correlation between fantasizing and susceptibility to hypnosis.
   e. internalizers are better hypnotic subjects than externalizers because they have a rich fantasy life.

6. Ernest Hilgard and his associates at Stanford have found that you are more responsive to hypnosis if you
   a. were reared by punitive, authoritative parents.
   b. are unlikely to become involved in imaginative experiences.
   c. continually question authority.
   d. are of lower intelligence.
   e. have narcolepsy.

7. Hilgard believes hypnosis is
    a. an abnormal or intense form of sleep.
    b. an altered state of consciousness in which consciousness is split, or "dissociated," from the body.
    c. closely connected to hysteria in extremely suggestible women patients.
    d. a parlor trick or black magic used to fool patients and observers.
    e. one of many conscious strategies for reducing the intensity of pain.

8. Braid's belief that the healing power of hypnosis proved that pain is as much a mental phenomenon as a physical one led other scientists to
    a. believe that hypnosis was much overrated.
    b. experiment with baths taken in electrically magnetized water.
    c. experiment with hypnosis in the control of pain.
    d. conclude that hypnotic "cures" were closely akin to black magic.
    e. turn to the investigation of astrophysical forces.

Objective 4: Describe some of the effects and limitations of hypnosis.

9. Recent studies of hypnosis made by the University of Kentucky's Robert Baker suggest strongly that hypnotic "age regression"
    a. is chiefly role playing by hypnotized subjects.
    b. depends entirely upon the suggestibility of the subjects.
    c. is an authentic effect of hypnosis.
    d. allows us to study past history in accurate detail.
    e. is risky because the subject may become "arrested" at an earlier age and be unable to return to the present.

Objective 3; and *Objective 5:* Compare "conscious strategies" and hypnosis as methods of dealing with pain.

10. Barber found that
    a. people could not consciously reduce pain.
    b. conscious strategies for pain reduction are not as effective as hypnosis.
    c. hypnosis is superior to mental discipline as an analgesic.
    d. conscious strategies for reducing pain are at least as effective as hypnosis.
    e. you get four unique psychological experiences from stimulating your skin—warmth, cold, pressure, and pain.

11. The experimenter is using _____ when he asks a subject to mentally dissociate himself from the pain of a hand held in extremely cold water.
    a. conscious strategy techniques
    b. hypnosis
    c. a placebo
    d. the "spinal gate" theory of pain
    e. Pavlovian conditioning techniques

12. Unlike hypnosis, cognitive strategies for pain control
    a. teach patients to consciously block pain input at the spinal gate.
    b. are more effective for internalizers than they are for externalizers in cases of chronic pain.
    c. depend on the subject's desire to please the experimenter.
    d. are described by all of the above statements.
    e. are described by only the statements in a and b.

Objective 6: Describe the biological processes involved in experiencing pain, including the "spinal gate" theory.

13. The Melzack-Wall theory of pain holds that there is a pain-control "gate" located in the
    a. cerebral cortex.
    b. spinal cord.
    c. limbic system.
    d. sympathetic nervous system.
    e. parasympathetic nervous system.

14. Of the two sensory input pathways in your spinal cord, one transmits _____ messages via _____ axonic fibers that are **insulated**; the other transmits _____ messages via _____ axonic fibers that are **not** insulated.
    a. fast, slow; pain, touch
    b. slow, fast; touch, pain
    c. touch, slow; pain, fast
    d. touch, fast; pain, slow

15. Melzack and Wall suggest that the perception of pain is controlled by closing or opening of the "spinal gate" by
    a. the particular gate the sensory inputs pass through.
    b. the relative amount of activity in fast and slow fibers.
    c. hypnosis or placebos.
    d. the body's natural pain-killers.
    e. both b and c.

16. When rubbing your bumped elbow relieves the pain, you are demonstrating
    a. the "spinal gate" theory.
    b. a conscious strategy for reducing pain.
    c. localized hypnosis.
    d. a decrease in emotional significance.
    e. the placebo effect.

17. Endorphins and other chemicals secreted by the body
    a. increase stimulus input along the fast-fiber axons.
    b. slam shut the spinal gate at the top of your spinal cord.
    c. decrease the emotional significance of painful inputs.
    d. decrease stimulus input along the slow-fiber axons.

Suggestions for Extra Credit

1. If you suffer severe headaches, back pain, some other chronic or recurring discomfort (or even a toothache on your dentist's day off), you might find it worthwhile to apply the London and Engstrom pain- control techniques outlined for you on page 433 of your text. (You could also try to help a friend or family member, if he or she is willing.) Review the techniques, then decide exactly how you will proceed, step by step. And, as Skinner would ask, what is your exact goal? Think about what kind of surroundings you would select for practicing relaxation techniques. What "tools," if any, would you use? Is time a factor in any of the four techniques? If so, how?

   Before you begin, you should review briefly what you have learned about operant conditioning. If you are really serious about learning how to cope directly with pain, read London and Engstrom's own account of their work, "Mind Over Pain," *American Health*, 1, 4 (1982): 62. As London and Engstrom recommend, be sure to keep a precise log or chart of your progress.

2. Not all pain responds to non-drug strategies, of course, and the scientists whose work you are studying in this lesson do not suggest that it does. What kinds of pain problems do you think might not yield to non-drug treatment? Advanced cancer, for example? You may be surprised to learn that the World Health Organization (WHO) complains that the management of pain in cancer patients has been largely neglected. In December 1984, pain experts from twenty-two countries called for worldwide educational programs to inform the public that cancer patients have the "right to be free of pain" and to tell cancer patients and their families that pain is not "inevitable," but is almost always controllable. The pain experts also pointed out that "drugs are still the mainstay of pain management. Used correctly (the right drug in the right dose at the right time interval), drugs are

effective in a high percentage of cancer patients." In the United States, there are a growing number of clinics that specialize in the management of pain, particularly chronic pain. Most of these are associated with universities and large medical centers. Locate and read an article that describes the techniques and successes (or failures) of one or more of these clinics. If there is a pain clinic in your area, perhaps you can obtain pamphlets or other literature that describe its work. What management techniques do they use? Are there limitations on the kinds of patients (or pain problems) they treat?

3. You will remember from Lesson Seventeen ("Memory") that the questions you ask someone about an event can actually **transform** the person's memories of what really happened. Hilgard, head of Stanford's Laboratory of Hypnosis Research, says that a hypnotist actually can make a hypnotized person believe that ideas implanted by the hypnotist are his or her own ideas. And Martin Orne, a former president of the International Society of Hypnotists, notes that what people remember under hypnosis is often entirely inaccurate. On text pages 427-428, McConnell asks what problems these findings raise about the use of hypnotism by police to "recover forgotten information." Locate and read "Investigative Hypnosis," by R. W. Dellinger, in the April 1978 issue of *Human Behavior*, page 36. Dellinger's article is a description and defense of the work of Los Angeles Police Department staff psychologist Martin Reiser in using hypnotism to "enhance the recall of both witnesses and victims of crime" and to solve some crimes. Reiser founded the Law Enforcement Hypnosis Institute and has trained and advised many other officers and court officials on the use of hypnosis in criminal investigations. Take a position on McConnell's question and write a report on your opinions.

4. For an interesting and colorful account of the experiences of a controversial medical doctor who claims to have hypnotized and treated at least 30,000 patients during his lifetime, read "Secrets of a Modern Mesmer," by Daniel Goldman in the July 1977 issue of *Psychology Today*.

Answer Key

True-False

1. T	9. T
2. F	10. F
3. T	11. F
4. T	12. F
5. F	13. T
6. T	14. F
7. T	15. F
8. T	16. T

Completion

1. psychological, receptor, spinal, fast, on, off;   2. scientifically, measured, description, drugs, placebos, belief, endorphins;   3. Mesmer, hypnosis, regression, role-playing, consciousness, unconscious, suppressing;   4. gate, closed, relative, more, less;   5. input, conscious, operant, suppressing, reduces.

Short-Answer Questions

1. Julian Rotter related the kinds of coping to each person's locus of control, which, he said, could be either internal or external. He explained that persons with an internal locus of control saw themselves as being in control of their own lives and of what happened to them, while persons with an external locus of control viewed themselves and their lives as being in the hands of God, fate, or Lady Luck. Rotter called these two groups internalizers and externalizers, respectively. Children whose parents are rigid and uncompromising are likely to feel they have no control over their own destiny and to become, therefore, externalizers. Externalizers have been conditioned to be obedient to authority (do what they are told to do), and they learn to retreat into their own imaginations and play a great many roles to escape punishment —or to **please** others. Hypnosis is considered by some psychologists to be primarily role-playing behavior.

   Recent studies by Barber, Hilgard, and others do show that the best hypnotic subjects usually have rich fantasy lives, and Barber concludes that there is a high correlation between the ability to fantasize and the ability to be hypnotized. He also notes that an ''intense desire'' to please the hypnotist is a major factor in the success of hypnotism.

2. Placebos seem to work best when patients believe in their effectiveness as a medication, when the patients to whom they are given are externalizers (look to others for relief), and when neither the patient nor the doctor (or researcher) is aware that the medication is a placebo. Research shows that placebos may actually trigger increased release of the body's natural pain-killers, the endorphins.

3. Cognitive strategies of pain control are based upon learning to activate the body's emotion-suppressing system and the input-blocking mechanisms. The first of four major techniques used by London and Engstrom teaches the patient to relax and otherwise reduce tension by deep, slow breathing—which encourages the release of endorphins and decreases the significance of painful inputs. The remaining three techniques focus on operant conditioning to train patients to close their spinal gates voluntarily before pain inputs reach the brain.

Self-Test

1. a (television program)
2. c (text pages 423-425)
3. e (text page 425; television program)
4. b (text page 425)
5. d (text page 426)
6. a (text page 426)
7. b (text page 428)
8. c (television program)
9. a (text page 427)
10. d (text page 429)
11. a (text page 428)
12. e (text pages 432-433)
13. b (text page 432)
14. d (text page 430)
15. b (text page 430; television program)
16. a (television program)
17. c (text pages 431-432)

Genetic Influences and Physical Development 19

Viewer's Guide for Program Nineteen

As you view the television program, watch for:

The film sequence of a fertilized egg dividing, then attaching itself to the uterine lining when it has grown to be a fluid-filled ball of cells called a blastula. Note also the film sequence showing the human fetus maturing.

The demonstration of an infant's reflexive responses, including blinking, the startle response, visual tracking, the head-turning response, the cheek-stroking response, the grasping reflex, the hand-to-mouth reflex, and crying. What survival value do these natural responses have? What social value?

The animated sequences showing the way in which the placenta allows the transfer of nutrients from mother to baby and demonstrating what happens when certain harmful chemicals cross the placental barrier. Certain illnesses suffered by the expectant mother and some chemicals ingested by her during pregnancy—such as German measles, narcotic drugs, and alcohol—can have harmful effects on the fetus.

The film sequence demonstrating the phenomenon of imprinting in ducks. During the first sixteen to twenty-four hours after it is hatched, the duck attaches itself emotionally to the first moving object it sees. In this film, a windup toy dog becomes the duck's "mother." Imprinting suggests that in animals, and perhaps in humans, there are "critical periods" of development when certain kinds of learning can best occur.

Preview

If you were given the opportunity to change one of your inherited characteristics or to acquire a particular natural ability, what would you choose? What would you change? Would you be taller? Slimmer? Better coordinated? Have an "eye" for color and design, or an "ear" for music?

Genetic counseling and engineering may one day offer us the opportunity to make such choices, not for ourselves, but for our children or our grandchildren. And once we are able to choose, we will be held responsible for the choices we make. What characteristics do we value most in human beings? And how do we ensure the precise combination of internal temperament and external environment to guarantee that any child's genetic potential will be realized? The story which opens and closes Chapter 17 raises a number of moral questions which will have to be faced when human genetic engineering becomes practicable.

Your genes determine your basic physical characteristics, specify your initial behavior patterns, and define your natural abilities. Thus, they give you a potential, something you can become. But the environment in which you grow up and your own intrapsychic development determine how you express your genetic potential and, indeed, how much of that potential you are willing and able to realize.

The means by which an organism moves toward its genetic potential are maturation and development. Maturation is the process by which an organism moves from infancy to adulthood, from youth to age. Development is the process by which it acquires and enhances special skills and abilities along the way. It is these processes that you will be studying in the next three lessons.

In this lesson, you will take a look at the process of human egg fertilization and fetal growth. You will see how a baby develops in the first environment, the womb, and how certain chemical substances cross the placental barrier to threaten and thwart this development. We know that the fetus is capable of learning while still in the uterus, and there is great likelihood that it also "hears" before birth. What "learned" behavior and natural reflexes does the baby then bring into the world with him or her? What skills does he or she acquire? And are there "critical periods" for the teaching and learning of these skills?

In this lesson, you will take a look at chromosomes and genes and at how they determine sex and other physical characteristics. You will learn what happens when chromosomes are abnormal or when genes are defective and how genetic counseling could be helpful to parents and prospective parents in coping with genetic defects in their children.

Learning Objectives

When you have finished viewing the program and studying your text assignments, you should be able to:

1. Recognize the role of genetic transmission in the development process.
2. Briefly outline early development from fertilization to birth.
3. List substances and conditions known to be dangerous to a developing fetus.
4. Discuss the research findings describing the effects of early training on motor development.
5. State the evidence for and against the critical-period hypothesis in human development.
6. Define and cite examples of imprinting.

Assignments

Before Viewing the Program

Read the preview at the beginning of this lesson and look over the learning objectives that precede the assignments.

Check the section "Did You Know That. . ." at the beginning of Chapter 17, "Infancy and Early Childhood: Physical and Emotional Development," and look over the subtitles for the chapter.

Read that portion of Chapter 17 which begins with the vignette on page 439 and concludes on page 455. Also read the section "Does Imprinting Exist in Humans?" (pages 459-460). As you read, note the boldfaced terms and those that are defined in the upper right corners of right-hand pages.

View Program 19, "Genetic Psychology"

After Viewing the Program

Review the text assignments.

Read through the summary at the end of the chapter. Then review all of the boldfaced terms. In particular, note the terms: XYY condition, nucleus, chromosomes, DNA, RNA, trisomy-21, identical twins, embryo, fraternal twins, fetus, placenta, prenatal learning, neonatal learning, schema, motor skill, critical-period hypothesis, imprinting.

Complete the study activities that are included here as an additional study aid for you.

Now evaluate your understanding of the lesson material by reviewing the learning objectives and taking the self-test in this study guide. Check your answers against the answer key.

According to your instructor's assignment or your own interests, choose and complete activities from among the suggestions for extra credit. You might also consider the recommended readings listed at the end of the chapter.

"I'll tell you why you're bald and I'm not. It's the genes. I read up on the genes, and, boy, do I know my genes! Take me. I got _good_ genes."

The New Yorker, November 17, 1975. Drawing by Ross; © 1975
The New Yorker Magazine, Inc.

Study Activities

Matching

Match each phrase in the column on the right with the appropriate term in the column on the left, writing the letters of the phrases in the appropriate blanks.

___ 1. XYY condition	a. nucleic acid that controls cell functioning
___ 2. chromosomes	b. messenger nucleic acid that carries instructions from cell nucleus to cytoplasm
___ 3. DNA	
___ 4. RNA	
___ 5. nucleus	c. an unusual genetic condition characterized by above-average height, early sexual maturity, severe acne, and impulsiveness
___ 6. trisomy-21	
___ 7. identical twins	
___ 8. fraternal twins	
___ 9. placenta	d. denotes three chromosomes in the twenty-first position; leads to a condition called Down's syndrome
___ 10. imprinting	
	e. center portion of the cell
	f. strings, or strands, of genes
	g. single fertilized egg
	h. the process by which some very young animals form a strong emotional attachment to the first moving object they see
	i. organ that nourishes the fetus and screens out harmful chemicals
	j. two fertilized eggs

Completion

1. Genes given you by your parents at conception helped to shape your physical development, your intellectual development, and some of your basic _____ patterns as well. Genes will continue to play a basic role throughout your life. Your _____ blueprint sets the limits for what you can do and what you will become, but it also gives you your _____ for growth and development. It does not specify what you might become, only what you _____ become. You are the product of both your _____ potential and your environmental experiences.

genetic
hereditary
can
personality
potential

2. The tiny units of heredity we call genes form _____ by coiling together in large chain-like structures. Genes and chromosomes are found in the _____ of almost every cell in your body and are made up chiefly of a nucleic acid called DNA, which controls the functions of the cell by making another nucleic acid, _____, that acts like a messenger to carry out the orders of the DNA. Every cell in your body except your _____ or sperm cells has 46 (or 23 pairs of) chromosomes. Your sex cells contain only _____ the chromosomes needed to survive and multiply.

half
RNA
chromosomes
nucleus
egg

3. You received your own unique genetic blueprint when a sperm from your father penetrated and _____ a tiny egg cell in your mother's body. The sperm and the egg cell, which are called _____ cells, each had only half the usual 46 chromosomes, but when the egg was fertilized by the sperm, their chromosomes _____ and the new cell life that was created had a normal complement of 46 chromosomes, or 23 pairs. If the sperm was a Y-type sperm you are male; if it was an _____ sperm you are female. During fertilization, however, genetic "mistakes" associated with chromosome _____ sometimes cause the new cell to receive either only one chromosome or one too many (three). Such errors result in the physical deficiencies known as Turner and Klinefelter's syndromes and trisomy-21, or Down's syndrome. These syndromes are often associated with mental and behavioral problems as well as physical ones.

sex
X-type
division
joined
fertilized

4. Because chromosomes split and recombine at _____, the number of possible combinations is endless. Each sperm and each egg is different from all other sperm and eggs; therefore, the new cell that is created when the egg is fertilized by the sperm is _____ any other. It is unique. Soon after fertilization, the new cell begins to _____ and it multiplies into cells that are similar. In about two weeks the process known as cell _____ begins and the new types of cells that are formed organize into tissues that will later become the organs and other parts of the body. In about eight weeks, the elementary outlines of most body structures have appeared. Before the mass of growing cells begins to resemble a human form, it is called an _____; after about the second or third month, it is called a _____.

unlike
embryo
differentiation
random
divide
fetus

5. The mother's placenta is the developing baby's first _____. Oxygen and food are given to the baby through the placenta, and most of the chemicals that come in contact with the developing child come through the placenta. Most harmful _____ are screened out, but if the mother is taking heavy amounts of alcohol, using narcotics, or has German measles, the unborn child can be severely retarded, malformed, and even _____ to drugs taken by the mother. Thus a developing human who has a genetic blueprint that is normal can have its potential tragically altered by the _____ even before it leaves the womb. The research also shows that fetuses can be _____ to respond to specific stimuli, and they may also be able to "hear" sounds, such as the mother's voice and heartbeat.

environment
addicted
conditioned
environment
substances

6. Thus, we arrive at birth with an innate set of behaviors known as _____ behaviors (some of which, such as sucking, are essential to survival) plus an uncertain amount of influence from the uterine environment which may include _____ behaviors. Newborns (neonates) are capable of a wide variety of behaviors. At birth, we can see, hear, move our eyes, heads, hands, and fingers, and—of course—cry. We can also distinguish _____ language, recognize our mothers, and imitate some _____ expressions within a very short time after birth.

learned
reflexive
facial
human

7. Our head and neck muscles mature and come under the control of the motor centers long before those of the legs and feet. Therefore, complex activities involving the lower parts of the body occur _____ in development than those involving the head region. Because this growth pattern is genetically determined, early training and encouragement by parents seem to have _____ effect on motor abilities. A considerable body of research seems to support the theory that there is an important and _____ time span during which the organism best learns certain skills or behaviors. This theory is known as the _____ hypothesis. A special kind of learning called _____ does occur in ducks, some birds, and some mammals soon after birth. For example, a newly hatched duck that has not yet seen its mother will become emotionally _____ to any moving object that crosses its line of vision within twenty-four hours after birth. The question of whether imprinting occurs in humans has not yet been resolved.

critical-period
attached
little
later
limited
imprinting

Short-Answer Questions

1. Explain how drugs, such as alcohol or narcotics, or a disease, such as German measles, can affect the fetus of a pregnant woman.

2. Describe the complex behaviors with which human infants are born.

3. Don Stanhope's determined efforts to teach his eleven-month-old son Rudi to walk in the television program vignette probably had nothing at all to do with the time at which Rudi actually did begin to walk. Explain why this would be true.

Self-Test

(Select the one best answer.)

Objective 1: Recognize the role of genetic transmission in the development process.

1. Your _____ determined your gender and your earliest behavior patterns, as well as both your potential and your limits for physical and mental development.
   a. chromosomes
   b. X and Y chromosome balance
   c. genes
   d. cellular feed-forward
   e. cytoplasmic RNA

2. Genes are composed chiefly of _____. They are found in the cell _____ and are strung together in strands called _____.
   a. DNA, nucleus, chromosomes
   b. chromosomes, DNA, nucleus
   c. DNA, chromosomes, nucleus
   d. nucleus, DNA, chromosomes
   e. chromosomes, nucleus, DNA

3. The sex of a child is detemined by
   a. the chromosome composition of the egg in the mother.
   b. both the egg and the mother's chromosomal pattern.
   c. the mother's diet during pregnancy.
   d. the chromosome composition of the sperm from the father.
   e. the father's diet before conception.

4. When an X-type sperm fertilizes the female egg cell, the child that is conceived will always be
   a. male.
   b. a male with female characteristics.
   c. female.
   d. an XXY male.
   e. an XYY female.

5. Research studies show that the XYY condition is found in
   a. about one-third as many women as men.
   b. disproportionately great numbers of criminally insane males.
   c. disproportionately great numbers of white males.
   d. all of the above.
   e. both b and c.

Objective 1; and *Objective 2:* Briefly outline early development from fertilization to birth.

6. A person with an XY chromosome pattern will be
   a. impulsive.
   b. male.
   c. taller than average.
   d. retarded.
   e. none of the above.

7. Trisomy-21 is a genetic defect which is caused when a chromosome fails to split and a baby develops with
   a. a single X twenty-third chromosome.
   b. a single X twenty-first chromosome.
   c. an XYY genetic defect.
   d. three twenty-first chromosomes.
   e. Klinefelter's syndrome.

8. If a child is born with an extra X twenty-third chromosome (XXY), the child will be
   a. physically female with strong male characteristics.
   b. physically male with strong female characteristics.
   c. short and fat.
   d. sexually precocious.
   e. institutionalized.

9. Which of the following statements does not describe the male child born with an extra Y chromosome (the XYY condition)?
   a. He reaches sexual maturity much earlier than normal (XY) males.
   b. He grows taller than normal males.
   c. His brain matures much sooner than that of normal males.
   d. He lacks control over his impulses.
   e. His adrenal glands secrete an abnormal amount of testosterone.

Objective 2

10. When the male sperm penetrates the female egg cell, _____ has occurred and _____ is soon triggered.
    a. cell differentiation, fertilization
    b. cell division, fertilization
    c. fertilization, cell division
    d. fertilization, cell differentiation
    e. cell division, cell differentiation

11. At the precise moment of _____, a complete genetic blueprint, or set of plans, was created for you.
    a. fertilization
    b. cell division
    c. cell differentiation
    d. chromosomal split
    e. birth

12. About two weeks after fertilization, _____ begins to occur.
    a. cell division
    b. cell differentiation
    c. RNA production
    d. DNA production
    e. morning sickness

13. The human fetus has developed the rudiments of all its body organs
    a. within twenty-four hours after conception.
    b. by about the fifth month of pregnancy.
    c. before the formation of the ectoderm, the endoderm, and the mesoderm.
    d. by about the eighth week of pregnancy.
    e. when cell differentiation begins.

14. As the embryo and fetus develop, the placenta screens out
    a. most of the substances in the mother's blood that might be harmful.
    b. narcotic drugs, such as morphine, in the mother's blood.
    c. enkephalin, the "natural pain-killer."
    d. excessive amounts of alcohol in the mother's blood.
    e. different chemicals secreted by a mother who has German measles.

Objective 3: List substances and conditions known to be dangerous to a developing fetus.

15. Excessive drinking by the mother during pregnancy
    a. will not affect the baby because of "placental protection."
    b. will turn the baby into an alcoholic.
    c. may help the mother to relax during labor.
    d. may deprive the fetus of oxygen and thus cause brain damage.
    e. may cause toxemia of pregnancy.

16. If a baby is born abnormally small, it may be because the
    a. chromosomes split too soon.
    b. chromosomes failed to split.
    c. fetus had German measles.
    d. fetus became addicted to drugs.
    e. fetus was malnourished.

Objective 4: Discuss the research findings describing the effects of early training on motor development.

17. Parents who spend time teaching their infants to walk at an early age
    a. accelerate the child's motor development.
    b. raise athletically superior children.
    c. tend to harm the child psychologically.
    d. tend to harm the child physically.
    e. probably do not accelerate the child's motor development.

State the evidence for and against the critical-period hypothesis in human development.

18. The critical-period hypothesis
    a. refers to the first three months of embryonic development.
    b. refers to the last six to eight weeks of fetal development.
    c. states that the organism's readiness to respond determines the best time for learning to occur.
    d. adequately explains the sequence of motor development for both humans and animals.
    e. suggests that trisomy-21 usually occurs in mothers over forty.

19. Evidence that a newly hatched duckling will accept a mechanical toy dog or a human as its "mother" tends to
    a. support the critical-period hypothesis.
    b. refute the theory of imprinting.
    c. prove that ducks learn best when young.
    d. prove that imprinting can be reversed.
    e. refute the critical-period hypothesis.

20. According to the television program, there may be critical periods in human development which
    a. apply only to the learning of foreign languages.
    b. govern the early acquisition of certain reflexes, such as sucking.
    c. are, in reality, stages in motor development.
    d. are longer and less time specific than in birds and other animals.
    e. do not exist.

Objective 6: Define and cite examples of imprinting.

21. The special form of learning called imprinting
    a. is rare in ducks and geese.
    b. is a photographic means of studying psychological subjects.
    c. is the process by which very young animals form a strong emotional attachment to the first moving object they see.
    d. is widespread among babies of primitive cultures.
    e. confirms the critical-period hypothesis with regard to human development.

22. If a newborn duckling begins to follow a large cat and behaves as if the cat is its mother, we can assume that
    a. the duckling has Klinefelter's syndrome.
    b. the duckling has imprinted on the cat.
    c. the duckling's genetic blueprint is defective.
    d. the duckling will never accept its real mother.
    e. the duckling has lost its mother.

Suggestions for Extra Credit

1. Early in text Chapter 17, author McConnell reminds you that the old "nature-nurture" controversy is one of four major theoretical issues that underlie the study of developmental psychology. You were, in fact, introduced to this thorny issue at the very beginning of this course and reminded of it at frequent intervals. This is perhaps a good time for you to pause long enough to analyze and collect your own opinions on this issue. You will, of course, confront the problem again before you complete this course, but you have already been exposed to the theories and findings of dozens of psychologists and other scientists.

   As we asked in earlier lessons, do your genes (your heredity) determine all of your thoughts and behaviors, or are you mainly the product of all your experiences and all you have learned from your environment? If you are interested in assessing your thoughts at this juncture, you might begin by taking a very quick look back at Lessons Two, Three, Four, and Five to refresh your memory. Before organizing (and defending) your thoughts in a brief paper, you might read "The Instinct to Learn," by J. L. and C. G. Gould, in the May 1981 issue of *Science 81*, pp. 44-50. As you might guess from the title, the Goulds take an "interactionist" position.

2. There is currently considerable activity in the area of prenatal (in utero) learning, but, so far, the studies are mixed in their emphasis. Nonetheless, what the investigators are finding is "that every time they look for fetal learning, it is there." This is the conclusion of Gina Kolata, reached after a survey and analysis of current research. As noted in your text, one thing fetuses learn is to distinguish their mothers' voices and to prefer one Dr. Seuss story over another. Prenatal learning research offers significant implications for the study of fetal development, particularly in the case of premature birth. Kolata's article, "Studying Learning in the Womb," can be found on pages 302 and 303 in the July 20, 1984, issue of *Science*.

3. Suppose you are considering having a child and you learn that you or your spouse, and perhaps both, are carriers of a serious genetic defect that your child has a 50-50 chance of inheriting. What do you do? Play "roulette," then cross your fingers during pregnancy? Suppose you or your spouse discovers, **after** becoming pregnant, that you carry defective genes which are certain to damage your child. Do you abort—or play roulette again and hope for the best? Then, finally, suppose you learn that the fetus has a serious handicap and likely will be born under sentence of retardation, physical handicap, suffering, and perhaps even death. Do you abort and try again?

   As Yvonne Baskin points out grimly in her 1984 book, *The Gene Doctors: Medical Genetics at the Frontier*, published by William Morrow and Company, Inc., these are precisely the decisions parents must make as well as the only options available to them when faced with these situations. Baskin reports that medical science now can screen for 200 hereditary diseases and at least 100 chromosome defects **before birth**, but medical science still cannot "fix" what is found. Gene therapy is, however, medicine's next frontier. Baskin's book is at once a comprehensive report on the progress and status of prenatal screening, genetic engineering, and a careful examination of the ethical and moral issues involved in gene manipulation. Baskin's book also has an excellent bibliography in her "Source Notes." Read and write a report on this book.

Answer Key

Matching

1. c	6. d
2. f	7. g
3. a	8. j
4. b	9. i
5. e	10. h

Completion

1. personality, genetic, potential, can, hereditary;   2. chromosomes, nucleus, RNA, egg, half;   3. fertilized, sex, joined, X-type, division;   4. random, unlike, divide, differentiation, embryo, fetus;   5. environment, substances, addicted, environment, conditioned;   6. reflexive, learned, human, facial; 7. later, little, limited, critical-period, imprinting, attached.

Short-Answer Questions

1. The mother's placenta blocks out most substances in her blood that could cause harm to the fetus. Alcohol is an exception, however. In 1982, research studies showed that the fetus's blood supply can be shut off temporarily if the mother drinks as many as three to five drinks. About one child in a thousand is born with a set of physical defects known as "fetal alcohol syndrome," which includes brain damage, stunted IQ, and clumsy physical coordination. For these reasons, the U.S. Surgeon General has issued a warning advising pregnant women to avoid alcohol entirely. Narcotic drugs, such as morphine, can pass through the placenta and cause the fetus to be addicted before birth. At birth, such a child suffers serious withdrawal symptoms. German measles can cause the expectant mother's body to secrete different chemicals than usual, and either the chemicals or the measles germs could infiltrate the placenta. If this happens during the third

month of pregnancy, deafness, cataracts, and severe mental retardation of the child may occur. Malnutrition in the mother can also mean a malnourished child.

2. Human infants are born with an array of reflexive behaviors, many of which are essential to survival. These include the sucking reflex; crying; the startle response, which includes blinking, throwing up the hands, and turning the head away from danger or toward a source of noise; the ability to see clearly; turning in the direction of touch stimuli; and clutching objects placed within the hands. As you learned in previous lessons, a newborn can recognize its mother's face shortly after birth and soon show some ability to perceive depths. Recent research seems to indicate that the fetus can also hear some sounds before birth and, after birth, the infant can distinguish human language from artificial language or sounds, recognize its mother's voice, and imitate facial expressions. As the infant matures, it develops more complex reactions that are the product of both heredity (the genetic blueprint) and environmental learning.

3. Don Stanhope's efforts probably had nothing to do with Rudi's walking because genetic schedules govern most physical development. Head and neck muscles of the growing child mature much sooner than those of the legs and feet. Therefore, such complex activities as walking are mastered later than activities involving the upper part of the body. Most children begin to walk between twelve to eighteen months after birth, and parental training has little or no effect in speeding up the process. However, some environmental influences can and do have other effects. For example, children who are encouraged by parental attitudes will be more active physically and more outgoing in exploring their environments. Special skills, such as skating or playing an instrument, also require special training and practice.

Self-Test

1. c (television program)
2. a (text page 445; television program)
3. d (text page 446)
4. c (text page 446; television program)
5. e (text page 447)
6. b (text pages 447, 470; television program)
7. d (text pages 448, 470)
8. b (text page 447)
9. c (text pages 447-448)
10. c (text pages 445-446, 449; television program)
11. a (television program)
12. b (text page 449; television program)

13. d (television program)
14. a (text pages 449-470; television program)
15. d (text page 450; television program)
16. e (text pages 450, 470; television program)
17. e (text page 451; television program)
18. c (text pages 451-452, 470)
19. a (text pages 451-452; television program)
20. d (television program)
21. c (text pages 451-452, 459-460; television program)
22. b (text pages 451-452; television program)

Emotional Development 20

Viewer's Guide for Program Twenty

As you view the television program, watch for:

The surrogate mothers designed by Harry and Margaret Harlow for their laboratory-raised infant monkeys. Not only did these substitute mothers fill the need of the babies for "contact comfort," they also enabled the Harlows to observe what maternal qualities the young animals found most appealing.

Close-ups of infant monkeys behaving much like newborn humans and of monkeys displaying human-like behavior disturbances when they are isolated and deprived of contact and stimulation by other monkeys. Also note explanations that the Harlows' extensive experiments with monkeys are very important to the study of human emotional development because monkeys seem to have the same emotional structure as humans, and they react to similar situations in similar ways.

Foundlings, ages six to twelve months, who were placed in institutions, then moved from institution to institution as often as six or seven times while they were still toddlers. The results you see are what some psychologists call "anaclitic depression."

Scenes of new approaches to childbirth based on recognition of the newborn's need for sensory stimulation. Studies indicate that immediate and prolonged physical contact with the mother, or primary caretaker, is not only reassuring to the infant but may be essential for normal mental and emotional development.

Glimpses of new fathers nurturing their babies and providing support for the young mothers.

Preview

What is love? Love, like death, is an area of human experience that is seldom studied scientifically. Love is, in part, an internal feeling or emotional "process." This aspect of love has been described with eloquence and erudition by poets and pundits. But, while their descriptions have done much to enhance our delight, they have done little to increase our understanding.

To be sure, love **is** an internal state, but it also is a response (or ways of responding) to persons or objects in the environment. As is all human behavior, love is shaped by the interaction of biology, intrapsychic aspects, and one's environment, but we do not yet know **which** aspects of emotional development are governed primarily by genes and which are shaped more by the mind and the world about us.

We do know that loving **behaviors** are conditioned in response to satisfaction and reward—or to pain, punishment, and lack of reinforcement; they increase with the one, decrease with the other. We therefore can study and measure these behaviors objectively, as we can all observable behavior. We can't, of course, deprive humans of love to observe the effects, but we can observe the behaviors of persons who have been so deprived by circumstances. And, as you will see for yourself in this lesson, experiments with monkeys in the laboratory tell us a great deal about emotional development under varying conditions.

We know, for example, that parental love is not pure instinct, as is often thought, but it does begin with a hormonally based predisposition and **develops** into an attachment (or "bond") which is shaped as much by the response of the infant to the mother as it is by maternal behavior and input from the environment. Maternal behavior, in turn, is shaped in part by the mother's own childhood experiences. You will learn that poor nurturance, or the lack of nurturance, in human and animal infants can distort social and emotional development and is sometimes associated with psychotic behaviors.

In this lesson, you will also consider some thoughts and findings about how love can, in many instances, repair such damage.

Learning Objectives

When you have finished viewing the program and studying your text assignments, you should be able to:

1. Identify the significance of the "nature-nurture" and "mind-body" controversies to emotional development.
2. Describe the Harlow "surrogate mother" experiments and tell what factors were found to be important for explaining an infant's attraction to a mother.
3. Describe the importance of "contact comfort" and nurturance for human emotional development.
4. Describe the importance of peer relationships to monkeys and humans.
5. Cite evidence against the proposition that loving parental behavior is instinctive (innate).
6. Describe the effects of the presence or absence of the father on child development.

Assignments

Before Viewing the Program

Read the preview at the beginning of this lesson and look over the learning objectives that precede the assignments.

Check the section "Did You Know That . . ." at the beginning of Chapter 17 in the text, and look over the subtitles for the chapter.

Read Chapter 17, beginning with "Emotional Development," page 456, and review pages 443-445. As you read, note the boldfaced terms and concepts that appear in the text and are defined in the upper right corners of right-hand pages. Use the accompanying definitions or descriptions to increase your knowledge or refresh your memory concerning these terms.

View Program 20, "Emotional Development"

After Viewing the Program

Review the text assignments.

Read through the summary at the end of Chapter 17 and consider the thought questions in the chapter. Then to aid your understanding of the materials presented in this lesson, review the boldfaced terms and concepts. In particular, note these terms carefully: primate, surrogate, contact comfort, psychotic, anaclitic relationship, anaclitic depression, bonding process, nurturance, infant-mother love, peers, paternal love, deprivation, plateau, Down's syndrome.

Complete the study activities included here as an additional study aid for you.

Now evaluate your understanding of the lesson material by reviewing the learning objectives and taking the self-test in this study guide. Check your answers against the answer key.

According to your instructor's assignment or your own interests, choose and complete activities from among the suggestions for extra credit. You might also consider the recommended readings listed at the end of the chapter.

Study Activities

True-False

1. T F The responses typically seen between a mother and her newborn child appear to be genetically determined behaviors.
2. T F Love is an emotional bond that is not subject to objective study in the laboratory.
3. T F Differences between maternal and paternal parenting behaviors are mainly culturally determined.
4. T F Studies of monkeys can tell us very little about loving behavior in humans.
5. T F Most recent studies have shown that boys raised without a father tend to have difficulty in being assertive.
6. T F Girls apparently need the presence of an adult male in their homes to help them learn appropriate responses to males.
7. T F Over a period of time, Harlow's socially isolated male monkeys showed increasingly normal behavior after spending time with normal infant female monkeys who were younger.
8. T F According to the Harlows, the first quality an infant monkey seeks in a mother is her warmth.
9. T F Research shows that retardation in Down's syndrome children may be the fault of environmental factors as much as biological or hereditary determinants.
10. T F Researchers agree that imprinting and maternal-infant bonding are really the same thing.

Completion

1. Difficulties in trying to study human emotions are compounded by some familiar problems: Do physical reactions or mental experiences dominate

emotional development? Does a child's heredity bestow all his or her potential emotional responses on him or her at birth, allowing only a minor role for influences from the environment? You will recognize these as the so-called _____ and _____ controversies. They can be re-combined for purposes of this study, thus becoming the "body-nature" and "mind-nurture" perspectives. Which of these positions is taken determines how you _____ and treat other people. If you believe that you were born with your set of emotional responses complete at birth and thereafter you merely reshape these _____ responses, then you have adopted the _____ position; if you believe that your emotions at birth were under the control of neural activity in your lower brain, but that somewhere along the way your cortex took command, making you an active participant in your own development, then you subscribe to the _____ position.

innate
mind-nurture
body-nature
mind-body
nature-nurture
perceive

2. We do not yet know which aspects of emotional development are controlled more by genes and _____ physical responses and which aspects come more under the control of your _____ and your environment. But numerous research studies, such as those of Margaret and Harry Harlow with monkeys at the University of Wisconsin, tell us a great deal about loving behaviors in primates. The Harlows found that infant monkeys would cling to, and develop a strong attachment for, an artificial mother, called a _____ mother, if neither their own mothers nor other adult female substitutes were present. During the first two weeks of life, the _____ of the surrogate seemed most important to the infant monkeys. After the first few weeks, Harlow noted that touch seemed more crucial to the infants, a factor which he called _____ comfort. Harlow concluded that the artificial mother monkeys gave the infants _____ and security.

confidence
surrogate
contact
innate
warmth
mind

3. When Harlow removed a substitute mother from an infant monkey, the infant immediately showed signs of distress. Spitz found similar behavior in human infants deprived of contact with their mothers. After a few weeks, the infants withdrew and became totally passive, a behavior which Spitz described as anaclitic _____. Other studies have suggested that there is a relationship between poor _____ in childhood and child _____ and psychotic behaviors in adult life.

nurturance
abuse
depression

4. The Harlow studies seem to show that the infant-parent relationship helps the child to develop _____ about the world and stimulates it to grow physically and emotionally. When and if female monkeys lacking in infant-parent experience become pregnant and give birth, they become poor mothers who frequently _____ their offspring. These studies suggest that the so-called _____ instinct is critically affected by experiences of the female organism with its own mother. The infant organism must also develop peer _____. Only from normal peer relationships can the infant progress to normal sexual adjustments and from there to a stage of normal parental behavior. Infant monkeys who do not _____ with peers show excessive aggression and other types of _____ social behaviors. These monkeys also never developed the _____ necessary for successful sexual relationships.

abuse
inappropriate
maternal
expectancies
relationships
behaviors
interact

5. Recent data suggests that fathers contribute _____ to the child's emotional growth, particularly in the role of _____. Fathers are as capable of nurturance as mothers, and the differences in maternal and paternal behaviors are largely a matter of _____. Studies of paternal deprivation are inconclusive, though at least one seems to show that father-daughter _____ during childhood help teach girls how to respond appropriately to men when they reach puberty.

playmate
relationships
significantly
culture

Short-Answer Questions

1. Why are the mind-body and nature-nurture problems important to the study of human emotionality? Give an example.

2. Discuss the role and significance of consistent parental response in the emotional development of the child.

3. Remembering what you learned about imprinting in Lesson Nineteen and about infant-mother bonding in this lesson, how would you answer the question: Does imprinting occur in humans? (See Suggestions for Extra Credit.)

Self-Test

(Select the one best answer.)

Objective 1: Identify the significance of the ''nature-nurture'' and ''mind-body'' controversies to emotional development.

1. Theorists who take the body-nature perspective tend to
    a. believe you actively participate in your own emotional development.
    b. believe you learn to change your thoughts and feelings **voluntarily**.
    c. believe that you possess a complete repertory of emotional responses at birth and do not develop **new** ones.
    d. believe that you **learn** to alter your environment as you develop.
    e. deny all of the above statements.

2. Which of the following statements is **not** true?
    a. Mind-nurture theorists believe that emotions of the newborn are controlled by neural activity in the lower brain.
    b. Body-nature positionists believe that you consciously and actively help to shape your own emotional development.
    c. Mind-nurture theorists believe that you create new emotions as you grow.
    d. Body-nature positionists believe that you are a passive recipient of whatever your genes and your environment hand out.

3. Current research shows that mental retardation associated with a Down's syndrome child can be
    a. overcome to a great extent if we change our perception of the child as a helpless victim of genetic fate.
    b. overcome only if we view the child as a helpless victim of genetic fate.
    c. treated effectively only with specific drugs.
    d. treated most effectively with institutional care.
    e. caused by factors other than chromosomal defects.

Objective 2: Describe the Harlow ''surrogate mother'' experiments and tell what factors were found to be important for explaining an infant's attraction to a mother.

4. On the basis of his studies with monkeys, Harlow concluded that love is best understood as a function of
    a. instinct.
    b. developmental stages.
    c. the infant's nutrition.
    d. basic biological needs.
    e. sexual needs.

5. When they were first born, Harlow's motherless monkeys clung first to surrogates with
    a. warm bodies and milk.
    b. cloth bodies and milk.
    c. cool bodies made of wire.
    d. bodies made of cool cloth.
    e. warm milk and cool bodies.

6. After the first few weeks of life, Harlow's baby monkeys were more interested in mothers
    a. that provided warmth.
    b. made of a particular kind of plastic.
    c. that gave them physical contact.
    d. that fed them when they were hungry.
    e. built with the ability to rock them.

7. Harlow's "surrogate-mother" experiments would be most likely to yield objective evidence about love in
    a. parent-child relations.
    b. adult males.
    c. adult females.
    d. adolescent monkeys.
    e. lower animals.

Objective 3: Describe the importance of "contact comfort" and nurturance for human emotional development.

8. The "contact comfort" given infant monkeys by surrogate mothers appeared to be rewarding to the babies because it
    a. changed the physical development of their brains.
    b. gave them feelings of trust and confidence.
    c. gave them warmth and food.
    d. helped them to love other monkeys.
    e. compensated them for maternal deprivation.

9. Violent tendencies in adult humans seem related to
    a. mistreatment by a "monster" surrogate mother.
    b. being reared with peers but no mother.
    c. poor nurturance or social deprivation.
    d. infant-parent bonding.
    e. abnormal brain development.

Objective 4: Describe the importance of peer relationships to monkeys and humans.

10. Monkeys that lack skill in adult sexual behaviors probably
    a. were raised in social isolation.
    b. were maternally deprived.
    c. were reared by a surrogate mother.
    d. suffered anaclitic depression as infants.
    e. have defective brain development.

Objective 4; and *Objective 5:* Cite evidence against the proposition that loving parental behavior is instinctive (innate).

11. Monkeys reared without interaction with other monkeys show all of the following abnormalities except
    a. stereotyped behaviors.
    b. excessive aggression toward other monkeys.
    c. inability to respond sexually.
    d. abusive treatment of offspring.
    e. learning deficiencies.

Objective 5

12. Female monkeys reared in isolation prior to being bred will often abuse their offspring cruelly because
    a. their behavior is stereotyped in infancy.
    b. they simply do not know how to treat other monkeys.
    c. they are victims of anaclitic depression.
    d. such behavior is instinctual for most animals.
    e. they are mentally retarded and cannot learn normally.

13. The fact that some of Harlow's monkeys who were motherless themselves were able to take adequate care of their second babies (if not of their first) demonstrates
    a. that anaclitic depression can be cured.
    b. that maternal behavior is largely instinctive.
    c. a lack of physical affectional stimulation.
    d. the importance of learning in maternal behavior.
    e. the importance of peer interaction.

Objective 6: Describe the effects of the presence or absence of the father on child development.

14. Which one of the following statements is false?
    a. Daughters of divorced mothers seek more attention and praise from males.
    b. Daughters of divorced mothers have more noticeable behavior problems.
    c. Daughters of divorced mothers appear to be more openly receptive to males.
    d. Daughters of widowed mothers seem less receptive to males.
    e. Young girls need an adult male from whom to learn appropriate responses toward men when they reach puberty.

15. According to some psychologists, fathers
    a. are motivated by instinct in treatment of their babies.
    b. are not as capable of nurturing behavior as are mothers.
    c. do not contribute significantly to the child's emotional growth.
    d. differ innately from mothers in parenting behaviors.
    e. contribute significantly to the child's emotional development in the role of playmate.

Suggestions for Extra Credit

1. Family violence has become America's national scandal. As the magazine *Parents* noted in December 1984, "if family violence were a communicable disease, such as swine flu, the government would declare it an epidemic." Americans are more likely to be killed, injured, physically attacked, or emotionally abused by someone related to them, often **in their own homes**, than by strangers or outside the home. *Parents* reports that research indicates that at least sixteen million Americans are assaulted each year by members of their families, but researchers believe that these statistics only hint at much more extensive violence that goes unreported. Parents and relatives beat, kick, starve, bite, stab, shoot, burn, kill, and heap verbal cruelty on children. Children throw things, shove, hit parents and grandparents with objects, kick or slap, threaten or kill with guns, knives, and clubs. Siblings abuse siblings. With the possible exception of death itself, the worst of these tragic and sorry behaviors is the **sexual abuse** of children. According to a report in the March 1985 issue of *Psychology Today*, as many as 250,000 children are sexually assaulted in their homes each year, and 75 percent of the assaults are by fathers on their own daughters.

The situation is indeed so bad that in 1983 President Reagan appointed a special task force to study ways to help cope with abuse of spouses, children, and the elderly. The task force was to make a public report on its findings and recommendations. Try to determine whether the task force has completed its work and has issued a report. If so, obtain a copy and report on the work of the group, especially recommendations for coping with the problem.

2. There are, of course, many books and articles that approach the distressing subject of violence and abuse. Some you may wish to read include: "Violent Families," by Roberta Roesch, page 74, *Parents*, and "Emotional Abuse," by Nicholas Putnam, M. D., in the same issue of *Parents*, page 77. Putnam observes that psychological abuse may be the "common pathway" to all other forms of child abuse. Both articles take a studied approach to causes and examine ways to help the situation. Others worth your time include: "Fathers and Daughters: The Broken Bond," *Psychology Today*, March 1985, page 10, and "Somebody Help Me! I'm Going to Do Something Awful to My Kids," *Family Circle*, August 13, 1985, page 48. You may also want to look up and select other articles or books that address the problem of family violence and abuse. Some of the causes of such violence were suggested in the lesson you've just completed. Are they the same as some causes noted in these articles? (Note the questions McConnell asks on text page 465: "What does the Harlows' research tell us about possible causes of child abuse in humans? What kind of maternal 'model' did the motherless monkeys have when they were young?") In view of your reading, together with what you have learned from the lesson, why do you think this kind of behavior has reached such shocking proportions? What are some specific things you or others among your family, friends, or community might do about it?

3. If you or someone you know or love needs help with a problem related to abuse or other violence—or you wish to volunteer to help someone—write or call the National Coalition against Domestic Violence, 1500 Massachusetts Avenue, N.W., Suite 35, Washington, D.C. 20005.

4. In the summer of 1985, the Marvel Comics Group began publishing a new comic strip, called "Spider-Man and Power Pack," which is designed to teach children about sexual abuse and how to prevent it. The new strip is sponsored by the National Committee for Prevention of Child Abuse (NCPCA), has been endorsed by the National Education Association, and is reviewed by child abuse experts before publication. Copies of the comic book can be had for a tax-free donation of $1.00 per copy (check or money order), which you send, with your name and address, to "Spider-Man and Power Pack," P.O. Box 94283, Chicago, Ill., 60690. If you are interested, you might obtain copies to give to children, grandchildren, or children of friends. After reviewing a copy, you might want to spearhead a small project and work with others to obtain and distribute copies of "Spider Man" in your neighborhood, church, school, workplace, and so on.

5. It isn't exactly news that what goes on in our minds can affect the health of our bodies; we know, after all, that tension causes headaches and worry irritates ulcers. For some time, psychologists and physicians have suspected that there is a mind-body connection with cancer. Writing in the August 13, 1985, issue of *Family Circle*, page 28, Dr. Bruce Hensel, an internist who teaches at UCLA, reports that current data tends to support the hypothesis that mental attitudes, thoughts, and feelings play a role in susceptibility to cancer, just as do genetics, diet, smoking, and environmental conditions. Dr. Hensel quotes studies that show a disproportionate number of cancer patients are people who seem to live their lives in what he calls an ''emotional crouch,'' feeling worried, pessimistic, and helpless to change things.

The good news is that it is a risk factor we can do something about, he says. (Dr. Hensel is also the medical host for the television program ''Alive and Well.'') What Dr. Hensel means is that doctors and psychologists have constructed a ''Type C Personality'' test which measures proneness to cancer, as doctors some years ago proposed a ''workaholic Type A,'' who is prone to heart attacks, and a ''laid-back Type B'' who isn't. Fortunately, Type C persons can change their feelings and behaviors and they respond well to therapy, according to Dr. Hensel. (The Type A and B profiles are controversial and widely debated.)

The Type C questionnaire, excerpted from Dr. Hensel's article, is printed in this exercise, along with instructions for using and interpreting it. If you wish to experiment with the questionnaire as a way of learning about yourself as well as about the validity and effectiveness of such ''typing,'' you should read Dr. Hensel's entire article, then follow his instructions after taking the quiz. Write a detailed report about your experiences with this exercise and your feelings about it.

Type C Questionnaire

Answer true or false to the following twenty statements as honestly as you can.
1.   T F   I have difficulty showing anger.
2.   T F   I often feel overwhelmed by my problems.
3.   T F   I often lie in bed in the morning feeling depressed, thinking it's just not worth it to get up.
4.   T F   I have trouble confronting people when I think they've hurt me.
5.   T F   When I fail at something, I blame myself for a long time afterward.
6.   T F   When I make plans, I usually assume they will be canceled or turn out badly.
7.   T F   If I have a symptom such as a cough or a pain, I will delay going to the doctor, hoping it will go away.
8.   T F   When I have a symptom that doesn't go away, I assume it can't be cured, so I avoid telling the doctor about it.

9.   T F   I often feel alienated, separated, or different from other people.
10.   T F   I put on a "happy face" even when I feel unhappy.
11.   T F   I tend to have few close relationships.
12.   T F   I feel as if I can do little to change my life.
13.   T F   When I have an argument, I usually feel guilty.
14.   T F   I sometimes think that life is just not worth living.
15.   T F   As a child, I often felt lonely or alienated from my family.
16.   T F   When a disappointment occurs, I tend to dwell on it for a long period of time.
17.   T F   I would rather not attempt a really difficult task than run the risk of failing at it.
18.   T F   I often deal with stressful situations by having a drink or two, or by taking tranquilizers.
19.   T F   I pride myself on being in control and don't reveal my true feelings to anyone.
20.   T F   When I'm unhappy or depressed, I feel I have no one I can talk to.

If you answered "true" to more than fourteen of these statements, you're probably a Type C personality and need to make a conscientious effort to change your ways of dealing with emotional stress, anger, and disappointment. If you answered "true" to between seven and fourteen of the statements, you should be alert to your Type C tendencies, though you're probably doing a good job of keeping them in check. If you answered "true" to fewer than seven statements, you're probably not a Type C at all, but perhaps you can help someone you love who is.

If you think you fit the Type C profile, don't panic; you can get rid of most of the Type C tendencies by practicing these techniques:

Study your responses. Periodically ask yourself these questions about each one: Have I done anything to resolve that tendency or situation? If you have trouble getting started, consider going for professional help; you may simply need a few sessions with an expert to get you on the right track.

Learn to open up.

Set up family meetings on a regular basis to discuss everyday difficulties. Consider seeking professional family counseling, if needed, especially in times of crisis.

Practice stress reduction.

Try not to isolate yourself from other people.

Learn to forgive yourself. If you make a mistake, learn from the experience, then let yourself off the hook. You'd do that for someone else, wouldn't you?

Answer Key

True-False

1. F
2. F
3. T
4. F
5. F

6. T
7. T
8. T
9. T
10. F

Completion

1. mind-body, nature-nurture, perceive, innate, body-nature, mind-nurture;
2. innate, mind, surrogate, warmth, contact, confidence;   3. depression,
nurturance, abuse;   4. expectancies, abuse, maternal, relationships, interact,
inappropriate, behaviors;   5. significantly, playmate, culture, relationships.

Short-Answer Questions

1. According to McConnell, the study of emotionality requires that we do so
   within a framework built from the mind-body problem since we must decide
   whether to emphasize physical reactions or mental experiences. (Does the
   mind control the body or vice versa?) But, when considering the
   development of emotional responses in children, we also must contend with
   the nature-nurture "thorn." Those who emphasize the physical dominance
   of emotions (the body-nature theorists) believe that emotional reactions are
   chiefly inherited and are the result of animal instincts. We are born with a set
   of undifferentiated emotional responses which are shaped and reshaped by
   contact with others, but we cannot originate new emotions. We are, then,
   passive recipients of our genetic and environmental worlds.
   Those who emphasize mental experiences (the mind-nurture position)
   believe that emotions once were controlled by neural activity in the lower
   brain, but that with growth and development, the cortex takes over, and we
   actively participate in changing and directing our emotions and thoughts.
   Whatever position we take determines both how we perceive other people
   and how we treat them—and thus we can drastically influence the course of
   some lives. For example, until recently, most psychologists assumed Down's
   syndrome children were doomed to suffer physical deformities and mental
   handicaps because of damage from defective chromosomes. However,
   recent work with these children shows conclusively that medical experts
   can correct some of the physical deficiencies previously thought to be
   untreatable, and special programs of intensive stimulation during early
   childhood can result in enormous "jumps" in IQ scores.

2. Sensory stimulation enables the infant to build up psychological expectations about what its environment is like. Much of this input about what the world is like comes usually from the child's mother or a substitute mother-figure. If what the child learns is pleasant and satisfying, and if the parents respond to the child with consistent behavior patterns, the child rapidly builds a strong emotional attachment that serves as a base for learning to predict and control the environment and its own behavior as it grows up. Mothers or fathers who are inconsistent in their response—perhaps loving the child one day, punishing it the next, and later ignoring it—will prevent the child from knowing what to expect and from finding consistent ways of satisfying its needs.

3. The question is not yet resolved, and the only conclusion that can be drawn is that there is no clear evidence that imprinting takes place in humans, though there is considerable evidence that it does occur in a number of animals, including sheep. Scientists do not agree, either, that an event such as "bonding" exists. Many psychologists, including Klaus and Kennell (whose writings are noted in your text), insist that there is a critical period in the first hour or so of an infant's life during which an infant-mother bond is formed which is vital to both mother and baby. Many doctors now advocate providing time immediately after birth for the mother to cradle her child and facilitate bonding. Despite these and other data, however, other researchers, such as Michael Lamb, author of the 1982 book, *The Role of the Father in Child Development*, claim that "bonding" research is seriously flawed and "shows no clear evidence of lasting effect of early physical contact between mother and infant." He also points out that most adoptive mothers are at least as loving as "bonded" mothers.

Self-Test

1. c (text pages 456, 468-469)
2. b (text pages 456, 468-469)
3. a (text pages 468-469)
4. b (text pages 460-465; television program)
5. a (text page 461; television program)
6. c (text pages 461-462; television program)
7. a (text pages 460-463; television program)
8. b (text pages 461-462; television program)
9. c (text page 463; television program)
10. a (text page 465; television program)
11. e (text pages 464-465; television program)
12. b (text page 465; television program)
13. d (text page 465; television program)
14. b (text page 467)
15. e (text pages 465-466)

Cognitive Development 21

Viewer's Guide for Program Twenty-one

As you view the television program, watch for:

Film footage of infants and children who seem to be functioning at each of Piaget's four stages of mental development. As you learn more about Piaget's theory of cognitive development, try to decide whether you think children really function exclusively on one level at a time.

Lana, a chimpanzee who has been taught to construct sentences in an artificial symbol language called Yerkish and now uses it to express all of her needs and many of her feelings. Research in language learning in chimpanzees and other primates has taught us a great deal about human language patterns.

Individual children being interviewed by psychologists to determine the stage each has reached in his or her cognitive development. Why does the little girl think the tall, thin glass holds more than the short, squat glass? In Piagetian terms, what is she unable to "conserve"? Why is the boy John able to solve the "riddle" of the birds and animals? What intellectual skills are being demonstrated by the teenagers who argue ethical and moral issues of immigration of minorities to the United States? Can you identify which of Piaget's four stages of intellectual development all of these youngsters have probably reached?

Preview

What was your mind doing before you learned to speak? Do you remember? Probably not. Some psychologists believe that it is language that allows us to remember past events. What was your mind doing before it learned to think, to reason? And how does a mind become a reasoning one? At what age can a child **say**, with Descartes, "I think, therefore I am" and **understand** what has been said? Along what path does the mind journey between saying and understanding? The incredible journey of the mind from simply **being** to thinking, knowing, and reasoning is called cognitive development, the subject of this lesson.

If you have watched a young animal or a small child grow, you are very well acquainted with physical development. And you have probably been struck by its apparent abruptness, by the fact that what is clearly impossible one day becomes an accomplished fact the next. One day the baby cannot walk, and the next day he toddles eagerly about in search of new worlds to explore and conquer. One day the foal wobbles uncertainly beside her mother, and the next day she frolics across the meadow. But what manifests itself externally as an abrupt change may actually be the culmination of many gradual internal changes. Slowly, nerve pathways have matured, muscles have gained strength, parts of the body have been brought under voluntary control, and awkward, random movements have become coordinated and purposeful.

Similarly, the mind matures. Like physical development, cognitive development seems to manifest itself in abrupt, observable changes. In successive stages, the child utters a "first" word, two words, then a "sentence," building expectations, acquiring language, beginning to visualize a complex sequence of operations, and at last developing the ability to reason. This journey of the mind from passive observer to active thinker is difficult to study because it cannot really be observed and can seldom be remembered by the person making the "journey." It is yet another aspect of the mind-body and nature-nurture issues discussed in earlier lessons.

In this lesson you will survey leading theories advanced to explain and describe this human journey from innate reflex and tendency to concept formation, abstract thought, and problem solving. You will make a thorough examination of the ideas and work of Jean Piaget, among others, and you will learn about some weaknesses and strengths in Piaget's conclusions. You will also become aware of the role and importance of play in the life of the developing child.

Learning Objectives

When you have finished viewing the program and studying your text assignments, you should be able to:

1. Identify the special importance of the nature-nurture and continuity-discontinuity issues to the study of cognitive development.
2. Describe Piaget's view of mental development in children and review some criticisms of his theories.
3. Define assimilation, accommodation, conservation, and egocentrism as used by Piaget.
4. Name Piaget's four stages of intellectual development and trace a child's developing abilities through these stages.
5. Describe the acquisition of language and identify its importance to cognitive development.
6. Name several types of play and suggest why play is important for the development of children.

Assignments

Before Viewing the Program

Read the preview at the beginning of this lesson and look over the learning objectives that precede the assignments.

Check the section "Did You Know That . . ." at the beginning of Chapter 18 in the text and look over the subtitles for the chapter.

Read Chapter 18, "Cognitive Development: Early Childhood and Adolescence." As you read, note the boldfaced terms and concepts that appear in the text and are defined in the upper right corners of right-hand pages. Use the accompanying definitions or descriptions to increase your knowledge or refresh your memory concerning these terms.

View Program 21, "Cognitive Development"

After Viewing the Program

Review the text assignments.

Read through the summary at the end of Chapter 18, and consider the thought questions inserted at intervals in the chapter. Then to aid your understanding of the materials presented in this lesson, review the boldfaced terms and concepts.

In particular, note these terms carefully: cognitive, schemata, assimilation, accommodation, sensory-motor period, object permanence, pre-operational stage, egocentric reasoning, conservation of quantity, stage of concrete operations, stage of formal operations, linguistic, Yerkish, pre-social play, social play, ambiguity, concept, critical periods, American Sign Language, equilibrium.

Complete the study activities included here as an additional study aid for you.

Now evaluate your understanding of the lesson material by reviewing the learning objectives and taking the self-test in this study guide. Check your answers against the answer key.

According to your instructor's assignment or your own interests, choose and complete activities from among the suggestions for extra credit. You might also consider the recommended readings listed at the end of the chapter.

"According to this, you're a neat, punctual, healthy, well-behaved stupid kid."

Study Activities

Matching

Match each phrase in the column on the right with the appropriate term in the column on the left, writing the letters of the phrases in the appropriate blanks.

____ 1. cognitive
____ 2. phoneme
____ 3. accommodation
____ 4. pre-social play
____ 5. nature-nurture
____ 6. pre-operational stage
____ 7. conserve
____ 8. knowledge
____ 9. concept
____ 10. stage of concrete operations
____ 11. sensory-motor period
____ 12. stage of formal operations
____ 13. Yerkish
____ 14. assimilation

a. includes exploratory activities
b. infant correlates sensory inputs with motor outputs
c. an artificial language
d. child begins to visualize series of operations independent of its own actions
e. intellectual, having to do with thoughts rather than feelings
f. child can reason and handle abstract concepts, such as truth, honor, responsibility
g. question of whether cognitive abilities are entirely innate or programmed by environment
h. adjusting your thoughts and behaviors to fit external realities
i. schema that includes some ideas and excludes others
j. understanding the abstract idea that an object can undergo certain types of changes and still remain the same object
k. basic sounds of human speech
l. accumulation of facts plus strategies or rules for using them
m. the process of making sensory inputs fit your own internal structures
n. child learns to speak and to manipulate the world symbolically

Completion

1. As you learned in earlier lessons, **cognition** refers to those conscious mental activities that include perception, memory, imagery, language, concept formation, problem solving, reasoning and decision making. The growth

process by which you acquire and use these abilities is called _____ development. In the study of cognitive development, all four of the major philosophical issues that trouble psychologists are important, as they are to all human development; however, the issues known as _____ and _____ ' are especially vital. The first issue asks whether we are born with ability to think and process language, or are these skills almost entirely _____ . The second asks whether the stages of development are governed primarily by physical maturation and are therefore determined by genes, or does the _____ direct and shape developmental stages. As McConnell notes, which position is taken is important, since theory determines _____ .

practice
cognitive
nature-nurture
learned
continuity-discontinuity
environment

2. Children do not develop "piecemeal," of course; they develop mentally at the same time as they are developing biologically and emotionally. However, we do not know precisely how development occurs. A noted Swiss biologist and child psychologist, Jean _____, developed a comprehensive theory to explain the cognitive development process. According to Piaget, the human mind has the innate ability to develop _____, which are _____ structures that represent reality. If these structures and external reality do not match, one is literally driven to achieve _____ by achieving such a match. One of the functions of the mind is organization, by which it can develop complex schemata from simple ones; another function is _____, the manner in which the mind processes sensory inputs. As Piaget sees it, your mind processes inputs in two ways: You either _____ (make inputs from the outside world fit your own internal needs) or _____ (change your response outputs to fit the realities of the external environment). Mental growth results from the continuous active interplay between these two processes.

adaptation
mental
Piaget
equilibrium
accommodate
schemata
assimilate

3. For Piaget, there are four stages of cognitive development. The first is the
_____ period in which the infant responds directly to its environment,
tries to correlate its sensory inputs with its physical efforts, and builds up
initial expectations about objects and people. The second is the _____
stage. It lasts from about two until six years. During this stage the child gains
greater control over its muscular responses and learns to speak. It is able to
substitute sounds and _____ for things, but cannot _____ physical
properties. Piaget's third stage is the stage of _____ operations. During
this stage, the child begins to visualize a complex series of operations
independent of its own actions. The fourth stage is the stage of _____
operations. In this last stage, which begins about age twelve and continues
throughout life, a person can _____ and handle abstract concepts.

formal
conserve
pre-operational
reason
concrete
symbols
sensory-motor

4. During what Piaget calls the pre-operational stage, we acquire _____.
Some investigators consider language _____ to be the most important of
human accomplishments. While some primates can be taught to talk using
computers and symbols and a form of sign language, only human brains seem
to be uniquely suited for language learning. Vocalizations made by monkeys
and chimpanzees are controlled by the limbic system, not by the _____,
as speech is in humans. Humans also talk _____; animals do not. Babies
begin to talk by making babbling sounds, which are single syllables. These
basic sounds of human speech are known as _____. Language acquisition
also involves learning the meaning of words (semantics); mastering syntax,
the rules by which words can be combined into sentences; and learning the
pragmatics, or appropriate social use of speech. During the infant's first
months, the mother usually begins to _____ language learning, first by
attracting the infant's attention and naming objects, and, later, by _____
the child for learning the names. During language learning, the mother also
makes bargains, or social _____, in which she may "promise" play for
learning and use praise as well.

contracts
shape
spontaneously
acquisition
rewarding
phonemes
cortex
language

5. Recent studies suggest that a child learns as much from random play as it does in a schoolroom. Most psychologists regard play as vital because it _____ children and adults for learning cognitive skills and behaviors and _____ **all** growth and development.

stimulates
rewards

Short-Answer Questions

1. Briefly, how would you summarize the weaknesses and strengths of Piaget's theory?

2. What did Piaget mean when he said "the child is the teacher"?

3. Describe the purposes and importance of play for the child's cognitive development.

4. If a very young child seems confused when he or she sees his or her mother in a bathing suit for the first time, then soon thereafter sees her dressed for a formal ball, what difficulty might the child be struggling with (according to Piaget)?

Self-Test

(Select the one best answer.)

Objective 1: Identify the special importance of the nature-nurture and continuity-discontinuity issues to the study of cognitive development.

1. Which of the following statements best describes the importance of the nature-nurture issue to the study of cognitive development?
   a. The "nature" theory holds that we are not born with the ability to think and process language.
   b. The "nature" theory holds that "mental structures" are programmed into the mind by the environment.
   c. Whatever position in the nature-nurture controversy is adopted can have strong influence on educational methods.
   d. All of these statements describe the importance of the nature-nurture issue.
   e. None of these statements describes the importance of the nature-nurture issue.

2. Which of the following does not belong in a list of processes by which cognitive development occurs?
   a. perception, imagery, problem solving
   b. imagery, reasoning, decision making
   c. problem solving, reasoning, decision making
   d. perception, mind, memory
   e. language, concept formation, problem solving

Objective 2: Describe Piaget's view of mental development in children, and review some criticisms of his theories.

3. Piaget believed that _____ shape and motivate cognitive development.
   a. imitative play and epistemology
   b. predetermined schemata
   c. innate mental structures
   d. equilibrium and development of language
   e. equilibrium and play

4. Which of these, according to Piaget, is the drive which urges a child to match inner abstractions with reality?
   a. equilibrium
   b. adaptation
   c. schema
   d. altruism
   e. epistemology

5. One main objection to Piaget's theory centers on the point that
    a. biological factors do not account completely for cognitive development.
    b. actual mental development does not necessarily proceed along an established sequence of discrete stages.
    c. behavioral factors do not account completely for cognitive development.
    d. his conclusions were based on observation of children, not adults.
    e. his descriptions of child behavior were inaccurate.

6. Piaget's work is criticized because
    a. of his astute observations and interpretations of children's behavior.
    b. he acknowledged the influence of Baldwin on his theories.
    c. he believed that cognitive abilities are developed from both innate structures and environmental influences.
    d. he emphasized the importance of cognitive skills rather than rote learning in education.
    e. other scientists have not been able to support some of his findings.

Objective 2; and *Objective 3:* Define assimilation, accommodation, conservation, and egocentrism as used by Piaget.

7. According to Piaget, assimilation and accommodation are both aspects of which mental function?
    a. innate reflexes
    b. organization
    c. equilibrium
    d. adaptation
    e. epistemology

Objective 3

8. Piaget would call the act of making sensory inputs fit your own needs
    a. assimilation.
    b. accommodation.
    c. conservation.
    d. egocentrism.
    e. goal achievement.

9. Piaget would call the act of adjusting your responses to fit realities of the external environment
    a. assimilation.
    b. accommodation.
    c. conservation.
    d. egocentrism.
    e. object permanence.

10. Piaget describes as _____ the inability of the infant to differentiate itself from the environment.
    a. assimilation
    b. accommodation
    c. conservation
    d. symbolism
    e. egocentric reasoning

11. The term Piaget uses for the ability to understand that an object can undergo certain types of changes and still remain the same object is
    a. conservation.
    b. accommodation.
    c. assimilation.
    d. symbolizing.
    e. egocentric reasoning.

Objective 4: Name Piaget's four stages of intellectual development and trace a child's developing abilities through these stages.

12. Which of the following is **not** one of Piaget's four stages of intellectual development?
    a. sensory-motor period
    b. stage of formal operations
    c. phallic stage
    d. stage of concrete operations
    e. pre-operational stage

13. During the sensory-motor period, the child acquires
    a. conservation.
    b. language.
    c. the concept of number.
    d. object permanence.
    e. the ability to reason.

14. During the pre-operational stage, children usually acquire
    a. conservation.
    b. language.
    c. the concept of number.
    d. the ability to reason.
    e. object permanence.

15. Although the child may have previously learned to count, it first acquires the concept of number during the
    a. sensory-motor period.
    b. pre-operational stage.
    c. phallic stage.
    d. stage of concrete operations.
    e. stage of formal operations.

16. The first stage in which the child can correctly perform experiments requiring "conservation" is
    a. sensory-motor.
    b. pre-operational.
    c. phallic.
    d. concrete operations.
    e. formal operations.

17. The child is first capable of abstract thought during the
    a. pre-operational stage.
    b. sensory-motor period.
    c. phallic stage.
    d. stage of formal operations.
    e. stage of concrete operations.

Objective 5: Describe the acquisition of language and identify its importance to cognitive development.

18. The fact that babbling occurs in infants from many different cultures suggests that
    a. language ability is innate.
    b. cultural environments are similar.
    c. linguistic environments are similar.
    d. language ability is almost totally learned.
    e. mothers are responsible for verbal shaping.

19. Psychologist Jerome Bruner's theory of language development cites the importance of _____ in the language acquisition process.
    a. cultural differences
    b. cultural similarities
    c. reinforcement
    d. innate factors
    e. biological factors

20. Research suggests that _____ begin to shape language learning soon after birth of their babies.
   a. brothers
   b. sisters
   c. fathers
   d. mothers
   e. teachers

21. The basic sounds of speech common to infants everywhere are called
   a. semantics.
   b. syntax.
   c. phonemes.
   d. telegraphic speech.
   e. holophrastic speech.

22. What is one important difference between humans and primates in the acquisition of language?
   a. Primates can learn to use phonemes but not semantics.
   b. The cortex seems to control the primate's ability to make sounds, while in humans speech is controlled by the limbic system.
   c. Primates learn sign language much faster than humans do.
   d. Primates learn to talk spontaneously, while humans have to be coaxed.
   e. Humans learn to talk spontaneously, while primates must be coaxed to master communication skills.

Objective 6: Name several types of play and suggest why play is important for the development of children.

23. Piaget believes that _____ play is the child's way of learning to manipulate symbols rather than objects.
   a. creative
   b. parallel
   c. exploration
   d. formal
   e. free

24. Today, most psychologists agree that play is necessary to the child because it
   a. recapitulates the behavioral history of the human race.
   b. stimulates all aspects of human development.
   c. is the source of all art.
   d. releases the child's surplus energy.
   e. serves all of the purposes listed above.

Suggestions for Extra Credit

1. By now you've become quite aware that human babies come into the world with a surprisingly good deal of equipment and potential for coping with their new world. Otto Friedrich has written in the August 15, 1983, issue of *Time*, "What Do Babies Know?" (pages 52-59), that babies are born with much more sophisticated skills than anyone ever thought they have. Newborns have "minds," Friedrich says. They can learn and hear **before** birth. When they are born, they can see and smell. They know and understand more than we realize, and they are genetically "prewired to make friends with any adult who cares for them." Harvard's Dr. T. Berry Brazelton, who has authored many books and is sometimes referred to as the new "Dr. Spock," comments, "We used to see the parents shaping the baby, now we see the **baby** shaping the **parents**. Author Friedrich agrees: "At birth...a tiny, dark, wet head thrusts out into the world. . .**Then comes the first squall**." Friedrich's *Time* article is an easy-to-read survey of what is known currently about the cognitive state of the newborn. You might wish to read the article and consider what the conclusions about newborn knowledge mean to medicine, education, philosophical theories, and—of course—parenting. What about Locke's "blank mind" and William James's "great blooming, buzzing confusion"?

2. In this lesson, it is emphasized that the acquisition of language is a uniquely human faculty that is vital to cognitive development. Children are programmed by their genes to learn to talk, and they do so spontaneously. Learning to talk changes the child's world profoundly, allowing him or her to direct and control his or her own being, to know what to expect, to interact with the environment. But is there a critical period during the child's infancy when the ability to learn to talk is enhanced—or, when it can be blighted and forever denied its potential? The work of UCLA linguist Susan Curtiss over a period of years with a thirteen-year-old "wild girl," Genie, seems to strongly support the theory of just such a critical period for language learning. Genie was imprisoned by her parents in a small room—isolated, naked, and in silence—at the age of about one and was not rescued until she was thirteen years old. Genie was able to develop only limited language abilities under the extensive tutelage of Curtiss but the fact that she could talk at all reaffirms the resilience of the human personality, and it disproves one theory—that language learning takes place only between the ages of two and puberty. Curtiss has written several books, including *Genie: A Psycholinguisitic Study of a Modern-Day "Wild Child"* (New York: Academic Press, 1981). Several journal articles about Genie have also been published. Try to locate one or more of these sources and tell what you think Genie's tragic case has to say about critical periods, learning theories, and child development in general.

3. Many of Piaget's theories, including that of conservation, are, as you know, disputed by other scientists. Review Piaget's ideas about transformations and conservation on pages 496-497 of the McConnell text, and, if you are interested in seeing for yourself whether children of the pre-operational age (two to seven) are unable to "conserve," or understand transformations, as Piaget thought, try a simple replication of the "penny exercise" shown on page 497. Lay out ten pennies in two equal rows on a table, making sure the pennies and the rows are equal, and show them to a couple of children (your own or a friend's) of appropriate age. Ask if the rows are the same and contain the same number of pennies. Then spread the pennies in one row farther apart, to left and right (to "transform" their appearance), and ask the same children the same questions. Observe and record what the children say and do, then chart or graph your results and present your findings in a brief report. Do the ages and abilities of the children tested agree with Piaget's ideas? Remembering what you learned about optical illusions in an earlier lesson, what would you say about the possibility of an illusory effect in this particular exercise with the pennies?

4. Many psychologists have investigated the role of fantasy and creative play in child development. Bruno Bettelheim, in his book, *The Uses of Enchantment: The Meaning and Importance of Fairy Tales* (New York: Knopf, 1976; Random House, 1976), describes how fairy tales educate, support, and liberate the emotions of children. Read Bettelheim's book and one or two of the fairy tales he analyzes. Explain his interpretations of these tales or write your own analyses if you wish.

5. A different kind of play is presented in the August 13, 1985, issue of *Family Circle*. Read the article, "Mom, I'm Bored!" (25 Ways to Keep Kids Age 3 to 12 Busy), on page 66. What kind of "play" do you think is represented here? Evaluate the article against what you know about the purposes of play.

Answer Key

Matching

1. e	8. l
2. k	9. i
3. h	10. d
4. a	11. b
5. g	12. f
6. n	13. c
7. j	14. m

Completion

1. cognitive, nature-nurture, continuity-discontinuity, learned, environment, practice;   2. Piaget, schemata, mental, equilibrium, adaptation, assimilate, accommodate;   3. sensory-motor, pre-operational, symbols, conserve, concrete, formal, reason;   4. language, acquisition, cortex, spontaneously, phonemes, shape, rewarding, contracts;   5. rewards, stimulates.

Short-Answer Questions

1. Piaget's work has profoundly influenced educational practices in the United States, particularly in focussing on the development of cognitive skills. Piaget insisted that knowledge is more important than reflexes or rote learning and that teachers should help children to develop better "schemata." Today Piaget is respected most for his astute observations of children's behavior, not for his "stage" theory of development. Ironically, because he depended on observations and not controlled experiments, however, Piaget's methodology is flawed, and, as a result, many of his findings have not been supported by subsequent research. For example, there is little or no evidence that Piaget's "mental structures" exist. Critics also find that cognitive development does not necessarily occur in separate stages or in any formal sequence. And Piaget's findings were biased by the fact that his subjects for observation were white, middle-class European children.

2. Piaget was an interactionist who believed that the child is born with innate mental structures that provide guidance and motivation for growth, but that the mind is **shaped** partly by the environment. However, he did not believe that the child is moulded by parents and teachers; rather the child is actively involved in its own cognitive development, doing its **own** interpreting and shaping of input from the social environment.

3. According to recent studies, young children may learn as much from random play as they do from classroom "conditioning." Some thinkers and scientists have considered play to be the source of "all art," or a means of releasing "surplus" energy, but most psychologists do agree that play stimulates the physical, emotional, and social development of the child as well as intellectual development. As McConnell notes, play also rewards the child for learning the cognitive and behavioral skills expected of him.

4. The child's thinking may still be perception-bound, and, according to Piaget, he or she may be having difficulty in dealing with the fact that objects (even the child's mother) can undergo "transformations," yet remain the same. The change from familiar clothing to beach wear and formal attire might indeed cause a young child to think his or her mother had been "transformed" if he or she had not yet developed the ability to "conserve."

Self-Test

1. c (text pages 477-478)
2. d (text pages 477-478)
3. c (text page 490)
4. a (text pages 490-491)
5. b (text page 498; television program)
6. e (text page 497)
7. d (text pages 492-493)
8. a (text page 492; television program)
9. b (text pages 492-493; television program)
10. e (text page 496)
11. a (text page 496; television program)
12. c (text pages 495-497; television program)
13. d (text page 495; television program)
14. b (text pages 495-496; television program)
15. d (text page 496; television program)
16. d (text page 496; television program)
17. d (text page 497; television program)
18. a (text page 479; television program)
19. c (text page 479)
20. d (text page 482)
21. c (text page 479)
22. e (text pages 482-484)
23. a (text page 499)
24. b (text pages 500-501)

Personality Theory 22

Viewer's Guide for Program Twenty-two

As you view the television program, watch for:

A series of stills and animations depicting constellations of the zodiac, ancient myths, and Renaissance ideas. For centuries, scientists and philosophers, sages and seers have sought to explain why individuals behave as they do. In their efforts to chart the chaotic course of human life, they have looked to the stars and planets, to the gods and goddesses, and to other **external** conflicts and forces.

Actual scenes of Sigmund Freud's consulting rooms in Vienna and animated cartoons dramatizing his ideas about the levels of consciousness and about the regions of the mind—id, ego, and superego. Freud was among the first to explain personality in terms of **internal** conflicts and forces.

The interview with Erik Erikson and the animated sequence illustrating the eight developmental stages through which, he believes, each human must pass on the way to full maturity.

The interview with Carl Rogers, a humanist who believes that personality growth and development continues throughout life. He believes you become a fully functioning individual when you gain conscious awareness of, and are completely comfortable with, all parts of your behavior.

Preview

What distinguishes you from the people around you? What makes you interesting? Different? Refreshing? Unique? What makes you YOU?

Even more than your appearance, your personality sets you apart from those around you and gives you your identity. It is the characteristic way in which you think and behave as you adjust and respond to the world around you. It is something you have in common with all other human beings and, at the same time, something that is unique to you.

For centuries, scientists and philosophers, sages and seers have sought to explain personality. They have looked to the stars and planets of astrology, to the gods and goddesses of mythology, and to other **external** influences and forces. But the theories they have derived have answered special needs and thus have proved useful only to a particular age and have failed to explain the entire personality and all of its many behaviors to all who would inquire for **all** ages.

In fact, no theory is yet adequate to the task; and so the search goes on, but in new directions. Some personality theorists have concentrated their attentions on **internal** forces, on the urges and conflicts within.

Among the first to do so was Sigmund Freud. Seeing pleasure as resulting primarily from the satisfaction of biological urges, he viewed personality as being entirely and almost immutably the product of conflicts, experienced during early upbringing, between these urges and social approval. Thus, he viewed the disturbed minds he treated as casualties of a battle within, of the struggle between the desire for pleasure and the demands of daily living. Freud gave psychology its first comprehensive theory of personality. He still dominates twentieth-century psychology, and, though his ideas are attacked from many sides and his theories are disputed (and, in some cases, supported), his scientific theories remain "alive and well" after repeated scrutiny by modern investigators.

Although influenced by Freud, later personality theorists disagreed with his emphasis on unconscious biological instincts and on the almost unchangeable influence of early upbringing. Among them were Carl Jung, Alfred Adler, Erik Erikson, and humanists (such as Carl Rogers and Abraham Maslow), who view persons as being capable of continual psychological growth and development toward self-actualization.

Personologists, such as Murray, and the social-learning theory, which developed from Murray's ideas, now say that development and learning are a lifelong process and that you are not the passive tool of your needs **or** your environment but an active decision-maker in an interactionist relationship which leaves **your** imprint upon how you see your needs and how the environment responds to **you**. Today, the emphasis is on cognitive processes—not unconscious ones—upon differences between individuals, not similarities, and upon extending the concept of development to include the entire life span, not just the childhood years.

In this lesson, we shall describe and evaluate a variety of these theories of personality. In the three lessons that follow, we shall see how personality is measured, attempt to define normal and abnormal behavior, and then examine the means we have for treating abnormalities.

Learning Objectives

When you have finished viewing the program and studying your text assignments, you should be able to:

1. Describe Freud's concept of psychosexual development in terms of the conscious, preconscious, and unconscious minds and the functions of the libido, id, ego, and superego.
2. List Freud's defense mechanisms and explain their role in psychosexual development.
3. Analyze the approaches of Skinner in relation to Freud, the humanists, and Erikson's theory of developmental stages.
4. Compare Murray's "personology" and social learning theory to traditional personality theories developed by Freud, Jung, Adler, Skinner, Erikson, Rogers, and Maslow.
5. Identify some recent trends in personality theory and relate or apply these trends to traditional concepts of personality, particularly as they relate to maturity and old age.

Assignments

Before Viewing the Program

Read the preview at the beginning of this lesson and look over the learning objectives that precede the assignments.

Check the section "Did You Know That. . ." at the beginning of Chapter 19 in the text, and look over the subtitles for the chapter.

Read Chapter 19, ''Personality Theories: Psychoanalysis, Humanism, and Social Learning Theory.'' As you read, note the boldfaced terms and concepts in the text and glossed at intervals in upper right corners of right-hand pages. Use the accompanying definitions or descriptions to increase your knowledge or refresh your memory concerning these terms.

View Program 22, ''Personality Theory''

After Viewing the Program

Review the text assignments.

Read through the summary at the end of Chapter 19 and consider the thought questions inserted in the chapter. Then to aid your understanding of the materials presented in this lesson, review the boldfaced terms and concepts. In particular, note these terms carefully: personality theory, libido, reality principle, id, pleasure principle, ego, superego, psychosexual stages, Oedipus complex, Electra complex, defense mechanisms, extroversion, introversion, inferiority complex, life-style, psychosocial theory of development, autonomy, humanistic psychologists, behaviorism, social learning theory, self-actualization, personology, needs and need integrates, interactions, senility, expectations, ''no-go,'' ''go-go.''

Complete the study activities included here as an additional study aid for you.

Now evaluate your understanding of the lesson material by reviewing the learning objectives and taking the self-test in this study guide. Check your answers against the answer key.

According to your instructor's assignment or your own interests, choose and complete activities from among the suggestions for extra credit. You might also consider the recommended readings listed at the end of the chapter.

Study Activities

True-False

1. T F Freud's theory of psychosexual development explains how the ego learns to resolve the conflicting demands of the id.
2. T F Freudian theory places heaviest emphasis on the role of the unconscious mind in personality development.

3. T F Recent trends in personality theory show a shift away from the interaction theories of Murray and the social-learning viewpoints.
4. T F Personology is the scientific study of what personality actually is and how it grows and develops over an individual's life span.
5. T F In Freudian psychology, much of our repression of unacceptable thoughts and behaviors is the result of censoring by the ego.
6. T F Forgetting in older people may be a problem only because of society's expectations about the behavior of old people.
7. T F The oral stage is the earliest of Freud's stages of psychosexual development.
8. T F During the latency period, according to Freud, a person begins to seek out heterosexual relationships.
9. T F Even the best theories of personality limit our conception of life-span development.
10. T F Erikson's work encouraged the development of humanistic psychology.
11. T F The most important of Freud's defense mechanisms is denial, the process by which the ego blocks off threatening thoughts or desires.
12. T F Adler believed that the social environment is a more important determinant of personality than the genetic blueprint.
13. T F In contrast to Freud's view that one's personality is immutably fixed by adulthood, Erikson insists there is hope and possibility for change throughout life.
14. T F Skinner limited the scope of his work in behaviorism by discarding the roles of physiological and psychological influences on behavior.
15. T F Freud built his theories upon the differences between individuals, while the humanistic psychologists emphasize the similarities betweeen us.

Completion

1. Although his theories have been—and are continually being—altered, Sigmund Freud remains the most famous personality theorist of the twentieth century. As a personality theory, Freudian psychoanalysis is still the most _____ yet developed. Recent reviewers report that, while research casts doubt on some Freudian conclusions, Freudian _____ is still scientifically "alive and well." Freud suggests that there are three levels of mental functioning. That part of the mind which is operating whenever we are awake, allowing us to respond to the world around us, is the _____ mind. A second level of mental functioning that is usually concealed from our awareness, but can be easily called into consciousness, is the preconscious mind. The third level of functioning is the _____ mind which includes memories that cannot be recalled. Reflexes, autonomic functioning, emotional reactions, and insight originate in the _____ mind.

unconscious
conscious
comprehensive
theory
unconscious

2. Freud also suggested that three structures of the mind operate on the three levels of consciousness. The _____ is responsible for pleasure seeking and is a collection of instinctual biological _____ that are the source of our _____ energy. Once an infant begins to learn that there are differences between the desires of its own id and the desires of other people, it begins to distinguish between itself and the outer world, bringing into being a conscious self, or _____. The ego helps you to communicate with the external world, reason, make judgments, and solve problems. As you mature, your ego is influenced more by the _____ principle, or the practical demands of daily living. A part of the ego that splits off and acts on its own as your conscience, helping you to adjust to society's rules and regulations, is your _____. Psychic energy from the id, which Freud called _____, powers the functions of all the structures.

drives
ego
libido
libidinal
superego
id
reality

3. Since the instincts of the id often come into conflict with the _____, libidinal tensions may build up and you may suffer the discomforts of what Freud calls "signal anxiety." To help handle conflicts and reduce anxiety, the ego builds _____ mechanisms. The most important of these defenses is _____, the process by which the ego blocks out and keeps out of your conscious mind extremely threatening thoughts or desires.

repression
superego
defense

4. Like Freud, Carl Jung believed in instincts, but he was convinced that we are motivated more by _____ needs than by primitive sexuality. According to Jung, we are born with "racial _____" or unconscious "mental fragments of past human history," that are lodged in what he termed the _____ unconscious. Jung's most important contribution to personality theory is the concept of introversion versus extroversion. The _____ personality focuses on the outside environment, while the _____ personality is oriented to an inner, personal world.

memories
extroverted
collective
introverted
religious

5. In disagreement with both Freud and Jung, Adler emphasized the _____ environment. He thought people could shape their own destinies and saw life as a conscious struggle to achieve _____. We have an instinct for _____ and through training and experience, we develop our own style of life. Knowledge about what we cannot do creates in us what Adler called an _____ complex, which motivates us to succeed.

self-realization
superiority
inferiority
social

6. Erikson's psychosocial theory also emphasizes the _____ motives rather than the sexual drives that Freud thought critical. Erikson is best known for his detailed description of eight stages of _____, each of which occurs in sequence and is characterized by a typical conflict for that period. Personality development continues throughout life and personality is always a _____ adjustment to _____ situations. The human personality is motivated less by blind sexual hungers than it is by the need for determining _____ and a place in the world.

psychological
identity
social
development
social

7. The two best-known subscribers to humanistic theories of personality are Carl Rogers and Abraham Maslow. Where Freudians emphasize the similarities between individuals, the humanists stress the _____. They reject most _____ concepts, claiming that an individual's greatest innate tendency is toward a process of continual psychological growth and improvement, which is called _____. This process is at the peak of what Maslow calls a _____ of needs. With maturity, our self emerges from the totality of our experience and is the _____ part of our experience.

conscious
self-actualization
hierarchy
psychoanalytic
differences

8. By showing us ways in which behavior can be changed effectively and by emphasizing the role of the _____ in shaping behavior, B. F. Skinner has contributed much to theories of personality. But, as a behaviorist, he rejects both the _____ and intrapsychic determinants of behavior. Personology, a viewpoint associated most often with Harvard's Henry Murray, and a movement described as the social-learning approach have adopted an interactionist approach. This approach regards needs as conscious, not unconscious, and the way you _____ your needs as important, rather than the needs themselves or the way you _____ to these needs. Therefore, personality is seen as the _____ of _____ perceptions and _____ interactions.

person-environment
conscious
respond
perceive
biological
environment
interaction

Short-Answer Questions

1. Briefly define personality as it is discussed in the television program and the text chapter for this lesson.

2. How do you think Freud would be likely to interpret the following information one young college male shared with his class when asked to tell something about his personality?

   I can distinctly remember often withholding my bowel movements when I was a toddler—I now realize that it must have been because I was afraid of making a mess. To this day I am an extremely neat and orderly person, and I budget my money down to the last penny. I know this probably has something to do with toilet training, but I'm not sure. I don't remember.

3. Describe the recent trends in personality theory which McConnell lists in your text.

Self-Test

(Select the one best answer.)

Objective 1: Describe Freud's concept of psychosexual development in terms of the conscious, preconscious, and unconscious minds and the functions of the libido, id, ego, and superego.

1. Freud believed that the human psyche functioned on which of the following three levels?
   a. oral, anal, and phallic stages
   b. id, ego, superego

    c. unconscious, conscious, preconscious

    d. primary, secondary, ego process

    e. libidinal, reality principle, introjection

2. According to Freud, preconscious experience is
    a. found only in infants and children.
    b. difficult to bring into awareness.
    c. the same as the id.
    d. a border between unconscious and conscious experience.
    e. responsible for logic and reasoning.

3. You have a choice of studying for an exam or going out for a pizza with friends. According to Freud, which part of your personality would argue for the pizza? Which for the exam?
    a. id, superego
    b. id, ego
    c. ego, id
    d. ego, superego
    e. superego, id

4. According to Freud, the _____ is the source of all of your psychic energy and obeys the _____.
    a. id, pleasure principle
    b. ego, pleasure principle
    c. id, reality principle
    d. superego, reality principle
    e. ego, id

5. The correct sequence of psychosexual development is
    a. genital stage, oral stage, anal stage.
    b. anal stage, latency stage, genital stage.
    c. oral stage, anal stage, phallic stage, latency stage.
    d. phallic stage, genital stage, latency stage.
    e. oral stage, latency stage, puberty.

Objective 2: List Freud's defense mechanisms and explain their role in psychosexual development.

6. The ego develops what Freud called _____ to cope with anxieties built up by tensions between the id and the superego.
    a. libidinal energy
    b. a hierarchy of needs
    c. self-actualization
    d. a style of life
    e. defense mechanisms

7. Which of the following characteristics does not describe defense mechanisms?
    a. They operate at a conscious level, and the ego is usually aware of them.
    b. They are the ego's way of trying to reduce anxiety.
    c. The ego is not always aware of them because they operate at an unconscious level.
    d. They may deny or distort reality.
    e. They are employed by the ego to defend itself against conflicting commands from the id and the superego.

8. The most important defense mechanism, the process by which the ego blocks off below the level of consciousness certain threatening thoughts and desires, is called
    a. denial.
    b. repression.
    c. reaction formation.
    d. sublimation.
    e. rationalization.

9. If you attribute an unacceptable motive of your own to someone else, you may be
    a. projecting.
    b. displacing.
    c. regressing.
    d. rationalizing.
    e. sublimating.

10. According to Freud, libidinal energy
    a. resides in the superego.
    b. is that part of the mind that imposes social norms and values on the personality.
    c. is the primary content of the conscious self.
    d. is a psychic force that motivates the structures of the personality.
    e. is a force that originates during the phallic stage of development.

11. Freud thought that the child creates a(n) _____ during its psychosexual development in order to control the libido.
    a. superego
    b. conscious self (ego)
    c. defense mechanism
    d. Oedipal attachment
    e. Electral attachment

Objective 3: Analyze the approaches of Skinner in relation to Freud, the humanists, and Erikson's theory of developmental stages.

12. Which theorist suggested that we all possess a drive to compensate for our fears of inferiority?
    a. Freud
    b. Adler
    c. Skinner
    d. Erikson
    e. Jung

13. Which theorist emphasized the effect of past human history and instinct on personality development?
    a. Freud
    b. Jung
    c. Erikson
    d. Adler
    e. Skinner

14. According to Erikson, finding your true identity is the critical task of
    a. latency.
    b. the phallic stage.
    c. childhood.
    d. adulthood.
    e. puberty.

15. The view that motivation to improve may be more important than the past in shaping our personality is an important contribution of _____ theory.
    a. dynamic
    b. Skinnerian
    c. humanistic
    d. structural
    e. Freudian

16. According to Rogers and Maslow, the most important innate drive is the need for
    a. finding one's true identity.
    b. solving the crisis of generativity.
    c. achieving autonomy.
    d. self-actualization.
    e. developing a style of life.

17. Which of the following theorists believed in considering only things that can be measured objectively?
    a. Jung
    b. Freud
    c. Skinner
    d. Adler
    e. Erikson

18. In contrast to the Freudians and the humanists, Skinner demonstrated the importance of _____ factors in shaping personality.
    a. intrapsychic
    b. social/behavioral
    c. biological
    d. unconscious
    e. moral and spiritual

19. Which personality theorist would make the statement that self-actualized people "have relative independence of their physical and social environments, and they rely on their own development and continued growth"?
    a. Maslow
    b. Skinner
    c. Freud
    d. Jung
    e. Murray

20. Which personality theorist would make the following statement: Human behavior is controlled by external forces rather than free will?
    a. Freud
    b. Jung
    c. social-learning theorists
    d. Rogers
    e. Skinner

Objective 3; and *Objective 4:* Compare Murray's "personology" and social learning theory to traditional personality theories developed by Freud, Jung, Adler, Skinner, Erikson, Rogers, and Maslow.

21. If you believe that you have a great deal of conscious control over your life, then your ideas are closest to those of
    a. the psychoanalysts.
    b. Jung and "racial memories."
    c. the social-learning theorists.
    d. Skinner and the behaviorists.
    e. the body-nature viewpoint.

22. Erikson's psychosocial theory of development proposed that every person passes through eight stages of life, each of which is characterized by
    a. a particular type of crisis or conflict.
    b. direct control of actions by external stimuli.
    c. a struggle to achieve superiority.
    d. the necessity to release libidinal energy.
    e. a focus on continuing interaction between conscious self and environmental inputs.

Objective 4

23. Which theorist (or theorists) would disagree with the statement, "Needs are conscious, but it is not the need itself that determines how you respond—it is how you perceive the need and your response"?
    a. Freud and the psychoanalysts
    b. Murray and the social-learning theorists
    c. the Skinnerians
    d. Freud and Murray
    e. Freud and Skinner

24. Which of the following statements does **not** describe the social-learning theory of personality?
    a. Murray's personology does not explain how we learn things.
    b. Social-learning theory emphasizes the importance of organism-environment interactions.
    c. Social-learning theory offers an effective way of teaching people new behaviors.
    d. Your perceptions are an important part of personality development.
    e. You are not passive, but active, in relation to your environment.

Objective 5: Identify some recent trends in personality theory and relate or apply these trends to traditional concepts of personality, particularly as they relate to maturity and old age.

25. Decreasing interest in fixed developmental stages plus lack of support for the belief that personality structure is "set" by age fifteen may help us to recognize that
    a. most healthy older Americans are as physically capable of learning new things as are younger individuals.
    b. all older individuals don't become senile or infantile.
    c. some memory behaviors are considered problems only because we associate them with old age.
    d. we need to change our traditional conceptions about old age.
    e. all of the statements listed above are true.

Suggestions for Extra Credit

1. Sigmund Freud was an authoritarian professor, and Carl Jung was, for a time, his disciple. The correspondence between them provides insight into the warm, intensely fruitful, and finally savage encounter between these two giants in the psychoanalytic movement. Read *The Freud/Jung Letters: The Correspondence Between Sigmund Freud and C. G. Jung,* edited by William McGuire (Princeton, N.J.: Princeton University Press, 1974) or excerpts from these letters in the February 1974 issue of *Psychology Today*.
2. By himself, Jung is fun and provocative to read. His theories on inherited "racial memories" are intriguing, though little or no credence is accorded these views in modern psychology. If you are interested, spend a few hours of time reading and analyzing Jung's book, *Psychological Types*. You might find it intellectually stimulating to mount a criticism or a defense of his ideas.

3. Make a chart or table like the one below in which you compare Erikson's psychosocial development with Freud's psychosexual development and Piaget's stages of cognitive development. You might, for example, have one column be the specific conflict or crisis identified by Erikson, a second column be the psychosocial stage in which it occurs, a third column be the Freudian equivalent (if there is one), and the fourth column reserved for Piaget. Review what you have learned in this and previous lessons about the theories of Piaget, Freud, and Erikson before you try to fill in the columns. Once you have done so, study your chart, then write a brief analysis of your findings. What relationship, if any, do you find among the three ideas of stages? Erikson's causes? How do you think Piaget's stages of cognitive development relate to Erikson's psychosocial stages and Freud's psychosexual stages?

Erikson's Crisis or Conflict	Erikson's Psychosocial Stage	Freud's Psychosexual Stage	Piaget's Stages of Cognitive Development

4. The point is made in this lesson that ideas about the abilities of older people in America may be more a function of the way we see the aging process than it is in reality. Not only the scientific and professional literature contribute to these perceptions; fiction also paints the over-sixty-five individual as a nonproductive, useless, physically impaired, and childlike person of low status and insignificant role in society. Select one or more of the following readings listed here—or choose some from your own sources—and take a position either supporting or challenging the contention that society must find new conceptual models for aging: "Conceptual Models of Aging: The Challenge of a New Frontier," Carl Eisdorfer, February 1983, *American Psychologist*, page 197; "Love through the Ages," Elizabeth Stark, *Psychology Today*, December 1984, page 16; "Sex after Fifty," Francesca Lunzer, *Forbes* magazine, November 5, 1984, page 238; "Memory and Mental Tempo," Nancy C. Waugh and Robin A. Barr, in *New Directions in Memory and Aging*, proceedings of the George A. Talland Memorial Conference, 1980, published by Lawrence Erlbaum Associates, Inc., page 251; "Cognitive Skill Training for the Elderly: Why Should 'Old Dogs' Acquire New Tricks?", Elizabeth Anne Robertson-Tchabo, in *New Directions in Memory and Aging*, proceedings of the George A. Talland Memorial Conference, 1980, published by Lawrence Erlbaum Associates, Inc., page 511; and the following articles from the *Handbook of Developmental Psychology*, 1982, Prentice-Hall, Inc.: "Old Age and Behavioral Changes," page 791; "Aging and Cognitive Changes," page 807; "Learning and Memory in Later Life," page 828; "The Aging of Human Abilities," page 847; and "Social Behavior and Aging," page 871.

Answer Key

True-False

1. T	9. T
2. T	10. F
3. F	11. F
4. T	12. T
5. T	13. T
6. T	14. T
7. T	15. F
8. F	

Completion

1. comprehensive, theory, conscious, unconscious, unconscious;   2. id, drives, libidinal, ego, reality, superego, libido;   3. superego, defense, repression;   4. religious, memories, collective, extroverted, introverted;   5. social, superiority, self-realization, inferiority;   6. social, development, psychological, social, identity;   7. differences, psychoanalytic, self-actualization, hierarchy, conscious;   8. environment, biological, perceive, respond, interaction, conscious, person-environment.

Short-Answer Questions

1. Since human communication began, singers, storytellers, artists, writers, philosophers, and (later) scientists and humanists have been creating definitions and theories that will explain the human personality. Myths, natural events, signs of the zodiac, gods and goddesses, internal and external forces—all have been woven into definitions that are sometimes elaborate, sometimes simple. No definition or theory has as yet been universally accepted as a complete explanation of the human personality. Cantor and Kihlstrom propose that personality can be thought of as "the distinctive patterns of thought, behavior, and experience which characterize the individual's unique adjustment to his or her life situation." Your particular "personality" is revealed in the way you understand, respond to, and change your world.

2. Freud probably would surmise that the young man's mother interfered with his normal ego development during his anal stage by her insistent demand for toilet training. Freud has identified obstinance, excessive neatness, and stinginess as hallmarks of what he called the **anal character**. Freud would try to make the young man understand that his behaviors were attempts to punish his mother for the traumas of toilet training. In response to her insistence that he be "clean," he rebelled by withholding his feces. Withholding his pennies as an adult is the young man's "adult" way of rebelling.

3. McConnell sees at least six different major trends developing in personality theory. These include:
   1. shift from the nature-nurture views to the interactionist approach of the social-learning theorists;
   2. movement toward regarding the individual as an active participant in the shaping of his personality;
   3. increasing emphasis on cognitive processes rather than emotion;

4. tendency to see conscious processes as the central elements in personality;

5. growing belief that human individuals continue to learn and to grow throughout life (personality is not ''fixed'' in adolescence);

6. less interest in developmental stages and more interest in viewing personality as a continuous interplay between individual and environment.

Self-Test

1. c (text pages 513-514; television program)
2. d (text page 514)
3. b (text pages 515-517; television program)
4. a (text page 515; television program)
5. c (text pages 517-518; television program)
6. e (text pages 519-520; television program)
7. a (text page 519; television program)
8. b (text page 519; television program)
9. a (text page 520)
10. d (text pages 515-517; television program)
11. b (text page 516)
12. b (text page 523)
13. b (text pages 521-522)
14. e (text page 527; television program)
15. c (text page 529; television program)
16. d (text pages 529-539; television program)
17. c (text page 534)
18. b (text page 534)
19. a (text page 530)
20. e (text page 532)
21. c (text pages 532-534)
22. a (text pages 525-528; television program)
23. e (text pages 532-534)
24. a (text page 532)
25. e (text pages 535-538)

Individual Differences: 23
Measurement and Meaning

Viewer's Guide for Program Twenty-three

As you view the television program, watch for:

Scenes of early twentieth-century classrooms and playing fields, children being tested, and photos of French scientists Alfred Binet and Theophile Simon. Binet and Simon devised a test that would enable teachers to identify retarded children and thus created the first in what has become a proliferation of so-called "intelligence" and personality tests.

Scenes that illustrate the many factors that influence intelligence, such as socioeconomic status, deprivation, culture, race, contact with parents. Scenes of different people using many different abilities that are not measured by standard intelligence tests.

Footage of subjects describing an inkblot and taking a personality test known as the Minnesota Multiphasic Personality Inventory (MMPI). The inkblot is a device used in what is called the Rorschach personality test, a projective measure; the MMPI, an objective test, is possibly the most widely used personality measure in the United States today.

Preview

Where is your mind located? This question, asked often in earlier lessons, will be asked here once again in an effort to determine where the essential YOU resides. And we might confront an even more penetrating issue: **Who are you**?

In Lesson Twenty-two, we equated that essential YOU with your personality. We said it is your characteristic way of thinking and behaving, even more than your unique appearance, that sets you apart from those around you and gives you your identity. But where do we find that personality and how do we describe and categorize it?

We have developed a fairly accurate set of measures to describe appearance. Using height, weight, and other observable physical characteristics, it is possible for one person to describe a suspect so accurately that a second person can sketch a recognizable portrait of him or her. And some of our early attempts to categorize personality relied on our knowledge of body structure and physical type. Greek scientist Galen thought personality was determined by humors, or secretions of the heart, lungs, and liver. Both William Shakespeare and W. H. Sheldon observed a relationship between personality and body shape. More recently, theorists have sought to profile personality by measuring and grouping traits.

The real you is the sum of your genes, your past experiences, and your present environment. How well have we succeeded in discovering this real you?

Only moderately. We have devised standardized tests to measure your intelligence, but intelligence is not a single trait. Rather, it is a composite of traits, perhaps as many as 20,000 traits. Intelligence quotient seems to be a good predictor of academic success but to be less well correlated with creativity and success outside the classroom. Most IQ test scores fluctuate widely under personal and environmental differences. These measures are usually biased for culture and social class, and many investigators believe they measure achievement, not "intelligence." We have devised tests to profile personality type, and these are useful in helping normal people achieve self-actualization. The Minnesota Multiphasic Personality Inventory is regarded as the most reliable personality test, and it is useful for identifying a large number of personality characteristics which may reveal emotional problems. The MMPI, as it is popularly called, is a so-called test because it is made up of multiple-choice items.

We have also devised projective tests to identify personality problems. By association and projection, clinicians help clients express deep-seated needs and uncover unpleasant memories long repressed. But these tests place a heavy burden on the interpreter and may actually yield more information about the person doing the interpreting than about the person taking the test.

In short, few, if any, psychological tests have either the reliability or the validity that we take for granted in the instruments we use to measure body size and weight and to describe appearance. While each of these tests may be useful and may provide interesting psychological feedback, it is important to remember that each has its biases and limitations. More important than delimiting personality is recognizing its potential. As psychologist Leona E. Tyler has optimistically observed, "Individuals create themselves." Many psychologists regard your intelligence as part of your personality, and—in truth—both are the products of your genes, your past experiences, and your environment in an interactive relationship.

As McConnell observes, trait theory is dominant in personality psychology today. Therefore, in this lesson, we will examine IQ and personality tests that try to measure traits, and we will consider some of their values and strengths as well as their weaknesses and potential for misuse. Above all, we will find that IQ is not a number with which you are "branded" for the rest of your life. The evidence is that IQ can fluctuate sharply in either direction.

Learning Objectives

When you have finished viewing the program and studying your text assignments, you should be able to:

1. Describe theories reflecting the view that personality is related to body type, and indicate problems with this approach.
2. Briefly describe Allport's theory of traits and Cattell's factor analysis approach.
3. Discuss how Binet and Simon chose to define and measure intelligence.
4. Define normal distribution, reliability, and validity, and discuss how these apply to intelligence tests.
5. Discuss the following influences on intelligence scores: early environmental deprivation, birth order, family size, practice and training in test-taking, culture, race, and coercive discipline.
6. Distinguish between IQ (intelligence quotient) and intelligence.
7. Distinguish between objective and subjective tests, citing examples of each, and discuss the usefulness and limitations of each kind.

Assignments

Before Viewing the Program

Read the preview at the beginning of this lesson and look over the learning objectives that precede the assignments.

Check the section "Did You Know That . . ." at the beginning of Chapter 20 in the text and look over the subtitles for the chapter.

Read Chapter 20, "Individual Differences: Measurement and Meaning." As you read, note the boldfaced terms and concepts and the glossary items that appear throughout the chapter. Use the accompanying definitions or descriptions to increase your knowledge or refresh your memory concerning these terms.

View Program 23, "Personality Tests"

After Viewing the Program

Review the text assignments.

Read through the summary at the end of Chapter 20. Then to aid your understanding of the materials presented in this lesson, review the boldfaced terms and concepts. In particular, note these terms carefully: eugenics, morphologies, endomorphs, mesomorphs, ectomorphs, factor analysis, individual and common traits, cardinal traits, central traits, secondary traits, mental age, chronological age, intelligence, intelligence quotient (IQ), normal distribution, bell-shaped curve, reliability, validity, Thematic Apperception Test, Rorschach, projective tests, MMPI, fluid and crystallized intelligence, social class.

Complete the study activities included here as an additional study aid for you.

Now evaluate your understanding of the lesson material by reviewing the learning objectives and taking the self-test in this study guide. Check your answers against the answer key.

According to your instructor's assignment or your own interests, choose and complete activities from among the suggestions for extra credit. You might also consider the recommended readings listed at the end of the chapter.

"He won't let me on. He says I show all the hijacker's personality traits."

Study Activities

Matching

Match each phrase in the column on the right with the appropriate term in the column on the left, writing the letters of the phrases in the appropriate blanks.

_____ 1. morphologies
_____ 2. trait
_____ 3. Binet-Simon
_____ 4. IQ
_____ 5. bell-shaped curve
_____ 6. test validity
_____ 7. secondary traits
_____ 8. projective test
_____ 9. Boston Study
_____ 10. enriched environment

a. personality measure in which subject is presented with unstructured situation
b. indication that a test measures what it says it measures
c. Allport's term for responses that are learned
d. can increase IQ scores dramatically
e. body structure types which are believed to predispose personality structure
f. first intelligence test
g. normal distribution of test scores
h. indicates that social class accounts for differences in IQ scores
i. mental age divided by chronological age and the quotient multiplied by 100
j. tendency to respond to many different stimuli in the same way

Completion

1. What determines our personalities has long puzzled human beings, resulting in the development of some interesting theories. Galen, a Greek physician, believed that the fluids secreted by the body, known as humors, were primarily responsible for human personality. And a scientist named Sheldon studied male college students to determine if their _____, or body type, and _____ traits were correlated.

personality
morphology

2. Psychologists have generally rejected Sheldon's _____ approach toward personality, and have focused instead on _____ traits, such as intelligence. How to measure intelligence became a major problem for psychologists. Among the first to face the issue were _____ and _____, who developed what is known as the IQ test. By means of this test, your _____ is determined by dividing your mental age by your biological age, and multiplying the result by 100. This test was considered so effective in predicting a child's _____ performance it became a standard part of educational psychology.

Simon
mental
academic
morphological
intelligence quotient
Binet

3. Psychologists at this time were also influenced by Darwin's theory of evolution, which suggested that intelligence is _____. Most intelligence tests were based on a normal _____—or bell-shaped _____—of test scores in which most students would get average grades, or Cs. However, intelligence consists of many different traits, which are expressed as interactions among _____, past experiences, and present _____. Thus, there is no reason why all IQs should fit into a _____ curve.

environment
distribution
curve
innate (inherited)
bell-shaped
genes

4. Psychologists today feel most intelligence tests are fairly reliable, especially in predicting academic achievement, but their _____ is questionable since not all psychologists agree on what intelligence actually is. There is one basic problem, however, concerning reliability: Traits are _____, part of your inner self; IQ tests measure performance, not your inner condition. While IQ tests can predict academic success well, they do not predict "real-life" success very well. Another problem with intelligence tests is built-in cultural and racial biases; that is, they simply do not take into account the past experience or the social environments of the persons taking the test. Therefore, IQ tests as we know them tend to _____ the innate intelligence of socially deprived groups. Children raised in deprived areas usually have lower IQ scores than do children brought up in stimulating environments.

subjective
underestimate
validity

5. Psychologists continued to measure personality by studying a person's past until a Harvard psychologist named Allport began studying those traits that look to the future. He believed the important traits are those that _____ a person, as well as provide structure to the individual's personality. The psychologist identified two classes of traits: _____ and _____. He believed individual traits could be broken down into three types: cardinal, _____ and _____.

secondary
common
motivate
central
individual

6. _____ (or subjective) tests present a subject with a variety of unstructured or ambiguous situations and measured reactions to them. This tests physiological reactions in response to words. The Thematic Apperception Test, or _____, consists of pictures depicting potentially emotional situations designed to elicit expressions of an individual's perception of the world. The most famous of the projective tests is the inkblot test developed by a Swiss psychiatrist named _____. In this test, a series of inkblots is shown, and the subject describes the inkblots in terms of personal experiences. These three tests are all composed of ambiguous stimuli that you "structure" in terms of your own _____.

366

7. A second type of personality test is the _____ test. A prime example is the Minnesota Multiphasic Personality Inventory, or the _____, which is a set of scales standardized on a fairly large population. The test consists of short statements to which a person agrees, disagrees, or says he or she cannot respond. This approach to studying personality judges people almost entirely by their objective responses and has been considered to be very _____. However, recent studies criticize the MMPI for comparing today's subjects to a limited group established as "normal" forty years ago.

Short-Answer Questions

1. What is the difficulty psychologists have in defining intelligence? How may this difficulty affect the validity of intelligence tests?

2. Can you raise your own IQ? Discuss evidence that supports your answer.

3. Summarize the evidence reported in the text that environment can have a great effect on the IQ scores of black and white children.

Self-Test

(Select the one best answer.)

Objective 1: Describe theories reflecting the view that personality is related to body type, and indicate problems with this approach.

1. According to Sheldon, personality is determined mainly by
   a. early childhood experiences.
   b. body type.
   c. your environment.
   d. intrapsychic forces.
   e. body type and environment.

2. Sheldon's classification of types includes
   a. endomorph, mesomorph, ectomorph.
   b. phlegmatic, choleric, melancholic.
   c. introverted, extroverted, nonextroverted.
   d. schizothymia, confidence, dependence.
   e. the categories described in both a and b.

3. Sheldon's theory of body types is criticized because it
   a. failed to explain why body type influences personality.
   b. insisted that all people can be classified into "pure" types.
   c. overemphasized intrapsychic forces.
   d. did not include all the possible body types.
   e. was never tested on human subjects.

Objective 2: Briefly describe Allport's theory of traits and Cattell's factor analysis approach.

4. Which of the following theorists suggested that important human traits are related more to the future than to our genetic past?
   a. Jung
   b. Allport
   c. Binet
   d. Kretschmer
   e. Sheldon

5. Cattell, through factor analysis, reduced personality traits to only _____ which he called _____ traits.
   a. 15, cluster
   b. 16, cluster
   c. 16, source
   d. 35, secondary
   e. 35, source

Objective 3: Discuss how Binet and Simon chose to define and measure intelligence.

6. The original "mental" tests designed by Binet for French schoolchildren were constructed to
    a. identify the exceptionally talented child.
    b. distinguish smart children from problem learners.
    c. identify the mental characteristics of the normal child.
    d. identify the chronological age of the child.
    e. predict the intelligence quotient of the child.

7. At first, Binet related intellegence to
    a. body types.
    b. intrapsychic influences.
    c. environmental influences.
    d. head size.
    e. learning in school.

8. Binet and Simon described a child's level of intelligence, based on test performance, as
    a. motor ability.
    b. standard score.
    c. chronological age.
    d. physical age.
    e. mental age.

Objective 4: Define normal distribution, reliability, and validity, and discuss how these apply to intelligence tests.

9. When scores of any measurable variable assume a bell-shaped curve on a graph, the curve is described as a(n)
    a. intelligence quotient.
    b. reliable test.
    c. normal distribution.
    d. test of validity.
    e. culturally biased test.

10. A test is said to be _____ when it measures what it is supposed to measure.
    a. reliable
    b. error free
    c. normally distributed
    d. predictive of real-life performance
    e. valid

11. There is considerable question about _____ in IQ tests because there is no agreement on what intelligence really is.
    a. validity
    b. reliability
    c. validity and reliability
    d. ethics

Objective 5: Discuss the following influences on intelligence scores: early environmental deprivation, birth order, family size, practice and training in test-taking, culture, race, and coercive discipline.

12. Zena Blau's recent studies of the relationship between IQ scores, strong religious beliefs, and harsh discipline reveal that
    a. children whose mothers hold strong religious beliefs and are overly strict tend to score higher on IQ tests.
    b. children whose mothers hold strong religious beliefs and are overly strict in punishment tend to score the lowest on IQ tests.
    c. there is no correlation between religion, strictness of discipline, and IQ.
    d. social class affects performance on IQ tests more than religion or punishment.
    e. children whose mothers hold strong religious beliefs but are not overly strict score highest on IQ tests.

13. Skeels was able to raise the IQ scores of "retarded" orphanage children to near-normal levels by placing them in a situation where they received
    a. better nutrition.
    b. psychological counseling.
    c. mothering and massive stimulation.
    d. training in test taking.
    e. practice in problem solving.

14. Bloom and Broder found that
    a. low-IQ students could not be helped.
    b. high-IQ students were good guessers.
    c. low-IQ students could think problems through, but were not smart enough to solve them.
    d. low-IQ students did not have the patience to think problems through.
    e. high-IQ students did not need to think problems through.

Objective 6: Distinguish between IQ (intelligence quotient) and intelligence.

15. Your intelligence quotient is
    a. identical with your intelligence.
    b. a measure of your creative abilities.
    c. a good predictor of your future success in life.
    d. impossible to change once it is fixed.
    e. a score derived from your actual age and your performance on a test.

16. An intelligence quotient score is probably not a complete indicator of a person's intelligence because
    a. intelligence is a mixture of many different traits.
    b. an intelligence quotient score is entirely determined by genetic factors.
    c. no two intelligence tests yield identical scores.
    d. of the factors described in both a and c.

Objective 7: Distinguish between objective and subjective tests, citing examples of each, and discuss the usefulness and limitations of each kind.

17. Which of the following is not a projective test?
    a. the Thematic Apperception Test (TAT)
    b. the Rorschach (inkblot)
    c. the Minnesota Multiphasic Personality Inventory (MMPI)
    d. the Word Association Test
    e. the Milwaukee study

18. A test that asks you to express your feelings by drawing a picture and then interpreting it is
    a. an objective test.
    b. a projective (subjective) test.
    c. an intelligence test.
    d. not regarded as valid.
    e. not helpful to psychologists.

Suggestions for Extra Credit

1. By creating a test of your own with which you attempt to measure someone's personality, you might learn more about the problems and failures (and successes, of course) which psychologists and educators have experienced in more than a century of trying to devise a workable, reliable,

valid instrument that fairly and objectively measures **all** aspects of personality—including intelligence. If you are interested, design a short, simple personality test that you can use with a few willing friends, fellow students, or fellow workers. Which traits would you choose to measure? Cattell has condensed potential human traits into sixteen categories (see text Table 20.1, page 550), but some scientists claim there are at least 20,000 traits. Would you choose an objective-type test (such as the multiple-choice MMPI), or a projective measure (Rorschach, TAT)? How would you score your test? Can you make sure that your instrument is free of cultural, racial, or gender bias? Finally, how will you test its reliability and validity? You will find it helpful and instructive to check the literature for readings on how some of the more popular personality tests (such as the MMPI and the Rorschach) are administered, how they are interpreted, and what they find.

2. Creativity has long been a favorite subject for psychological research, and recent years have seen a renewal of interest in this topic—what creativity is, how it is related to intelligence, how it is nurtured, whether it can be taught, and whether it can really be measured in objective terms. Author Robert Shankland has observed that creative people ''discern previously unseen patterns; they see in new ways. They also make connections where no connection had seemed possible. They take risks; seize upon chance; form networks of people who interact in creative ways. What all this seems to come to is the curious mind, the fresh eye, the receptive heart, and the unafraid personality.'' How would you go about developing that personality in yourself or in another? How would you measure your success? In this connection, see *Creativity and the Unconscious* by Sigmund Freud (New York: Harper & Row, 1925; 1958); *Applied Imagination* by Alex F. Osborn (New York: Scribner's, 1979); *Guiding Creative Talent* by E. Paul Torrance (Englewood Cliffs, N.J.: Prentice-Hall, 1976); *Cradles of Eminence* by V. Goertzel and M.G. Goertzel (Boston: Little, Brown, 1978); and ''Family Influences in the Development of Creativity in Children: An Integrative Review,'' in *The Family Coordinator*, 1979, 28(3), 295-312.

   If you didn't work with Extra Credit exercise 4 in Lesson Nine, you might want to experiment with it now. The exercise involves a pair of simple tests that are widely used in psychology to assess creativity and are easy to administer. Merely follow the directions given in the exercise, and be sure to share your findings in a report or brief paper of some kind.

3. In recent years it has become fashionable to categorize people in personality ''types'' according to a particular constellation of behaviors. (You will recall the ''workaholic Type A,'' the ''laid-back Type B,'' and from Lesson Twenty, Suggestions for Extra Credit, the new ''cancer-prone Type C.'') Dr. Pauline Rose Clance, Georgia State University psychologist, in her book, *The*

Imposter Phenomenon, Peachtree Publishers, Ltd., 1978, identifies a new syndrome which she calls the "IP (for imposter phenomenon) personality." People with IP personalities are highly successful men and women who believe that underneath it all they are really frauds and they deserve to be "unmasked" one day, to be seen for the "failures" they actually are. (Dr. Clance thinks she once was an IP personality.) Dr. Joan C. Harvey, a Philadelphia clinical psychologist, working from Clance's theory, has devised the Harvey IP scale, a fourteen-question self-evaluation instrument which psychologists use to measure (and treat) IP tendencies. Dr. Harvey describes the scale in her book, *If I'm So Successful, Why Do I Feel like a Fake?*, St. Martin's Press. If you can secure a copy of Harvey's book, you might be able to decide whether you, or anyone you know, fits the IP syndrome.

4. If science does not yet quite have the ability to control all genetic aspects of human reproduction, it soon will have such control. But, aside from scientific and medical issues to be considered, there are moral and ethical ramifications of enormous import. Do you believe, as some do, that we should exercise genetic controls to assure the birth of babies with superior intelligence and bodies—and prevent the birth of children with lesser intelligence and imperfect bodies? Should we use eugenics to improve the intelligence and creativity of the human race? Yvonne Baskin's 1984 book, *The Gene Doctors*, William Morrow and Company, New York, is first of all a readable and comprehensive survey of research and the current status of genetic technology; second, it is a straightforward examination of the moral, ethical, and philosophical questions to be raised. Of special interest are Section I, "Genetic Choices"; Chapter 17, "New Genes for Mice and Men"; Chapter 18, "Injecting Embryos"; Chapter 19, "Building Mighty Mice"; Chapter 20, "The Genetic Bureaucracy"; Chapter 25, "Improving the Species?"; and Chapter 26, "Choosing Our Future." There is much here that you might wish to pursue. What, for example, are Baskin's conclusions . . . and what are yours?

5. Adrian Dove, a black psychologist, developed the "Chitling Intelligence Test" a few years ago as a sarcastic comment on the middle-class, white bias of most existing intelligence tests. The test is **not** intended as a culture-free (or culture-fair) test for blacks; rather, it is a spoof whose purpose is to show how different can be the language and experiences of black and white children. Here is an abbreviated version of the Chitling Test. Use it to see how well you and your friends or fellow students perform. You can find a discussion of the test in "Taking the Chitling Test," *Newsweek*, July 15, 1968, pp. 51-52. (Incidentally, is "chitling" defined in your dictionary? Are any of the other terms?)

The Chitling Intelligence Test

1. A "gas head" is a person who has a
   a. fast-moving car.
   b. stable of "lace."
   c. "process."
   d. habit of stealing cars.
   e. long jail record for arson.

2. "Bo Diddley" is a
   a. game for children.
   b. down-home cheap wine.
   c. down-home singer.
   d. new dance.
   e. Moejoe call.

3. If a pimp is uptight with a woman who gets state aid, what does he mean when he talks about "Mother's day"?
   a. second Sunday in May
   b. third Sunday in June
   c. first and fifteenth of every month
   d. first of every month
   e. none of these

4. A "handkerchief head" is a(n)
   a. cool cat.
   b. porter.
   c. Uncle Tom.
   d. hoddi.
   e. preacher.

5. If a man is called a "blood," then he is a
   a. fighter.
   b. Mexican-American.
   c. Negro.
   d. hungry hemophile.
   e. red man, or Indian.

6. Cheap chitlings (not the kind you purchase at a frozen-food counter) will taste rubbery unless they are cooked long enough. How soon can you quit cooking them to eat and enjoy them?
   a. 45 minutes
   b. two hours
   c. 24 hours
   d. one week (on a low flame)
   e. one hour

(The answer to all the above questions is "c.")

Answer Key

Matching

1. e
2. j
3. f
4. i
5. g

6. b
7. c
8. a
9. h
10. d

Completion

1. morphology, personality;   2. morphological, mental, Binet, Simon, intelligence quotient, academic;   3. innate (inherited), distribution, curve, genes, environment, bell-shaped;   4. validity, subjective, underestimate; 5. motivate, individual, common, central, secondary;   6. Projective, TAT, Rorschach, personality;   7. objective, MMPI, reliable.

Short-Answer Questions

1. If intelligence were a single trait, psychologists would probably have little trouble defining it. In general, a person is considered intelligent if he or she is good at solving many kinds of problems and adapts easily to many kinds of challenges. Scientists do not agree, however, on what intelligence is, or on how to measure it. Many studies indicate that intelligence results from a great number of talents and abilities. J. P. Guilford, in fact, has identified 120 different factors of intelligence.

Intelligence tests do give valid results by predicting success in school studies and in occupational **levels**. Because many of them measure past learning, or achievement, they are not helpful, and therefore not valid, in predicting success within a given occupation, nor in predicting the improvement in school performance that could occur if special training is given to students. Most IQ tests also can and do fluctuate widely under personal and environmental influences. In order for intelligence tests to better predict future success, the specific traits which promise success would have to be identified and some way found to test for them. Korchia and Schuldberg believe that future tests will have to measure how traits and the environment interact.

2. Many psychologists believe that you can add significantly to your IQ scores by learning how to reason and how to take IQ tests. In a study of how University of Chicago students with low and high IQ scores react to mental challenges, Bloom and Broder found significant differences in the ways in which the two groups approached problem-solving tasks and in the patience with which they persevered. In contrast to low-IQ students, those with high IQ scores read instructions carefully, used step-by-step deduction, and worked patiently at their tasks. After an intensive retraining program, students in the lower IQ group were able to achieve better grades in their college classes. Bloom and Broder concluded that the students had never acquired mental habits necessary for good performance. Whimbey concluded that individuals can improve their IQ scores as much as twenty to thirty points with a great deal of practice with a tutor and immediate positive feedback.

In the 1930s, Skeels was able to raise the IQs of ''mentally retarded'' children from below 50 to near normal ranges by removing the children from institutions and matching them with retarded women who gave them massive attention and stimulation. Minnesota's Steinberg and Scarr, in a more recent study, reported dramatic results in raising the IQs of foster children who, from their genetic backgrounds, were believed to have IQs well below the average. When placed in foster homes with parents who were well educated and had professional jobs or responsibilities, the adopted children scored well above average and close to what might be expected of children brought up in similar natural homes.

3. A number of studies have shown that black children who move from culturally deprived environments to more stimulating ones show a marked improvement in IQ scores, and so do children of all other races and nationalities. Although some studies have shown that black children average lower IQ scores than white children, these differences are probably the result of cultural and racial biases in the tests themselves, not of differences in the average abilities of children of the two races. Black children raised in advantaged environments generally have higher IQs than white children raised in deprived environments. The Boston study of paired black and white children from upper- and lower-class social levels suggests that social class, rather than race, accounted for almost all differences in the scores of 304 black and white children who were tested.

Self-Test

1. b (text page 546)
2. a (text page 546)
3. a (text page 546)
4. b (text pages 549-550)
5. c (text pages 550-551)

6. b (text page 552; television program)
7. d (text page 552; television program)
8. e (text page 553; television program)
9. c (text page 554)
10. e (text page 557)
11. a (text pages 557-558)
12. b (text pages 555-556)
13. c (text page 555; television program)
14. d (text pages 556-557)
15. e (text page 553; television program)
16. d (text pages 551-552, 555; television program)
17. c (text pages 563-567; television program)
18. b (text pages 561-562; television program)

Abnormal Psychology 24

Viewer's Guide for Program Twenty-four

As you view the television program, watch for:

Scenes of people engaged in unusual and even bizarre behavior. One problem we must confront when we discuss abnormality is that of defining the term. Whether an action is considered normal or abnormal often depends on the actor's age, the immediate situation that provoked the action, and the larger culture in which it takes place.

Slides depicting a history of madness and our ways of dealing with it. Over the years, its victims have been variously treated and tortured as the means to an end, if not a cure. Centuries ago, the Greek physician Hippocrates advocated a scientific approach to the treatment of psychological abnormality.

Scenes showing a variety of "abnormal" behaviors originating from multiple causes. Behavior which we agree is abnormal may be variously attributed to biological, intrapsychic, or social causes. For example, the behaviors we associate with stroke, retardation, and senility have biological causes. Obsessive neurosis has intrapsychic roots, and alcoholism may be socially caused. Yet, in many instances, the line between causes may not be distinct. Stroke victims and alcoholics may suffer from intrapsychic problems, and senility may be minimized or even eliminated by changes in social setting and expectancies.

The segment on schizophrenia, a psychosis which takes a variety of forms.

Preview

How "normal" are you? How do you know? What makes you so sure?

According to McConnell, some therapists and theorists would probably consider you "normal," while others would find you just a little "abnormal." And, upon examination, some of us would be found to be more abnormal than others. More important, you could be labeled as "mentally disordered" when you really are not.

Recent estimates suggest that three to four million Americans suffer from severe mental disorders and the lives of millions of others are disrupted by less severe, though significant, mental problems. "I do not believe that there is, or can be, anywhere, any normal person," commented Bertrand Russell. "We all have something queer about us." It is the **quantity**, or amount, of queerness that distinguishes the mental patient from the average citizen, not the **quality** or the type of psychological problem.

R. D. Laing has observed that madness, or insanity, is "a perfectly rational adjustment to an insane world." While sociologists and political theorists might disagree as to the date of onset of the world's "insanity," anthropologists would have no trouble finding signs of troubled minds among ancient ruins. For centuries, we have been confronted by madness. In one age or another, we have revered it as divine and condemned it as demonic. We have viewed it as a sign of genius and used it to excuse or explain dissent. Throughout the ages, we have sought ways to cope with it or to coop it up.

In this lesson, we will take a look at the *Diagnostic and Statistical Manual of Mental Disorders*, the American Psychiatric Association's standard reference for diagnosing a wide range of abnormal behaviors. Always a controversial document, the DSM is in its third edition. We will attempt to define abnormality and to discuss some of the forms it takes. We will see that there are many mental disorders which the medical model, on which the DSM is based, may be inadequate either to explain or to treat, and we will learn that even psychiatrists and psychologists do not always agree on DSM's "labels" or on how to apply them with accuracy.

Critics who viewed surrealist Salvador Dali's paintings often proclaimed him utterly mad. He responded by pointing out that "there is only one difference between a madman and me. I am not mad." The question raised by Dali's response is: How does Dali know whether he is mad or not? How does a psychologist or psychiatrist know? And, finally, does anyone know—really?

Learning Objectives

When you have finished viewing the program and studying your text assignments, you should be able to:

1. Discuss some of the problems involved in defining "normal" and "abnormal."
2. Define range, mean (average), and standard deviation and show how these terms can be used to define "normal" and "abnormal."
3. Describe the purpose and basic assumption of the *Diagnostic and Statistical Manual of Mental Disorders* (DSM-III).
4. Describe how DSM-III has modified the traditional classifications of neuroses and psychoses.
5. Briefly define and give an example of organic mental disorders, substance-induced disorders, schizophrenic disorders, and affective disorders.
6. Discuss the general meaning of "neurosis" and list examples of neurotic disorders.
7. List some of the criticisms and strengths of DSM-III.

Assignments

Before Viewing the Program

Read the preview at the beginning of this lesson and look over the learning objectives that precede the assignments.

Check the section "Did You Know That . . ." at the beginning of Chapter 21 in the text and look over the subtitles for the chapter.

Read Chapter 21, "Abnormal Psychology." As you read, note the boldfaced terms and concepts that appear in the summary and are glossed in upper right corners of right-hand pages. Use the accompanying definitions or descriptions to increase your knowledge or refresh your memory concerning these terms.

View Program 24, "Abnormal Psychology"

After Viewing the Program

Review the text assignments.

Read through the summary at the end of Chapter 21, then consider the thought questions in the chapter. Then to aid your understanding of the materials presented in this lesson, review the boldfaced terms and concepts. In particular, note these terms carefully: deviate, neurosis, psychosis, mode, mean, median, standard deviation, norm, medical model, DSM-III axes, organic psychoses, functional psychoses, senile psychosis, schizophrenia, disorganized schizophrenia, catatonic schizophrenia, paranoid schizophrenia, undifferentiated schizophrenia, paranoia, depression, neurotic disorders, psychosexual disorders, antisocial personality disorder, anxiety disorders, somatoform disorders, validity, reliability, pseudo patients.

Complete the study activities included here as an additional study aid for you.

Now evaluate your understanding of the lesson material by reviewing the learning objectives and taking the self-test in this study guide. Check your answers against the answer key.

According to your instructor's assignment or your own interests, choose and complete activities from among the suggestions for extra credit. You might also consider the recommended readings listed at the end of the chapter.

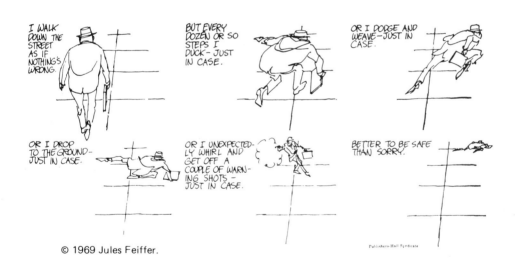

© 1969 Jules Feiffer.

Study Activities

True-False

1. T F Any well-educated person can accurately determine whether a specific behavior is "normal" or "abnormal."
2. T F Psychologists should be aware of what behaviors are common in their culture before labeling a specific one "abnormal."
3. T F To psychologists, the word "mean" is another term that means "norm" or the middle range of scores.
4. T F When a standard deviation is determined for the range of scores on a test, approximately one-half of all the scores will be found in the interval from one standard deviation below the mean to one standard deviation above the mean.
5. T F A score or frequency within one standard deviation above or below the norm is considered within the normal range.
6. T F A score or frequency just at two standard deviations above the norm would be considered within the normal range.
7. T F DSM-III is intended to provide a system for classifying and diagnosing all mental disorders.
8. T F DSM-III assumes that most mental disorders are social in origin.
9. T F A stroke is an example of a biological factor which may cause a mental disorder.
10. T F A fairly mild but permanent emotional disturbance has generally been termed a "psychosis."
11. T F DSM-III has eliminated the term "neurosis" and makes little use of the term "psychosis."
12. T F A patient with a conversion disorder suffers organic symptoms caused by subconsciously repressed or unacceptable desires.
13. T F An unreasoning fear of closed places is an example of a phobic neurosis.
14. T F A feeling of panic experienced whenever a specific activity is anticipated may be an example of an obsessive-compulsive neurosis.
15. T F A patient with schizophrenia experiences extreme "highs" and "lows."
16. T F An affective psychosis is marked by extreme mental disorganization.
17. T F Homosexuality is considered an alternate life-style, rather than a deviation, by many psychologists.

Completion

1. Most of the great personality theorists, such as Freud, Jung, and even Rogers, developed their ideas from studies of people who were mental patients and had exaggerated mental and behavioral problems. They therefore presumed that all of us probably _____ from the norm in certain ways and that the mental patient differs from the average person in the quantity, or amount, of deviation, not in the _____ or type of psychological problem. But if everyone deviates from the the norm, what is normal? What is abnormal? Some psychologists insist, however, that definitions of abnormal must be based on some _____ of what is normal or abnormal for a given person in a given _____. For example, when you describe your problem (or problems) to a therapist, you are implying some standard, or _____, which is characteristic of you. If your usual behavior is "normal," as defined by the culture, then any _____ from your usual ways of thinking, feeling, or behaving can be considered an indication of psychological abnormality. But a therapist must have some way of measuring how _____ you depart from your own and societal _____ of normality.

quality
deviation
culture
definition
concept
norm
much
deviate

2. The statistical approach to defining what is normal is related to the average or middle range, which is called the _____, median, or mode. If an individual score is within the first one-third of the scores above or below the norm, the performance is considered within normal range. Such a score is said to be within one standard _____ above or below the mean. A score that is more than two standard deviations above or below the _____ is considered significantly _____.

mean
abnormal
deviation
mean

3. *The Diagnostic and Statistical Manual of Mental Disorders*, or DSM, as it is called, is a complex diagnostic scheme that attempts to classify people according to their problems. First published by the American Psychiatric Association in 1952, the DSM is now in its third edition, which is popularly referred to as DSM-III. In the traditional system of classifying mental disorders, less serious conditions were termed _____. More severe disorders which prevent effective functioning were termed _____. However, "Axis 1" of the DSM-III includes both neuroses and psychoses under "Severe Mental Disorders." Some less severe conditions included in "Axis 2" are termed _____ disorders.

personality
psychoses
neuroses

4. Neuroses are relatively mild emotional disturbances. Someone who converts a mental or emotional problem to a body symptom suffers from conversion (formerly called hysteria). A person who feels that a separate personality takes charge of his body to perform unacceptable acts has a _____ disorder. Frequent repetition of a symbolic act is called _____ neurosis. Irrational fear of a certain situation or environment is experienced in a _____ neurosis. Freud and and earlier editions of DSM had classified the psychoses as either functional, based in emotional causes, or organic, based in biological causes. Psychosis is marked by mental disorganization, extreme deviation from normal _____ of acting, thinking, and feeling, and, most important, a break with _____. One form of functional psychosis is known as schizophrenia. Another example of a functional psychosis is marked by feelings of persecution and is called _____.

phobic
paranoia
obsessive-compulsive
reality
patterns
dissociative

5. Addictive use or overdose of many drugs can cause both abnormal behavior and _____ mental disorders. Other causes of organic _____ include strokes, Alzheimer's disease, onset of senility, and traumatic head injuries.

psychoses
organic

6. While DSM-III fills the vital need for a scheme of _____ for human problems, its orientation is strongly biological and, as a medical _____, it tends to suggest the use of _____ (or pills) rather than psychotherapy.

model
chemotherapy
classification

Short-Answer Questions

1. What is "normal" as you interpret it from your text and the television program for this lesson?

2. Describe some dangers inherent in pinning psychiatric labels on anyone who may seem to be suffering from psychological pain or disorder.

3. Discuss the problems with DSM-III identified by McConnell, and explain why it is useful despite these criticisms.

4. By drawing lines from one to the other, match the disorder indicated in the left column with the appropriate description in the right column.

phobic disorder   bodily symptoms

obsessive-compulsive   delusions and feelings of being persecuted

paranoia   repetition of thoughts and acts

conversion   irrational fear of harmless objects

Self-Test

(Select the one best answer.)

Objective 1: Discuss some of the problems involved in defining "normal" and "abnormal."

1. In order to determine whether a particular behavior is normal or abnormal, you need to be aware of
   a. your own opinion or judgment.
   b. the behavior of the majority of members of the society in which the behavior occurs.
   c. the opinion of a majority of members of society.
   d. the judgment of professional persons.
   e. a theory of personality that explains all behavior.

2. One difficulty in defining "abnormality" as a deviation from some standard or norm is that
   a. this definition considers only cultural norms, not personal ones.
   b. this definition considers only personal norms, not cultural ones.
   c. attributes such as high intelligence and great beauty also could be said to be abnormal.
   d. attributes such as high intelligence and great beauty are seen as normal for some people.
   e. this definition fails to specify who sets the standards.

Objective 2: Define range, mean (average), and standard deviation and show how these terms can be used to define "normal" and "abnormal."

3. Those scores that are said to be within one standard deviation of the mean will include the first _____ of those above and below the mean.
   a. one-eighth
   b. one-sixth
   c. one-fourth
   d. one-third
   e. one-half

4. Behavior (or test results) is considered within the "normal range" statistically if it falls within that of the middle _____ of the population.
   a. one-third
   b. one-half
   c. two-thirds
   d. three-quarters
   e. nine-tenths

Objective 3: Describe the purpose and basic assumption of the *Diagnostic and Statistical Manual of Mental Disorders* (DSM-III).

5. The DSM-III seems to view all
   a. personality disorders as social problems.
   b. mental disorders as medical problems.
   c. physical conditions as results of mental problems.
   d. mental disorders as social problems.
   e. mental disorders as the results of parental influence.

6. Which of the following best summarizes the purpose of DSM-III?
   a. classification of all physical and mental conditions
   b. classification of "healthy" and "disordered" behaviors
   c. a holistic approach to mental illness
   d. classification of all conditions that might be referred to a doctor
   e. classification of all conditions that might be referred to a psychiatrist

Objective 4: Describe how DSM-III has modified the traditional classifications of neuroses and psychoses.

7. The DSM-III classifies mental disorders as either
   a. psychoses or neuroses.
   b. emotionally caused or socially caused disorders.
   c. severe mental disorders, personality disorders, or physical disorders and conditions.
   d. biological abnormalities or social abnormalities.
   e. schizophrenia or neuroses.

Objective 4; and *Objective 6:* Discuss the general meaning of "neurosis" and list examples of neurotic disorders.

8. In the traditional classification of mental disorders,
   a. a neurosis or a psychosis may be equally severe in affecting the individual's ability to function.
   b. a neurosis is considered to be caused by biological factors while a psychosis is considered to be caused by emotional factors.
   c. a psychosis is a learned behavior and a neurosis is an inherited behavior.
   d. a neurosis is more incapacitating than a psychosis.
   e. a psychosis is more incapacitating than a neurosis.

387

Objective 5: Briefly define and give an example of organic mental disorders, substance-induced disorders, schizophrenic disorders, and affective disorders.

9. Which of the following is marked by manic periods, depressive periods, or both?
    a. an affective disorder
    b. drug addiction
    c. schizophrenia
    d. paranoia
    e. phobia

10. Organic mental disorders include which of these conditions?
    a. those appearing first in childhood
    b. those showing general mental disorganization
    c. those in which the patient experiences extreme "ups and downs"
    d. those for which there are evident physiological causes
    e. those for which there are no apparent physiological causes

Objective 6

11. Excessive repetition of a symbolic act, such as washing your hands, may indicate
    a. a conversion disorder.
    b. a phobic disorder.
    c. a dissociative disorder.
    d. an obsessive-compulsive disorder.
    e. a major depression.

12. Multiple personality is an example of a (an)
    a. psychosexual disorder.
    b. somataform disorder.
    c. dissociative disorder.
    d. affective disorder.
    e. paranoid disorder.

Objective 7: List some of the criticisms and strengths of DSM-III.

13. On the basis of experiments in which "pseudopatients" pretended they heard voices and were admitted to mental hospitals, Stanford's Rosenhan suggests that
    a. psychiatric judgment of what is normal and what isn't is not always reliable.
    b. what the patient says has very little bearing on eventual diagnosis.
    c. most professional personnel can't be deluded easily.
    d. there is considerable agreement among psychiatrists on diagnosis of schizophrenia.

14. Which of these is not one of the criticisms of DSM-III discussed in the text?
    a. Its validity has not yet been established.
    b. The reliability of psychiatric diagnosis has been questioned.
    c. It follows a medical model.
    d. It does not take accompanying physical conditions into account.
    e. The classifications do not discourage placing labels on people.

15. A major flaw of DSM-III is that it
    a. does not attempt to deal with the mentally retarded.
    b. is expected to have a strong influence on the future of psychology.
    c. classifies all mental disorders in a medical model and ignores other important factors.
    d. does all of the above.
    e. does only b and c.

Suggestions for Extra Credit

1. As you might suppose, Rosenhan's experiments in getting a group of "normal" men and women admitted to mental hospitals on the basis of no other information than their complaints that they were "hearing voices" roused the ire of many professionals, amused others, and gave rise to serious concerns about our ability to distinguish the sick from the "sane" (see pages 591-592 in your text). Rosenhan's eight pseudopatients included one psychiatrist, three psychologists, a pediatrician, student, painter, and a homemaker. They were admitted to twelve different hospitals on the east and west coasts and were detained from seven to fifty-two days before they could "negotiate" their release. All but one were **labeled** "schizophrenic" on admission, and on release, their records were marked "schizophrenia in remission." Some psychiatrists said they were merely showing "humanistic concerns" in admitting these pseudopatients. Rosenhan said, "If you're in an insane place, you're insane. Some doctors can't distinguish sanity from insanity." Read Rosenhan's own findings for yourself, then draw some conclusions of your own. (Rosenhan, D. L., "On Being Sane in Insane Places," *Science*, 179, (1972): 250-258.)

2. DSM-III classifies anorexia nervosa (and other eating disorders) under the Axis 1 heading "Severe Mental Disorders." Since the manual now subscribes to the so-called medical model, which implies biological causes and treatment appropriate to biological causes, how do you think this ailment might be seen and treated in the future? If you were unable to read Anne Fadiman's article ("The Skeleton at the Feast: A Case Study of Anorexia Nervosa," *Life*, 5, 2, February 1982: 62.) earlier in this course, you might find it interesting to do so now. Fadiman's article tells of the long and lonely struggle of a teen-ager and her therapist to restore her to health.

3. Ken Kesey's novel *One Flew over the Cuckoo's Nest* (New York: Macmillan, 1962; Viking, 1964) is about every man's struggle to be himself within a society that uses guilt and shame as means of control. More specifically, it is the story of the titanic struggle between a male inmate and a female nurse for the spirits and hearts of a group of people "labeled" insane (some wrongly) and forgotten by the world. It is made memorable by the haunting questions it raises about the credibility of our theories of "normalcy" and the efficacy of our state mental institutions. The novel was made into an Academy Award-winning movie starring Jack Nicholson and Louise Fletcher. Read the novel and/or see the movie, then write about your reactions to either one or both. How is the outcome of this story a tragic example of McConnell's oft-expressed warning that theory is important because it decrees how we perceive people, thus how we **treat** them?
4. Some persons believe that DSM-III and the medical model reflect sex-role stereotyping and a male bias and that diagnosis and treatment of mental and emotional disorders is likewise biased because most psychiatrists are men and the psychiatrists who created DSM were mainly men. (Freud also gets some blame for this bias.) Do **you** think sex-role stereotypes influence conceptions of mental health? If you want to find out, copy the short questionnaire below and adapt it for a simple experiment.

Mental Health Questionnaire

In the list below, check the six characteristics that best describe a mature, healthy, socially competent adult.

____	aggressive
____	gentle
____	logical
____	tactful
____	independent
____	does not hide emotions
____	competitive
____	religious
____	does not cry easily
____	aware of others' feelings
____	adventurous
____	emotional
____	ambitious
____	easily expresses tender feelings

To adapt the questionnaire, make three or more copies on which you write (or type) "male" where it reads "adult" in the instructions; make the same number of copies using the word "female" instead of adult; then, of course, make sure you have an equal number of the original that has only the word "adult." You might hypothesize that conceptions of a healthy male will differ from those of a healthy female, and that the differences show sex-role stereotyping, but you could also make a second hypothesis related to this exercise. What do you think it would be? Ask equal numbers of friends or fellow students to fill in your questionnaires, then record and analyze your results. What implications might sex-role stereotyping have for diagnosis and treatment of mental disorders?

4. Hannah Green's *I Never Promised You a Rose Garden* (New York: New American Library, 1970) is the haunting story of a young girl's torturous journey through schizophrenia to some semblance of "normalcy" and a life of her own with the help of a sensitive and gifted woman psychiatrist. Write a few pages giving your impressions of the girl's fight for health. In what category of DSM-III do you think this young girl would fit? What would the medical model say about the cause of her illness? What you would **you** say?

Answer Key

True-False

1. F	10. F
2. T	11. T
3. T	12. T
4. F	13. T
5. T	14. F
6. F	15. F
7. T	16. F
8. F	17. T
9. T	

Completion

1. deviate, quality, concept, culture, norm, deviation, much, definition;
2. mean, deviation, mean, abnormal;   3. neuroses, psychoses, personality;
4. dissociative; obsessive-compulsive, phobic, patterns, reality, paranoia;
5. organic, psychoses;   6. classification, model, chemotherapy.

Short-Answer Questions

1. "Normal" is often described as those behaviors that are defined by the society as being characteristic of most of the people who live and function in the society. But most of the best personality theories developed by men such as Freud, Erikson, and Rogers assume that most of us deviate from the norm in some way. And if that is true, then what is normal? If most of us engage in deviant behavior, according to society's definition, then these behaviors would be **normal** because they are characteristic of most of us. The

difficulty with this reasoning is that it is perilously near being circular. It is perhaps a bit easier to define "normal" in terms of our usual way of thinking, feeling, or behaving according to some personal or social standard or norm. Any deviation from these patterns could be said to be "abnormal." But normalcy also can be regarded as a continuum along which moderate deviations would be classified as neuroses and greater deviations as psychoses. Abnormality, then, is a matter of how great the deviation is.

2. When we label someone as neurotic or psychotic, we tend to ignore the individual's healthful behaviors and make our perceptions of him or her fit the label. We also equate the person with the problem: the person is a "thing" or a disease ("James is psychotic"). Once labeled—whether erroneously or not—a person will often try to fit his or her behavior to the perceptions that are created by the label. In labeling, we are implying that we know more about the causes and cures of the problem; we are also usually assuming that the problem is either in the mind, the environment, or (as with DSM-III) in one's biological being. We may ignore not only the interplay of these factors, but also others that may be the true cause.

3. DSM-III fills a great need for a way of classifying and dealing with the problems that beset millions of people, thus it helps to standardize the fields of psychiatry and psychology throughout the world. DSM-III was widely tested and has been accepted by numerous professionals in many countries. Its classifications are also much broader than those of previous editions. DSM-III de-emphasizes psychoanalytic theory in favor of a biological orientation, or "medical model." In doing so, the manual swings toward the current view that pills (chemotherapy) are the treatment of choice for mental disorders. According to McConnell, many professionals (non-psychiatrists) see DSM-III as an attempt by psychiatrists to dominate the field. There are also questions of reliability and validity. While DSM-III correlates well with other tests, or has **construct** validity, some observers think it is not a good predictor of real-life situations. Some disorders are not well defined. Worse, professionals disagree often in diagnosing specific patients according to the manual's labeling system, and experiments show that some psychiatrists are unable to distinguish "real" mental patients from those who are pretending to be disturbed.

4. If you drew your lines correctly, your chart should look like this:

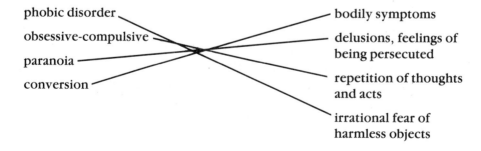

phobic disorder — bodily symptoms

obsessive-compulsive — delusions, feelings of being persecuted

paranoia — repetition of thoughts and acts

conversion — irrational fear of harmless objects

Self-Test

1. b (text pages 572-573)
2. c (text pages 572-573)
3. d (text pages 575-576)
4. c (text page 576)
5. b (text pages 589-591)
6. e (text page 579)
7. c (text pages 578-579)
8. e (text page 574)
9. a (text pages 583-584)
10. d (text pages 578-581)
11. d (text pages 585-586)
12. c (text pages 578, 586-587)
13. a (text page 592)
14. d (text pages 589-591)
15. c (text pages 589-590)

Psychotherapy I 25

Viewer's Guide for Program Twenty-five

As you view the television program, watch for:

An African witch doctor "curing" a patient. Primitive people in Africa and elsewhere have believed, and still do believe, that mental disorders are caused by curses, hexes, spells, and evil spirits. The accepted treatment is an elaborate ritual whereby the spell is broken and the demon banished, but not without inflicting great physical pain and suffering on the patient.

The historical film of Sigmund Freud's life and work. Termed the father of psychoanalysis, Freud developed the first truly modern theory about the origins and treatment of mental illness. Although there are now a number of other accepted therapies for use in the treatment of emotional disorder and mental illness, Freud's theories still dominate the field.

Carl Rogers counseling clients. Rogers is a humanistic psychologist. His approach is a client-centered one in which he attempts to become a "psychological mirror" for the client, reflecting back the client's own thoughts in a slightly different form and without criticizing or making value judgments. In this way, the client can examine his or her own mental functioning in a supportive atmosphere and decide what he or she wants to become.

Preview

What would you do if someone close to you exhibited obvious symptoms of serious physical illness? You would probably suggest without hesitation that he or she call a doctor and seek immediate medical treatment. But what would you do if someone you knew appeared to have a serious mental or emotional disorder? Would a course of action be obvious to you and would you be confident of a cure?

Mental illness and emotional disorder have long plagued human beings, who have sought comfort and cure in a variety of rites and rituals, tonics and treatments, depending upon whom or what they viewed as the cause. In primitive societies both past and present, where mental disorders are seen as the work of witches and evil spirits, the accepted treatment is an elaborate and sometimes painful ritual designed to cast out demons or break spells.

In our more modern and more complex society, both madness and method, cause and cure, seem less well defined. Because we have asked more searching questions, we have found fewer answers. Over a period of years and on the basis of observation and experimentation, trial and error, psychologists and psychiatrists have formulated theories to explain why people become mentally ill and have developed methods for restoring them to sound mental health. These methods are called psychotherapies, meaning ''mind treatments.'' Practitioners choose among them on the basis of their personal biases and their beliefs about the cause of mental disorder. If they blame social/behavioral factors, they may try to alter the group or the environment in which the patient lives. And if they accept an intrapsychic explanation, they may try psychoanalytic or humanistic therapy.

In general, all that can be said about these therapies is that each one of them is effective in some instances, no one of them is effective in all instances, and in still other instances, patients seem to recover spontaneously, without treatment of any kind. In particular, it is possible to evaluate various forms of therapy. In this lesson, we shall examine some biological and some intrapsychic therapies and seek some answers to the questions: How successful is any particular therapy? How reliable is it? What are its side effects? And what do we mean by **cure**? We will also see how some recent important studies are attempting to answer questions such as these.

395

Learning Objectives

When you have finished viewing the program and studying your text assignments, you should be able to:

1. List four issues raised in the text that should be considered when evaluating any form of therapy.
2. Describe the following biological therapies: electro-convulsive therapy, drug therapy, and psychosurgery.
3. Describe the major characteristics of the two types of intrapsychic therapies, psychoanalytic and humanistic.
4. Analyze and evaluate the biological therapies reviewed in this lesson.
5. Analyze and evaluate the various intrapsychic therapies reviewed in this lesson.

Assignments

Before Viewing the Program

Read the preview at the beginning of this lesson and look over the learning objectives that precede the assignments.

Check the section "Did You Know That . . ." at the beginning of Chapter 22 in the text, and look over the subtitles for the chapter.

Read Chapter 22, "Psychotherapy," text pages 599-616. The remainder is covered in the next lesson. As you read, note the boldfaced terms in the text and those that are defined in the upper right corners of right-hand pages. Use the accompanying definitions or descriptions to increase your knowledge or refresh your memory concerning these terms.

View Program 25, "Psychotherapy, Part I"

After Viewing the Program

Review the text assignments, and you might also review Lesson 22 and text Chapter 19, especially the sections on Freud and the humanists.

Read through the summary at the end of Chapter 22 and consider the thought questions in the chapter. Then to aid your understanding of the materials presented in this lesson, review the boldfaced terms and concepts. In particular, note these terms carefully: psychosurgery, lobotomy, transference, client-centered therapy, unconditional positive regard, biotherapies, major and minor tranquilizers, side effects, reflective ''mirror,'' cure rate, and spontaneous recoveries. You should also be able to define humanistic therapy, free association, psychoanalytic therapy, drug therapy, and electro-convulsive therapy.

Complete the study activities included here as an additional study aid for you.

Now evaluate your understanding of the lesson material by reviewing the learning objectives and taking the self-test in this study guide. Check your answers against the answer key.

According to your instructor's assignment or your own interest, choose and complete activities from among the suggestions for extra credit. You might also consider the recommended readings listed at the end of the chapter.

"The Electra complex is always a toughie, and on top of that, you were born under Aquarius. Let's see what the 'I Ching' says."

Playboy, November 1974. Reproduced by special permission of PLAYBOY Magazine; copyright © 1974 by Playboy.

Study Activities

True-False

1. T F   Our therapies almost always stem from our theories of what causes mental illness.
2. T F   Excessive use of electro-convulsive therapy can cause damage to the brain, heart, and lungs.
3. T F   Psychosurgery has proven to be the most effective means of treating mental illness.
4. T F   Librium and valium are called "minor tranquilizers," but they are among the drugs most frequently abused.
5. T F   In his research on psychotherapy, Werner Mendel discovered that reserpine had a distinctly more dramatic effect on the behavior of psychotic patients than the way he responded to the patients.
6. T F   Psychoanalysis focuses on changing the patient's personality.
7. T F   Transference is the method by which analysts prevent strong emotional dependence between themselves and their patients.
8. T F   Freud believed that many psychic conflicts express themselves in fantasy.
9. T F   Humanistic therapy consists primarily of making you aware of your present state of functioning.
10. T F   In Carl Rogers's client-centered therapy, the client determines the goals of therapy, but the therapist decides at what speed they will be met.
11. T F   Intrapsychic therapy concerns itself with objective changes that occur in the environment.
12. T F   In 1952, H. J. Eysenck reported that the improvement rate of patients given psychotherapy was significantly lower than that of patients given no treatment.
13. T F   R. Bruce Sloane's study demonstrated that patients treated by psychotherapists showed far greater improvement than those who received behavior therapy.

Completion

1. In our modern society, both madness and method, cause and cure, seem less well defined than they were by the harshness of some primitive societies. Our choice of therapies is usually based on our _____ about what _____ human behavior, and our theories, in turn, are often shaped by what therapies we have available or have found to be useful. There are, however, four questions that can be asked about any therapy: How useful is it? How _____ is it? What are its side effects? What do we mean by _____?

reliable
theories
"cure"
causes

2. The causes of mental illness and emotional disorder can be viewed as being primarily biological, social/_____, or _____. Therapies for illnesses with biological origins include _____ therapy (ECT), psychosurgery, and _____ therapy. Proponents of the intrapsychic view have employed _____, humanistic, and _____ therapy.

psychoanalytic
intrapsychic
drug
electro-convulsive
client-centered
behavioral

3. Because Hungarian psychiatrist Ladislaus J. Meduna noted that very few schizophrenics were epileptics, he tried using drugs to induce seizures as a means of preventing schizophrenia. Although Meduna met with some success, the side effects of his treatment were alarming. In 1938, Italian psychiatrists Ugo Cerletti and L. Bini began using electrical current rather than drugs to induce seizures. Their method became known as _____ therapy (ECT). Excessive use of ECT can actually damage the _____, the heart, and the lungs. The idea that a diseased brain is responsible for psychosis has led to a form of treatment, that of _____, in which the damaged, diseased, or disease-causing portion of the brain is removed. Today, psychosurgery is generally regarded to be neither as effective nor as _____ as hoped.

psychosurgery
brain
reliable
electro-convulsive

4. Another physiological therapy involves the use of _____. Tranquilizers have been used with some success to calm patients with _____ and those with bipolar disorders. Patients suffering from depression may be helped with _____, although these may have serious side effects. Drugs alone usually _____ cure, and Werner Mendel's experience suggests that the attitudes of the patient and the doctor may have greater influence on improvement than the physical effects of the drugs.

do not
drugs
antidepressents
schizophrenia

5. Adherents to the _____ viewpoint believe mental illness has a physical cause that can be cured or eliminated. They focus on making physical changes. On the other hand, proponents of the _____ viewpoint seek to make changes in the structure or functioning of the patient's personality. Basically, intrapsychic therapy follows one of two approaches. Either it examines what has gone wrong in the _____ to help you understand your present self or it focuses on _____ goals to help you adjust your present attitudes and behaviors. Psychoanalysts, following the lead of Sigmund Freud, usually subscribe to the first approach. Through an emotional relationship between client and therapist, called _____, and through free association, they attempt to bring about a reconstruction of the client's personality.

past
transference
biological
intrapsychic
future

6. Modern humanistic therapists, such as Carl Rogers, have rejected the directive approach of psychoanalysts and substituted instead a client-centered therapy in which the client determines both the _____ of treatment and the speed at which they will be met. In an atmosphere of unconditional positive regard, these therapists reflect, or _____, the client's thoughts back to him or her to help the client perceive where he or she is and what he or she wants to become.

mirror
goals

7. Evaluating psychotherapies is difficult, partly because there are no accepted definitions for "cure" and "value." "Cures" suggest measurable changes of some kind, but values, self-understanding, and "feeling better" are subjective, not accessible to objective measurement. Some comparison studies of various therapies do yield some results, however. H. J. Eysenck reported, for example, that _____ therapy was better than psychotherapy given to some patients, but his studies ignored basic alterations in personality that are often the goals of _____ treatment. In a major investigation by Temple University's R. Bruce Sloane, the conclusion was that behavior therapy is _____ effective as, and possibly _____ than, psychotherapy for patients with moderately severe neuroses and personality disorders.

at least as
psychoanalytic
no
more so

Short-Answer Questions

1. List and explain what four issues McConnell says must be considered in evaluating any therapy.

2. What are the major differences between psychoanalytic and humanistic therapy?

3. Briefly describe the findings of the 1952 Eysenck report, Garfield's interpretation of the 1972 Menninger study, and the work of R. Bruce Sloane evaluating the effectiveness of various forms of therapy. Add a two- or three-line summary.

Self-Test

(Select the one best answer.)

Objective 1: List four issues raised in the text that should be considered when evaluating any form of therapy.

1. Which one of the following is not suggested by McConnell as a question to be asked in evaluating any therapy?
   a. How successful is it?
   b. Who developed it?
   c. How reliable is it?
   d. What are its side effects?
   e. What is meant by **cure**?

2. If a form of psychotherapy is consistently effective with many types of patients, we say it
   a. is reliable.
   b. is successful.
   c. is valid.
   d. has few side effects.
   e. leads to spontaneous recovery.

Objective 2: Describe the following biological therapies: electro-convulsive therapy, drug therapy, and psychosurgery; and *Objective 4:* Analyze and evaluate the biological therapies reviewed in this lesson.

3. Today, some psychiatrists believe that improvement caused by electro-convulsive therapy (ECT)
   a. justifies more frequent use.
   b. is more important than possible damage to the brain or the heart and lungs.

c. cures certain forms of forgetting.
d. may be due to a placebo effect.
e. proves that it is the most effective treatment for schizophrenics.

4. Long-term treatments with antidepressants can
   a. prevent the need for psychosurgery.
   b. alleviate most symptoms of schizophrenia.
   c. result in irreversible damage to the brain.
   d. be effective with most of the severe mental disorders listed in DSM-III.
   e. be used when psychiatrists cannot agree on a patient's diagnosis.

Objective 2

5. Which of the following is the best description of prefrontal lobotomy?
   a. removal of the higher centers of the brain
   b. removal of the lower centers of the brain
   c. cutting nerve connections between the thalamus and prefrontal lobes
   d. cutting most nerve connections between the left and right hemispheres
   e. cutting nerve connections between the prefrontal lobes and sensory receptors

6. While drug therapies may be helpful in reducing symptoms of various mental illnesses,
   a. they have been proven to "cure" only cases of manic-depression.
   b. they are most effective in treating schizophrenia.
   c. they have been shown to be ineffective in treating depression.
   d. they are not a substitute for psychological and social help that might be needed by the patient.
   e. their side effects render them too dangerous to use.

7. One problem of existing drug therapies is that
   a. research has not always controlled for the placebo effect.
   b. all of them produce serious side effects.
   c. they increase serotonin production.
   d. too many patients die during therapy.

Objective 3: Describe the major characteristics of the two types of intrapsychic therapies, psychoanalytic and humanistic.

8. The goal of intrapsychic therapy is to
   a. show how biological factors cause mental illness.
   b. control moods with meditation.
   c. get a group of patients to interact.
   d. change the patient's personality.
   e. explain the effect of environmental forces on mental health.

9. Which of the following is not a feature of psychoanalysis?
   a. transference
   b. free association
   c. interpretation
   d. dream analysis
   e. rapid symptom removal

10. Freud based the technique of free association on the assumption that
   a. our most important thoughts are conscious and are expressed in random speech.
   b. relaxing conscious control allows unconscious impulses and memories to surface.
   c. treatment must proceed whether or not causes have been identified.
   d. an unrestrained personality is a healthy personality.
   e. thoughts are far more important than emotions.

11. In psychoanalytic therapy, transference is the term used to describe the fact that the patient
   a. transfers his or her attention from present problems to future goals.
   b. transfers his or her attention from past problems to present problems.
   c. transfers intense emotions to the therapist rather than to figures from the past.
   d. relieves guilt by shifting the blame for past mistakes from himself or herself to others.
   e. changes from therapist to therapist as his or her condition improves.

12. In contrast to psychoanalysts, humanistic psychologists emphasize
   a. dream analysis.
   b. conscious determinants of behavior.
   c. free association.
   d. transference.
   e. past experiences.

13. In the client-centered approach to psychotherapy, the therapist
   a. gives the patient detailed instructions to follow.
   b. acts as a transference object for inappropriate emotions.
   c. usually sits behind a couch where the patient cannot see him or her.
   d. acts as a "psychological mirror" so that the patient can "see" and come to understand himself or herself.
   e. sets the goals of treatment and determines the speed at which they will be met.

14. Which of the following statements about the side effects of electro-convulsive therapy is **not** true?
    a. The patient usually does not remember the shock or events that immediately precede it.
    b. The treatment does not affect the brain permanently; there are no harmful side effects.
    c. Some depressed patients do show minor improvement after ECT.
    d. ECT patients experience seizures like those of epileptics.

15. How reliable is psychosurgery as a therapeutic tool?
    a. Sloane's studies showed lobotomies to be more effective in curing schizophrenia than was psychoanalysis.
    b. The fatality rate from lobotomies is about 4 percent.
    c. Lobotomies are not as effective as researchers hoped.
    d. The statements in b and c are true.
    e. None of these statements is true.

Objective 4; and *Objective 5:* Analyze and evaluate the various intrapsychic therapies reviewed in this lesson.

16. What is one factor in patient care that none of the therapies studied in this course attempts to explain?
    a. why people develop mental disorders
    b. why some people recover spontaneously, while others don't
    c. why some therapies are more successful for some kinds of disorders
    d. why some people develop one kind of disorder and others develop other kinds
    e. why therapists don't always agree on diagnoses and treatments

17. Which of the following is **not** a problem in evaluating the effectiveness of various psychotherapies?
    a. spontaneous remission rates
    b. symptom substitution
    c. measurement of the therapist's empathy
    d. criteria for cure or improvement
    e. the placebo effect

18. The results of H. J. Eysenck's study of disturbed servicemen and women in British hospitals led some scientists to suggest that
    a. psychoanalysis should be universally adopted as a treatment for mental disorders.
    b. some patients are better suited for analysis than others.
    c. hospitalized psychotics make good clients for analysis.
    d. the effectiveness of psychoanalysis cannot be determined.
    e. psychoanalysis might actually retard the progress of some patients.

19. In his comparison of various therapeutic approaches, psychiatrist R. Bruce Sloane found that _____ therapy may not be as effective as _____ therapy.
    a. psychoanalytic, behavior
    b. humanistic, drug
    c. client-centered, electro-convulsive
    d. behavior, psychoanalytic
    e. group, client-centered

20. In evaluating the success (or "cure" rate) of the psychotherapy approaches, scientific investigators
    a. have difficulty because they don't agree on the nature of therapy.
    b. encounter difficulties in defining "cure" or success.
    c. don't always consider the viewpoints of both clients and therapists.
    d. experience all of the problems described above.
    e. always base judgments on measurable behaviors.

Suggestions for Extra Credit

1. On page 603 of Chapter 22, McConnell asks the question: "Under what diagnostic category would a psychiatrist using the DSM-III put koro?" Koro, you will recall, is an affliction peculiar to some Chinese men whose morbid fear about their penises dominates and distorts their entire lives. To answer McConnell's question, look back through the DSM-III classifications in Chapter 21, then recall what you have learned about phobias early in this course. You might then say that the man with koro has an irrational fear (phobia) about losing his sex organ and that DSM-III classifies such a phobia as a form of anxiety and lists it under "Severe Mental Disorders." As you also know, therapists have had considerable success in treating phobias with desensitization techniques and counter-conditioning, but would these be effective in a "koro-minded" Chinese culture? (Would Freud have considered this to be a form of castration anxiety? What might Freud conclude about the wife's role in koro?) Prepare a brief diagnosis (label) for the koro victim, suggest how you would treat the problem, tell your reasons

for your decisions, then submit your work to your teacher or a psychologist of your acquaintance and ask for comment.

2. This exercise involves a fictional case history devised by a well-known professor and author of textbooks on abnormal psychology. It is commonly used as a learning tool for students of introductory psychology and is intended only to illustrate the difficulties of labeling and deciding upon a choice of treatment. In this case history, you are given somewhat more information than in the koro case.

The case of Dr. A, a dentist

After ten years of very successful practice, a thirty-four-year-old dentist noted that his practice had declined very slightly during the closing months of the year. Shortly after this he began to experience mild anxiety attacks and complained of continual worry, difficulty in sleeping, and a vague dread that he was "failing." As a result, he increased his hours of practice during the evenings from one to five nights and began driving himself beyond all reason in a desperate effort to "ensure the success of his practice." Although his dental practice now increased beyond what it had been previously, he found himself still haunted by the vague fears and apprehensions of failure. These, in turn, became further augmented by frequent heart palpitations and pains which he erroneously diagnosed as at least an incapacitating if not a fatal heart ailment. At this point his anxiety became so great that he voluntarily came for assistance.

What types of behaviors do you think are indicated in Dr. A's case? Psychologists would probably suggest neurosis rather than psychosis, but which one? Anxiety? Yes, but which kind? What other aspects of neurosis can you see? (Psychologists might say conversion and obsessive-compulsive.) Is there a break with reality? No. (The dentist continues to function in his culture, and he maintains a successful business operation.) Do you see any relationship between this dentist's behavior and Harvey's IP Personality, to which you were introduced in Lesson Twenty-three?

When you finish your description of what you think Dr. A's problem might be and have added some suggestions as to what treatment approach should be taken (if you think one is indicated), submit your work to your teacher or to a professional therapist of your acquaintance for comment.

3. Elinor Lander Horwitz, a graduate of Smith College and a free-lance writer who is married to a neurosurgeon, has written a brief but fully researched study of our approaches to mental illness, from the Old Testament "music therapy" that soothed King Saul through phrenology, Freud, "faradization," and psychosurgery, to encounter therapy and the human potential movement. Her book, *Madness, Magic, and Medicine: The Treatment and Mistreatment of the Mentally Ill* (New York: Lippincott, 1977), traces the development of our approaches to mental illness and the

technology for curing it and points out the age-old superstitions that underlie current practices. It includes interesting and unusual illustrations from the National Library of Medicine and the American Psychiatric Association Archives, a three-page list of suggestions for further reading, and a useful index. If you are interested, read Horwitz's book and write a brief paper relating what you read to some aspect of this lesson.

4. The licensing procedures for psychiatrists, psychologists, counselors, sociologists, social workers, and psychotherapists are quite different. Find out what classifications the law recognizes in your state, what schooling and qualifications each must have to practice, and what each is allowed or expressly forbidden to do (for example, perform surgery, prescribe medication). Summarize the results of your research and tell if the present system is fair or unfair to the practitioner and provides too much, too little, or sufficient protection for the client.

Answer Key

True-False

1. T	8. T
2. T	9. T
3. F	10. F
4. T	11. F
5. F	12. T
6. T	13. F
7. F	

Completion

1. theories, causes, reliable, "cure";   2. behavioral, intrapsychic, electro-convulsive, drug, psychoanalytic, client-centered;   3. electro-convulsive, brain, psychosurgery, reliable;   4. drugs, schizophrenia, antidepressants, do not;   5. biological, intrapsychic, past, future, transference;   6. goals, mirror;   7. no, psychoanalytic, at least as, more so.

Short-Answer Questions

1. The four issues are: (1) How successful is the therapy? (2) How reliable is it? (3) What are its side effects? (4) What do we mean by cure? **Success** must be measured in terms of actual cure rate adjusted for the expected number of spontaneous recoveries, those patients who would have recovered in time without treatment of any kind. In evaluating **reliability**, we must look at how often it works and in how many different cases or with how many different types of illness. **Side effects**, too, must be considered. If they are

sufficiently severe or undesirable, the "cure" may be worse than the ailment or may leave the patient with more serious problems to be solved. And then there is the question of what is meant by **cure** and who decides. Is a marked improvement the same as a cure? If the symptoms return, does that invalidate the cure? And whose responsibility is it to determine when a cure has taken place—the therapist's, or the patient's, or some outside observer's?

2. Although psychoanalytic therapy and humanistic therapy seek the same goal—mental health and effective functioning—they differ in at least two respects: (1) the emphasis and direction of the analysis and (2) the roles played by client and therapist. In psychoanalytic therapy, the therapist determines the goals of the treatment and the speed at which these goals will be reached. Through the process of transference, the therapist becomes a power figure. Then, using the techniques of free association and interpretation, the therapist encourages the client to recall and explore what has gone wrong in the past in order to understand his or her present self. In the more client-centered humanistic therapy, the client determines both goals of treatment and the speed with which they will be met. The therapist provides a warm and supportive atmosphere in which the client is encouraged to talk about his or her problems. The therapist may restate some of what the client says to help the client examine his or her thoughts but will seldom give advice or offer suggestions about what ought to be done. The client is encouraged to set future goals and then to examine present behavior to see how it can be changed to make these goals achievable.

3. After investigating the cases of several thousand servicemen and women hospitalized in British institutions after World War II, behaviorist H. J. Eysenck suggested that psychoanalytic treatment of mental disorders might actually retard the progress of the patient. Eysenck reports an improvement rate of about 44 percent for patients treated with psychoanalytic techniques, compared to a 64 percent improvement rate for patients given other forms of psychotherapy, and a rate of about 72 percent for patients whose bodily ills were treated but who were given no form of psychological therapy. Sol Garfield reviewed the results of a Menninger Foundation study released in 1972. The study followed 21 patients who had undergone psychoanalysis and another 21 patients who had received insight therapy. According to Garfield, the results are not really favorable toward psychotherapy, because slightly less than one-half of these patients showed either moderate or marked improvement after several years. Temple University's R. Bruce Sloane divided a group of patients into two treatment groups and a control group. Patients in all groups were interviewed and given personality tests. One group was then treated with psychoanalytic "insight" therapy, a second group was given behavior therapy, and the third group became an untreated control group. Patients in the treatment groups were given one hour of therapy each week for four months. At the end of the treatment period, all patients were retested and

reinterviewed. Sloane found that 80 percent of patients in the treatment groups showed improvement of symptoms, but about half of the untreated control group exhibited spontaneous improvement. Compared to those who had received behavioral therapy, the patients with insight therapy showed less improvement in their work situations and social adjustment.

Sloane concludes that behavior therapy is at least as effective as, and possibly more so than, psychotherapy with moderately severe neuroses and personality disorders that are typical of clinical populations. His work dispelled the theory that behavior therapy has only limited application to such disorders as "phobias" and established that behavior therapy is clearly a generally useful technique.

In summary, it might be said that, despite difficulties with definitions, problems with methodologies, subjective factors, and other "non-measurables," most types of "talk" therapies can be of value to some patients, and behavioral therapies seem to work better than psychoanalytic approaches in some situations, but that a large percentage of patients seem to get well on their own.

Self-Test

1. b (text page 603)
2. a (text page 603)
3. d (text pages 604-605)
4. c (text page 608)
5. c (text page 605)
6. d (text pages 606-607)
7. a (text page 607)
8. d (text pages 608-609; television program)
9. e (text page 610; television program)
10. b (text page 609; television program)
11. c (text page 609; television program)
12. b (text pages 610-611; television program)
13. d (text pages 610-611; television program)
14. b (text pages 604-605)
15. d (text page 605)
16. b (text pages 609-613)
17. c (text pages 609-613)
18. e (text pages 612-613)
19. a (text pages 613-615; television program)
20. d (text pages 611-613)

Psychotherapy II 26

Viewer's Guide for Program Twenty-six

As you view the television program, watch for:

An armchair tour of therapy groups. You will see Frederick G. ("Fritz") Perls working with a Gestalt therapy group, watch a transactional analysis (TA) group analyze the "scripts" and "games" that often characterize interpersonal transactions, and witness some encounter groups in action.

Actual scenes of a modern "token economy" system in practice. Patients in mental hospitals frequently develop a childlike dependency on the staff, an attitude that is called "institutional neurosis." The token economy is a technique used to encourage patients to accept responsibility for their own improvement.

A photo of psychiatrist Adolf Meyer and scenes from a holistic health center. Meyer, who is often called the "dean of U.S. psychiatry," recognized that there were multiple causes for even the simplest of behaviors and believed in a holistic approach, wherein he sought to determine and build upon the normal aspects of the patient's behavior.

Have you ever taken part in a group therapy session?

If your answer is a hasty and definite no, you may want to pause and think for a moment about what a group therapy session is. You may be surprised to learn that you actually take part in one regularly.

Until fairly recently, we assumed that mental illness existed **within** an individual—whether in the brain or in the mind—and could best be cured by working from the inside out in some sort of one-to-one analysis. Within the past century, another view has emerged, the view that mental illness is as much a disruption of relationships **between** people as it is a disruption of the thought and behavior control processes **within** a person. Abnormal behavior is usually expressed in social situations; and to be of lasting value, treatment must help the patient function more effectively in these situations. Put simply, it must help the patient get along better with others.

In response to the emergence of this view, therapeutic techniques have been developed in which the patient is seen and treated as part of a group. Group therapy takes many forms, including psychoanalytic groups, inspirational groups, encounter groups, transactional analysis (TA), psychodrama, Gestalt groups, and environmental therapies such as token economies and milieu therapy. What these groups seem to share is a belief that intimate sharing of feelings, ideas, and experiences in an atmosphere of mutual respect and understanding enhances self-respect, deepens self-understanding, and helps the individual to get along better with others. While most participants seem to find group experiences rewarding and satisfying at first, studies show that group therapy has little long-term therapeutic value and may even result in harm.

In this lesson, we will examine some of these forms of therapies in action and form our own opinions as we understand their dynamics. We will also learn what successful psychotherapies have in common and be introduced to the new technique of meta-analysis, which seems to affirm the general effectiveness of psychotherapy as treatment.

Learning Objectives

When you have finished viewing the program and studying your text assignments, you should be able to:

1. Describe the characteristics of various group psychotherapies: psychodrama, transactional analysis, Gestalt and encounter groups.

2. Describe milieu therapy and the use of token economies as forms of environmental therapies.
3. Evaluate the benefits and limitations of the various social/behavioral therapies.
4. Explain Meyer's holistic approach and the results of applying "critical common sense" to the analysis of strengths and weaknesses of existing therapies.

Assignments

Before Viewing the Program

Read the preview at the beginning of this lesson and look over the learning objectives that precede the assignments.

Check the section "Did You Know That . . ." at the beginning of Chapter 22 in the text and review the subtitles for the chapter.

Read Chapter 22, "Psychotherapy," from page 616 through 626. As you read, note the boldfaced terms and concepts that appear in the text and are defined in the upper right corners of right-hand pages. Use the accompanying definitions or descriptions to increase your knowledge or refresh your memory concerning these terms.

View Program 26, "Psychotherapy, Part II"

After Viewing the Program

Review the text assignments.

Read through the summary at the end of Chapter 22 and consider the thought questions. Then to aid your understanding of the materials presented in this lesson, review the boldfaced terms and concepts. In particular, note these terms carefully: group therapy, milieu therapy, psychodrama, transactional analysis, Gestalt therapy, encounter groups, institutional neurosis, token economy, holistic therapy, team therapy, meta-analysis.

Complete the study activities included here as an additional study aid for you.

Now evaluate your understanding of the lesson material by reviewing the learning objectives and taking the self-test in this study guide. Check your answers against the answer key.

According to your instructor's assignment or your own interests, choose and complete activities from among the suggestions for extra credit. You might also consider the recommended readings listed at the end of the chapter.

"Leave us alone! I am a behavior therapist! I am helping my patient overcome a fear of heights!"

© 1975 Medical Tribune. Reprinted by permission of Sidney Harris.

Study Activities

True-False

1. T F Mental illness is now viewed as a disruption of relationships between people as well as the individual's intrapsychic maladjustment.
2. T F Identification of destructive "games" is an important goal of transactional analysis therapy.
3. T F In psychodrama, the group leaders enact situations to illustrate their meanings for the participants.
4. T F Gestalt therapy teaches participants to recognize three basic "game plans": parent, adult, and child.

5. T F Encounter groups are so named because they are largely unplanned and undirected.
6. T F Encounter groups frequently focus on nonverbal experiences.
7. T F Environmental therapy is practiced by encouraging the patient to look at the environment in a new way, no matter how unpleasant it may seem.
8. T F In milieu therapy, attempts are made to structure the patient's surroundings to encourage better adjustment.
9. T F In a token economy, patients are given concrete awards for approved behavior.
10. T F According to research, the majority of participants in group therapy show long-term personality change and improvement.
11. T F Despite the limitations of social and behavioral therapies, a mentally disturbed person seldom improves without some kind of treatment.
12. T F No form of psychotherapy can be shown to "cure" more than 60 percent of its patients.
13. T F Adolf Meyer believes in a holistic approach to psychotherapy.
14. T F A critical and demanding environment does not encourage psychological change.
15. T F While the attitude of the therapist is important to success in therapy, the patient's attitude seems to make little difference.
16. T F According to Meyer's "critical common-sense approach," most successful forms of treatment have at least five major characteristics in common.
17. T F Meta-analysis supports the belief that psychotherapy is ineffective.

Completion

1. Prayer meetings, revivals, and seances were the earliest forms of _____ therapy. The concept of group therapy originated from a discovery by a Boston physician that patients in treatment for tuberculosis seemed to profit more from intensive discussions than from his lectures. Present-day group therapy techniques vary widely, although there are some strong similarities among them. Participants in _____ act out roles with each other. Learning to identify and avoid destructive ego games is important in _____ analysis groups. _____ therapy is based on perceiving the world as wholes and encourages exploration of one's perceptions and behavior. Members of _____ groups often meet for an intensive day or weekend of activity.

Gestalt
group
encounter
transactional
psychodrama

2. _____ therapy might be thought of as a psychological ecology. In the past, institutions such as insane asylums, which are, in reality, _____ systems, often had a very poor rate of "cure" because the _____ itself was so abnormal. One's social environment is one's milieu, and therapy directed toward changing the patient's environment to change behavior is known as _____ therapy. So-called token economies have been designed to counter the "free economy" typical in a mental hospital. It has been found that patients in institutions tend to become increasingly dependent upon the hospital and staff—a condition called _____ neurosis. In a token economy, approved behaviors are _____ while inappropriate or abnormal behaviors are _____. The token economy environment seems to have a definite effect on a patient's _____, but this approach is criticized because it does not deal with _____ psychological problems.

milieu
ignored
Environmental
rewarded
underlying
ecological
institutional
behavior
environment

3. A majority of participants are usually _____ enthusiastic about group therapy experiences immediately after the experience. As time goes on, however, this degree of enthusiasm tends to _____. Recent studies indicate there is little scientific evidence that group therapy has much _____ value. Indeed, it may often cause real _____.

decrease
harm
highly
therapeutic

4. Adolf Meyer called his _____ approach to psychotherapy "critical common sense." He believed the therapist should work to change the patient's _____ as much as his or her inner feelings or behaviors.

Applying Meyer's approach, McConnell points out that most successful forms of treatment provide _____ to the patient, giving the patient more information than he or she had before about himself or herself and the world. A successful therapy will probably build on the patient's _____ rather than by attacking weaknesses.

_____

feedback
holistic
strengths
environment

Short-Answer Questions

1. What is the basic point of view upon which the social/behavioral therapies are founded?

2. What is the future potential of a team approach to psychotherapy, considering the current track records of the various therapies now in use?

3. What does meta-analysis reveal about psychotherapeutic approaches to the treatment of mental problems?

Self-Test

(Select the one best answer.)

Objective 1: Describe the characteristics of various group psychotherapies: psychodrama, transactional analysis, Gestalt and encounter groups.

1. In which of the following types of group therapy does the participant become a "hero" or "heroine"?
   a. Gestalt therapy
   b. psychodrama
   c. transactional analysis
   d. encounter
   e. nondirective group therapy

2. Which of the following would be most typical of an encounter group?
   a. The leader would attempt to serve as a psychological mirror, reflecting the participants' attitudes and emotions back to them.
   b. Emphasis would be placed on the games being played as parent, adult, or child.
   c. Group members might explore their emotions, attitudes, or perceptions through a variety of activities.
   d. Participants would learn to identify behavior that is manipulative.
   e. Participants would be encouraged to identify their own emotional reactions and learn ways to communicate these to others.

3. Which of the following is **not** accurately descriptive of a particular group therapy approach?
   a. In transactional analysis, the leader would not attempt to control the activities of the group in any way.
   b. In psychodrama, many activities resemble the staging of a play.
   c. In Gestalt psychotherapy, emphasis is on growth through exploration.
   d. In an encounter group, emphasis may be on nonverbal awareness and communication.
   e. In Gestalt therapy, attention is primarily directed toward the here and now.

Objective 2: Describe milieu therapy and the use of token economies as forms of environmental therapies.

4. Which of the following is **not** true of a "token economy" therapy?
   a. Appropriate behavior is rewarded.
   b. Emphasis is on changing the patient's behavior.
   c. Token rewards may be used to obtain privileges and pleasures.
   d. No attempt is made to encourage patients to modify their behavior.
   e. Patients are often strongly motivated to improve their behavior.

5. Which of the following describes milieu therapy?
   a. Patients are taught to discover "games" they and others play.
   b. The patient's total environment is designed to encourage increased self-confidence and self-esteem.
   c. Patients are under strong pressure to change their behavior.
   d. Patients are taught in a short play how to express their feelings and experiment with new behaviors.
   e. Patients are given tangible rewards for appropriate behavior.

Objective 3: Evaluate the benefits and limitations of the various social/behavioral therapies.

6. According to a study by Lieberman, Miles, and Yalom,
   a. traditional insight therapy far surpasses group therapy in effectiveness.
   b. group therapy might best be used as an opportunity for exploration and intense interpersonal experiences.
   c. group therapy has a significantly higher cure rate than other forms of therapy.
   d. there is virtually no danger of harm to an individual from group therapy.
   e. only one variety of group therapy has been demonstrated to be effective.

7. Of the environmental therapies discussed in this lesson,
   a. only milieu therapy concentrates on the changing of behavior rather than inner states.
   b. none significantly affects behavior.
   c. token economy therapy tends to encourage dependence on the institution and staff.
   d. token economy therapy concentrates significantly on changing behavior rather than inner states.
   e. each has a strong immediate influence on the behavior of most patients.

8. Which of the following statements is true?
   a. Most mentally disturbed individuals tend to improve, even without therapy.
   b. Half or more of mentally disturbed individuals tend to become more seriously impaired without therapy.
   c. It is likely that an individual with a neurosis or psychosis will not improve without therapy.
   e. Most mentally disturbed individuals change very little one way or the other.

9. A chief criticism of _____ therapy is that it successfully changes behavior, but does not get at underlying psychological problems.
   a. encounter group
   b. Gestalt
   c. nondirective
   d. transactional analysis
   e. token economy

10. The application of meta-analysis to studies of psychotherapeutic treatment of mental disorders
   a. proves that the medical model, as exemplified by DSM-III, is the best approach.
   b. indicates that all successful therapies have certain aspects in common.
   c. supports the belief that psychotherapy is an effective form of treatment.
   d. refutes the belief that psychotherapy is an effective form of treatment.
   e. suggests that a combination of therapies might be more effective than any one approach.

Objective 4: Explain Meyer's holistic approach and the results of applying "critical common sense" to the analysis of strengths and weaknesses of existing therapies.

11. By "critical common sense," Adolf Meyer meant that
   a. a therapist should be critical of the patient's weaknesses and set new goals for him or her.
   b. the therapist should build on the patient's assets, allow the patient to set goals, and give the environment as much attention as psyche or behavior.
   c. patients should be taught to be critical of their environments and of other people's games.
   d. every type of psychotherapy should be evaluated critically in testing an individual.
   e. the therapist should be able to diagnose patients' conditions accurately and determine exactly what is occurring in their psyches.

Suggestions for Extra Credit

1. Consult your library, chamber of commerce, or perhaps your secretary of state to obtain a list of therapy or so-called "self-help" groups organized and active in your community or your state. You may be surprised to find how many of these are in existence and what wide areas of interest they embrace—for example, religious groups and those organized around families with children or spouses who are suffering a debilitating or fatal disease (such as Alzheimer's). Try to locate a good literature reference or two on some of these groups (or others like them). Then, from your reading

and what you've learned in this lesson about the benefits and limitations of these kinds of groups, try to draw some conclusions about why they seem to be so persistent and so widespread. What appeal do they seem to have? What success, if any? If you are interested, attend one or more meetings of one or two groups and read any literature they offer.

2. If you have taken part in group therapy, write a one-page summary of your experience, stating what kind of group therapy it was, how long it lasted, what procedures were followed, how you felt immediately after the sessions were over, and how you felt six months later. Compare your reactions with what your text reports about the success of such groups.

3. Psychologist Jerry Greenwald has applied Gestalt group therapy principles in his work with patients and has advocated them in his books. For a clearer understanding, read *Be the Person You Were Meant To Be* or *Is This Really What I Want To Do?* (Pasadena, Calif.: Ward Ritchie Press, 1977). In this latter volume the author states that the ongoing question we should ask ourselves is whether the activity in which we are presently engaged is the way we want to use up this hour, this evening, or this day of our lives, or whether there is something more nourishing and creative we would rather be doing. Read this book and write a review of it. Do you agree or disagree with what the author has to say?

Answer Key

True-False

1. T	10. F
2. T	11. F
3. F	12. F
4. F	13. T
5. F	14. T
6. T	15. F
7. F	16. T
8. T	17. F
9. T	

Completion

1. group, psychodrama, transactional, Gestalt, encounter; 2. Environmental, ecological, environment, milieu, institutional, rewarded, ignored, behavior, underlying; 3. highly, decrease, therapeutic, harm; 4. holistic, environment, feedback, strengths.

Short-Answer Questions

1. Historically and philosophically, it was assumed that mental illness resided in the brain or the mind of the individual. Thus, most forms of biological and intrapsychic therapies attempted to treat the patient "from the inside out." The social/behaviorists have come to believe, however, that mental illness is as much a disruption of the "outside"—the relationships between people—as it is a disruption of one's inner psychodynamics. Abnormal behavior is almost always expressed in social situations and mentally ill persons are rarely banished to institutions unless they upset others. In fact, people who surround the person who is ill may actually be contributing to the problem without being aware of it, and the best therapy may be to change the environment or change the way the people in the environment behave. Treatment must not only alter the patient's behavior, it must help the patient to get along better with people.

2. It seems likely that a team approach, in which the patient is treated as a whole individual functioning within a complex environmental system, will be the most promising form of mental therapy for the future. In some treatment centers, therapists work with individual patients in teams—one therapist dealing with physical or biological problems, one concerned with intrapsychic dynamics, a third helping to change behavior patterns, and a fourth working with alteration of the social environment. Ideally, the goals of therapy should be spelled out in a written contract signed by the patient and all members of the therapy team. One way of recording progress could be to use a graph.

3. In 1977, Smith and Glass reported that meta-analysis, a new technique for trend analysis, shows that there are more studies that suggest positive results for psychotherapy in the treatment of mental disorders than there are studies that indicate negative results. Although it is disputed, this trend seems to support the efficacy of psychotherapeutic approaches in the treatment of mental disorders. Because behavioral psychologists in particular are highly critical of the meta-analysis technique, there is, according to McConnell, still some doubt about the effectiveness of psychotherapy.

Self-Test

1. b (text page 617)
2. e (text page 620)
3. a (text pages 619-620)
4. d (text page 622; television program)
5. b (text pages 621-622)

6. b (text page 621)
7. d (text page 622; television program)
8. a (text page 623)
9. e (text page 622)
10. c (text page 622)
11. b (text page 624)

Person Perception and Social Roles 27

Viewer's Guide for Program Twenty-seven

As you view the television program, watch for:

Scenes of people from various cultures engaged in a variety of tasks requiring a variety of roles. Throughout life, we play many parts, assume many roles as we move in and out of different social settings and situations.

Women playing traditional roles and women in roles once reserved for men. Convenient contraceptive methods and an awakening awareness of their potential have caused women to seek expression and fulfillment outside the home. A woman's place is no longer, as W. C. Fields once wryly observed, exclusively "in the stove."

Actual film sequences of Stanford psychologist Albert Bandura's experiments on role modeling. Bandura believes that **observing** and **modeling** may be the primary ways we learn how to play our social roles. He has observed that children will pattern their treatment of an inflatable doll after the violent example set by a grown-up model. And he has successfully used modeling therapy to help people lose their fear of snakes.

Footage of Zimbardo's controversial "jail" experiment, in which subjects appeared to "become" the roles they were expected to play. "Guards" became abusive and "prisoners" grew increasingly submissive.

Preview

Liking and being liked is one aspect of normal, healthy behavior. Of course you like other people, and you want others to like you. But why do you like the people you care for? Why do you like your closest friends, and what is it about you that causes them to like you? What, exactly, do you mean when you use the word like?

The word like means to feel attraction toward or to take pleasure in. Thus, to like someone means to want to be around that person and to genuinely enjoy his or her company. Harvard psychologist Zick Rubin suggests that we like persons for whom we have affection or respect.

And how do other persons win your affection or gain your respect? By the roles they assume and the ways in which they play them. As Jacques observed in Shakespeare's *As You Like It*, "All the world's a stage, and all the men and women merely players: they have their exits and their entrances; and one man in his time plays many parts." The ways in which these parts are played may attract or repulse you, cause you to view the "player" with respect or disdain.

How do you form your opinion? For one thing, you see what you expect to see. Your initial impressions are often strong and are likely to be colored by stereotypes and by social expectations. That is, you may have a preconceived notion of how someone of a particular sex, age, or social class should act, and you form your opinion, in part, on the basis of how the person conforms to or deviates from your notion. But, according to psychologist Donn Byrne, the major factor that attracts you to someone is similarity. In short, to be "like" is to be liked.

According to some psychologists, there are specific sequences in social interaction which we can study—and interrupt, if we wish or need to change role behaviors or learn new ones. In this lesson, you will read about these sequences. You will also learn a bit about the qualities that make for effective performance in leadership roles and a lot about the power and pervasiveness of social roles in general. After reading about the Zimbardo studies, you will become aware, perhaps uncomfortably so, that many otherwise normal persons will engage in sadistic behaviors simply because their role and social setting seem to demand it of them.

Learning Objectives

When you have finished viewing the program and studying your text assignments, you should be able to:

1. Describe some of the factors that affect person perception, including first impressions, attitudes, reputations, stereotypes, primacy and recency effects, autistic hostility, and self-fulfilling prophecy.
2. Describe various ways in which physical appearance, nonverbal communication (such as body language), personal space, territoriality, and the attribution process influence perception of other persons.
3. Define the concept of social roles and identify some examples of roles.
4. Discuss leadership roles and describe the influence on leadership of factors such as learning, gender, ''specialist'' types, and participatory management techniques.
5. Explain the behavior of the participants in the Zimbardo prison experiments in terms of social roles.

Assignments

Before Viewing the Program

Read the preview at the beginning of this lesson and look over the learning objectives that precede the assignments.

Check the section ''Did You Know That . . .'' at the beginning of Chapter 23 in the text and look over the subtitles for the chapter.

Read Chapter 23, ''Person Perception, Attribution, and Social Roles.'' As you read, note the boldfaced terms and concepts that appear in the text and are defined in the upper right corners of right-hand pages. Use the accompanying definitions or descriptions to increase your knowledge or refresh your memory concerning these terms.

View Program 27, ''Interpersonal Attraction''

After Viewing the Program

Review the text assignments.

Read through the summary at the end of Chapter 23, and consider the thought questions in the chapter. Then to aid your understanding of the materials presented in this lesson, review the boldfaced terms and concepts. In particular, note these terms carefully: person perception, first impressions, attitude, autistic hostility, stereotypes, primacy effect, recency effect, body language, behavioral congruence, personal space, body posture, eye contact, attribution process, social role, dyad, participatory management, exchange theory, task specialist, depersonalization, learned helplessness, sadistic.

Complete the study activities included here as an additional study aid for you.

Now evaluate your understanding of the lesson material by reviewing the learning objectives and taking the self-test in this study guide. Check your answers against the answer key.

According to your instructor's assignment or your own interests, choose and complete activities from among the suggestions for extra credit. You might also consider the recommended readings listed at the end of the chapter.

"Well, frankly, no, Miss Kramer, I didn't answer all the questions honestly at the computer-mate office."

427

Study Activities

True-False

1. T F First impressions are usually discarded by a person as he or she quickly perceives new information about a new acquaintance.
2. T F Experiments have shown that students form opinions based on actual information about a new acquaintance rather than on reports about the person's reputation.
3. T F A stereotype is a fixed perception based upon a person's membership in a class or group.
4. T F The concept of **primacy effect** indicates that the first information a person receives about another will most strongly influence perceptions and attitudes.
5. T F In American culture, a new acquaintance will probably make a better impression if he or she stands less than two feet distant when introduced.
6. T F Usually, a person will attribute the behavior of others to rational responses to changes in the environment.
7. T F In the story that introduced the chapter for this lesson, the student who played "guard" attributed many negative traits to his roommate.
8. T F People from the American middle class tend to look a speaker in the eyes to show interest and respect while listening. This behavior is true of most other classes.
9. T F Research shows that whether we perceive persons as attractive or unattractive exerts a powerful influence on how we judge their behavior.
10. T F The most successful managers were found in a study to be those meeting self-actualization needs.
11. T F The most successful managers in one study were those who did not need to seek advice or cooperation from their subordinates.
12. T F In the Zimbardo "prison" experiment, some otherwise "normal" guards tended to develop increasingly sadistic behavior toward prisoners.
13. T F In the "mock prison" experiment, it was found that "prisoners" and "guards" all behaved as tests had predicted they would.

Completion

1. Your _____ of a person is often influenced by a number of factors. First impressions are usually lasting, and what you learn about the reputation of people you are to meet may determine your _____ toward them. These are both examples of _____ effect—that is, the first information you receive about another person creates the most _____ impression. Perhaps one reason that our attitudes about a person do not change easily is our tendency to avoid someone that we feel we will not like. This response is called autistic _____.

attitude
lasting
perception
hostility
primacy

2. People's perceptions are influenced by appearance. More positive traits and motives are attributed to _____ people than to unattractive people. Our perceptions are also influenced by _____ language, and other _____ communication, such as eye contact, posture, facial expressions, and how _____ to you another person stands. Married couples sometimes also "stake out" personal or individual areas of the home, or _____ where their rights are respected. If the way people act tends to confirm our first impressions of them, we say their behavior is _____; if later actions do not conform to first impressions, we experience behavioral discongruence.

congruent
close
body
attractive
non-verbal
territories

3. In addition to appearance, we perceive people through _____ of age, sex, skin color, dress, nationality, and a great many other factors. We expect people to behave in ways that _____ these stereotypes, and when they do, we tend to get a _____ first impression; when they don't, we don't find them very likeable. We also tend to believe that our own personal actions are deliberate responses to the environment, while the behavior of others is caused by their motives and personality _____. We call this tendency to explain behavior by projecting motives and traits onto others the _____ process.

confirm
stereotypes
attribution
traits
favorable

4. We also explain our personal actions in terms of social expectations, or _____. Traits are perceived as intrapsychic factors, but roles, which are basically _____ sets of responses made to similar situations, are largely learned. For example, leadership skills appear to be more a matter of training than _____ ability.

innate
roles
stereotyped

5. Hall's research revealed that managers who were identified as most successful were motivated by needs relating to _____, while least successful managers were seeking to meet _____ needs. Most successful managers sought advice and agreement of subordinates, which is a pattern called _____ management.

identity
participatory
self-actualization

6. In Zimbardo's "mock prison" experiment, one-third of the guards behaved so cruelly that their behavior was described as _____. Prisoners became submissive and less active, displaying what is termed _____ helplessness. Despite the belief of many critics that such behavior was due to "character flaws" in the subjects, it is believed that the participants were actually just conforming to the expected role required by the _____.

environment
sadistic
learned

Short-Answer Questions

1. What similarities do you see between Jay Hall's findings on women managers and Werner Mendel's discovery that his patients at St. Elizabeth's suddenly showed improvement when he started to perceive them differently? (Note: Review Lesson 22.)

2. How might Harold Kelley's research on reputation help explain the difficulty that David L. Rosenhan's "pseudopatients" had in convincing mental hospital staffs that the "pseudopatients" were really normal or sane? (Review the Rosenhan studies in text Chapter 21.)

3. We are often frightened by people whose behavior is highly unpredictable. How might the theory of the attribution process explain why deviant individuals often end up in prisons and mental hospitals?

4. Why did Zimbardo's "prisoners" and "guards" never seem to realize that their behaviors were the result of role playing?

Self-Test

(Select the one best answer.)

Objective 1: Describe some of the factors that affect person perception, including first impressions, attitudes, reputations, stereotypes, primacy and recency effects, autistic hostility, and self-fulfilling prophecy.

1. Forming an opinion of another individual based primarily on his or her membership in a race, religion, or other group is an example of
   a. stereotyping.
   b. autistic hostility.
   c. primacy effect.
   d. cultural expectation.
   e. reputation.

2. Primacy effect is most closely related to
   a. cultural expectation.
   b. stereotypes.
   c. first impressions.
   d. body language.
   e. intelligence.

3. Which of the following best defines "attitude"?
   a. feeling based on the person's membership in a particular group
   b. the importance of the first information obtained about a new acquaintance
   c. cultural expectations placed on persons of specific ages, sexes, body builds, or occupations
   d. a consistent way of responding to a specific aspect of our environment
   e. tendency to avoid a person that we believe we will not like

Objective 1; and *Objective 2:* Describe various ways in which physical appearance, nonverbal communication (such as body language), personal space, territoriality, and the attribution process influence perception of other persons.

4. After people have developed an attitude toward a new acquaintance, they tend to
   a. revise their opinion based on new information and the actions of that person.
   b. rationalize or ignore any behaviors that do not support the attitude.
   c. expect the person to respond to events in unpredictable ways.
   d. modify their attitude further, based on the person's membership in a group or class.
   e. be more aware that their own behavior is based on their internal traits and motives.

Objective 2

5. When a person has a negative reaction to a stranger standing too close, or possibly touching him or her, it is probably because the
   a. person has a phobia about being touched.
   b. stranger has misleading body language.
   c. person's personal space has been violated.
   d. stranger was too passive.
   e. stranger has a bad reputation.

6. We often assume that we understand the inner causes of another's behavior, and these assumptions help us to predict this individual's future behavior. What term best describes this?
   a. stereotyping
   b. role playing
   c. congruence
   d. primacy effect
   e. attribution process

7. Why are conflicts in the attribution process said to be "irresolvable"?
   a. Most people believe that their opinions and explanations for behavior are correct because they are based in "fact."
   b. When we explain our behavior, we see ourselves as filling the approved role of "peace-maker."
   c. There is really no way we can prove whose attributions are right or wrong.
   d. All of these statements are true.
   e. None of these statements is true.

8. If you are riding in an elevator in a large building in the downtown section of a prosperous city, you can probably expect that
   a. other passengers will probably stare at the wall instead of you.
   b. the passengers probably will be middle-aged and middle- or upper-class persons.
   c. people will want to make eye contact with you if you are attractive.
   d. the passengers will be middle- or upper-class persons who will not make eye contact with you.
   e. the passengers will be lower-class persons who will wait for you to look at them first.

Objective 3: Define the concept of social roles and identify some examples of roles.

9. Social role is best described as
   a. whatever set of goals you are trying to reach at a given moment.
   b. a stereotyped set of responses made to related or similar situations.
   c. whether or not you are stingy or generous, kind, or cruel.
   d. your genetic tendency to behave in certain ways prescribed by your culture.
   e. the interaction of your personality traits and your motives.

10. Triandis's studies of exchange theory indicate that
   a. most people assume everyone else shares their expectations and intentions.
   b. most people assume that people from different cultures or countries will have different intentions and expectations.
   c. most people can make a fairly accurate guess of the intentions of a new acquaintance.
   d. understanding someone else's role expectations is of little help in making new friends.

Objective 4: Discuss leadership roles and describe the influence on leadership of factors such as learning, gender, "specialist" types, and participatory management techniques.

11. Which of the following statements about leadership roles is false?
   a. Managers described as "idea generators" or "social facilitators" rate high on leadership scales.
   b. Social facilitators appear to encourage group solidarity.
   c. The most successful managers listen to the opinions of employees and are concerned with their needs.
   d. There are no differences between men and women in the way they administer the management process.
   e. People are born to leadership roles; they cannot be learned.

12. In one study, successful managers generally displayed all of the following except
    a. little commitment to organizational goals.
    b. concern for needs of employees.
    c. personal self-actualization needs.
    d. perception of employee needs as similar to their own.
    e. perception of employees as resources.

Objective 3:

13. Which of the following is one effective way of learning or changing a social role?
    a. adopting new behavioral intentions and habits
    b. relying on familiar stereotypes and reputation
    c. formal study and informal discussion of roles
    d. asking others' opinions
    e. questioning your own behavior

Objective 5: Explain the behavior of the participants in the Zimbardo prison experiments in terms of social roles.

14. In the "mock prison" experiment, virtually all guards behaved in
    a. abusive, dehumanizing ways.
    b. a sadistic manner.
    c. a supportive manner.
    d. an inconsistent manner.
    e. a resentful manner.

15. Prisoner behavior in the "mock prison"
    a. varied widely from rebellious to humorous and depressed.
    b. was generally consistent, becoming more depressed, dependent, and subdued.
    c. varied predictably with the less authoritarian becoming more rebellious, the more authoritarian conforming to expected roles.
    d. was generally consistent, with all prisoners becoming vocally more resentful, but willingly conforming to the rules.
    e. was somewhat varied, with several behaving more like guards.

16. Zimbardo's research indicates that the behavior of guards and prisoners in the "mock prison" was caused almost entirely by
    a. character traits of each participant.
    b. willingness of each participant to follow the rules.
    c. the social roles expected in that environment.
    d. Zimbardo's failure to explain what was expected of the participants.
    e. personality inadequacies in some of the students selected as guards.

Suggestions for Extra Credit

1. Near the end of text Chapter 23, after describing the Zimbardo "prison" studies, author McConnell asks the questions: If you had been a "guard" or a "prisoner" in Zimbardo's experiment, would you have played the roles the way Zimbardo's subjects did? If you were Zimbardo, what could or should you do to convince people the results of the studies are valid? Before trying to answer these questions, you should read more about the Zimbardo studies. McConnell lists Zimbardo's 1975 article, "On Transforming Experimental Research into Advocacy for Social Change," in M. Deutsch and H. Hornstein (eds.), *Applying Social Psychology*, Hillsdale, N. J.: Erlbaum. But you will get a broader perspective of the experiment, Zimbardo's defense, and implications of the study for prison reform by reading Chapter 4, "The Stanford Prison Experiment: Zimbardo's Hell," in *Mindwatching, Why People Behave As They Do*, Garden City, N.Y.: by Hans J. and Michael Eysenck, Anchor Press/Doubleday, 1983, pp. 62-78. You might also read the vignette with which McConnell begins text Chapter 23, "The Best of Intentions." When you have had time to read and think about the issues, you might then want to ask a few more questions. For example, if attempts were made to change role behaviors, how could the social interaction sequence (page 637 in your text) be useful? Think about whether there is a relationship between role playing and the punitive, abusive behaviors of some parents.

2. Note that Zimbardo dressed his "prisoners" and "guards" quite differently. It has long been known that clothing has a profound effect on both group and individual behavior, as does language, but you may be surprised to find that some studies have revealed the existence of an entire prison language, or "jargon," which prisoners are forced to use. What do you suppose is the purpose, and the effect, of special clothing and language in the prison environment? If you can locate *The Importance of Wearing Clothes*, by Lawrence Langner, Hastings House Publishers, New York, 1959, you will find it a valuable discussion of the history and psychology of clothing. Especially relevant to this study are the sections devoted to the relationship between clothes and civilization, social conduct (behavior and conformity), and sexual attitudes and behavior. If you are interested, try also to locate not only other, more recent writings on clothing and behavior, but also some references on prison language systems. You might also look again at the vignette for Chapter 23. Describe your findings, and your feelings about what you have learned, in a brief paper which you might wish to share with fellow students and friends, as well as your instructor.

3. Actors often speak of "getting **into** the part," and sometimes they devote considerable time and trouble to studying the personality and behavior of the individual (either fictional or real) whose role they will play. Do you think that actors ever **become** the roles they play?

4. By observing yourself and your own reactions, develop a chart or a card index of some of the composite trait stereotypes you use to understand others and predict their behavior. For example, what do you expect of an "old man," "young, blonde woman," or "redheaded boy"? Do you expect the redhead to have a quick temper or be full of mischief? And would your picture change if we added other descriptors, for example, if we called the woman "shapely" or "beautiful," or said that the man was "bearded" or "handsome"? Although it often seems that stereotypes and stereotyping are all "bad," you know, of course, that these "expectancies" do serve important purposes in social relationships and are often helpful. Can you think of a few examples of stereotyping that might be of benefit to you and others?

5. Aristotle once argued that beauty is a greater recommendation than a letter of introduction. From this lesson, you probably have a pretty good idea about what Aristotle meant. Everyone knows that being physically attractive has a great many advantages, especially during a first encounter, but—according to the two psychologists who wrote *Mindwatching*—the effects of being beautiful or handsome are much more far-reaching than people suppose. Not just romance, but jobs and jail sentences, among other things, are all too often handed out on the basis of "looks." If you are interested, read Chapter 2, "Why Some People Get Away with Murder," pp. 29-41, in *Mindwatching*. (See exercise 1 in this section for full reference.)

Answer Key

True-False

1. F
2. F
3. T
4. T
5. F
6. F
7. T
8. F
9. T
10. T
11. F
12. T
13. F

Completion

1. perception, attitude, primacy, lasting, hostility; 2. attractive, body, non-verbal, close, territories, congruent; 3. stereotypes, confirm, favorable, traits, attribution; 4. roles, stereotyped, innate; 5. self-actualization, identity, participatory; 6. sadistic, learned, environment.

Short-Answer Questions

1. Werner Mendel is professor of psychiatry at the University of Southern California School of Medicine. While a resident at St. Elizabeth's Hospital in Washington D.C., he was involved in a series of experiments to test the effectiveness of a drug called reserpine. He reports that, almost as soon as the study began, his patients calmed down dramatically. He did not learn until later that his group was the control and did **not** receive medication. His patients did improve—not because of the drug, but because he **expected** them to improve and treated them accordingly, and they responded to his expectations.

   Texas psychologist Jay Hall conducted studies dealing with male and female executives. He discovered that women seem to be more "achievement oriented" and to be less open in relating to colleagues than men are, though they do not differ significantly in the way they administer the management process. He also discovered that one of the main problems women managers have is the way they are **perceived** by men. Men view women as being poor at task achievement but skilled at handling social-emotive resources, and this misperception determines the way that men treat—and promote—women. Both Mendel and Hall discovered that it is the perception, not the reality, that determines the treatment and, thus, the response to it.

2. Psychologist Harold Kelley tested the importance of reputations and discovered that once you are convinced you will not like a person you tend to avoid further contact with him or her, a response Michigan psychologist Theodore Newcomb termed **autistic hostility**.

   Stanford psychologist David L. Rosenhan undertook research on the reliability of psychiatric diagnoses; he had pseudopatients check themselves into state and private mental hospitals, explaining that they "heard voices." Once they had been admitted, they found it all but impossible to convince the hospital staff that there was nothing wrong with them. In fact, they could not even get the staff's attention. The psychiatrists (who spent less than one percent of their time on the wards) apparently accepted without question the "reputations" (the label "schizophrenic") of the pseudopatients, and when the patients' behavior failed to confirm their expectations, the psychiatrists treated them with avoidance and hostility.

3. Social psychologist Fritz Heider feels that our tendency to stereotype arises from our need to predict the way people will react to us. He says we all become alarmed when we cannot guess fairly accurately what will happen to us next. And so, to avoid stress, we seek not only to know **what** but also to know **why**, to ascribe some cause or motive. While we assume our own actions are highly controlled by our environment, we perceive the actions of others as being an expression of their character. In this way, we actually "attribute" personality traits to these persons on the basis of their outward appearance or some few actions we have observed. Most of these attributed "traits" are, in reality, stereotypes.

Because we do need to predict what will happen to us, we are uncomfortable around persons whose behavior is unpredictable or irrational to us. When we cannot "accommodate" to the unexpected behavior and it continues to defy seemingly logical explanation, fitting no familiar stereotype, we may finally label the person as mentally ill; view the behavior as dangerous and unpredictable; and lock the person away where the unpredictable behavior will no longer be a bother or a threat.

4. Heider says that we tend to attribute the behavior of **others** to intrapsychic factors such as motives and personality traits—particularly the latter—while we excuse **ourselves** as behaving in appropriate response to the behavior of others. Mainly we see attributed traits through stereotypes, over which we can often exercise some degree of prediction and control. In the "prison" experiments, both guards and prisoners began responding to one another in terms of stereotypical role expectancies. However, prisoners saw the behavior of guards as the result of certain personality traits and motives and their own actions as being caused by the behavior of the guards; guards saw prisoner behavior as the product of flawed traits and faulty motives and their own actions as merely responding to prisoner behavior in ways that were expected of them ("I was just doing my job."). Neither saw themselves or others as playing roles which they perceived as expected of them.

Self-Test

1. a (text page 639; television program)
2. c (text page 641; television program)
3. d (text pages 635-636; television program)
4. b (text page 643)
5. c (text pages 643-644)
6. e (text pages 646-647)
7. d (text pages 648-649)
8. d (text page 645)
9. b (text page 649)
10. a (text pages 652-653)
11. e (text pages 650-651)
12. a (text pages 650-651)
13. e (text pages 654-656)
14. a (text pages 653-654)
15. b (text pages 653-654)
16. c (text page 654)

Viewer's Guide for Program Twenty-eight

As you view the television program, watch for:

Footage of people in many kinds of group situations, visualizing for you that man is a social animal and grouping is a universal behavior. Can you see from these scenes how difficult it is to define "group"?

Footage of passersby responding to group pressure to conform. As the behavior of one individual becomes the impetus for others to gather and stare at the top of a tree, we see that conformity is sometimes unavoidable.

Reenactments of experiments on obedience conducted by psychologist Stanley Milgram. When asked to deliver successively stronger shocks to students who failed to memorize a list of words, 65 percent of Milgram's subjects were completely obedient in spite of inner conflict over the students' apparent increasing discomfort.

Scenes of laboratory animals whose brains are implanted with electrodes. These scenes introduce us to a consideration of the ethics involved in experiments with human subjects as well as animals.

Footage of communal projects and a farm family working together. The host reminds us that conformity is not always necessarily negative—that some forms of cooperation are not only desirable, but essential to social goals.

Preview

You belong to dozens, if not hundreds, of groups. You became a part of some of these groups by chance. Others, you joined by choice. You were born into some, accidentally joined some, and applied for membership in others. Your relationship with some of these groups has been brief, while your relationship with others will last throughout your lifetime.

What is a "group"? According to McConnell, "A group is a system of two or more individuals who are psychologically related, or are in some other way dependent on one another." The group may be formal or informal, and membership within it may be temporary—the result of a brief sharing of the same experience—or enduring. The most important groups in your life are those that are made up of people with whom you have frequent face-to-face encounters and that last a long time.

We observed in Lesson Twenty-seven that it is important to us to be able to predict how others will respond and what will happen to us. One of the most reinforcing aspects of group membership is knowing what other members are likely to think and do, at least in certain kinds of situations. Thus, group rules are almost always stated in terms of shared attitudes and expected behavior, and members are under tremendous pressure to conform.

Most of us yield to this pressure in some situations but not in others. However, children whose authoritarian parents gave them little independence training are inclined to conform fairly consistently, to be followers rather than leaders.

Perhaps to your dismay, you will find that most people, under command of higher authority, will obey orders to a point where they would actually do harm to themselves or others. **If there are other people around**, many people would not go to the aid of a person in dire distress—which is precisely what happened during the grisly murder of a young woman in New York a few years ago. Researchers found, as you will learn, that the thirty-eight people who saw and heard the murder probably felt only a "diluted" responsibility for what happened.

In this lesson, you will take a look at some theories advanced to explain these behaviors, and you will examine some aspects of group conflict. Some ethical issues about experimentation will also be raised.

Learning Objectives

When you have finished viewing the program and studying your text assignments, you should be able to:

1. Define "social group" and cite several examples.
2. Describe factors operating in a group, such as rules, norms, cohesion, and commitment, that affect its functioning and structure.
3. Describe experiments which indicate that group pressure may lead to conformity.
4. Describe adaptation-level theory as one explanation of conformity.
5. Briefly describe Milgram's research and his conclusions regarding conformity and obedience to authority.
6. Discuss the issues involved in deceiving human subjects for psychological research.
7. Describe research on and conclusions about bystander apathy.
8. Describe "cognitive dissonance" as an explanation of why groups alter their beliefs or perceptions.
9. Explain Sherif's conclusions from his research on conflict between groups.

Assignments

Before Viewing the Program

Read the preview at the beginning of this lesson and look over the learning objectives that precede the assignments.

Check the section "Did You Know That . . ." at the beginning of Chapter 24 in the text and look over the subtitles for the chapter.

Read Chapter 24, "Social Groups." As you read, note the boldfaced terms and concepts that appear in the text and are defined in the upper right corners of right-hand pages. Use the accompanying definitions or descriptions to increase your knowledge or refresh your memory concerning these terms.

View Program 28, "Social Groups"

After Viewing the Program

Review the text assignments.

Read through the summary at the end of Chapter 24 and consider the thought questions in the chapter. Then to aid your understanding of the materials presented in this lesson, review the boldfaced terms and concepts. In particular, note these terms carefully: social group, interaction groups, group norms, consensus, homogeneous, heterogeneous, reference groups, adaptation-level theory, negative conformity, bystander apathy, cognitive dissonance, obedience, intergroup conflict, group pressures, good Samaritans.

Complete the study activities included here as an additional study aid for you.

Now evaluate your understanding of the lesson material by reviewing the the learning objectives and taking the self-test in this study guide. Check your answers against the answer key.

According to your instructor's assignment or your own interests, choose and complete activities from among the suggestions for extra credit. You might also consider the recommended readings listed at the end of the chapter.

The New Yorker, December 6, 1976. Drawing by Lorenz; © 1976
The New Yorker Magazine, Inc.

Study Activities

True-False

1. T F If a group is homogeneous with strong cohesion, a good deal of disagreement among members about rules can be tolerated.
2. T F To be considered a member of a group, an individual must always consciously accept the rules and values (norms) of the group.
3. T F Some persons who are pressured into group conformity yield without realizing how they have been influenced by the group.
4. T F A group can be said to be homogeneous if many of its members dissent from the rules.
5. T F According to adaptation-level theory, you will be more susceptible to group pressure to conform if you have to make an important decision from memory.
6. T F Research evidence shows that, when given orders from a higher authority, most "normal" people will obey, even if it means hurting themselves or others.
7. T F If you are asked to stand up, state your name to your group, and give your vote publicly on a controversial subject, you are more likely to vote the same way as the rest of the group.
8. T F Most people are more likely to go to the aid of someone in distress if others in the group do not feel responsible for taking action.
9. T F Darley and Latané's experiments indicate that, given a choice between our conscience and our fears of violating group expectancies, most of us would violate our conscience.
10. T F When you do something that conflicts with your moral code, you may be more likely to change your behavior than to change your perception of yourself.
11. T F The studies and experiments that are discussed in this chapter, such as Milgram's obedience experiments and the study of bystander apathy in the murder of a New York woman, all testify to the fact that most of us do not recognize the tremendous control our social environment exercises over our behavior.
12. T F Sherif showed that extremely hostile behavior between two rival groups can be changed if the groups can be persuaded to work together for a common goal and if they are rewarded for doing so.

Completion

1. A group can be broadly defined as a set of persons whose members are psychologically related to or _____ upon one another. A group is considered as a single entity, or _____. Most people belong to several groups, including _____ groups, such as religious, political, or athletic organizations, _____ or _____ groups. Most important are _____ groups, those that last and are composed of people with frequent face-to-face encounters. These group members have similar interests and attitudes. The study of how people think, feel, and behave toward one another is called social psychology because it focuses on relationships or _____ rather than on individuals.

family
ethnic
dependent
interaction
system
formal
groups

2. One major group characteristic is the shared acceptance of group _____. If the group is a lasting one, there must be minimal agreement, or _____. Group rules are usually stated in terms of attitudinal or behavioral _____ that specify the average behavior of each member, or what role each plays. Being able to predict what members are likely to do in given situations is a _____ aspect of group membership. If the members of a group are similar, the group is said to be _____; if not, the group is _____. The more homogeneous the group, the more its members stick together, a trait called _____. An important function of the group is to encourage _____ from its members, for the more members support the group's norms and goals, the more cohesive and homogeneous the group will be.

cohesiveness
heterogeneous
rules (or norms)
homogeneous
reinforcing
consensus
commitment
norms

3. Kelley has identified the groups we belong to as our _____ points, or guides, for our standards of thought and behavior. We evaluate ourselves by these groups and they reward or punish us according to whether we conform or not. Members who _____ from the standards are pressured by others to toe the line. Sherif studied the effects of group _____ on visual perception. In his experiments, Sherif asked subjects to estimate the "motion" of a stationery light that merely **appeared** to move. Tested singly, the subjects gave different estimates. Tested in a group, they gave answers that _____ with the group norm. Asch found that subjects were correct 99 percent of the time when solving a problem individually, but when tested in a group, they agreed with a judgment that was wrong. Asch concluded that some people feel compelled to conform to group _____, even if they are wrong, while others seem not to be _____ that they are yielding.

norms
pressure
deviate
reference
conformed
conscious

4. Helson's _____ theory is one explanation of conformity. Helson and his colleague Blake theorized that all behavior, including conformity, is influenced by three factors. (1) The task, problem, or _____ input confronting the subject is the first factor. The more difficult the task and the more confusing the instructions, the more likely you are to go along with group behavior. (2) The second is the social situation or context, which Helson called _____ factors, in which the stimulus is presented. For example, if your decision is very important and if you are told a decision must be unanimous, you will probably give in to group pressure. (3) The third factor is innate response patterns, traits, past experiences, and other _____ factors. While there is no "conformist" profile, some studies do show that "yielders" may be more _____ and more submissive.

stimulus
authoritarian
personality
adaptation-level
background

5. When we violate our ethical codes, or do not quite live up to our moral standards, many of us try to find some logical explanation that excuses our behavior—that is, we _____. Festinger refers to such conflict situations, or those in which we face the problem of explaining away something we should not have done, as cognitive _____. Because this state is uncomfortable, we must reduce it, and we do so by changing our _____ to fit our actual _____.

behaviors
rationalize
beliefs
dissonance

Short-Answer Questions

1. What is a negative conformer?

2. Why should juries, which often decide matters of life and death, always take secret ballots?

3. What similarities do you see between the people who "obeyed" Milgram and the young men in Zimbardo's experiment (Lesson 27) who became "brutal" in their behaviors toward men who were playing the role of prisoner?

Self-Test

(Select the one best answer.)

Objective 1: Define 'social group' and cite several examples.

1. Which of the following is **not** a social group?
    a. the New York Yankees
    b. your psychology class
    c. the President's family
    d. persons taller than six feet
    e. your car pool

2. Groups that are composed of people who have frequent face-to-face encounters over a fairly long period of time are called
    a. ethnic groups.
    b. formal membership groups.
    c. interaction groups.
    d. heterogeneous groups.
    e. dyadic relationships.

Objective 2: Describe factors operating in a group, such as rules, norms, cohesion, and commitment, that affect its functioning and structure.

3. For any group to last, it must
    a. be comprised of more than two individuals.
    b. have a shared acceptance of rules by its members.
    c. be heterogeneous.
    d. be homogeneous.
    e. face a threat from the outside.

4. A rule, or _____, specifies what the behavior of group members should be.
    a. conformity
    b. shared acceptance
    c. group norm
    d. adaptation-level
    e. attitude

5. A group of strangers caught in a stalled elevator for more than a few minutes probably would become
    a. cohesive.
    b. independent.
    c. heterogeneous.
    d. apathetic.
    e. aggressive.

6. If you and your neighbors spend the weekend raising money for the Cancer Society, you are
   a. becoming more homogeneous.
   b. becoming more heterogeneous.
   c. classified as a formal group.
   d. showing a high level of commitment.
   e. proving dissonance theory.

Objective 3: Describe experiments which indicate that group pressure may lead to conformity.

7. Yielding to group pressure is frequently observed in situations in which
   a. a person has little or no information about the group norm.
   b. a group is composed of strangers rather than friends.
   c. a person must state an opinion publicly rather than secretly.
   d. all of the above factors are present.
   e. the factors described in a and b are present.

8. Sherif showed that individual judgments about ''movement'' of a light were
   a. more homogeneous when subjects were tested in groups.
   b. more heterogeneous when subjects were tested in groups.
   c. about the same no matter how they were tested.
   d. strongly affected by the number in each group tested.
   e. always wrong because the light never actually moved.

Objective 3; and *Objective 4:* Describe adaptation-level theory as one explanation of conformity.

9. In Asch's experiment on conformity, the other subjects' opinions functioned as a _____ factor.
   a. response
   b. adaptation
   c. background
   d. personality
   e. stimulus

Objective 4

10. According to _____, all behavior, including conformity, is influenced by stimulus factors, background or situational factors, and personality factors.
    a. Asch's experiments
    b. Milgram's obedience studies
    c. cognitive dissonance theory
    d. the Darley-Latané studies
    e. adaptation-level theory

11. Subjects in a conformity experiment will give in to group pressure most often if they are called on to judge _____ stimuli.
    a. strong and intense
    b. vague or abstract
    c. common types of
    d. concrete types of
    e. many different kinds of

Objective 5: Briefly describe Milgram's research and his conclusions regarding conformity and obedience to authority.

12. If we are given orders from an authority whom we respect, most of us
    a. would remain apathetic and unresponsive to the orders.
    b. exhibit signs of autokinetic distress.
    c. might refuse to obey unless we agreed with the orders.
    d. would probably obey even if it meant hurt to others.
    e. tend to increase our group commitment.

Objective 6: Discuss the issues involved in deceiving human subjects for psychological research.

13. In the field of psychological research, what has been the response to the issue of deceiving subjects in an experiment?
    a. No code of ethics has been universally accepted.
    b. The American Psychological Association has declared itself against unwarranted deception.
    c. There is little criticism of this type of experimentation.
    d. The statements in both a and b describe the response.
    e. The statements in both a and c describe the response.

Objective 7: Describe research on and conclusions about bystander apathy.

14. If no one around you responds to an emergency situation that everyone is aware of, you
    a. probably are in a situation of intergroup conflict.
    b. most likely would be motivated to help the distressed person or persons yourself.
    c. may feel little responsibility to take action by yourself.
    d. most likely would ask the person nearest to the site of the emergency to help.
    e. likely would feel that you are being deceived about the emergency.

15. You would be most likely to help in an emergency situation if
    a. the situation is ambiguous.
    b. you are alone.
    c. two or more people are involved.
    d. you are with a friend.
    e. you are sure no one else will help.

Objective 8: Describe "cognitive dissonance" as an explanation of why groups alter their beliefs or perceptions.

16. According to Festinger's theory of cognitive dissonance, you can most likely change a person's attitudes if you
    a. force and coerce him or her to behave inconsistently.
    b. emphasize how much better other attitudes are.
    c. let him or her know that you belong to a lower level of status and prestige.
    d. put the person in a stimulus-deprived environment.
    e. subtly induce the person to behave in a manner inconsistent with his or her own attitudes.

17. Cognitive dissonance theory is most applicable to
    a. attitude change.
    b. problem solving.
    c. attribution.
    d. intergroup conflict.
    e. adaptation levels.

Objective 9: Explain Sherif's conclusions from his research on conflict between groups.

18. Sherif found that it is possible to unite two extremely hostile groups by
    a. presenting a problem that can be solved only by cooperation.
    b. giving the two groups a common problem.
    c. rewarding the groups for wanting to be together.
    d. changing their actions toward each other.
    e. doing all of the above.

452

Suggestions for Extra Credit

1. On a chart or table, such as the one below, list some of the groups to which you belong and then indicate with a check mark whether you joined by chance or choice and whether the group is formal or informal, large or small, temporary or enduring, and approximately how many members each has.

Name of Group	Joined by		Structure		Size		Permanence		Number of Members
	Chance	Choice	Formal	Informal	Large	Small	Temporary	Enduring	

You might wish to extend this chart to include the purpose of each group, the extent of your commitment, and approximately how much time you spend in some form of interaction with each group. How cohesive would you say these groups are? If you don't want to confine yourself to a chart, you might write a brief analysis of what you've recorded.

2. In the last several lessons particularly, you've undoubtedly become aware of grave questions about the use of human subjects and the deception of subjects in scientific experiments. Some of these ethical and moral issues have surfaced in connection with the Zimbardo experiments studied in Lesson Twenty-seven and the Milgram experiments in this lesson. Others might be concerned with the administration of placebos to some patients in pain studies or the provision of alcoholic drinks to alcoholics in studies designed to reduce excessive drinking. For additional information on which you might base opinions and judgments, refer to Heinze Schuler's 1982 book, *Ethical Problems in Psychological Research*; review the reading recommended for the Zimbardo studies in the extra-credit section of Lesson Twenty-seven; review the Milgram research; and try to locate a copy of the American Psychological Association's guidelines for research that involves human subjects. In addition to putting your thoughts on paper, you might want to organize a discussion with friends, family, or fellow students on the question of when and under what circumstances humans should be used as experimental subjects.

3. In Chapter 3, "The Dangers of Obedience," of *Mindwatching*, authors Hans J. and Michael Eysencks' (see Lesson Twenty-seven) note that Milgram's obedience studies raise a number of moral issues, and they suggest that it is "instructive to compare the experimental findings of Milgram and others with the horrific reality of Hitler's Germany." Milgram and others feel the studies might be relevant to other atrocious war crimes of this century and perhaps to such violent phenomena as the Charles Manson Family murders. For a more complete, and rather more shocking, picture of the behavior of subjects in the obedience studies, read the chapter mentioned above.

4. In *Mindwatching*, the Eysencks also offer an excellent discussion and analysis of research studies and findings in the case of Kitty Genovese, the young New York woman who was murdered on her doorstep within sight and sound of thirty-eight of her neighbors. Why did none of these people help—or even summon police? Read Chapter 1 in this book, "Where Has the Good Samaritan Gone?" pp. 14-18.

Answer Key

True-False

1. F	7. T
2. F	8. F
3. T	9. T
4. F	10. F
5. T	11. T
6. T	12. T

Completion

1. dependent, system, formal, family, ethnic, interaction, groups;   2. rules (or norms), consensus, norms, reinforcing, homogeneous, heterogeneous, cohesiveness, commitment;   3. reference, deviate, pressure, conformed, norms, conscious;   4. adaptation-level, stimulus, background, personality, authoritarian;   5. rationalize, dissonance, beliefs, behaviors.

Short-Answer Questions

1. Many persons who pride themselves on being independent thinkers and doers and insist that they "do things my way" are really as subject to group conformity pressures as the rest of us. Blake and Helson have found that these self-styled "independents" yield **negatively**; that is, they will depart

from the group norm no matter what it is and even if it means that they are forced to give up their preferred opinions and attitudes. Negative conformers reject group norms because they reject the group.

2. In a jury trial setting, pressure to conform can be particularly intense, especially if a unanimous decision is required of the jury and if the case is an important one. Studies show that the more importance a judgment is suppposed to have, the more likely it is that the individual will be swayed by incorrect or inappropriate group norms. The greater the prestige, status, or trustworthiness of other jurors, the greater is their power to sway the individual member of the group. And the more ''out in the open'' a juror is forced to make a decision, the more likely the juror is to abandon his or her own opinion in favor of the group decision. This is particularly true if the juror is required to state his or her name and to respond so that the rest of the group can hear.

3. As you will recall from Lesson Twenty-seven, Stanford psychologist Philip Zimbardo conducted an experiment in which students were randomly selected to act as ''guards'' and ''prisoners'' in the ''Stanford Jail.'' In this artificially created, dehumanizing environment, the guards became more and more authoritarian, even sadistic, and the prisoners were quickly reduced to a state of learned helplessness. Because psychological tests before the experiment had shown the participants to be normal with no measurable tendencies toward aggression or dependency, Zimbardo concluded that their ''abnormal'' behaviors were nothing more than role behaviors determined by the particular institutional setting in which they occurred.
In psychologist Stanley Milgram's experiments, subjects were asked to act as ''teachers'' and to teach a list of words to ''students.'' As Milgram carefully explained, in an effort to ''study the effects of punishment on learning,'' they were to deliver successively stronger shocks to students who failed to memorize the list of words. Amazingly enough, 65 percent of Milgram's subjects obediently delivered the shocks in spite of inner conflict over doing so.
In both experiments, the subjects no longer **played** but somehow **became** their assigned roles. As ''guards'' or ''punishing teachers,'' they were frighteningly willing to do what the rules decreed or the experimenter told them to do. The ''prison guards'' conformed; the ''teachers'' obeyed.

Self-Test

1. d (text pages 661, 663; television program)
2. c (text page 662; television program)
3. b (text page 662; television program)
4. c (text page 663; television program)
5. a (text page 665)

6. d (text page 665)
7. c (text page 666)
8. a (text page 666)
9. e (text pages 666-667)
10. e (text pages 668-669)
11. b (text page 668)
12. d (text pages 670-671; television program)
13. d (text page 674; television program)
14. c (text pages 674-677)
15. b (text pages 675-676)
16. e (text pages 677-678)
17. a (text page 678)
18. e (text pages 678-679)

Persuasion and Attitude Change 29

Viewer's Guide for Program Twenty-nine

As you view the television program, watch for:

Mrs. Mildred Cushman who, in the dramatization, nearly falls victim to the classic "bank examiner" con scheme. Every con artist prides himself on his ability to persuade. Fortunately for Mrs. Cushman, a bank security officer warns her about this misuse of persuasion.

Film footage of master persuaders at work. Dictators such as Adolf Hitler, television news commentators, and politicians all seek to achieve credibility in the eyes of their audiences and, thus, to become better able to persuade them to adopt certain attitudes, to alter their behaviors, or to buy certain products.

Physician Sam Sheppard who, with companion Carole Tregoff, was accused of murdering his wife. Sheppard allegedly became the victim of a propaganda campaign by a Cleveland, Ohio, newpaper whose editor is said to have perceived that his readers wanted to believe that Sheppard was guilty. What is your opinion of the newspaper's role in this case? Did the paper really sway the opinion of an entire major city?

Preview

What brand of toothpaste, shaving cream, or laundry detergent do you use? How did you happen to pick that particular brand? While you might like to believe that you are an independent thinker who makes such decisions only after careful consideration of all the facts, your opinions about these products and many others were probably created for you by advertisers.

According to McConnell, "Americans spend more money each year on advertising than they do on education, or on pollution control, mental health, poverty relief, or scientific research," with the result that you encounter about 1,500 ads on radio and television and in books, magazines, and newspapers each day of your life. Obviously, **someone** is trying to sell you **something**!

But how susceptible are you to this message bombardment? As you might imagine, psychologists, advertisers, public relations specialists, and others share an interest in the answer to this question. Their studies have shown that your receptivity to information is initially affected, for example, by the credibility you ascribe to the communicator of that information. It may also be affected by peer pressure and parental preference. In other words, you may simply have purchased the shaving cream your father used, bought the detergent your mother preferred, or voted for the candidate of the party they both espoused.

One observation opinion researchers find puzzling is that the pencil-and-paper attitudes you profess on a questionnaire may bear little relationship to your flesh-and-blood behavior. In other words, your attitudes in theoretical situations may be very poor indicators of what you would actually do, think, and feel in real-life circumstances. For this reason, attitudes are hard to analyze and evaluate. Are they predictors of future behavior or merely rationalizations of past actions?

In this lesson, we shall be looking at attitudes—at **what** they are, **where** they come from, **why** they are important, **how** they are related to behavior, **who** seeks to influence or change them, and with **what** results. And we shall be asking about the ethical questions involved in persuasion, this process of attitude formation and change. Is it ethical to indoctrinate children with religious or political theories? Is it right to persuade someone to buy something that is ill-suited to his or her budget or life-style? Is it reasonable to cling to and perpetuate a variety of potentially harmful myths? What rights and responsibilities have we in the process of influencing and persuading others?

Learning Objectives

When you have finished viewing the program and studying your text assignments, you should be able to:

1. Describe Newcomb's findings on factors supporting both attitude change and attitude stability.
2. Identify the four factors present in persuasive communication.
3. Discuss the effects of communicator credibility and the sleeper effect.
4. Outline the research and conclusions on fear-arousing messages and their effectiveness in changing attitudes.
5. Describe the approach taken by the Mills and Walter research to cause attitude change.
6. Describe several reasons why mass media campaigns may fail to change attitudes.
7. Describe examples which illustrate that attitudes and behavior may be inconsistent.

Assignments

Before Viewing the Program

Read the preview at the beginning of this lesson and look over the learning objectives that precede the assignments.

Check the section "Did You Know That . . ." at the beginning of Chapter 25 in the text, and look over the subtitles for the chapter.

Read Chapter 25, "Persuasion, Communication, and Attitude Change." As you read, note the boldfaced terms and concepts that appear in the text and are defined in the upper right corners of right-hand pages. Use the accompanying definitions or descriptions to increase your knowledge or refresh your memory concerning these terms.

View Program 29, "Persuasion"

After Viewing the Program

Review the text assignments.

Read through the summary at the end of Chapter 25 and consider the thought questions in the chapter. Then to aid your understanding of the materials presented in this lesson, review the boldfaced terms and concepts. In particular, note these terms carefully: reference group, persuasion, credibility, sleeper effect, fear-arousing messages, counter-propaganda, repression, deterrent, reciprocal determinism, communicator, feedback loop, mass hysteria, psychological traps.

Complete the study activities included here as an additional study aid for you.

Now evaluate your understanding of the lesson material by reviewing the learning objectives and taking the self-test in this study guide. Check your answers against the answer key.

According to your instructor's assignment or your own interests, choose and complete activities from among the suggestions for extra credit. You might also consider the recommended readings listed at the end of the chapter.

© 1977 United Feature Syndicate, Inc.

Study Activities

True-False

1. T F Americans spend more money each year on education and pollution control than they do on advertising.
2. T F In general, the more you know about a person, thing, or idea, the more stable your attitude toward it.
3. T F The Bennington College study demonstrates that students invariably maintain the attitudes taught them by their parents.
4. T F If maintaining a particular attitude is sufficiently important to a person, he or she will choose an environment that supports the attitude.
5. T F Without an outward flow of communication from your nervous system to the outside world, your attitudes probably will not change.
6. T F The sleeper effect has to do with the fact that after hearing or seeing a persuasive message you may later tend to be more influenced by the content of the message than its source.

7.   T F   Fear appeal is highly effective in changing attitudes because the strong emotional response it evokes sharpens memory.

8.   T F   People who prepare and present propaganda are often more persuaded by it than are members of their intended audience.

9.   T F   Research has shown that audiences are not passive and that responses must be studied to determine if a message is effective.

10.   T F   There is little consistency between the attitudes people profess and the actions they take.

11.   T F   In present-day society, it is impossible to free yourself of the influence of others or of the responsibility you have for influencing others.

12.   T F   Follow-up studies show that most activists of the 1960s have tended to become much more conservative in their attitudes and life-styles.

Completion

1. _____ are relatively enduring ways of thinking and feeling about an object, person, group, or idea and may predispose you to act in a certain way. They are useful because they allow you to predict future events. In general, the more you know about something, the more _____ your attitude toward that thing will be. And the more an attitude helps you make accurate predictions, the less susceptible it will be to _____.

stable
change
Attitudes

2. One type of attitude we hold is political opinion. In his studies of political attitudes among women students of Bennington College, a highly liberal institution, social psychologist Theodore Newcomb discovered that _____ students were looked down on, seniors were significantly more _____ than freshmen, and that many of the most liberal graduates deliberately sought to insulate themselves against _____ liberal influences.

less
conservative
liberal

3. According to Solomon Asch, to change your attitude toward something, you must either _____ the thing itself so that you will perceive it differently or somehow change your _____ about the thing. The most important aspect of persuasion is the communication process, which has four main factors: communicator, _____, audience, and the _____ loop between audience and communicator.

perceptions
change
feedback
message

4. _____ seems to be one of the most important characteristics of the communicator, be it print or person. You are inclined to move _____ the position of someone you trust and _____ from the position of someone you distrust, even when doing so means changing your own original attitude or position. You tend to believe persons whom you like, who appear to be sincere, and who have _____ social status.

high
Credibility
toward
away

5. Once you have forgotten the content source of a piece of information, you may yet remember the _____ and become less or more convinced of the truth in it depending upon how you see the credibility of the communicator. Carl I. Hovland and Walter Weiss termed this tendency to remember the facts of an argument while forgetting the source of those facts the _____ effect.

sleeper
argument

6. With regard to the message, many studies suggest that _____ communication is much more persuasive than use of the mails or mass media. Contrary to popular opinion, experiences with "Scared Straight" and other similar programs suggest that _____ communications are not effective because people tend to _____ frightening information and because such messages focus attention on problems rather than on solutions.

fear-inducing
repress
person-to-person

7. The third factor in persuasive communication is the _____, the person or group whose attitude is to be changed. Advertisers spend millions of dollars each year to learn about the personal characteristics of their target audiences. It has been shown that the more propagandists construct their message to fit the prior beliefs and attitudes of the audience and the more they pay attention to audience _____, the more successful will be their attempts to persuade. Interestingly enough, people involved in presenting propaganda are usually _____ affected by it than is their intended audience.

feedback
more
audience

8. A difference between the opinions many people profess on questionnaires and their actual flesh-and-blood behaviors suggests that they have inconsistent or conflicting _____ and that attitudes are very _____ indicators of what people actually do, think, and feel in real-life situations. Rather than being reliable predictors of future behaviors, they may merely be _____ of past actions.

rationalizations
attitudes
poor

9. Research on the methods involved in persuasion and attitude formation raise but leave unanswered a number of _____ questions. What seems clear, however, is that we are _____ by many others and must, in turn, bear some responsibility for the influence we exert in return.

influenced
ethical

Short-Answer Questions

1. In the Mills and Walter research on youthful offenders, why was job skills training more successful than punishment?

2. Why do fear and threat techniques not accomplish as much as people generally expect them to in changing attitudes?

3. List and discuss the four factors present in persuasive communication.

Self-Test

(Select the one best answer.)

Objective 1: Describe Newcomb's findings on factors supporting both attitude change and attitude stability.

1. Newcomb found in his study of Bennington College women that
   a. the entire college population acted as a reference group that rewarded liberal attitudes and punished conservative ones.
   b. women who resisted the liberal college tradition identified primarily with their classmates.
   c. many liberal students reverted to conservative positions after graduation.
   d. many conservative women became exceedingly liberal after graduation.
   e. it was easy to be both reactionary and intellectually respectable.

2. After his follow-up of the Bennington College study, Newcomb argued that the attitudes learned by students at college
    a. changed when they returned to their home environments.
    b. were effective in changing parental attitudes.
    c. were impossible to maintain outside the "ivory tower."
    d. determined the type of social environment the graduates sought out and preferred.
    e. crumbled under a combination of peer and parent pressures.

Objective 2: Identify the four factors present in persuasive communication.

3. Which of the following is not one of the four main factors in persuasive communication?
    a. communicator
    b. conformity
    c. message
    d. audience
    e. feedback

4. Many lecturers encourage questions during or after their speeches. In what way does their doing so enhance the persuasive communication process?
    a. It activates the feedback loop between audience and communicator.
    b. It allows audience members who disagree with the communicator to express their opinions.
    c. It allows audience members who agree with the communicator to say so.
    d. It offers audience members a chance to ask the lecturer about his or her background and, thus, to determine his or her credibility.
    e. It enables the lecturer to fill more time with less preparation.

Objective 3: Discuss the effects of communicator credibility and the sleeper effect.

5. The research of Carl I. Hovland and Walter Weiss on "trustworthiness" of sources indicates that credibility is particularly important for
    a. male audiences.
    b. female audiences.
    c. gaining initial acceptance for an idea.
    d. maintaining the attitude later.
    e. preventing the sleeper effect.

6. The sleeper effect discovered by Hovland and Weiss involves
   a. being so bored by a communicator that you fail to pay attention to the message.
   b. remembering arguments but forgetting sources.
   c. remembering the sources of an argument but not the argument itself.
   d. attributing an argument with which you agree to a high-credibility source.
   e. ascribing an argument with which you disagree to a low-credibility source.

Objective 4: Outline the research and conclusions on fear-arousing messages and their effectiveness in changing attitudes.

7. If you wanted desperately to persuade someone not to use a substance you believed would be harmful, or perhaps fatal, which of the following would you do?
   a. Develop a strong message designed to "scare the life" out of him or her.
   b. Develop a low-key and logical presentation of your argument.
   c. Suggest an alternative course of action.
   d. Combine a low-key and logical argument with a suggestion for an alternative course of action.
   e. Combine a low-key and logical argument with a positive suggestion for action and encourage questions after your message.

8. The use of high-fear lectures in persuasion efforts
   a. evokes strong emotional responses.
   b. is less effective in changing behavior than low-fear messages.
   c. tends to have an effect opposite to what is intended or expected.
   d. focuses attention on problems rather than on solutions.
   e. does all of the above.

Objective 5: Describe the approach taken by the Mills and Walter research to cause attitude change.

9. Which of the following tactics did Carolyn Mills and Tim Walter use in their efforts to teach social skills to youthful offenders?
   a. threats and other scare tactics
   b. peer pressure and verbal harassment
   c. job-skill training with daily positive feedback regarding performance
   d. isolation from parents and peers so that the juvenile offenders became a captive audience
   e. additional social studies classes in school and role playing

466

10. The program for juvenile delinquents operated by Mills and Walter demonstrated
    a. the effectiveness of combining scare tactics with positive feedback.
    b. the effectiveness of providing people with positive feedback regarding their accomplishments.
    c. that peer pressure eventually forces youths to return to delinquent behavior.
    d. that teaching people the skills that will allow them to maintain healthy attitudes is a useful strategy.
    e. that it is more important to change attitudes than to provide job-skill training.

Objective 6: Describe several reasons why mass media campaigns may fail to change attitudes.

11. Results of the Cincinnati study on attitudes toward the United Nations indicate that
    a. the more you know about something, the less you search for additional information.
    b. the more actively involved you are in a campaign, the more quickly you lose interest when it is over.
    c. the more feedback you get about propaganda, the more effective your campaign can be.
    d. the mass media are always an effective means of changing voter attitudes.
    e. the mass media are seldom an effective means of changing voter attitudes.

12. Results of this same Cincinnati study also indicate that
    a. a massive media campaign can be successful if the issue is not controversial.
    b. behavior change can be effectively produced by predictions of disaster.
    c. the easiest subjects to convince are those who are already interested.
    d. the "cold war" provided a ready context for changing political attitudes.
    e. political attitudes are too deep-seated to be affected by any type of media campaign.

13. Mass media campaigns may fail to change attitudes because
    a. audiences prefer person-to-person contact.
    b. the message is not tailored to meet the needs of the audience.
    c. the information is not sufficiently important to claim the attention of the audience.
    d. of the factors listed in both a and b.
    e. of the factors listed in b and c.

Objective 7: Describe examples which illustrate that attitudes and behavior may be inconsistent.

14. A growing body of experimental evidence suggests that attitudes, as measured by questionnaires,
    a. are poor indicators of what people think and do in real life.
    b. can pretty accurately predict what a person will think and do in real life.
    c. can be readily changed by changing the wording of the questionnaire.
    d. can be considered reliable research data.
    e. are harder to change after the questionnaire is administered.

15. The experimental evidence also indicates that
    a. there is often a significant relationship between attitude change and behavior change.
    b. most people eventually resolve the conflicts between their attitudes and their behaviors.
    c. professed attitudes are good indicators of what people will do in a given situation.
    d. there is often little or no relationship between attitude change and behavior change.
    e. attitudes and opinions are not related to needs.

Suggestions for Extra Credit

1.
                        "Caveat Emptor"
        "The buyer needs a hundred eyes, the seller not one."
**"Television watching is perhaps the most common (and
                        undiagnosed) addiction."**
**"We have been bludgeoned by [Congressmen who are] defenders of
the Constitutional freedom of three-year-olds to have access to
                critical information about cocoa crisps."**

What all of these quotations have in common is that they all touch upon the long-standing and hotly fought debate over whether advertising should be regulated or censored in some way. Advertising is, of course, an extremely powerful channel for communication and persuasion. You probably will have no problem recognizing the first quotation, an old Roman proverb, "let the buyer beware." The second quotation above is excerpted from *Jacula Prudentum*, by the seventeenth-century English poet George Herbert. The third quotation is the contribution of an anonymous textbook editor, who placed it under a photograph of several people whose eyes are riveted to a television screen. And the fourth is the complaint of a member of the Federal Trade Commission who tried to persuade the United States Congress that the content of television commercials aimed at children should be "regulated." The hue and cry over advertising and attempts or proposals to regulate it are not new, but the controversy has certainly intensified with the advent and proliferation of television. If you are interested in joining the ongoing debate over whether advertising should be regulated, you might begin by considering how the sentiments quoted above relate to the controversy. Read the complaint of former Federal Trade Commission Chairman Michael Pertschuk as it is very briefly reported in the March, 1982, issue of *Consumer Reports*, page 131. Then read "Freedom Needs Advertising," a speech made by Stuart Clark Rogers to the Sons of the American Revolution, Washington, D.C., September 19, 1984, reprinted in the November 15, 1984, issue of *Vital Speeches of the Day*, pp. 86-89. For a balanced view, you should also locate some references that include arguments in **favor** of limiting advertising messages. If you decide you are in favor of restricting advertising, write a short paper describing what you would limit and how you would do it. (You will want to remember that advertising includes messages from political, governmental, charitable, and religious sources as well as commercial ones.)

2. Indications are that in recent years the attitudes of Americans toward some of our major institutions and the people who lead them have been changing dramatically from feelings of trust to distrust. Polls show that, by and large, Americans don't particularly trust higher education, religion, medicine, the press, the White House, the military, or large corporations. To what would you attribute this loss of confidence? The University of Denver's Dr. Philip Shaver, a social psychologist, writes of this phenomenon in "The Public Distrust," *Psychology Today*, October, 1980, pp. 44-49.

3. As McConnell notes in this lesson, the literature is full of studies of the strange and interesting behavior known as "mass hysteria." A review of some notable cases is offered by author Wray Herbert in "An Epidemic in the Works," *Science News*, Vol. 122, September 18, 1982, pp. 188-190. You may wish to pursue other references and write a brief paper summarizing your findings.

4. Adolf Hitler was one of the master persuaders of history. In *Mein Kampf*, he described in detail his methods, which were frighteningly effective. An English essayist and novelist named Eric Blair developed a fierce hatred of Hitler's brand of totalitarianism. In protest and under the pen name George Orwell, he wrote *Animal Farm*, a satire on the ease with which a society allows itself to be subjugated by a totalitarian regime. Read either Hitler's *Mein Kampf* or Orwell's *Animal Farm* and write a brief paper comparing the propaganda methods outlined in either with the points McConnell makes about persuasive communication.

5. If Hitler was one of **history's** master persuaders, then Iago is one of **literature's** master persuaders. A character in Shakespeare's play *Othello*, Iago sets out systematically to destroy Othello's love for Desdemona by persuading him that she has been unfaithful. The tragedy lies in the fact that, although there is no truth in Iago's argument, he succeeds. He is a skillful communicator who knows his audience, is sensitive to feedback, and matches his message to Othello's weaknesses and needs. Read Shakespeare's *Othello*, and then write a short paper analyzing Iago's effectiveness as a persuasive communicator. What methods does he use? How is he able to change Othello's attitude and, at last, his behavior?

Answer Key

True-False

1. F	7. F
2. T	8. T
3. F	9. T
4. T	10. T
5. F	11. T
6. T	12. F

Completion

1. Attitudes, stable, change;   2. conservative, liberal, less;   3. change, perceptions, message, feedback;   4. Credibility, toward, away, high; 5. argument, sleeper;   6. person-to-person, fear-inducing, repress; 7. audience, feedback, more;   8. attitudes, poor, rationalizations;   9. ethical, influenced.

Short-Answer Questions

1. According to McConnell, the Mills and Walter experiment shows that teaching youthful offenders the skills they need to maintain healthy attitudes may be the best way of preventing antisocial behavior. An experimental group was given special training in appropriate behaviors, and these behaviors were reinforced with daily feedback from employers. Probably, the earnings received by the youths were a further reinforcement, because others in their peer group stopped criticizing the program and requested training for themselves when the paychecks started appearing. A comparison with a control group that has a similar history of arrests yields some contrast of the effectiveness of behavior training and punishment: Less than 10 percent of the youths in the experimental group were arrested again, while about 70 percent of the youths with no training had more trouble with the law.

2. "High-fear" messages may evoke strong emotional responses from subjects exposed to them, but the long-term effect of such messages seems to be opposite to that predicted. Janis and Feshbach report that subjects tend to repress or forget frightening information and, while fear messages may arouse subjects, arousal is not necessarily translated into behavior. Fear-inducing communications focus your attention on problems, not solutions.

3. The four factors in persuasive communication are the communicator, the message, the audience, and the feedback loop between the audience and the communicator. The communicator is the person or group trying to induce the attitude change. While it is important that the communicator be perceived as credible and sincere, and it is helpful if he or she is of high rather than low social status, in the long run it is probably what this person says or does, and not who or what he or she is, that has the greatest effect on attitudes.

The message is the information the communicator transmits to the audience. Studies have shown that person-to-person communication is far more effective than mass media communication. The audience is the person or group whose attitude is to be changed. Obviously, a clever communicator will find out as much as possible about the target audience's demographic makeup and personal biases before trying to change its attitudes. Last, and perhaps most important for successful persuasion, the communicator must have effective feedback loops to determine the effectiveness and success of the message.

Self-Test

 1. a (text pages 689-690)
 2. d (text page 690)
 3. b (text page 692; television program)
 4. a (text page 692)
 5. c (text page 693; television program)
 6. b (text pages 693-694; television program)
 7. e (text pages 695-700; television program)
 8. e (text pages 695-698; television program)
 9. c (text pages 697-698)
10. d (text page 698)
11. c (text pages 698-700)
12. c (text page 699)
13. e (text pages 698-699; television program)
14. a (text pages 701-702)
15. d (text pages 701-702)

Viewer's Guide for Program Thirty

As you view the television program, watch for:

Capsule reviews of the three major approaches to the study of psychology: biological, intrapsychic, and social/environmental. Host Paul Napier also reminds us that the aims of psychology are to help us to explain why we do what we do, how we learn, how we face and deal with reality.

The Kubler-Ross research on the stages of death and dying, the effects of death on the individual and the community, and the ethical questions raised by death. Footage of research emphasizing that adulthood is a time of change and challenge, not a static condition, and scenes depicting aging as a daily process that has major implications for psychology and for society as a whole.

Sequences stressing the importance of work as a basic reality for men and women today and noting great changes that have been occurring in recent years in social attitudes toward work and career.

In concluding the series, Paul Napier notes that career planning often is synonymous with life planning.

Preview

Science is, among other things, "the fine art of predicting the future in objective terms." It enables us to analyze, alter, and adjust ourselves and our environments to meet present demands and to reach future goals. Thus, it gives us some measure of control over our days and our destinies. We are no longer left at the mercy of the fates though, from time to time, we are, indeed, victims of the **facts**.

Because it is easier for most of us to be objective about "things" than about ourselves and because the struggle to survive was so contingent upon "things," the physical sciences were the first to develop. We observed the stars and planets, found ways to predict their motions, and learned what force bound us to the earth. We also began to invent "things," at first, to ensure survival, and then, to make survival more worthwhile. These inventions sparked the Industrial Revolution, which began in Europe in the mid-eighteenth century. Before the Industrial Revolution, we had little control over our physical environment or our own bodies, and even less over our psychological development. During the 1800s we turned our attention to living things and, at last, to the human body. Biology became a true science. A "Medical Revolution" began that gave us the ability to prevent, treat, or cure an increasing number of illnesses, and the ability to control and predict our physiological reactions, as well as to prolong the life span.

And then, in the early part of the twentieth century, we discovered ways to look at ourselves, our minds, and behaviors objectively. Now we are immersed in what McConnell believes is a "Psychological Revolution," which is bringing cultural changes that are as "mind-blowing" as those of the Industrial and Medical Revolutions. We are able to explore vast new areas of human behavior and potential; we know much more about the functions and abilities of the brain, and we understand that through our cortex we can bring under voluntary control all the passions, desires, and emotions of the lower brain centers; and we are beginning the foundations of a new applied psychology which will allow us to apply facts and theories to real-life problems of all kinds.

In biology, "genetic engineering" is becoming a reality of this century, and soon we will be able to change heredity before and after birth. We will know how to prevent genetic handicaps as well as how to help medical doctors help patients overcome the effects of brain damage and mental illness. Scientists now tell us that about 70 percent of deaths in the United States are blamed upon not **biologically** caused diseases but upon unhealthy **behaviors, life-style**, or **environmental** factors. A new behavioral medicine will confront these modern-day problems as a team; psychologists, doctors, and surgeons will work together with patients and employ a holistic approach that considers each patient in the light of his or her biological, intrapsychic, and social/behavioral being. Evidence of the dramatic success of this approach is offered in the story of Eliza, the teenager whose damaged cortex could not allow her to "see," though her eyes were still able to respond to stimuli. But we are reminded that each of us, individually, must also take responsibility for our own personal health—a responsibility that could demand profound changes in life-style for many Americans.

McConnell predicts that in the realm of intrapsychic psychology, scientists will devise improved intelligence tests that will measure **quality**—not just quantity—potential skills, and performance in "real-life" situations. Therapy, too, will change toward more emphasis on cognitive and behavioral skills and what we have learned about cognitive behavior modification and social-learning theory. Cognitive studies are one of the fastest-growing areas of psychology, and as we understand more about our cognitive processes, we will be able to help people learn better and to learn throughout their life spans as well.

Applying the techniques of social/behavioral psychology, we can enhance community mental health programs in many ways. We can help men and women to learn better parenting skills, and we can create much more effective treatment programs for those incarcerated in mental hospitals and prisons. There will be greater interest in—and more emphasis upon—the study of organizations, the work environment, job performance of the workers, and management techniques used by supervisors and administrators. There is hope that we will be able to reduce or solve our problems of "psychological pollution," such as war, hate, prejudice, violence, mental illness, unemployment, and crime—all that poisons personal growth.

In this lesson, which concludes our formal study toward an understanding of human behavior, we will discuss the growing need for psychological services and some new career opportunities possible for those who are interested.

For better or for worse, we now have the tools, the objective data, and the ability to predict and control the future—to change the future deliberately. Although we must, of course, be concerned with what is happening in the present, we must now look to tomorrow and the world we have the means to shape. We must give more thought to the person each of us can become, rather than to what we have been. For each of us to become all we are capable of being—to fulfill our potential—there is no other choice.

But what is human potential? And what are its limits?

Assignments

There are no specific objectives for Lesson Thirty and thus no test materials. However, as a fitting conclusion to your study of human behavior, you will want to complete the assignments suggested in this section. Your faculty instructor or your manager for the course may also elect to set learning objectives for you and require assignments.

Before Viewing the Program

Read the preview at the beginning of this lesson.

Look over the subtitles for Chapter 26, "A Conclusion," then read the chapter.

View Program 30, "Applied Psychology"

After Viewing the Program

Review the text chapter.

Complete the short-answer questions included here for thought or for written assignment, as your instructor desires.

According to your instructor's assignment or your own interests, choose and complete activities from among the suggestions for extra credit.

And, you might find it fun and interesting to read the statistical appendix with which McConnell concludes the text.

Short-Answer Questions

1. Briefly summarize the advances which McConnell foresees in each of the three major branches of psychology.

2. What are some major differences in the brains of men and women?

3. What is the significance of "Eliza's" case to the disciplines of medicine and psychology?

4. What is meant by the term "behavioral medicine," and how will it be important in the future?

5. Define "behavioral engineering" and give some possible applications.

"Excuse me, sir. I am prepared to make you a rather attractive offer for your square."

Drawing by Weber; © 1971 The New Yorker Magazine, Inc.

Suggestions for Extra Credit

1. If you tried the short true-false exercise on common misconceptions in psychology which we offered in the beginning lesson of this course (Extra Credit Suggestions), you might want to look up the exercise and see how you did. **All of the answers to the questions are false**, though you, like most new students, may have answered some of them incorrectly. If you wish to check the answers, you will find references for the questions as follows: a. page 239; b. page 141, television program 11, "Subliminal Perception"; c. page 129; d. pages 456-468, 719-720; e. pages 711-712 (also 38-39, 299, 301-303, 457-458); f. pages 71-72; g. pages 536-537; h. page 58; i. pages 230, 351-352.

2. If you wrote a short paper telling what psychology is, what psychologists do, and what makes people think and act the way they do, reread your paper. Do you agree or disagree now with what you wrote then? In what ways has your point of view changed? In what ways is it still the same?

3. If you wrote a paragraph stating your reasons for taking this course, what you hoped to learn, and how you planned to apply what you learned, add a few paragraphs explaining what you actually did learn and how you now plan to apply it.

4. Open your textbook and reread the table of contents. On a sheet of paper, write the titles of the chapters that interested you most and tell briefly why each interested you. If you did this suggested exercise for Lesson One, compare your list. What area or aspect of psychology interests you most?

5. If you made a list of the unfamiliar boldfaced terms glossed in the text, look at that list. How many of the terms are now familiar to you? Can you define and/or explain all of them?

6. From memory, try to list the names of some famous psychologists. Beside their names, write the theories, discoveries, and/or methods for which they are most famous. How many were you able to name? Compare your work with the notes you made for Lesson One.

7. Which of the differing approaches to explaining human behavior do you personally subscribe to, now that you are completing your work for the course? The physiological orientation, the intrapsychic views, the social/behavioral theories? Or the holistic approach? Briefly explain why and mention a few theorists with whom you particularly agree or disagree.

8. It is the year 2000 and you are employed as a genetic counselor. What advice would you give to prospective parents, both before and after marriage? In your answer, try to make suggestions based on what you already have learned in Lessons Nineteen, Twenty, and Twenty-one about ''parenting'' and genetic influences on development. You may wish to check your local library for pertinent and timely research material or consult the reading references listed for Chapters 19, 20, and 21.

9. University of Hawaii psychologist Jerrold Michael, writing in the August 1982 issue of *American Psychologist*, says that both individual behavior and medicine must change to meet the realities of death and disease in America. A definition and discussion of behavioral medicine are also offered by G. E. Schwartz and S. M. Weiss in *Psychosomatic Medicine*, 1977. And in 1975, the U.S. Department of Health, Education, and Welfare published a report, *Forward Plan for Health*, which points out the radical changes in mortality causes in the United States and stresses the importance of individual responsibility for health. Read one or more of these articles and write a report briefly explaining the concept of behavioral medicine, then give your own ideas about how and in what ways behavioral medicine might be applied. You might also speculate about what future you see for behavioral medicine.

10. Are you interested in becoming a psychologist? The American Psychological Association has a book entitled *A Career in Psychology*. It describes how to become a psychologist, details specialty areas in psychology, and assesses current opportunities. For a free copy of the book, write to: Order Department, American Psychological Association, 1200 Seventeenth Street, N.W., Washington, D.C. 20036. Read the book and then write a few paragraphs in which you explain what area of psychology interests you and why. You might also want to read the discussion of professional psychology by R. Fox, A. Barclay, and D. Rodgers in the 1982 *American Psychologist*.

Answer Key

Short-Answer Questions

1. In the chapter assigned for this lesson, McConnell discusses predicted advances in the biological, intrapsychic, and social/behavioral branches of psychology.

   His discussion of biological psychology anticipates progress in many areas. Genetic counseling and genetic engineering may make it possible to prevent or correct many inherited problems. Increased knowledge about the functioning of the brain's hemispheres may allow important advances in educational methods and in the treatment of conditions caused by brain damage and in mental ailments like autism and schizophrenia. In behavioral medicine, we may see advances which will change habits and behaviors leading to possible injury or death as well help to treat language and learning difficulties and physical handicaps. Drug therapy and devices to aid or improve sensory processing will also advance.

   McConnell sees significant changes of direction in the field of intrapsychic psychology. Testing is useful today, but McConnell believes new testing techniques will be developed which tell more about real-life situations and potentiality. Psychotherapy, on the other hand, may cease to be a treatment and become a ''psychic exploration'' for individuals who wish to discover more about themselves; new therapies will emphasize cognitive modification and behavioral skills and, in some cases, will be combined in a holistic approach. Research on the two hemispheres of the brain, together with advances in cognitive studies (the fastest-growing area of psychological research today) and the proliferation of the computer, is stimulating many concurrent developments in education. We can now teach people who were thought to be beyond the reach of learning; lifelong opportunities are being made available to adults who want them; and we are improving the learning process itself. We now should be able to tailor education to individual needs. McConnell foresees the expansion and improvement of community services to provide more effective care and treatment for the mentally ill and for criminal offenders as well as training for necessary skills such as parenting. A great interest in the study of organizations and their management has taken place in the last several decades, and McConnell notes that these are certain to result in additional applications of psychology to such vital areas as work performance, job satisfaction, and improvement of the work environment.

2. According to recent research, the right ear and eye in women are more sensitive to sensory input, the left ear and eye are more sensitive in men; the left hemisphere is usually dominant in women, the right hemisphere is dominant in men. Young women have fewer language problems, more

479

difficulties with spatial concepts; men have more language difficulties and are better with spatial concepts and math symbolism. Women also are better at integrating processes that involve both hemispheres. However, research also shows that these abilities are profoundly affected by maturity; thus, late-maturing women tend to develop the same range of cognitive abilities as do men, and early-maturing males are more proficient at verbal tasks than are late-maturing males.

3. Eliza's case is significant for three important reasons: (1) It is an example of the effectiveness of behavioral medicine; (2) it indicates that parts of Eliza's brain that were not previously involved in visual processing could assume these functions, and damaged visual areas learned to process information in new ways; (3) it demonstrated the usefulness of psychology as well as medicine in helping Eliza; and (4) the fact that Eliza did recover though doctors had considered her case "hopeless" demonstrates the problem inherent in labelling individuals diagnostically as they **are** rather than as they might **become** with appropriate treatment.

4. In their article in *Psychosomatic Medicine*, Schwartz and Weiss define behavioral medicine as the "field concerned with the development of behavioral science knowledge and techniques relevant to the understanding of physical health and illness and the application of this knowledge and these techniques to diagnosis, prevention, treatment, and rehabilitation." University of Hawaii psychologist Jerrold Michael has written that 50 percent of the deaths in the United States are due to environmental factors. Most behavioral medicine approaches assume, then, that the biological, intrapsychic, and social/behavioral aspects must be looked at as interacting systems that require a new psycho-technology to help coordinate the inputs and outputs of all three. Psycho-technology, or behavioral medicine, not only can help to "cure" such problems as cortical blindness (previously considered hopeless) but also can help to change thoughts and behaviors that produce adverse effects on physical health. Trained technologists can, for example, help patients to stop smoking; stay on diets; stay with medical treatment plans; and learn to reduce stress, relax, cope with pain, and develop a more positive self-image.

5. Behavioral engineering should be one of the important professions of the future. This is the science of using psychology to create new, more satisfying social and work environments. Some areas behavioral engineers may be involved in are community mental health, teaching parenting skills, rehabilitating the mentally ill, re-educating and rehabilitating criminal offenders, and improving work performance and job performance.

From Incas to Indios

From Incas

to Indios

Photographs by

Werner Bischof, Robert Frank and Pierre Verger

Introduction by Manuel Tuñon de Lara

Robert Delpire, Paris

Universe Books, New York

Text translated by James Emmons

Introduction

The snowy summits of the Andes tower into a sky whose only denizen is the condor, wheeling in graceful circles high above the interminable ranges and plateaux where the llama grazes. Yet even at these altitudes, like nests as boldly perched as the condor's roost, we find the age-old stones, palaces and sanctuaries of a shattered civilization, primitive and refined, authoritarian and humane, superstitious and astute. Nothing but stones and the rockbound plateaux that once echoed to the imperative voice of the Great Inca? No, there is something more; there are men like ourselves, but men taciturn and sullen, keepers of secrets that we shall never fathom. Heirs of a fabulous civilization to which a tissue of legend still clings, they go about their humble tasks stooping under the loads they carry on their backs, like the burden of the past. They wear the peculiar hats the Spanish colonists taught them to wear. Before the Spaniards came they lived in harmonious communion with the sun and the earth. Their life was not an easy one, but they accepted the good with the bad. Then the patterns of the Inca world were suddenly disrupted by strangers from overseas: the conquistadors, with their firearms and trinkets, their crucifixes and lust for gold, their ruthless way of smashing or changing what they found.

In this brutal collision of two worlds, a soldier of fortune from Estremadura named Pizarro imposed his stern law and iron will, to which the Indian bowed but never quite yielded. The Spaniard did not adapt his rule to the native way of life, and he met with that passive resistance which nothing can melt or overcome. The secret of a civilization, locked in each Indian's heart, remained untouched and even unsuspected by conquerors—soldiers and brigands, priests and traders—who, in order to profit by their conquest, founded colonies on the coast, pushed into the interior, overran the high plateaux, and even scaled the peaks of the Andes in search of El Dorado, the land of fabulous treasure. Many an Indian was massacred in the process, but the conqueror soon realized that he needed the Indian's help. Then began that symbiosis of Spaniards and Indians, that assimilation of two dissimilar peoples. The conquistador became a colonist. Where before he had merely offered the lead shot of his harquebus, he now offered Christian art. To some extent he continued to deal out death, but he also dealt out life. He continued to explore a new country, but now he also made it his own. Intermarriage soon became a common occurrence; from these the first mestizos, or half-castes, were born, and with them a new society. Far more than an intermarriage of races, it was a marriage of civilizations. Even the animal world of the new continent felt the effects. The llama was no longer left to graze and wander at will over the broad tablelands, but was domesticated. The horse and the donkey, hitherto unknown in America, were introduced from Europe. Where there are horses and riders, there is song, and the Indians were soon plucking the guitar with the best of the Spaniards.

The last of the Incas, Atahualpa and Tupac Amaru, and many thousands of Indians perished at the hands of Pizarro, Almagro and their like, but pre-Columbian civilization lived on. Peru, Bolivia and many other countries of South America bear witness to the survival of the Indian. The purity of the Inca blood has been affected, but not its vitality. More than four centuries have passed since the first encounter of Inca civilization, entrenched in the solitude of ancestral ways, with the civilization of Western Europe in the person of the Spaniards. That marriage of forces remains even today the tacitly acknowledged pact by which the future of all South America is guaranteed—a whole continent and its peoples, over 160 million strong, heirs of both the Cid and Huilcanota, of the founders of both Burgos and Cuzco, of both Don Quixote and the Popol-Vuh.

In the highlands of the Andes live today some five million Indians. They form over half the total population, the rest being mostly half-castes, whites of Spanish descent and Negroes. Can all these men be said to have merged homogeneously into the different national communities? That would be saying too much. But to infer on the other hand that those who came from afar have remained impervious to the culture and the way of life they found there, would be even more misleading. When at the dawn of the 16th century the Old and the New World collided, men fought and killed one another, palaces crashed to the ground, empires crumbled and new ones arose, but the spirit of man remained unchanged. A civilization ravaged and all but uprooted was promptly grafted on to the civilization that had attacked it. Therewith began a long process of interpenetration. Beside the Cyclopean ruins of Inca palaces arose the Baroque marvels of colonial architecture. Today excursion buses from the ultra-modern plants of Detroit, Michigan, climb the mountain roads, drive past these ruins and rumble over the passes of the Andes. The immense monotony of the plateaux, once broken only by the shadows of circling condors, is now also broken by those of passing airplanes. Have memories of the Inca world been able to hold their own against the energy and enterprise of the foreigner? The answer is Yes, those memories are fresh and compelling. The present has not wiped out the past.

No culture is immutably fixed. However stagnant or petrified it may seem, it continues to transmit its heritage and thus continues to live. On these immemorial Incan stones, seemingly deserted by life, new worlds are in the making. The life of a given culture—and that of the pre-Columbian Indians is a conspicuous example—proves its permanence not by lingering on indefinitely in a mummified state, impervious to time and the ferment of other cultures, but by a generous opening of its pores, by a generous imbibing of new life forces. So it is with the Inca culture, whose vestiges strike us as soon as we sight them on the plateaux of the "altiplano." The folk dancing we watch, though typically Indian, is full of Spanish touches. The clothes we see, though woven on the hand loom with the inimitable skill of the aborigine, betray the cut and the trim of Spanish costume in the colonial era. The pagan ritual of long ago remains very much alive beneath the outward forms of Catholic worship. If from us they accepted the Cross and the Mass, to them we owe the potato, coffee, corn, cacao and quinine. The shipping lanes along which these novelties flowed to the Old World became, in the course of time, lifelines by which two civilizations were reciprocally nourished. All that had not been crushed in the early struggles began to thrive anew. The days of Pizarro, Cortes and Valdivia have long since gone by, and the conquered, having withstood the early tests of adversity, have acceded to a common share in the conquest of the future, in the making of a civilization whose underpinning is a potent aggregate of peoples widely differing in race, in esthetic, in moral principles, in their notions of life and death.

This is not to say that that civilization has come of age. The Indian holds back, a figure hieratic and taciturn. What does he think about it all? Sparing of his words, he comments on things with characteristic terseness: "Bayeta rompiendo," replies the Indian shepherd, in his wretched rags and tatters, when the county sheriff questions him in Ciro Alegria's fine novel of life in the Andes.

His gold was stolen, his way of life disrupted. The Cuzco of the Great Inca was overshadowed by the Lima of the Spanish viceroys. The land he cultivated, the last of his possessions, remained his own for a time. Then, in the second half of the 19th century, an "agrarian reform" engineered by the generals in power at Lima and their friends the "gamonales" deprived the Indians of most of their land holdings. These were their ancestral property, but how could they prove their legitimate ownership when the officials demanded their deeds of property duly signed and sealed? They had no choice but to move out, to withdraw to the remote districts where their community farms, modeled directly on the "Ayllu" of the Incas, are still to be found. But these are isolated survivals. The Indians have been dispossessed of the very land acknowledged to be rightfully theirs by the "Leyes de Indias" drawn up at Salamanca, Seville and the Escorial. Even in early colonial times, the clan system of the Ayllus suffered the encroachments of the "Encomiendas," which were nothing more nor less than wholesale appropriations of land which obliged the Indian to pay an annual tribute to his overlord—in other words, a feudal system imported from medieval Spain and designed to exploit the "natives." Three centuries later, the "caudillos" imposed their own version of the Napoleonic Code on an economic and social structure inherited from the feudal age, thus legally completing the pillage that began with the conquistadors.

Today the Indian has a scantier ration of corn and wheat than in pre-Columbian days. To make up for it, he enjoys a plentiful supply of coca, a treacherous drug which, when chewed, anesthetizes the mouth and gives the comforting illusion of having a full stomach and not a care in the world. The addict, however, is finally reduced to a state of intoxicated inanity. There is not enough bread or corn to go around, but there is plenty of coca.

What does it matter if, as a result, the Indian suffers a premature death? He no longer has land of his own to work in the Ayllus of his ancestors. Under the Incas, in the Kingdom of the Sun, he was regimented into a system severe to the point of rigidity. But he ate his fill and wove the clothes he needed from the wool of the vicuña. Then came the conquest and colonization; the Indians were herded together and used as slave labor in the mines and lumber camps. In the early 19th century came the independence of Peru, Bolivia and the neighboring states. Independence is what the government officials proclaimed it to be, and what the city-dwellers, the Creoles and the "cholos" were pleased to call it. But there was no change in the Indian's condition. He continued to be a tenant on land that belonged to others more fortunate than he. In times of need he was conscripted to wage wars whose meaning was a mystery to him. Released—if he survived—he returned to the wilderness of the Sierra and the plateaux. He allowed himself to be converted to Christianity, but the outward rites of Christian worship have left the ancestral rites within him intact. The religion of the Quichua Indians (the dominant tribe of Peru in Inca times) was primarily a moral code. Bound up with the life of the soil and the earth, not with a life in heaven, with the here-and-now, not with the hereafter, that religion collapsed with the Inca Empire, only to be reborn with the Indians' conversion to Catholicism. Emilio Romero aptly writes: "The Indians were deeply moved by the solemnities of the Catholic church service. In the glittering, brocaded

9

chasuble of the priest, they saw the symbolic image of the sun." The cult of the Virgin took vigorous root in the region of Lake Titicaca (original seat of the Inca theocracy). The conversion of the men of the Tahuantinsuyo marked the outward triumph of the Catholic rite, its images being freely adopted by pagan souls that had never before made any distinction between the temporal and the spiritual, the religious and the political.

Over four hundred years have elapsed since the marriage of these two civilizations, but the world born of that union has yet to attain anything like its natural maturity. The Indian gazing at us here, mute and wary, has lost the thread of the life he led four centuries ago. He needs, and badly needs, a country of his own, land of his own. Democratic constitutions come and go, but the Indian remains dispossessed and homeless, because landless. The land, the soil, the earth—that to him is both God and Mother. It is, as he calls it, "Mama Pacha" or "Pachamama," the supreme god. His corn was created by "Viracocha," the spirit of the earth. And corn nourishes men; it is the sacred staple. The Indian gazing at us inquiringly, anxiously, is a man torn bodily from the land and the gods that gave meaning to his life. The day he recovers his farmland he will also recover the heritage of his ancestors, together with a new awareness of the tie binding him to his ancestral gods. Only then will the names of Belgrano and San Martin (the liberators of Peru, Argentina and Chile in 1817–1821) embroidered on their holiday ponchos have any meaning. According to José Carlos Mariategui, a great Latin American and a great Peruvian, the Indian is married to his land; he mourns its loss as a lover mourns, and will never be happy until he regains possession of it.

The Indian worships the earth as he worships the sun, instinctively. So long as he languishes in an aimless existence, or slaves in the mines and lumber camps, all our solemn declarations of the Rights of Man will be no more than a hollow mockery, and the question arises whether the Indian was better off before under the Incan autocracy or is better off now under the liberal State of modern times.

To answer that, it is enough to go among these men and see their tragic faces. Yet, without the Indians the Andean highlands would be no more than a vast geological landscape, a wasteland given over to the raiding condor. These temples and palaces are manmade. Men planted the crops of corn and potatoes, and created the dances and the rites of this region. Let us try to get better acquainted with these men, with their ancestors and their civilization, so as better to understand whence they came and whither they may be going, for they lift their dispirited faces with a lordly air as if the future held better things in store for them.

The Inca civilization dates from the 13th century. The name "Inca" is known to have designated the supreme head of the Empire. A lesser known fact is that it originally designated the head of each "Ayllu," or community farm, which constituted the basic unit of that society from remotest times up to the last decades of the 19th century. The Empire of the Incas was entirely made up of a vast network of such community farms. This system, as historical records prove, successfully guaranteed the people against famine and hardship. It is true, they lived obscure and industrious lives in out-of-the-way valleys hemmed in by lofty mountains; the rigid pattern of community life, regulated by the seasons, practically ruled out anything resembling individual initiative as we know it today. This is not the place to sing the praises of that primitive life, innocent of every stain, glorified by Jean-Jacques Rousseau, or to draw up an idyllic picture of that lost paradise so fondly evoked by Don Quixote as he discoursed with the goatherds. Yet perhaps his words are worth recalling here: "Happy age and happy century, on which the Ancients bestowed the name of Golden, not for that it abounded in gold (which in our iron age is so highly prized) but that the men alive in those days knew not what it meant to say 'thine' and 'mine'." Here, very likely, we have the distinctive feature of Inca society in its heyday, before the Spanish conquest, when it comprised some ten million Indians.

The Incas were an agricultural people. Their industries were those of the craftsman and farmer, while their public works invariably served religious, agrarian or military ends. Yet the Incas were not a warlike people. In their tongue the word "soldier" was simply synonymous with "stranger" or "outsider." Essentially tillers of the soil, they left behind them many traces of their labors in the form of irrigation ditches and terraced hillsides. Their outlook on life was based on the traditional belief that from the earth, the common mother, sprang not only the crops but man himself. And "Mama Pacha," deity of the sun, watched over no one in particular but all in common, without distinction or privilege. This conception of things accounts for their social organization. The Ayllu, a social unit grouping blood relations into a community or clan, assumed responsibility for all the arable land, even when this was divided into individual plots. The federation of Ayllus, a tribal organization, including all the Ayllus grouped around a given village or town, controlled the waters, forests and pasture land, which was collective property. (Strange though it seems, a similar system still prevails in certain provinces of Spain, where for the poor—and only for the poor, this being the great difference—private property is limited to a house in the village; the communal lands are worked by one and all for the collective benefit.) Labor, as conceived by the Incas, was carried out on the basis of joint cooperation toward a common goal. The harvest was gathered in common and shared out individually. The Indians raised potatoes, beans, pimentos and corn; the last-named was, and still is, the staple foodstuff of their diet. Llama-breeding was carried out on a large scale, including all three varieties: the vicuña, the alpaca, the guanaco. They wove the wool of the llama as well as cotton and pita fiber. Though the use of iron was unknown to them, they were skillful workers in the precious metals which they found to hand in abundance and which they also alloyed with each other.

On this social structure arose the empire of the Great Inca, son of the Sun. The Indians contributed a share of the fruit of their labors to the Inca and the Sun, and another share to the autocratic class that ministered to the Inca. The rest reverted to each family in proportion to the number of its members. Each family worked the plot of ground allotted to it. Persons over fifty years of age were exempt from work and supported by the State.

The conquest that began with the landing of Pizarro in 1531 came like a thunderbolt upon this secluded world scarcely two centuries old. Even today its remains are like those of a vast empire struck by lightning and burst apart. That, in fact, is what it must have looked like very soon after being overrun by Francisco Pizarro, his brothers Juan and Gonzalo, their fellow soldier of fortune Diego de Almagro, and the priest Hernando de Luque. They brutally seized and tortured the young Inca Atahualpa. In vain did his subjects bring forward the ransom of gold demanded in exchange for his life. On the 29th of August, 1533, he was condemned to death and executed. His most faithful subjects held out a few years longer at Machu Picchu, the hidden city which the Spaniards never found, but the Inca Empire, deprived of its ruler, rapidly declined and crumbled. The seeds of a new civilization were planted, but had to be watered by the blood of thousands of Indians, decimated by forced labor in the mines and plantations; many others took refuge in the mountains. Their daughters became the mothers of half-castes.

A second generation of half-castes was born, and hybrid social and religious forms also came into being. The Indian accepted without demur the religious rites put up to him and blended them with the rites of his ancestors. The ritual splendor of the Mass made an irresistible appeal to the mind and imagination of this primitive people. But conversion went no deeper than the display of images; it remained on the threshold of the unfathomable soul of the Indian. The silence of these men is nowhere more eloquent than on this point, and that very silence is a kind of barrier between the old, which is theirs, and the new, which is ours. Instead of spreading the Gospels, which require other methods to be effective, the missionaries merely familiarized the Indians with the ritual of the Mass, adapting it to native customs. So it is that the red-letter days of the Gregorian calendar coincide in the Andes with the great pagan festival days. This was the price of conversion.

As conquest gave way to colonization, the missionary gave way to the ecclesiastic. All the churchmen of the colonial era were not ruthless inquisitors, though the long arm of the Inquisition was by no means slow to reach out across the Atlantic. Many of them in fact were honest Christians more concerned with helping others than with judging them; they taught arts and handicrafts, they introduced new tools, new methods of working the soil, new species of plants and animals. It was a group of monks who founded the first university. Among such men the Indians found their loyalest friends and staunchest defenders.

Founded by Pizarro in 1535, Lima prospered to the detriment of Cuzco, the old capital of the Incas. Seat of the viceroys, stronghold of Spanish power in Latin America, cradle of colonial Baroque architecture, Lima was the exclusive preserve of the government officials, the priests, and hordes of profiteers. There a life of luxury and idleness was the order of the day. Meanwhile, in the wilderness of the Andes, the natives were condemned to extracting precious metals from the mines of Potosi. Gold and silver flowed steadily into the holds of the great Spanish galleons and were shipped across the ocean to Seville, or to Lisbon or Antwerp, where other profiteers took them in hand. Meanwhile the population of the Andes steadily diminished. In Peru alone, by the time the colonial era came to an end, the native population had been reduced to one million.

These Indians who today dance themselves into a state of intoxication, who scrupulously observe their traditional death ritual, who work long hard hours to scratch out a meager living, who haggle to their heart's content on their small, quaint-colored marketplaces—they are the descendents of Atahualpa, of Tupac Amaru, of the Indian labor battalions in the mines and plantations; they are the descendents of the Indians recruited to fight a War of Independence which meant absolutely nothing to them because it failed to better their lot in the slightest. In this book of pictures both pleasant and painful, you will find what may be described as a cross-section of the beautiful and the ugly, the uplifting and the pathetic, the gorgeous and the tragic. Both had to be included to show the Indians as they really are, for their faces make no secret of their distress and their eternal surprise at finding no relief from that distress. While there is no lack of the picturesque in these pages, one elementary fact must be borne in mind: everything that is picturesque, compelling and beautiful in these Indians derives from the remote past and has somehow maintained its vitality; it is their very own, it is the legacy of the Incas. As against this, everything that we have given them—or nearly everything—is paltry, dreary, ridiculous. Neither buses nor trains seem the indispensable attributes we take them for when they are surrounded by a throng of ragged Indians. The image of our world and our civilization that they produce is immediately distorted in these outlying regions, just as in those convex mirrors that reduce everything to a fantastic caricature. The disgraceful truth is that modernism is at home hereabouts only in the bars and their gaudy shopfronts. There the atmosphere of the Upper Andes is somehow powerless to act, powerless to distort the blatant and absolutely truthful image of our 20th century produced by the local bars where the Indians are free to drink as much "chicha" as they can pay for—with the result that the infant mortality rate among them runs into the tens of thousands.

No praise is too warm for the efforts undertaken by various public and private institutions in behalf of the Indians. Unfortunately, all their generous exertions are not enough to cope with the situation. The Indian of today is not only the child of the Incas; he is also the child of the colonial era, with all its abuses and oppression, and the ignoble spirit of that era lives on in him as it lives on in the big property owners of today who dismiss him as an inferior being—"indio bruto," they call him. The Indian is an object of contempt for men who are not above the influence of whisky and reproach him for getting drunk on chicha, the juice of the divine corn. The Indian is illiterate, and so he remains, only considered good enough to provide cheap labor and to chew coca leaves.

Here and there, it is true, there seems to be a change for the better. Now to be found in some of the remote villages around Lake Titicaca are schoolteachers, courageous men and women imbued with the true missionary spirit, who are teaching the people, both children and grown-ups, not only to read and write, but to apply the rudiments of medicine and improved methods of farming. At Warisata (on the Bolivian plateau, at an altitude of 10,000 feet, where the air is difficult to breathe) the schoolmaster has taught the Indians how to cook certain foods and to observe the elementary rules of child-bearing. Elsewhere in the Andes, at Vareuna, a community school has been established for the benefit of the whole region. The schoolmaster often takes it upon himself to bring in the children from outlying farms and hamlets, and to see them home again. Parents too receive instruction. Roads have been laid out to link the school with surrounding villages. A well has been dug, the first at Vareuna. Fruit trees have been planted and a regional dispensary established.

The Indian's confidence in himself and in others must be restored. It is undeniable, and a cause for alarm, that so far the Indian population of Latin America has not been assimilated into the various nations that have taken form. It is no exaggeration to say that in certain countries (Peru, Bolivia, Ecuador and Guatemala, for example), where the proportion of Indians is very high, the future depends to a large extent on their participation in the life of the nation. The day the Indian breaks his silence and steps forth from his solitude may well mark the dawn of a new age, and a new lease of life for peoples still engrossed in their past.

Here we see them in their own environment—in their own circumstances, as the late José Ortega y Gasset would have said. Against the Andean landscape, amidst the stones of their ancestors, there they are with their tools and their domestic animals, their lives permanently scarred by the clash of civilizations that relegated them to this no man's land of time, between a past lost forever and a future still void of promise. They go on working to keep body and soul together. They gather in the village marketplace to sell their products. And a quaint and pretty sight their markets are, until the charm is suddenly broken when we realize the aching poverty of it all.

Centuries-old sentinel of the Holy Valley of the Incas, Machu Picchu stands on a crag 2500 feet above the brisk waters of the Urubamba. The hidden city of the Incas, it is perched on the very brink of the cliffs, its roots of masonry sunk into the rockface, all its apertures facing toward the sky, toward which also faces the "Intihuatana," or holy stone graven with the image of the sun, to which the High Priests used to "attach" their Star God each year at the winter solstice.

> Mother of stone, foam of the condor,
> High reef of the dawn of mankind,
> Shovel lost in the pristine sand.
>
> This was the dwelling, this was the place.
> Here the fat seeds of corn came up
> And went down again like red hail.

These lines of Pablo Neruda glorify the city whose whereabouts was long a mystery, whose rediscovery and resuscitated traditions are now the pride of all Latin America. The conquistadors never reached Machu Picchu. To that fact alone it owes its survival, and the survival of the "Intihuatana," the sun stone fanatically destroyed wherever they found it by the conquistadors who desecrated the pagan places of worship with a rapacious lawlessness and arrogance that even in retrospect are frightening.

Today a little old railway that is something of an anachronism in its own right carries tourists up to these altitudes (11,500 feet above sea level). A bridge has been built across the river Vilcanota, and the road runs up as far as the former dwelling of Tupac Amaru, last of the Incas, beheaded by the Spanish viceroy in 1571. This bridge, road and railway, unlike so many modern innovations, have genuinely facilitated the give-and-take of civilizations. They are winning friends where the henchmen of Philip II spread terror and dismay.

It is known that the survival of Machu Picchu is not an isolated case. There exist other lost cities in the Andes, still intact, where survivors and descendents of a shattered civilization managed to find asylum and lived for generations secure from the ravaging soldiery of the colonial armies. In 1952 a group of Peruvian archeologists discovered such a city on the Vilcanota, some 14 miles from Machu Picchu and 56 miles from Cuzco. The Swedish explorer Ander Bolinder has discovered other Incan fortress cities hitherto unknown, located at an altitude of nearly 7000 feet, literally "above the mêlée" of three and four centuries ago.

This inspired and inspiring landscape exalts the solitude of the Indian, and also exalts his grandeur. The dimensions of the region overshadow man and are a challenge to his creative powers. The eye sweeps over boundless tablelands and up to the fretted line of unbelievable peaks capped with snow and wisps of cloud. These are cosmic dimensions, completely eclipsing those of daily life. But the earth beneath our feet is also an overwhelming presence. To yield, the soil only asks to be tilled. It is a curious fact that in Quichua, the Indian language, the verbs "to work" and "to toil" do not exist apart from their connection with the soil; they are identical with "cultivate" and "till." After the earth comes the sun, just as naturally as a man's eye lifts from the ground to the sky; and in the absence of sun, life slackens and declines on the earth. This the Indian observed in the rhythm of his own existence; hence his worship of the Earth and the Sun. There is no denying that even under the Incas the Quichua Indian learned that work meant more than cultivating the soil. The toil and the sweat of many thousands of men went into the building of these palaces and temples. Even today, as they carry their loads up the mountain, the Indians have all the same gait and the same peculiar way of throwing back their heads that betray both seasoned physical effort and pride in work accomplished. Four, five and six centuries ago, their forefathers carried the same stones on their backs, performing the same labors.

Inured to servitude, the Indian puts his trust in the earth and the sun. Treated for centuries as a human beast of burden, he has learned to distrust his fellow men. What he has given is out of all proportion with what he has received. True, he has received the donkey, that companion of the poor, unknown before the conquest. But he has always depended and still depends on the llama, the "camel of the Andes." Capricious but tough and serviceable, it is the one reliable means of communication and transport. For centuries, at the entrance of the mines, the llama has patiently, stoically shouldered its ritual payload of 100 pounds of silver. The limits of the Inca Empire reached out only as far as the llama could carry the Indians, and no farther. For centuries the llama has been their inseparable companion and ally. Together they peopled the plateaux and trail-blazed the remoter valleys of the Andes. The llama today, writes García Calderón, remains "the patient and compassionate brother of the Indian." "And," he adds, "when the white man and the half-caste move out of earshot, no one can guess the words of friendship that the master of the land and his animal companion exchange, or how they look into each other's eyes and cheer each other up."

The conquistadors arrived on prancing horses, but all they left behind was the plodding donkey—a steed good enough for Sancho Panza, but not for Don Quixote, the hidalgo. The horse made a tremendous impression on the Indians, who promptly idolized that noble animal which they were too poor to own. Legend has it that the image of the horse that belonged to Cortes, hewn in stone by the Indians, may still be seen in a cave beside the Lake of Peten in Guatemala. No such honor was paid to the humble donkey, though he has served the Indians well.

It is hardly a matter for surprise if the Indian women refuse to look us in the eye. They shrink away and cling to one another for that vague animal comfort that comes of flocking together with one's own kind. They all wear the round, derby-like hat characteristic of the Lake Titicaca region, and wear it drawn low over their faces. They still weave cloth that excites our admiration. They live and work for their menfolk. They sleep on the bare ground—one reason why relatively few of their frail children reach manhood. The resplendent, mysterious beauty of their seventeenth year blows over like a light mist, wiped out in a flash by married life. The average life expectancy in these regions hardly exceeds 30 years. Even so, a handful of oldsters is to be seen, majestic, enigmatic men and women with an absolutely ageless look on their wrinkled faces. But old folk are only to be found in such communities as have successfully held aloof from modern life, where work is still synonymous with the cultivation of the soil.

These Indians who keep step with the llama, who go and come around the huts of the patriarchal Ayllu, still partake of the Golden Age of the Inca world. But the glamour of that world is waning. There is no resisting the irruption of history, especially when it irrupts in the insidious form of material difficulties and inappeasable anguish of mind. Today the ancestral pattern of economic life and the peace of mind that went with it have been disrupted, and the Indian, like other people, is driven to earn a certain number of "soles" (the Peruvian unit of money) if he is to buy a few trifles from the itinerant vendors and a few indispensable tools which can only be obtained in the towns.

Work, often back-breaking work, provides the Indian children with the bulk of their education; they either help their parents on the farm or enter on an apprenticeship in town. This is the fate of half the children who, by rights, should be sitting in the schoolrooms. Most of those who begin their ABC's never even finish elementary school. It is not their fault if they are compelled to go to work almost as soon as they leave babyhood. They soon lose their childish smiles and their confident innocence. Their features are soon marked by a sorrowful, hangdog look which at first—like that of the guitar player hiding his instrument under his poncho, uncertain of the reception he will get—is tempered by a twitch at the corner of the mouth, by a fugitive gleam of merriment in the eye, by vague hopes that somehow continue to stir, though everything contributes to crush them. Finally, when they realize

16

that in this bitter world a useful life in normal society is denied them, they turn their gaze inward, nursing a grievance which only the llama seems to understand and share.

As for the little Indian girls in particular, obviously youth has passed them by. The art of being young—that is what changing times have robbed the Indians of. These little girls go straight from birth to the anguished maturity of womanhood. In their eyes, as in those of their mothers, is a look of accumulated pain and mourning deposited by the experience of centuries, whose meaning or whose lesson eludes them.

There is, to be sure, in spite of everything, a blithe and happy side to the heritage that has made these Indians what they are. Music, for example, represented chiefly by the guitar. The Spaniards introduced it and the Indians took to it so eagerly that they have made it an instrument peculiarly their own. A scrap of wood, an airhole, six strings, nothing more. But they have tuned it perfectly to their love of song and their need to sing, to chant, to relieve their hearts. The song of the guitar is the one breach in their wall of silence. Not that music was unknown in the Andes before the coming of the Spaniards, far from it. Even in early times, under the Incas, the period of rest after work was given over to music-making and the chants that soothe and elevate the mind. These were not war chants, but a pastoral music akin to the moist and fertile furrows of the fields, a music voicing love of life in the melodious Quichua language. Armed strangers on horseback had to trample their world underfoot for the Indian to take up his flute and pipe music of sorrow and revolt. In the "yaravi" he sings today mingle the remorseful melancholy of a lost happiness and dejection with life as he is condemned to live it now.

But with the guitar it is not quite the same. Around the guitar, as the Indians pluck it, a new folklore has sprung up, plunging its roots in the old-world soil of far-off Andalusia and uniting the voice of the cavaliers of Spain singing on horseback with that of the sons of the Incas singing on the mountain paths as they trudge beside the llama.

The Indian has behind him a long tradition of expert craftsmanship. Today, as seven centuries ago, he makes his own clothes, his own pottery and straw hats. The hat-maker is a craftsman of considerable importance in the Indian community. But the tall sombrero that so many Indians wear is not a native article, but an imitation of the classic Spanish headgear. It is not unusual, when an Indian doffs his sombrero, to see that hidden beneath it he wears the old Inca bonnet of the past. Thus the hat of one civilization covers the hat of another civilization, just as present-day life covers over the memory of ancestral life, though without blotting it out; that memory is very much alive in a people accustomed to honor the traditions of its ancestors.

On the marketplace, in the streets and lanes, in the houses, everywhere pottery proliferates. There are jugs and pots, often highly appealing in their rusticity, sometimes decorated with geometric patterns on burnished surfaces in the manner of the old Inca vases. Or, like the primitive Quichua vases, they are white, relieved only by a sober emblem in red.

Or they are reddish yellow, like freshly plowed earth. For the making of ceramics, the Indians mix their clay with ochre, coal dust and finely shredded corn straw. The results range from the truly ornamental amphora to a cup especially designed for drinking chicha, from the simplest type of pot to the most imposing of jugs. They also make a large gourd smoothly flattened on one side to fit against a man's back; filling it with chicha and passing straps through the holes on either side, the Indians carry it off to the fields where they drink it dry in the course of the day's work. Though it is very similar to the "botija" of the Andalusian peasants, this Inca gourd almost certainly dates from before the conquest. The fact is that it becomes increasingly difficult to distinguish what is Spanish from what is Indian, what is specifically indigenous from what is colonial. This is true of objects as it is true of faces, now that generations of interbreeding have wiped out so many racial distinctions.

It is also true of architecture. Here we have the Plaza Mayor of any Castilian town. The architecture imported by the colonists has taken its rightful place in the art history of these countries. But in this Spanish setting, instead of the "hidalgos" and "picaros" who lorded it during the conquest, we see Indians and "cholos." Take away the cars and strip these men of their modern dress, and we might believe ourselves back in the days of the viceroys. After all, this square is a crossroads of three, perhaps four worlds: that of the Incas, that of the colonial period, that of Latin American independence, and that of the future.

Nothing could be more impressive than the silence of the marketplace, though full of people. In this setting, straight out of old Castile, voices are strangely muffled. "Cholos" lean in the doorway of their shops, cutting the figure of big businessmen by contrast with the Indians. "Abarroteros" sell everything from beans to linen, from hats to spades, together with quack remedies; with these they proffer long-winded "medical" advice calculated above all to stimulate sales by adapting the symptoms to the concoctions at hand, by prescribing first a stimulant for the tapeworms of all these louse-eaten Indian children, then an antidote guaranteed to kill the worms. Indian women, down from the mountains with their babes on their back, go from vendor to vendor inspecting, calculating, haggling. Yet the sounds of the market are no more than an all but inaudible murmur relapsing into frequent silence; it is almost awe-inspiring. The colors of the place seem to make more noise than voices and movements. Yet haggling, an endless haggling over prices, is the immutable economic law of this crouched, shrinking, whispering world. Buyer and seller attempt to outwit each other in hushed voices, unwearyingly, but with that discretion which seems to remind bystanders that this is an exchange of words reserved only for the interlocutors and the brief space of air between them. Generous quantities of chicha helping, the barrier of timidity is gradually broken down, conversations are started up and grow almost lively, strangers meet and friendships are formed. But the Indian comes to market with the diffidence born of many rebuffs. Only yesterday he was the victim of a closed economy, ignorant of the art of buying and selling. Today the marketplace is like an open-air school where the Indian is initiated into the elementary rules of business. Arriving from miles around, peasants put out their beasts to graze beside the cemetery, while they themselves squat down in groups in front of the church and guzzle chicha beneath large inscriptions, posted on the whitewashed walls of brick and adobe, exhorting them to temperance and piety. Fortune-tellers thread their way through the crowd, accosting group after group, like nuns jingling the money-box amid the congregation. The marketplace is also a crossroads of rites and beliefs, though no one has the least concern for those of anyone else. Finally it is midday; the hot sun beats down from directly overhead. All morning, without a let-up, the men have been drinking chicha. Heavy-headed, unsteady on his feet, the Indian invariably leaves the market poorer than he came. He came to market with the innocent hope of taking home with him the value of his earnings. Home he goes befuddled with drink and not a "sol" left in his pocket. So far civilization has tempted him down from the plateaux and encouraged his craving for alcohol. That much has been accomplished. Might it not be possible to teach the Indians something more than that? Look at them: night falls over their empty lives after an empty day, they crouch beside the blighted walls and count their remaining pennies. The children look on with impassible faces. They too were at the market. They follow in the footsteps of their elders, whose example they in turn will imitate. But might it not be possible to provide them with other examples besides these? It is a shabby destiny indeed that lies before the child of the Indian plowman. To him are addressed these lines of Miguel Hernandez:

> He begins to live
> And to die from beginning to end . . .

Echoes of Castile are met with on every hand in the Andes. For the men of Castile brought with them not only the ways of the Western world, they transplanted some of its deepest roots. The "corrida," for example. Watching the "aficionados" go through their paces here, we might well believe ourselves in a Castilian village. The Spaniards not only introduced the bull, but succeeded in communicating their passion for bullfighting. The passion, the steps and movements, the costumes, but not quite the spirit of the thing. It was only natural for bullfighting to be eagerly taken up in countries where certain animal sacrifices were an immemorial custom. Perhaps no country has taken more lustily to the Spanish national sport than Mexico. But it thrills the crowds in Peru as well, above all at Lima. It is nonetheless a fact that the Indian fails to share in the spirit of the final kill. He has no heart for the final triumph of the matador. In this his attitude toward animals diverges from that of the Castilian or Andalusian. The Indian enthusiast takes his pleasure in the skill of the toreador in avoiding the charge of the bull, not in the victory and the sacrifice of the animal.

On the marketplace, cleared of its haggling groups of buyers and sellers, the spectacle offered by the bullfight is not so much that of the true Spanish "corrida," orderly and ritual, as that of an impromptu game of skill in which the poncho serves as the toreador's cape.

Needless to say, long bouts of chicha-drinking go hand in hand with every deal of the market and with every stage of the bullfight. Once the noble beverage of the Incas, chicha is now classed by general consent, along with coca, as the Indians' deadliest enemy. It was obtained by pressing out the juice of boiled corn with a stone cudgel, and when fermented served as a propitiatory offering to the Sun and the Great Inca. After the collapse of the Inca

Empire, it quickly became the favorite drink—no doubt the consolatory drink—of millions of Indians. The corn that before had nourished so well thus turned to poison; what was a blessing before became a curse. For centuries now, unchecked, it has sapped the vitality of the Indian people. This is not the place to decide whether it is the cause or the consequence of their downfall. It is enough to recall a few home truths. The Indian subsists on a diet that provides him with a daily average of 2219 calories, whereas the recognized daily minimum for a human being is 2410 calories. The Indian subsists on 57 grams of proteins daily, whereas the recognized minimum in temperate latitudes (and he lives in the highlands of the Andes!) is 75 grams. There is admittedly some excuse if such a man seeks to fill his stomach, in default of the actual food, at least with the consoling semblance of repletion imparted by the drinking of chicha and the chewing of coca leaves. The latter is a drug notorious for giving the impression of vitality while actually draining the body of its vital forces. The Peruvian Indian eats on an average 32 lb. of meat per year; the Bolivian Indian eats an average of 65.5 lb. of meat per year. Both live and work at an altitude of many thousands of feet, where breathing is difficult, and where other men would need an oxygen mask. While in the course of time the Indians have adapted their lungs and thorax to these conditions, that adaptation is being dangerously compromised by the drinking of alcohol.

Is the Indian a Christian or is he a pagan? The only immediate answer to that is the phrase the poet put into the mouth of the Indian who, when asked the same question, replied: "Quien lo sabe, Señor?" Who can say, Sir, who can say? The Indian's notions of religion—or, better, his religious emotions—are inextricably complex. Kneeling devoutly at the shrine of a Catholic chapel, he burns incense in the age-old manner of the Incas, Mayas and Aztecs. The Indian women can hardly contain their emotion at the sight of a procession in honor of the Virgin, in whom they venerate not only the Mother of Christ but also their ancestral Goddess of the Earth and the Intercessor of their own sorrows and wretchedness. There is an expression of genuine grief on the Indians' faces as they carry the image of the Madonna, of "Nuestra Señora." They obviously have an almost vehement sense of personally sharing, daily, in their own lives, the sufferings of their "goddess mother." This is the spirit in which they hold aloft the heavy polychrome image, richly sculptured and lavishly inlaid with gold and precious stones. Their ecstasy, if such it is, is in part merely an intense contraction of the muscles, while their grief-stricken countenance is that of an actor who deeply feels his part, for the honor of carrying the Virgin's shrine is reserved to the few already privileged to assist in preparing the Christian ceremonies and celebrations.

In a country evangelized and entirely refashioned by Spain there are, strangely enough, few priests to be seen. One reason is that, generally speaking, the Indians do very well without the ministers of a cult which they have only very imperfectly assimilated. Not that the Indians are lacking in the religious sentiment; it is the mystical sentiment that they lack. They look to the Catholic Church not for an outlet for pent-up religious ardor, not for an answer to burning metaphysical anxieties, but for an ordered social structure. And while

20

the Indians are strict and conscientious in observing their creed, it certainly is a creed peculiar to themselves. It is not unusual in the Aymara communities to find the priest receiving investiture not from his ecclesiastical superiors but directly from the tribe. In fact the priest is simply chosen from among the tribal elders. The Mass proceeds to the accompaniment of an outlandish jabbering of dog Latin, liberally mixed with broken Spanish and Quichua. To enlist the Indian in its cause, the Church had no choice but to sanction heterodox liturgy of this kind. Once converted, he relies heavily on the priest for certain things. However costly it is to be born (since there is no birth without baptism), to get married (since the sacrament of the Church consecrates the marriage tie), and to die (there being no death without a requiem Mass), the Indian is eager to pay for these things; he flatly refuses to see the most significant events of his existence go by without being solemnly, ritually observed in the manner prescribed by the creed he has embraced. And Christianity has its attraction for him. In the confusion of images which for him explain life and represent the world, he especially relishes the promise of a better life hereafter. It is, without a doubt, the vision of Paradise held up to his mind's eye that was instrumental in converting him. So it is that he does not hesitate to pay regularly for Masses that intercede for the deliverance of his soul or that of a loved one. In his novel "Huassipungo", Jorge Icaza describes an Indian named Andrès who pays with his own life the Masses intended to save the soul of the woman he loves. And Miguel Angel Asturias, in "Hombres de Maiz", draws a vivid picture of Don Casualidon, a terrifying Spanish priest in an Indian village, who meets only with hostility and derision where he expected to find a bed of roses. Yet these same Indians have a faith, or, lacking that, a thirst for faith whose sincerity cannot be questioned. Give them a chance to participate in the rites of the Church and they are won over at once. On feast days, the Alcalde (mayor) takes command of the community and, baton in hand, signifying his authority, presides over the ceremony. The tiny church with its stunted spire and profusion of wooden crosses is crammed to overflowing with a hushed crowd of copper-skinned figures wrapped in colorful ponchos. In many regions the old-established Indian communities have come to call themselves "confraternities" in imitation of religious brotherhoods. On feast days, the Indians vie for the signal honor of carrying the crosses and banners. With dreamy but impassible faces, they contemplate the image of Christ—it is exactly the same expression with which they gaze upon outsiders. What can they be saying to their new God? Whatever it is, they seem to find a much-needed solace in their worship of Him who suffered on the Cross for all mankind.

The persistance of primitive native beliefs is most strikingly seen in their death rites. Death, among the Indians, is a social event. Like a magnet, it tightens the family circle around the dead man, attracting even the most distant members of the family, together with the entire Ayllu to which the bereaved belong. The women tirelessly repeat the same monotonous phrases in praise of the deceased, while the men stand by in silence, munching coca leaves. From time to time a muttered prayer is audible. An elder takes charge, ceremoniously directs the saying of the Pater Noster and the Ave Maria, then in the next breath intones a native prayer intended to exorcise evil spirits, and lastly invokes the benevolence of the sacred animals. Who will draw the line between ancestral witchcraft and Christian piety?

Each visit of death in the immense solitude of the plateaux and each tombstone in the bleak cemetery where the Indians bury their dead is an outward sign of a struggle against nature which the living begin afresh each day in a region unfriendly to man. Familiarity with death inspires these people with a certain respect for the human person, while the stones, crosses and statues of their cemetery are like a terrible lesson that has left its indelible imprint on the landscape. The "velorio" (the wake, or vigil of the dead) is a memorable night. It is an occasion for hearty eating and copious drinking carried to the last degree of inebriation. Such macabre banqueting as this is the practice all over the South American continent, but its traditional rites are found in their purest state in the upper plateaux of Bolivia. There the Indians still observe the "last supper" of the friend or relative who has just died but has not yet been buried. Friends and family gather together, and all do justice to a big meal consisting of the favorite eatables of the deceased, carefully prepared in large earthenware pots. Once it is served up, each guest tackles his portion exactly as the dead man was wont to do; each guest does his utmost to respect the dead man's culinary preferences, to imitate his very gestures at table, to eat not only exactly the same dish or dishes, but to consume the very same quantities as he was accustomed to eating in his lifetime. This gastronomic rite is carried out beside the dead body. Only after this rite has been strictly observed, then, and only then, is it fitting to bury the body, which is thereupon conveyed to the cemetery and lowered to its grave in accordance with the Christian ceremony. The Bolivian Indians are extremely scrupulous in their observation of this rite, so scrupulous in fact that during the Bolivian revolution of 1952, when many Indians were killed in the fighting, burial was in every case postponed until such time as the "last supper" of each victim could be duly celebrated. No Indian could be found who was willing to omit or miss the last meal in honor of a friend or relative who had fallen. It is a remarkable fact that in Bolivia, where they constitute three quarters of the total population and where, as laborers, factory workers and above all miners, they are fast becoming a key factor in the productivity of the country, the Indians have sacrificed nothing of their ancestral traditions and heritage; they observe their old death rites and celebrate their own holidays with the time-honored ritual of each.

Thus we see their high-piled dishes of food in the shadow of the cross beside the bodies of the dead. For them the dead never quite vanish from the realm of the living, but come back to join in the dancing on feast days among or perhaps beneath the fantastic masks of birds and beasts whose power of magic is taken for granted by all.

The fiesta is by no means a mere throwback to bygone times, out of keeping with the Indians' destiny in the modern world. It is, on the contrary, one whole side of their life and an inalienable facet of their personality. While it is the direct expression neither of unhappiness nor of poverty, yet it is intimately bound up—by reaction, perhaps—with these all too frequent conditions of the Indians' existence; it is the outcry of their souls, the spiritual ferment of a people. No one resists the ardor and intensity of the fiesta. From the humblest to the most favored Indian, everyone is swept up in an irresistible display of showmanship, which is not to say that the show provided is mere artifice or a fraud. Nothing is more genuinely moving. The fiesta is like the image of a people, an image which fires the imagination and strikes up fresh contact between the individual and the collective soul. In the early days the Church attempted to outlaw these festivals in which the Indian personality finds freedom and fulfillment. But no such attempt could possibly succeed. Even the Inquisition was powerless to stifle that uprush of instinctive forces. The festivals of the Quichua and Aymara Indians sink their roots into the myths and ancient religious rites of pre-Columbian times, when nature and agricultural life were alone in inspiring men's thoughts and engendering men's visions. Today, as always, the Aymaras festively celebrate the dropping of young among the cattle. Mid-summer festivities herald the coming of harvest time; those celebrated on the feast day of St. Barbara (December 4th, which is summer in the southern hemisphere) hardly vary from the festivities of old in honor of the Inca goddess, Mama Pacha. It is a strange sight indeed to see a Christian feast day celebrated by libations in honor of Mother Earth and by the sacrifice of llamas. In the Huancayo region the annual animal dance takes place on December 25th, the day of the Nativity. For hours on end, masked dancers pretend to be the animals they represent, with which they strive to establish a sacred link of emotional sympathy. Once the dance is over, the dancers gather round the Manger and pay homage to the Christ-child.

No festival without music and dancing, and no dancing without masks. Mythical and symbolical, these dances hark straight back to the Incan, even to the pre-Incan world, despite the colonial Spanish influence that has left its mark on them. The masks were formerly worn by the "shaman," or medicine man, whose business it was to exorcise evil spirits. Fashioned out of gold, silver, wood, bronze, llama wool and bird feathers, these masks evoke a fantastic spirit world.

Dancing is of course the essential ingredient of an Indian festival. All the colonial chroniclers remark on this point. "When the Spanish came to America," wrote Pedro de Cieza de León, who traveled in South America from 1533 to 1550, "they were exceedingly surprised at the pleasure the natives took in dancing. They marveled that a people habitually sullen and apathetic should reveal such extraordinary sprightliness when indulging in its favorite amusement. It is true that for them dancing is not a mere amusement, but an earnest and important matter which has its place in every manifestation of their public and private life."

Today we find three distinct types of dancing among the Indians of the Andes: genuinely autochthonous dances, dances of Spanish origin, and dances of Negro origin. Chief among the first-named are the "Kahina" or love dance, performed by couples of boys and girls in a large circle, and the "Kachua," which represents a love-sick woman in search of her lover, with whom, when finally he is found, she triumphantly dances. The other dances, while retaining much that is strikingly Spanish or African, have nevertheless been freely adapted and embroidered upon. Many of these "cholitas" and "marineras," now so strongly marked by the rhythm of this people, prove that the creative faculty of the Indians still has surprises in store for us. In spite of poverty and illiteracy, in spite of coca leaves and chicha, their spiritual vitality remains intact. All they ask is a chance to pour that vitality into the task of building the Latin America of tomorrow and a happier future.

Grandiose and spectacular, the so-called "Diabladas de Oruro" take place each year at Carnival time. Oruro is a prosperous mining town in Bolivia (population 70,000). It is not, as some seem to think, a mere backwoods settlement cut off from the outside world and from the enjoyments of modern life. On the contrary, Oruro owes its development to the economic prosperity which, despite wars and slumps, has generally characterized the past few decades. Its rise began with the World War of 1914–1918 when—for destructive ends that certainly did us no credit—the Allied powers needed vast quantities of tin; these the mines of Oruro in part supplied and the town expanded. Since then, its prosperity has been assured by increased production standards and the increased demand for tin. Today the city boasts a modern university, several daily newspapers, and all the facilities that go with them. But Oruro and its Indian miners have not repudiated their traditions. And the most astonishing tradition they keep thoroughly alive is the annual "Diablada," invariably held on a Saturday. It gives the signal that Carnival time has at last arrived. The streets are packed with people, children and grown-ups, eagerly waiting for the "Devil" to appear on the scene with his wicked spouse, "China Supay," followed by the beneficent archangel St. Michael, and by the Condors and Bears. The entire population parades through the streets towing oxen and donkeys. The procession comes to a halt in front of the church dedicated to the Virgin of the Cave, on Socavon Square, where the offering to the Virgin is made, and where the Diablada properly so called takes place.

The Diablada is patterned after the medieval "autos sacramentales" (religious plays, especially popular in Spain, dramatically illustrating the mystery of the Eucharist), but it has come to reflect the spirit, mores and mentality of the Bolivian Indian in the highest degree. The theme on which it hinges is the struggle between Good and Evil, the Good winning out thanks to the providential intervention of the Virgin. But the vividness, rhythm and beauty of the Diablada have carried it leagues away from its original theme and meaning. The theological argument emphasized by the Spanish colonists has been largely overlaid by the exuberant fancy and pagan inventiveness of the Indians. In their hands the original Christian mystery play has been changed almost out of recognition. The Indian miner pays worshipful homage to the demon, the demigod, or demi-devil, whose presence he senses in the depths of the mine, and the tin he laboriously extracts from the bowels of the earth is the offering he is compelled to make to that demon. It is a fact that the men of Oruro, though their standard of living has undeniably risen, still feel themselves directly and inexorably in the grasp of the devil. Seventy per cent of them suffer from a dangerous lung ailment due to the unhealthy breathing conditions underground. When at work, down in the mines, the Indian contrives

24

to make light of his illness and even carves small caricatural statues of the devil, his challenge to the powers of darkness. Into the mouth of this diabolical effigy he sticks a lighted cigarette, and works on. If the cigarette goes out, that is an ill omen.

But coming back to the festival which, once a year, completely overshadows the anxieties and hardships of everyday life. The procession pours into Socavon Square, preceded by a Bear and a Condor. Then come Lucifer and China Supay, his spouse and helpmate, the only female impersonated, representing the temptations of the flesh (Supay is a native word for "devil"). In their wake is a boisterous throng of masked and costumed figures, whipped up into a frenzy of fiendishly rolling eyeballs, huge menacing horns, long flickering dragons' tongues. Now that the square has been reached, the show gets underway, and it is a gorgeous, inextricable complex of the Christian and the pagan, blending the imagery of both traditions into an unforgettable medley of color and symbol. The Archangel Michael stalks forward and summons the seven devils personifying the Seven Deadly Sins. Plied with liquor by China Supay, the seven devils are then upbraided by St. Michael, who threatens them with hellfire and brimstone. They acknowledge their unsatisfactory behavior and make ready to expiate their sins in the quenchless fire. But the Miraculous Virgin of Socavon, patroness of the miners, intercedes and decrees that the Good has duly triumphed. Whereupon all masks are dropped and all the miners file devoutly into the church, singing a hymn to the glory of their saintly protectress.

For the past century or so, the Diablada has been much as we see it now, danced rather than acted. But its origins go back many centuries earlier. One tradition has it that the Diablada originated about 1600 in the escapade of two Spanish settlers who, disguised in terrifying masks, attempted to frighten away the Indian proprietors of a mine which they hoped to appropriate for themselves. A more likely explanation lies simply in the deep-seated need of the Indians to exorcise the ills that dog them by performing rites that have issued from the primitive beliefs of their race. In their own minds, their fervid participation in the Diablada and their appeal to the Virgin serve to ward off the baleful influence of the devil they call Tiu, ruler of the dark underworld of the mine.

Whatever its origin, the Diablada is one of the most characteristic and certainly the most impressive of the fiestas to be seen in the Andes. Reveling goes on for three days. The entire city pours into the streets, singing and dancing like souls possessed. Everywhere are ponchos, "polleras" (skirts), blouses and shawls in colors that put the rainbow to shame, flamboyant colors whose secret is the Indians' alone. Released, once a year, from servitude to the mines and the earth, the people surge through the streets and give vent to their emotions. There is plenty to drink, that goes without saying. Yet it is a remarkable truth that, though the Indian workers continue to dote on chicha, they no longer overdo it and intoxication is rare. This fact was recorded by Dr. Paul Rivet during his last trip to Bolivia in 1954. No doubt improved living conditions alone have gone a long way toward stamping out alcoholism.

Taciturn and inscrutable, the Indians watch us as we go and come among them. Very close to the soil they till, keenly aware of the past, true to the spirit of their ancestors, these people have patiently domesticated the llama and patiently overcome the climatic handicaps of the highlands where they live. They are worthy of our admiration and respect. Living in tune with nature, they celebrate seed time and harvest time; they celebrate the good things of life with gusto. Though desperately poor and an easy prey to illness, they have somehow retained the proud and lordly bearing of their ancestors. These barefoot Indians—in present-day Peru 73 per cent of the people lack proper shoes, one half of the population still wear the primitive sandals known as "ojotas"—these Indians who were abject slaves until the emancipation of 1854, and who are still little more than serfs in their desolate Ayllus, these Indians have abundantly proved that they are men by the exercise of what is best in man: the ability to think independently, to celebrate joyfully and wholeheartedly, to keep tradition alive and responsive to the present and the future.

No man can decently serve as a mere museum piece to his fellow men. The Indians are not simply picturesque or quaint. Let us try to see them with open minds; let us try to see them as Miguel Unamuno wished them to be seen, not as the exotic inhabitants of a strange world, but as men of flesh and blood. The beauty of the spirit they embody will then seem all the finer to us.

Manuel Tuñon de Lara

First Chapter

1

2

3

4

9

11

1 Ruins of Machu Picchu, the lost city of the Incas in the Peruvian Andes. Shown here is that part of the city which dominates the valley of the Urubamba.

2 Upper plateaux at Maras, far above the tree-line. Atmospheric conditions characteristic of the Altiplano: the earth is intensely cold, the only heat comes from the sun, when it breaks through, and the only shadows are thrown by passing clouds.

3 Ruins of Chan Chan, in the Trujillo region of Peru. The only shadows are the result of man's handiwork. These rather rudimentary constructions date from pre-Columbian times, but stand apart from the great center of Inca civilization.

4 Fortress near Cuzco, the ancient Inca capital.
5 The stones of which it is made were brought from afar on the Indians' backs or, if too heavy, were dragged by teams of Indians. The method remains the same today. These stone-bearers use a harness more rudimentary than that of their donkeys.

6 Women of the Ayaviri region (between Puno and Cuzco, Peru). They are veiled and invariably wear their hat drawn low over their faces. Spanish women would consider the veil as sufficient to clothe their dignity and modesty, but here a hat is worn as a necessary and natural article of clothing. No Indian ever goes out without his hat, which protects both against sun and cold. Some even wear an extra head-covering, sometimes two of them, beneath their hat.

7 Suspension bridge near Chicla, in the Andes, made of rope and branches exactly as their ancestors made them in pre-Columbian times. The only things that have changed since then are the coat and hat of the men driving the llamas; otherwise this photograph shows Indian life exactly as it was five and six centuries ago before the Spanish conquest.

8 These houses belong to an Ayllu, or community farm. The two girls with a llama are on their way to the market at Pisac.

9
10 Market at Pisac. Man and beast face to face, profile to profile. They are old friends, though here their eyes do not meet. The haughtiest of the two seems to be the llama.

10 A more recent friendship: child and donkey. But the latter is patiently resigned to his drudgery, while the child is not. Look at his eyes: they express all the sadness and longing, all the gentle resentment of his race.

11 Packed like sardines on the back of a truck which serves as a bus.

12 A typical view of the Altiplano, which is like an exalted version of Castile. Everywhere here are striking reminders of the landscapes of Spain.

13 These little girls, at the age of ten, have already forgotten how to smile. Long before reaching womanhood they have experienced all the hardship of the Indian woman's life. Here they are about to step on to a bus. Each journey is an exodus and they take with them everything they can carry.

14 Carrying their spades (which they call by the old Moorish name, "almocafre"), these children are on their way to work on a sugar plantation at Abancay.

15 Women seated on a truck. Their mask-like faces of indeterminate age are typical of the Indian women after they have borne one or two children.

16 This guitar-player with his felt hat might almost be taken for a "cholo" (city-dweller). But the Indians are rarely "cholos" and the name is almost exclusively applied to such half-castes and whites who do not work in the fields, whether they actually live in the cities or not.

17 A half-caste. In his eyes is a last glimmer of the struggle between his Inca forefathers and his Spanish forefathers. On his face, as on the Indians' faces, the same mask of immobility. Not so much as a twitch of the muscles to betray the secret of that inscrutable silence deposited by all the centuries during which they have played the underdog.

Second Chapter

21

29

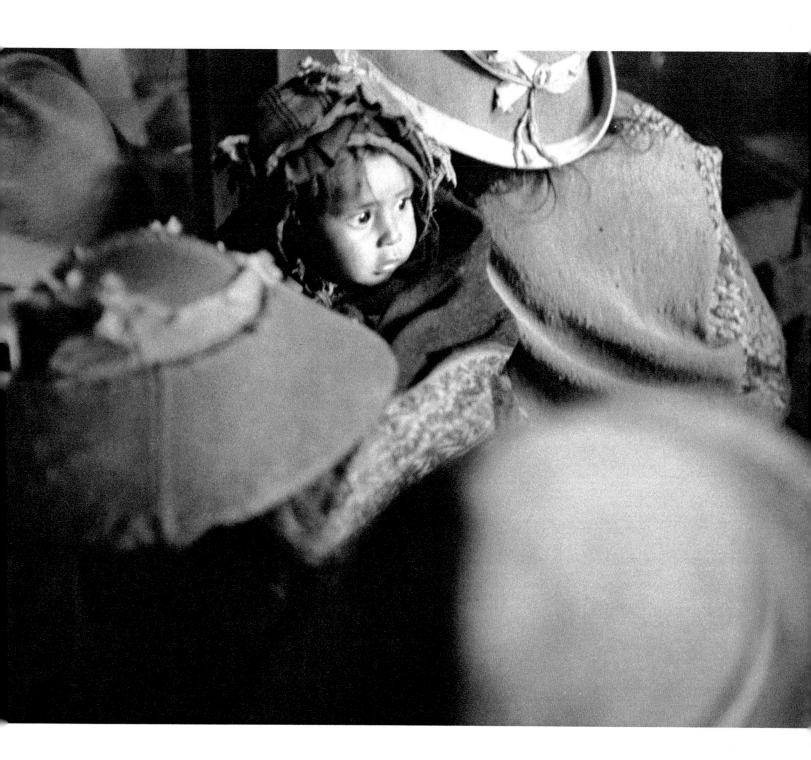

37

18 Hatmaker's shop at Cochabamba, Bolivia. Though introduced by the Spaniards, the sombrero as worn by the Indians has grown slightly taller than the classic Andalusian or Castilian type of sombrero. Its broad brim comes straight from the torrid Spanish countryside where the sun beats down fiercely, just as it does here, where the protection it offers is welcomed.

19 Square at Ayacucho. This town was the scene of one of the most famous battles against the Spaniards during the wars of independence in the early 19th century. The very name of Ayacucho symbolizes the liberation of South America.

20 Street at Cuzco, Peru. The atmosphere of the place is altogether Spanish, yet this town was once the capital of the Inca empire.

21 La Miscelanea, reads the shopsign. Here every conceivable article of local consumption is sold.

22 Marketday at Chincheros (Cuzco, Peru). These
23 women squat in front of their wares all day long without moving.

24 Old friends meet at the market. They greet each other in the Spanish fashion, with a hearty embrace or "abrazo". Visible beneath this Indian's sombrero is the old Inca cap, still worn today.

25 Girl tossing off a glass of chicha, of which the Indians consume unbelievable quantities. Fortunately it is not quite so strong an alcohol as might be supposed from the taste of it.

26 Two more chicha-drinkers. The small jug is a fine specimen of Indian pottery, and is certainly several centuries old.

27 These turkeys strut with something of the old conquistadorial swagger. The turkey (and many other fowls), the donkey and the horse were all introduced from Europe by the Spaniards.

28 A narrow street in Cuzco, gradually filling up with Indians come to market from miles around, their donkeys and llamas laden with corn and potatoes. After selling their produce, after drinking much chicha and mingling with the crowd, they load up their animals again with the few tools and small acquisitions made in town and trudge home at nightfall.

29 Outside a church a small ragged boy is watching a procession go by. He has stopped munching his stalk of sugar cane for a moment and has piously clasped his hands.

30 Indian women rarely put their children down. A baby leaves the womb for his mother's back, where he stays until old enough to walk. From his mother's back he discovers the world. Lying in their carriages, our babies see the sky and trees before anything else; the first things an Indian baby sees and grows familiar with are the earth and men squatting on the ground.

31 Night falls, and the Indians crouch in a silent circle beside the decaying wall of their house, while their women prepare the evening meal. The sadness of the scene speaks for itself.

32 The improvised stands of chicha-vendors spring up around the marketplace. Needless to say, they do a good business all day long.

33
34 Crowd at the yearly fair of Canicumca. There is not a man or woman in sight without a hat on his or her head.

35
36 A village bullfight. On the left, the spectators seen from behind. On the right, the aficionado in action, pursued by a young bull called a "capea". Such is the poor man's bullfight.

37 This fellow has passed out, dead drunk with chicha. A practised eye easily distinguishes the "healthy" drunkenness of the chicha-drinker from the morbid intoxication of the coca addict.

Third Chapter

51

38 Calvario on the heights above La Paz, Bolivia. At
39 noon, on three successive Thursdays, people come
up here to pray and burn incense. They believe
that from this elevated spot their prayers have a
better chance of reaching heaven, obtaining a
hearing and being fulfilled. They believe it, though
to judge by the monotonous poverty of their life
the heavens have so far turned a deaf ear to their
prayers.

40 Praying on the steps of St. Thomas, a church built
on the site of an ancient Maya temple at Chichi-
castenango, Guatemala.

41 Women following the procession, while their men-
42 folk shoulder the statue of Santiago at Cuzco,
Peru, on the feast day of St. James, July 25th.
This is wintertime in Peru and they are warmly
dressed.

43 The old church at Pisac, now hardly more than a
shaky ruin, slowly fills up with men, women and
children. The celebration of the Mass brings marketday to a climax. The Indians file inside from
the sunlit square and, while the slackening sounds
of talking and bargaining filter in from the marketplace, an Indian whispers a word in his companion's ear.

44 The Alcalde, or mayor, stands in a privileged place
near the altar with the other village notables, old
men with their black ponchos slung over their
shoulders.

45 The crowd, in a moment of hushed religious awe,
46 about to enter the church. These Indians—as al-
47 ways when men lead lives of hardship and poverty
without any promise of a change for the better—
look to religion for comfort and an answer to their
queries.

48 In the church of Pisac. Apparently returning from
49 a procession, these men have put their flower-laden
crosses down beside the altar. The Indians are submissive and dutiful in their observance of the
Christian rites, whose imagery appeals to their
imagination, but contained in all their offerings
and processions are instinctive allusions to the
sun-worship of their ancestors.

50 Not even standing room left in the church. The women and girls sit on the floor; beside them stand the men in respectful silence. Mass begins.

51 Incense-burners, called "quemaderos", in front of the cross of San Francisco el Alto (Guatemala).

52 Note the characteristic headdress of the Guatemala Indians. This "pañuelo" wrapped around the head was borrowed from the Spaniards in the 17th century. It was the headdress of the common Spaniard, of the settlers themselves, not of the conquistadors.

53 These crosses, near Camana in Peru, are the monument raised by the poor to the memory of their dead.

54 Juliaca cemetery, near Puno in Peru, on November 1st, All Saints' Day. "How lonely are the dead!" wrote Gustavo Adolfo Becquer, the Spanish romantic poet. On all other days, this cemetery seems like the loneliest spot in the world, in the middle of nowhere.

55 Altar for the dead, on All Saints' Day at Juliaca cemetery. Under small tents pitched along the walls, such portable altars as this are set up; on each is placed the dish of food for the dead required by pagan custom, which the Indians prudently continue to observe.

56 Indians at Tarabuco, Bolivia. Handsome and dignified, these men and women have retained all the noble purity of their race. Compare their features with those of the half-castes.

57 Carnival mask at Oruro, the Bolivian mining town. This type of mask is a throwback to the primitive death rites of the local Indians, and proves that those rites have by no means perished. Generally speaking, these masks betray one of two origins or a mingling of both: Inca and African.

Fourth Chapter

58 Kusilli (monkey) mask at Paucartambo, near Cuzco, Peru. Feast day of Our Lady of Carmel, July 16th.

59 The Mayordomo and his men, preparing to celebrate the feast day of St. Lawrence, August 10th, at Checacupe, near Cuzco, Peru.

60 This might be a street in any Andalusian village. Whitewashed walls, violent shadow contrasts.

61 Between Puno and Cuzco, the Peruvian village of Ayaviri celebrates the Nativity of the Virgin with colorful enthusiasm. These masked dancers play at being different animals, whose natural movements they imitate. The origin of this celebration is both catholic and pagan.

62 Indian women at Paucartambo, near Cuzco, Peru. These handsome, many-colored clothes are hand-woven. The secret of their bright colors is known only to the Indians.

63 Embroidered cape worn in the Waylillas carnival dance at Huancayo (central Peru). The patterns, of course, are modern, forming a curious medley of 19th century army uniforms and American automobiles, side by side. The cape also pays tribute to the wars of independence; visible at the bottom is the name Ayacucho (see plate 19), and at the top are the names of Belgrano and San Martin, two of the heroes of South American independence.

64 At La Paz, capital of Bolivia, the carnival is the most important holiday in the year. And dancing is the most important feature of the carnival. This girl is dancing the Wayno to show off the eight skirts she is wearing, which billow out around her like the petals of a flower.

65 Dances celebrating the Nativity, near Huancayo, Peru. They are full of pagan symbols, most prominent of which are whips and masks made of wool.

66 Dancing the Wayno in the Altiplano, where it is most popular. These high-altitude regions have so far had little contact with the modern world. This girl is perhaps a "cholita" from Ilave in the Puno region of Peru.

67 The white man's tuba has taken over where the Incan flute left off. Even so, this lustily blowing Indian is still wearing the Inca cap beneath his soft felt hat.

68 The dance of the Kenachos at Tiahumaco, Bolivia, on the feast day of St. Peter, June 29th. This dance harks back to the pagan celebrations of the winter solstice (June being wintertime in Bolivia). Again we find the eight-skirted dancer, though now she is barefooted.

69 Dancing the Wayno during carnival time at La Paz, Bolivia. For this the men always wear their tight-fitting Inca cap and the women their characteristic "derbies".

70 Dancing the Marinera at Huancayo (central Peru). This is a more modern dance, showing Spanish influence.

71 These dancers seem to have stepped straight out of the colonial era. Here there is hardly a sign of 20th century life. Yet many of these young people dancing at La Paz during carnival time will be off the next day to their jobs in mines and factories whose production standards are very much those of the 20th century.

72
73 Dance of the Sikuris at Copacabana (in the Lake Titicaca region of Bolivia) on the feast day of Our Lady of Copacabana, the Virgin of the Snows, August 5th. Music is provided (plate 72) by the "anthara", a native instrument resembling Pan-pipes but deriving from the purest Inca tradition. In contrast to that tradition is the inevitable archangel St. Michael (plate 73), with wings and helmets, brandishing a crooked sword intended to strike fear into any evil spirits that may be lurking in the vicinity.

74 A "contradanza" at Paucartambo, near Cuzco (Peru), on July 16th. This dance is partly Basque in origin.

75 The "Diablada" at Oruro, Bolivia. The devil's spouse, shrewish "China Supay", has lifted up her, or rather his, mask for a moment's respite after being tamed and chastised by St. Michael. Now "China Supay" will say a ritual prayer of repentance before the image of the Virgin of Socavon.

76 A tense moment in the Diablada. Satan is triumphantly borne aloft by his leering henchmen, who impersonate and symbolize the Seven Deadly Sins. This weird dance is not only a mixture of the Spanish "auto sacramental" and ancient Inca rites, but also seems to owe something to the tribal dances of the African Negros.

77 The dance of the Sikuris at Copacabana, Bolivia, calls for masks impersonating the birds held sacred by the Indians. This dance is one of the most faithful and colorful reflections of pre-Columbian folklore.

The captions were written by Manuel Tuñon de Lara

This volume, prepared by Robert Delpire, was printed by *Conzett & Huber, Zurich*. Finished the fifteenth day of July, nineteen hundred and fifty-six.

The photographs numbered 8, 28, 29, 30, 41, 43 to 50 were taken by *Werner Bischof*; 4, 5, 7, 9 to 17, 31, 60 by *Robert Frank*; 1, 2, 3, 6, 18 to 27, 32 to 40, 42, 51, 59, 61 to 77 by *Pierre Verger*.
Original printing of the photographs by *Pictorial Service*.
The cover is from a pre-Columbian vase found in Peru.

By the same publisher in the same series:
From One China to the Other. Photographs by Henri Cartier-Bresson. Text by Han Suyin.
Fiesta in Pamplona. Photographs by Inge Morath. Text by Dominique Aubier.